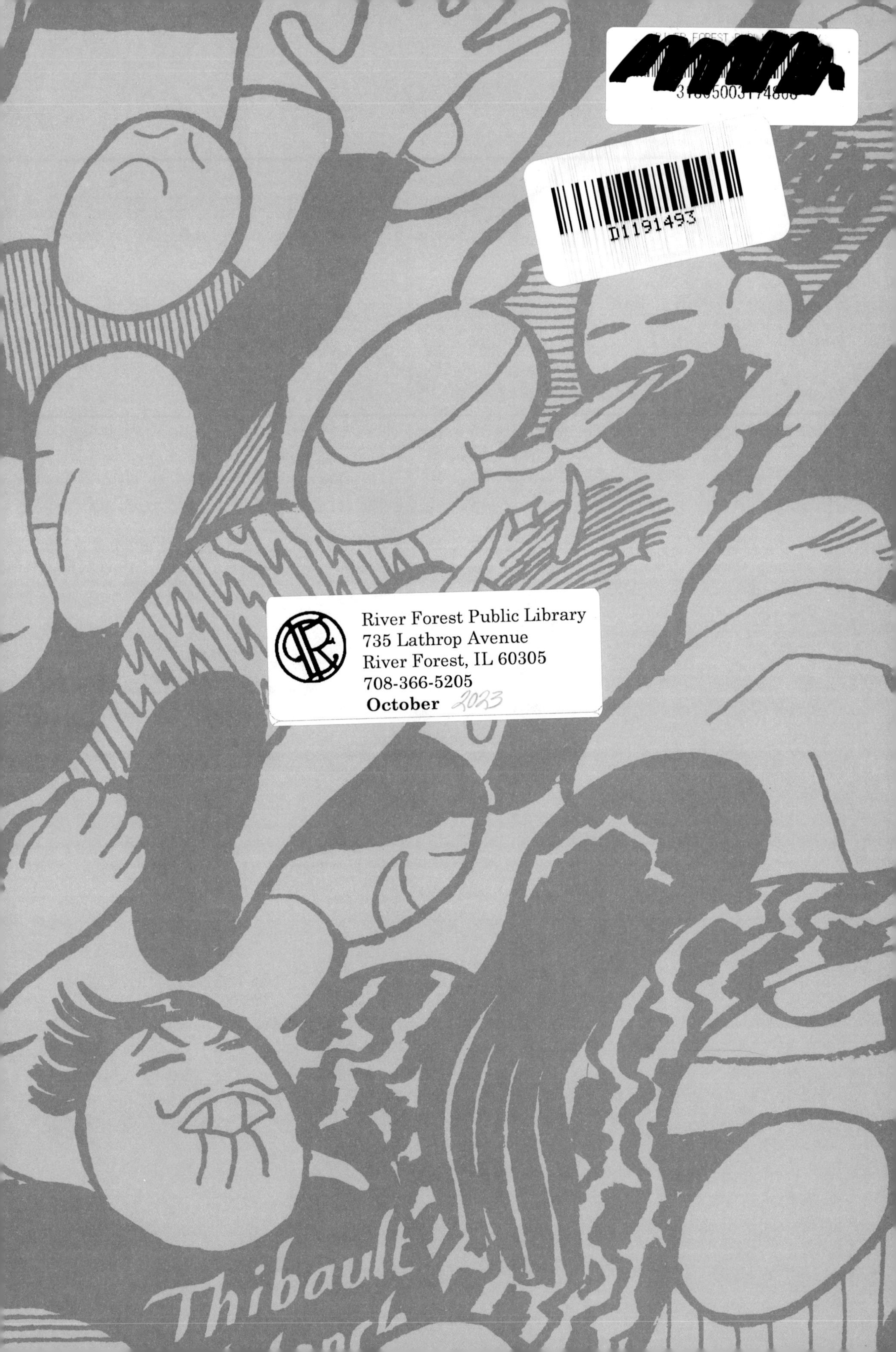
Thibault

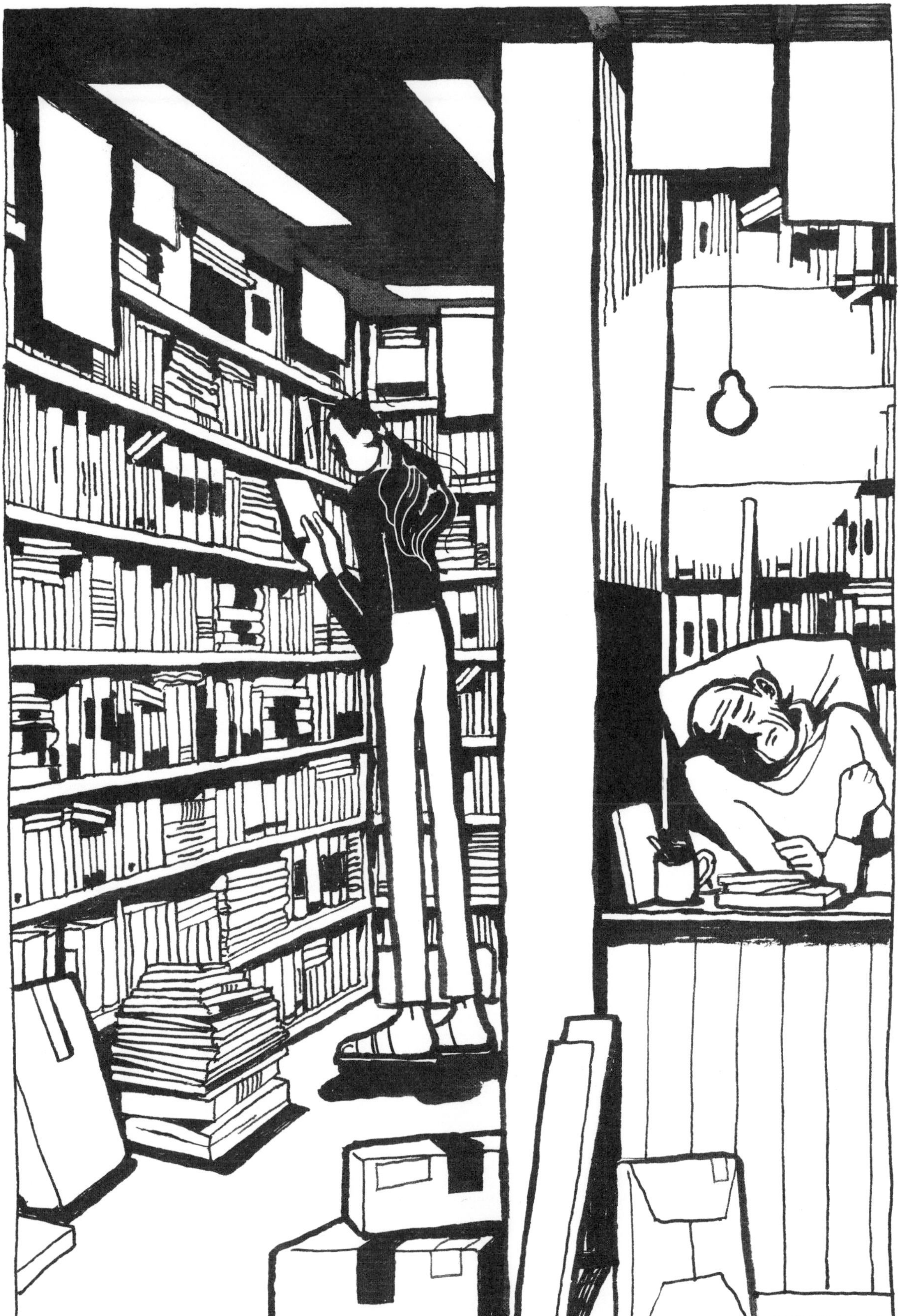

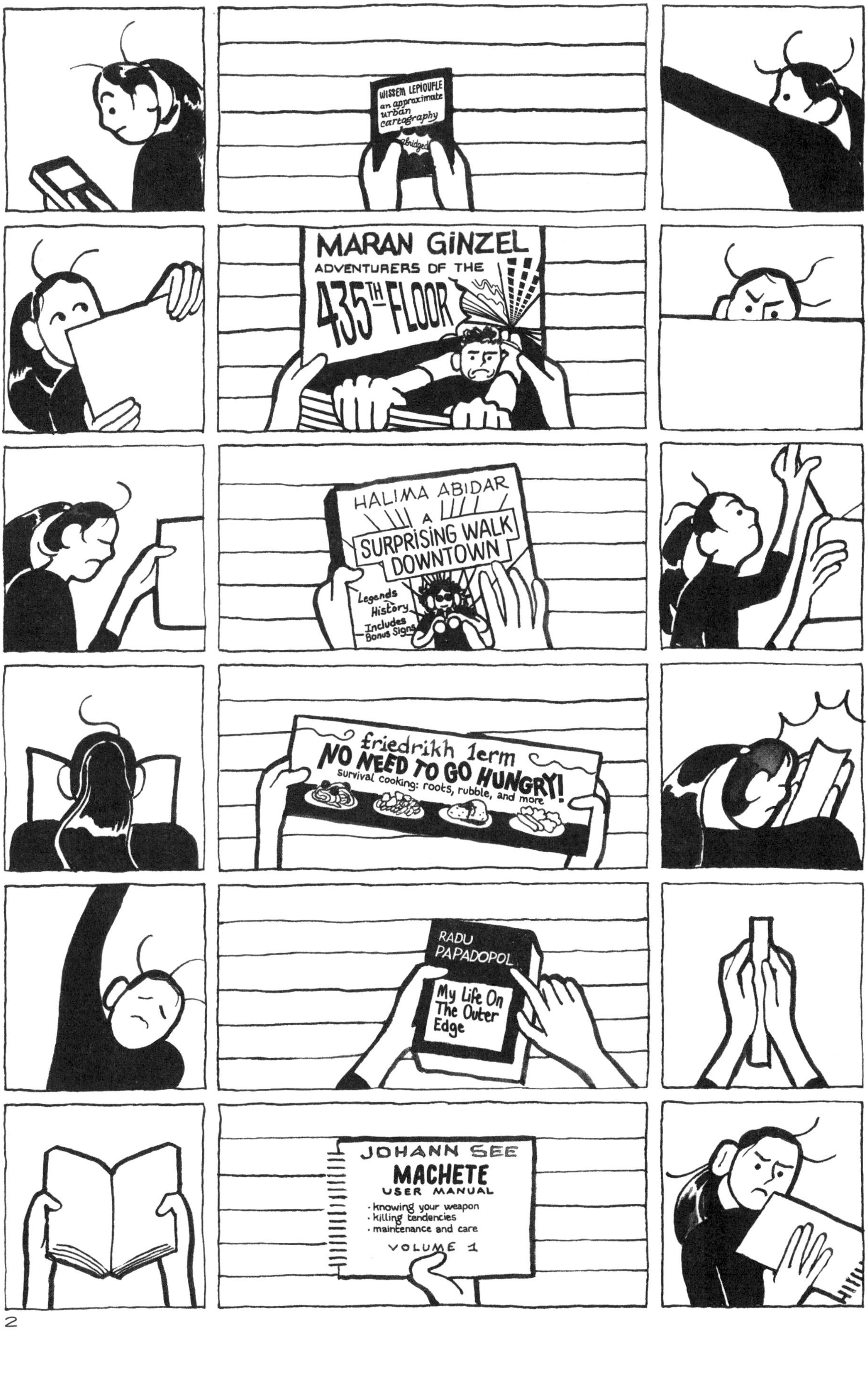
WISSEM LEPIOUFLE
an approximate urban cartography
abridged!
MARAN GINZEL
ADVENTURERS OF THE
435TH FLOOR
HALIMA ABIDAR
A
SURPRISING WALK DOWNTOWN
Legends
History
Includes Bonus Signs
friedrikh 1erm
NO NEED TO GO HUNGRY!
survival cooking: roots, rubble, and more
RADU PAPADOPOL
My Life On The Outer Edge
JOHANN SEE
MACHETE
USER MANUAL
· knowing your weapon
· killing tendencies
· maintenance and care
VOLUME 1

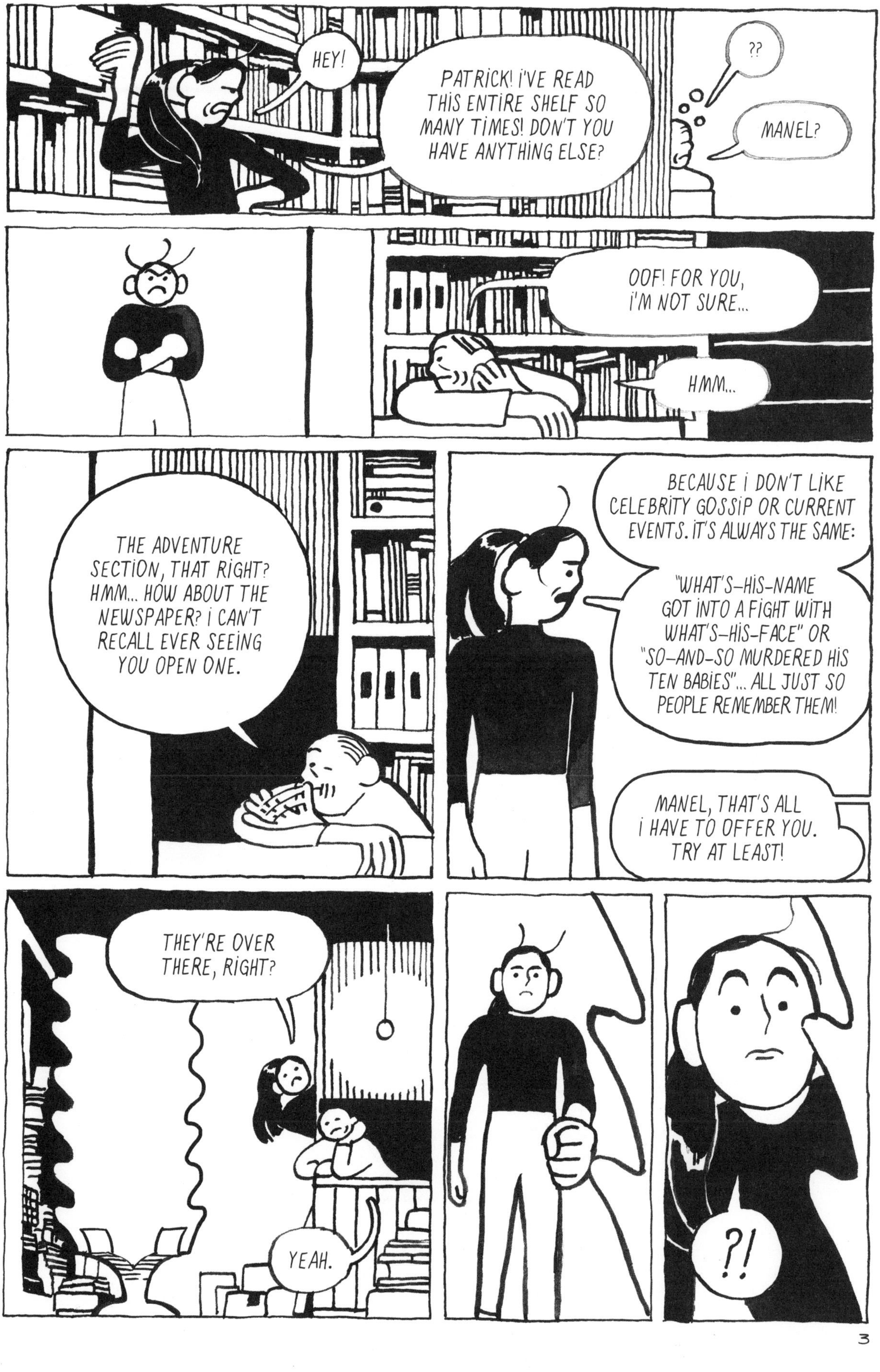
HEY!
PATRICK! I'VE READ THIS ENTIRE SHELF SO MANY TIMES! DON'T YOU HAVE ANYTHING ELSE?
??
MANEL?
OOF! FOR YOU, I'M NOT SURE...
HMM...
THE ADVENTURE SECTION, THAT RIGHT? HMM... HOW ABOUT THE NEWSPAPER? I CAN'T RECALL EVER SEEING YOU OPEN ONE.
BECAUSE I DON'T LIKE CELEBRITY GOSSIP OR CURRENT EVENTS. IT'S ALWAYS THE SAME:
"WHAT'S-HIS-NAME GOT INTO A FIGHT WITH WHAT'S-HIS-FACE" OR "SO-AND-SO MURDERED HIS TEN BABIES"... ALL JUST SO PEOPLE REMEMBER THEM!
MANEL, THAT'S ALL I HAVE TO OFFER YOU. TRY AT LEAST!
THEY'RE OVER THERE, RIGHT?
YEAH.
?!

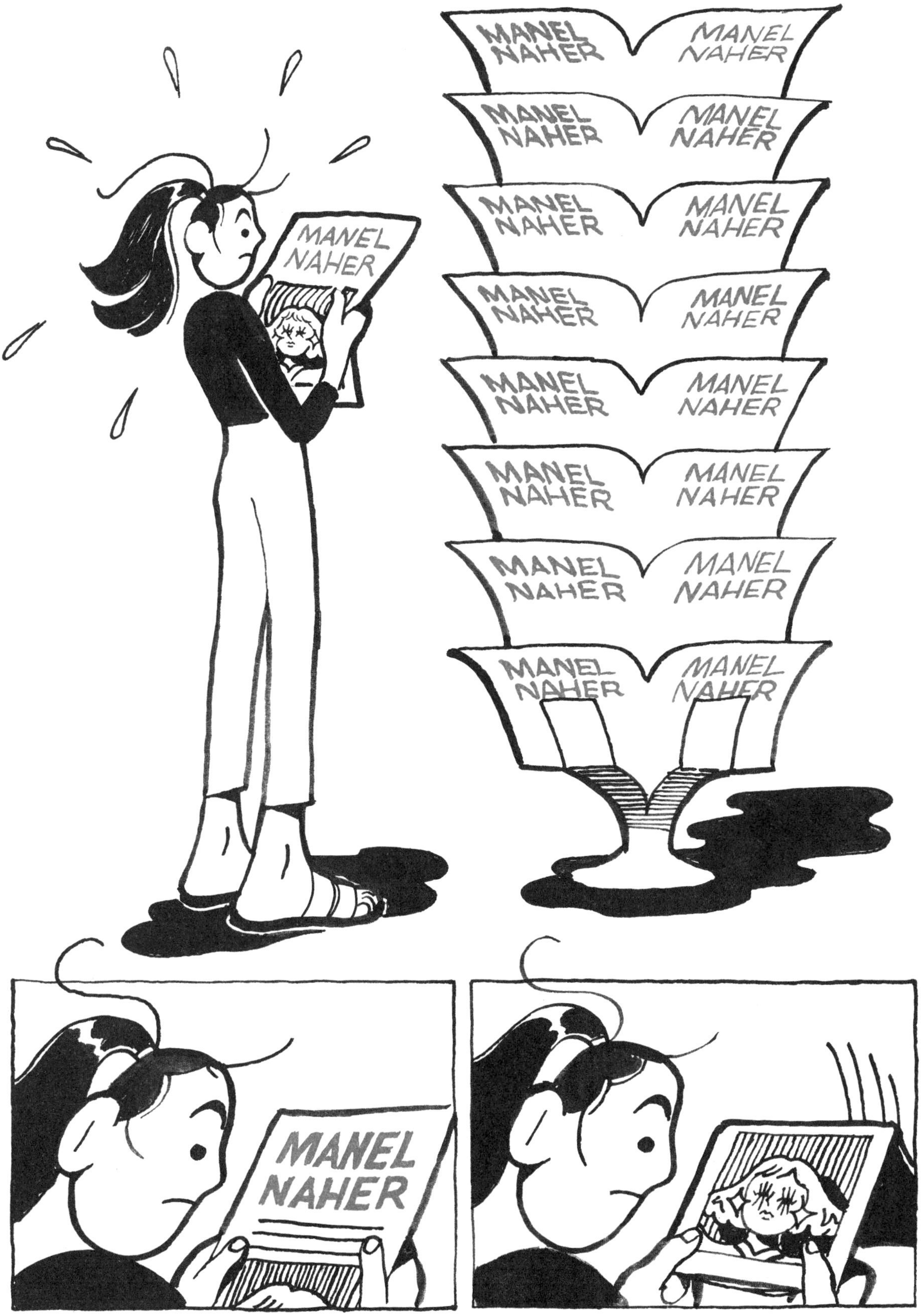
MANEL NAHER
MANEL NAHER
MANEL NAHER
MANEL NAHER
MANEL NAHER
MANEL NAHER
MANEL NAHER
MANEL NAHER
MANEL NAHER
MANEL NAHER
MANEL NAHER
MANEL NAHER
MANEL NAHER
MANEL NAHER
MANEL NAHER
MANEL NAHER
MANEL NAHER
MANEL NAHER

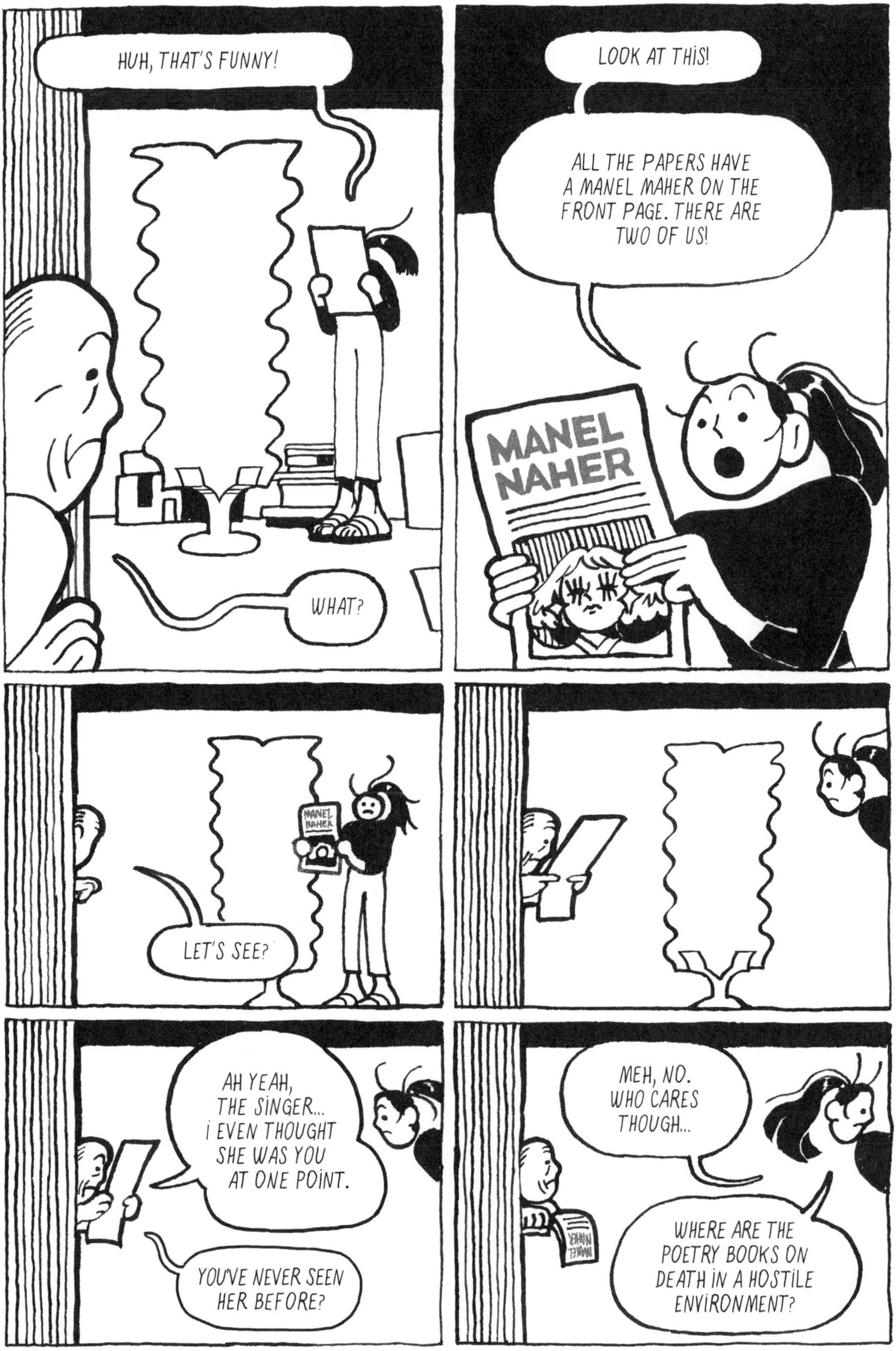
HUH, THAT'S FUNNY!
WHAT?
LOOK AT THIS!
ALL THE PAPERS HAVE A MANEL MAHER ON THE FRONT PAGE. THERE ARE TWO OF US!
MANEL NAHER
MANEL NAHER
LET'S SEE?
AH YEAH, THE SINGER... I EVEN THOUGHT SHE WAS YOU AT ONE POINT.
YOU'VE NEVER SEEN HER BEFORE?
MEH, NO. WHO CARES THOUGH...
WHERE ARE THE POETRY BOOKS ON DEATH IN A HOSTILE ENVIRONMENT?

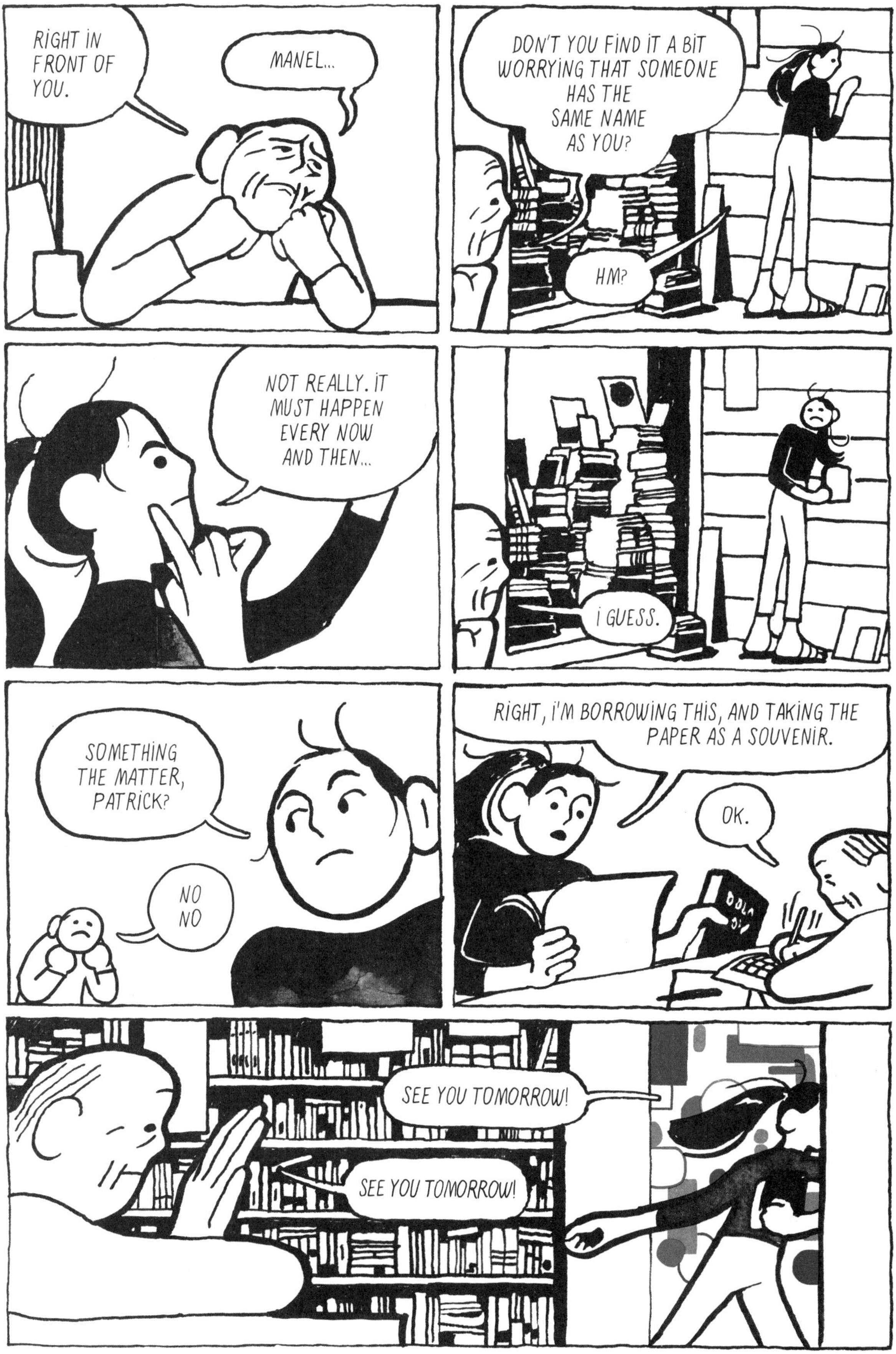
RIGHT IN FRONT OF YOU.
MANEL...
DON'T YOU FIND IT A BIT WORRYING THAT SOMEONE HAS THE SAME NAME AS YOU?
HM?
NOT REALLY. IT MUST HAPPEN EVERY NOW AND THEN...
I GUESS.
SOMETHING THE MATTER, PATRICK?
NO NO
RIGHT, I'M BORROWING THIS, AND TAKING THE PAPER AS A SOUVENIR.
OK.
SEE YOU TOMORROW!
SEE YOU TOMORROW!

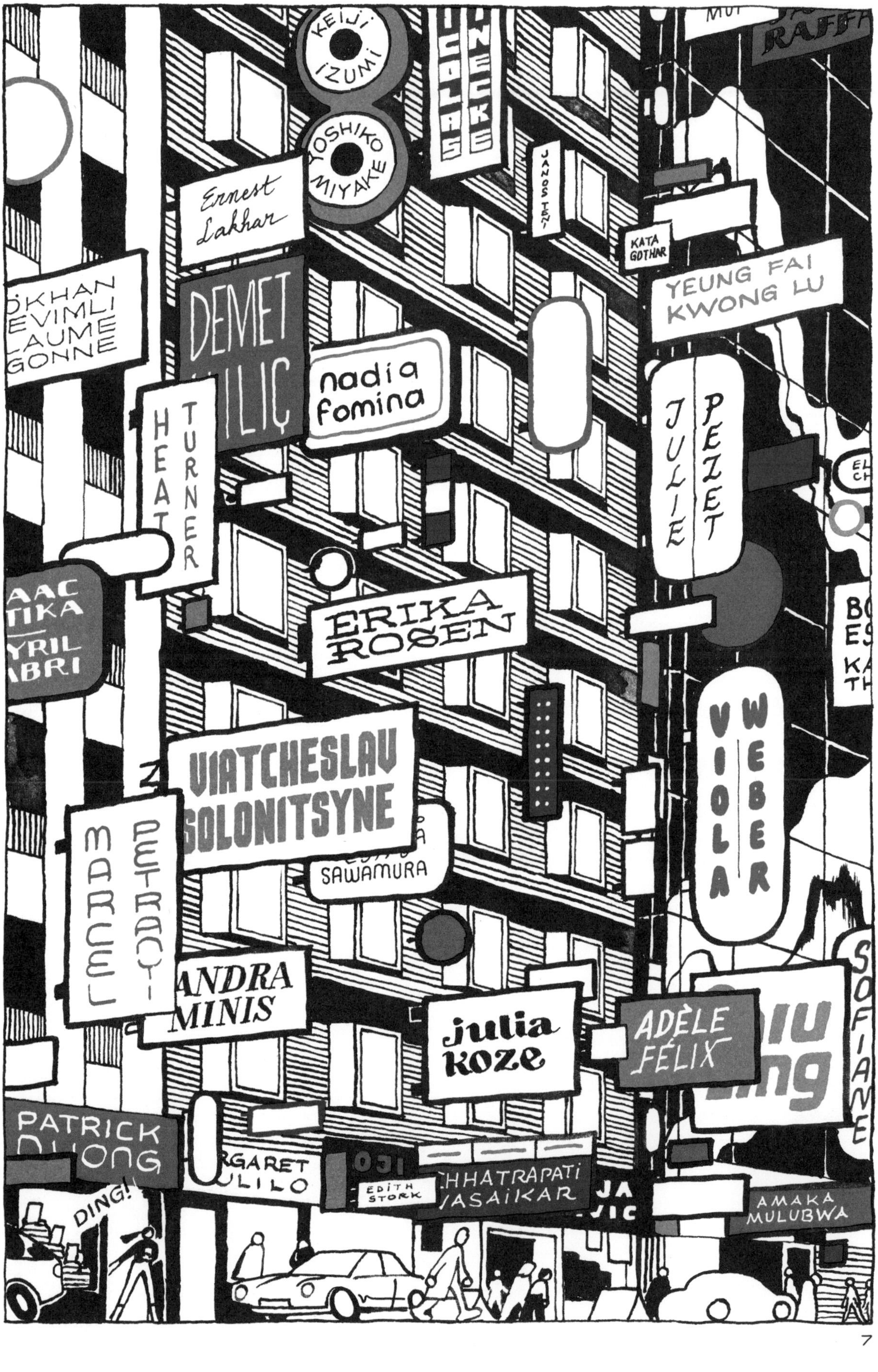
KEIJI IZUMI
YOSHIKO MIYAKE
NICOLAS
ANECKE
JANOS TENI
Ernest Lakhar
KATA GOTHAR
YEUNG FAI KWONG LU
nadia fomina
JULIE PEZET
HEAT TURNER
ERIKA ROSEN
VIOLA WEBER
VIATCHESLAV SOLONITSYNE
SAWAMURA
MARCEL PETRAQYI
ANDRA MINIS
julia koze
ADÈLE FÉLIX
SOFIANE
PATRICK DUONG
EDITH STORK
AMAKA MULUBWA
DING!

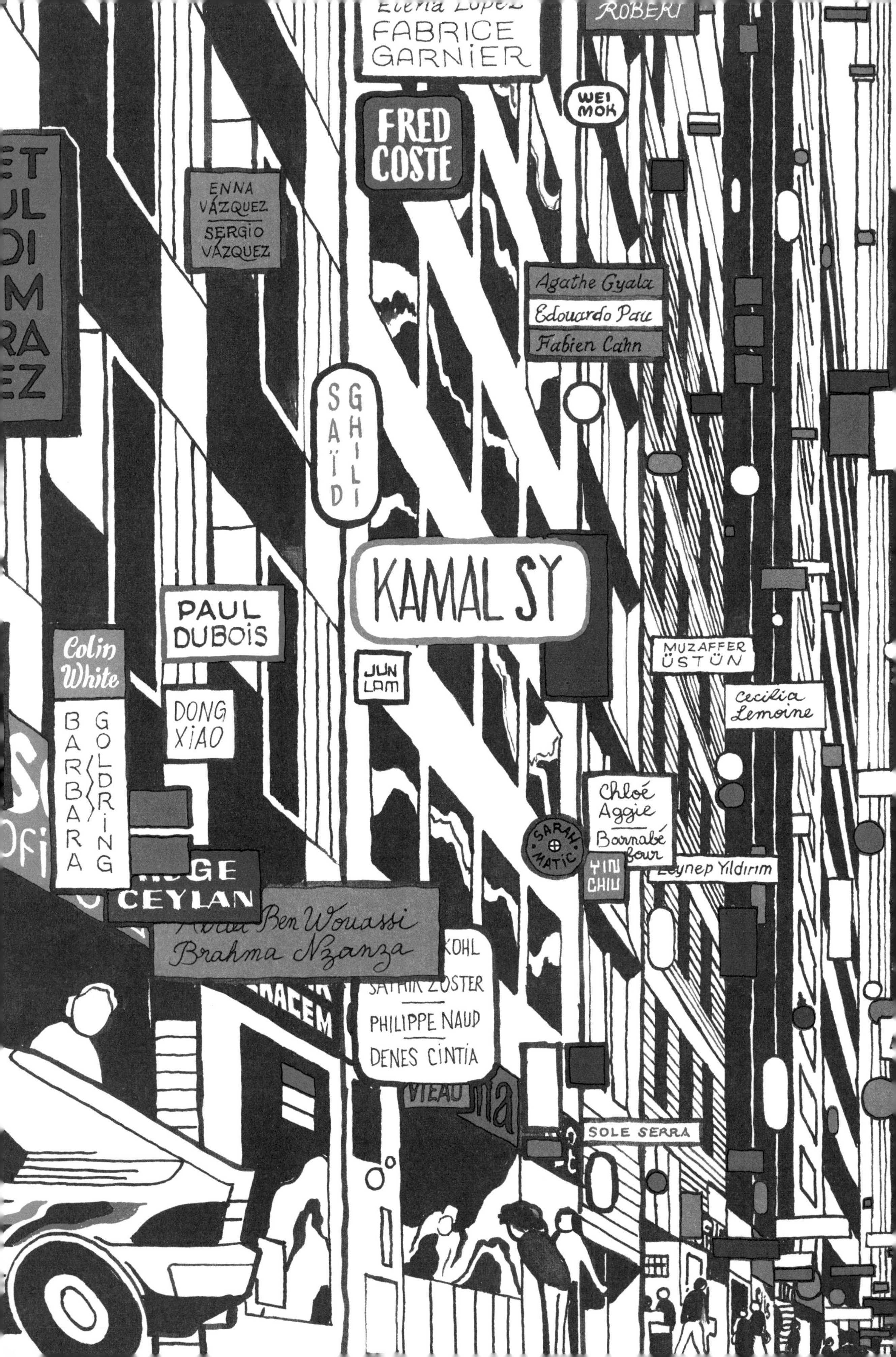

FABRICE GARNIER
ROBERT
WEI MOK
FRED COSTE
ENNA VÁZQUEZ
SERGIO VÁZQUEZ
Agathe Gyala
Edouardo Pau
Fabien Cahn
SAÏD GHILI
KAMAL SY
PAUL DUBOIS
Colin White
JUN LAM
MUZAFFER ÜSTÜN
Cecilia Lemoine
DONG XIAO
BARBARA GOLDRING
Chloé Aggie
Barnabé
SARAH MATIC
YIN CHIU
CEYLAN
Ben Wouassi
Brahma Nzanza
PHILIPPE NAUD
DENES CINTIA
SOLE SERRA

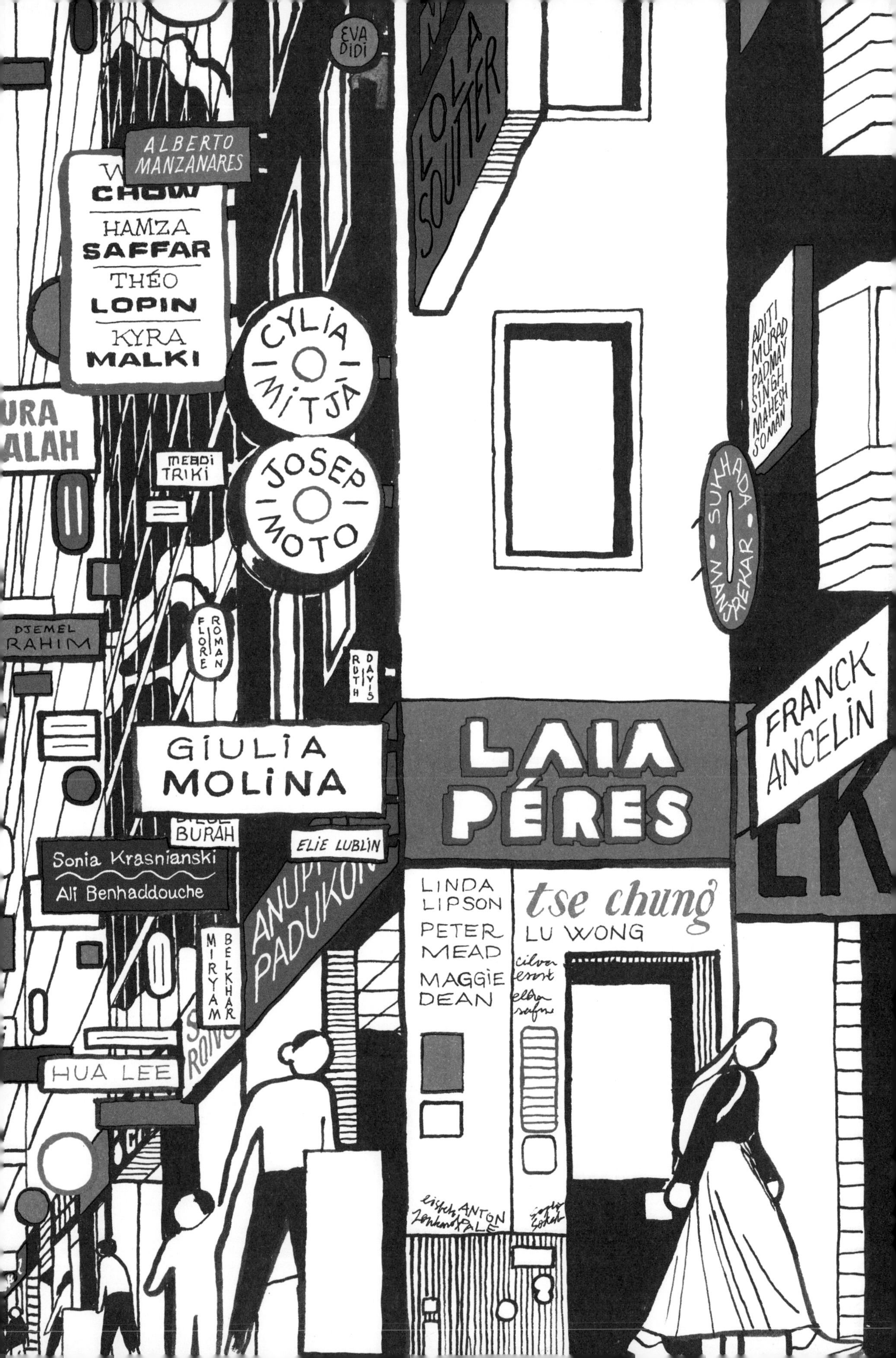

EVA DIDI
LOLA SOUTTER
ALBERTO MANZANARES
CHOW
HAMZA SAFFAR
THÉO LOPIN
KYRA MALKI
CYLIA MITJÀ
JOSEP MOTO
MEHDI TRIKI
SUKHADA MANJREKAR
DJEMEL RAHIM
FLORE ROMAN
RUTH DAVIS
GIULIA MOLINA
LAIA PÉRES
FRANCK ANCELIN
BURAH
ELIE LUBLIN
Sonia Krasnianski
Ali Benhaddouche
LINDA LIPSON
PETER MEAD
MAGGIE DEAN
tse chung
LU WONG
MIRYAM BELKHAR
HUA LEE

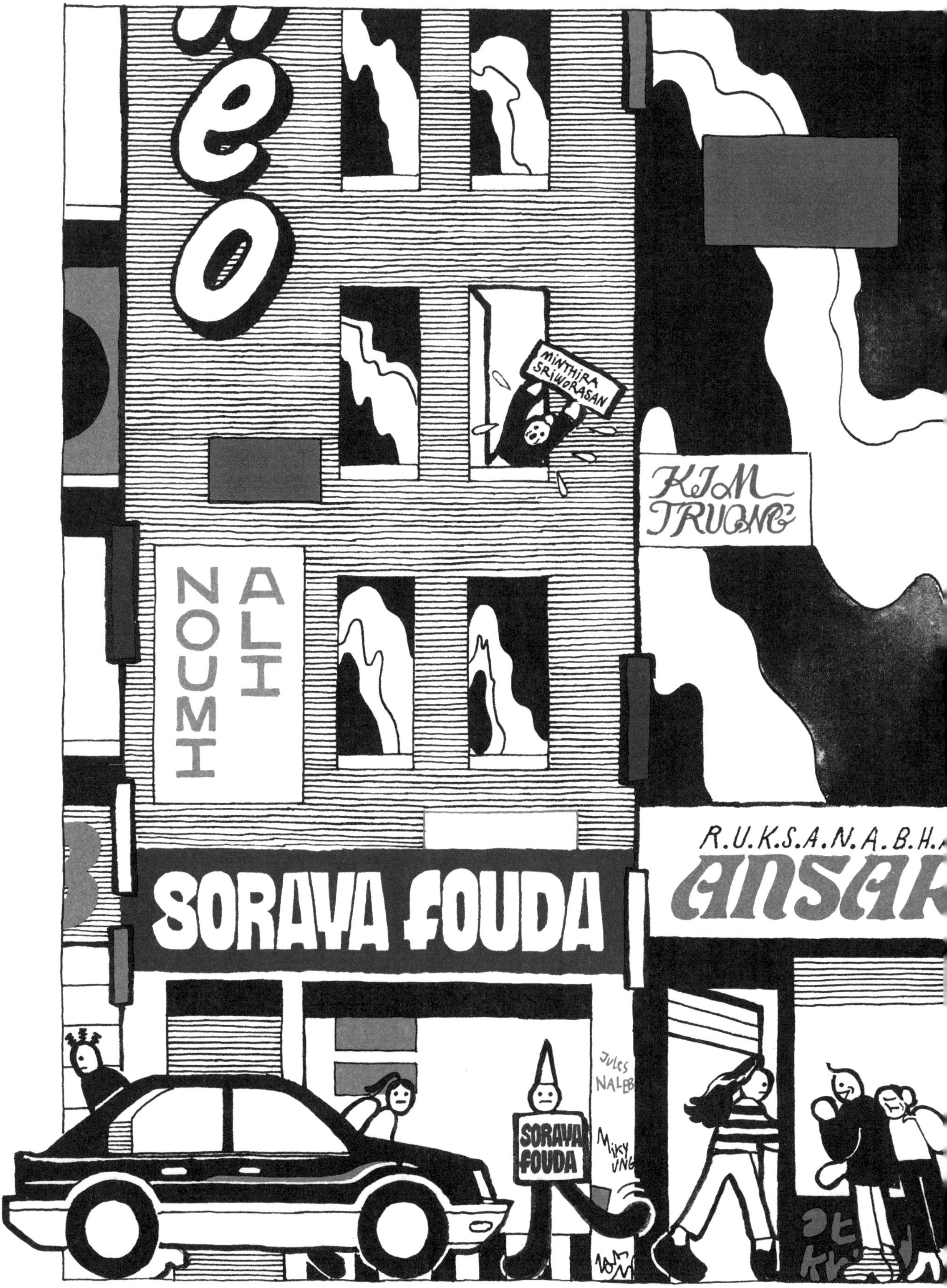

MINTHIRA SRIWORASAN
KIM TRUONG
NOUMI
ALI
R.U.K.S.A.N.A.B.H.
SORAYA FOUDA
Jules NALEB
SORAYA FOUDA
Miky UNG

THE GREAT BEYOND

LÉA MURAWIEC

TRANSLATED BY ALESHIA JENSEN

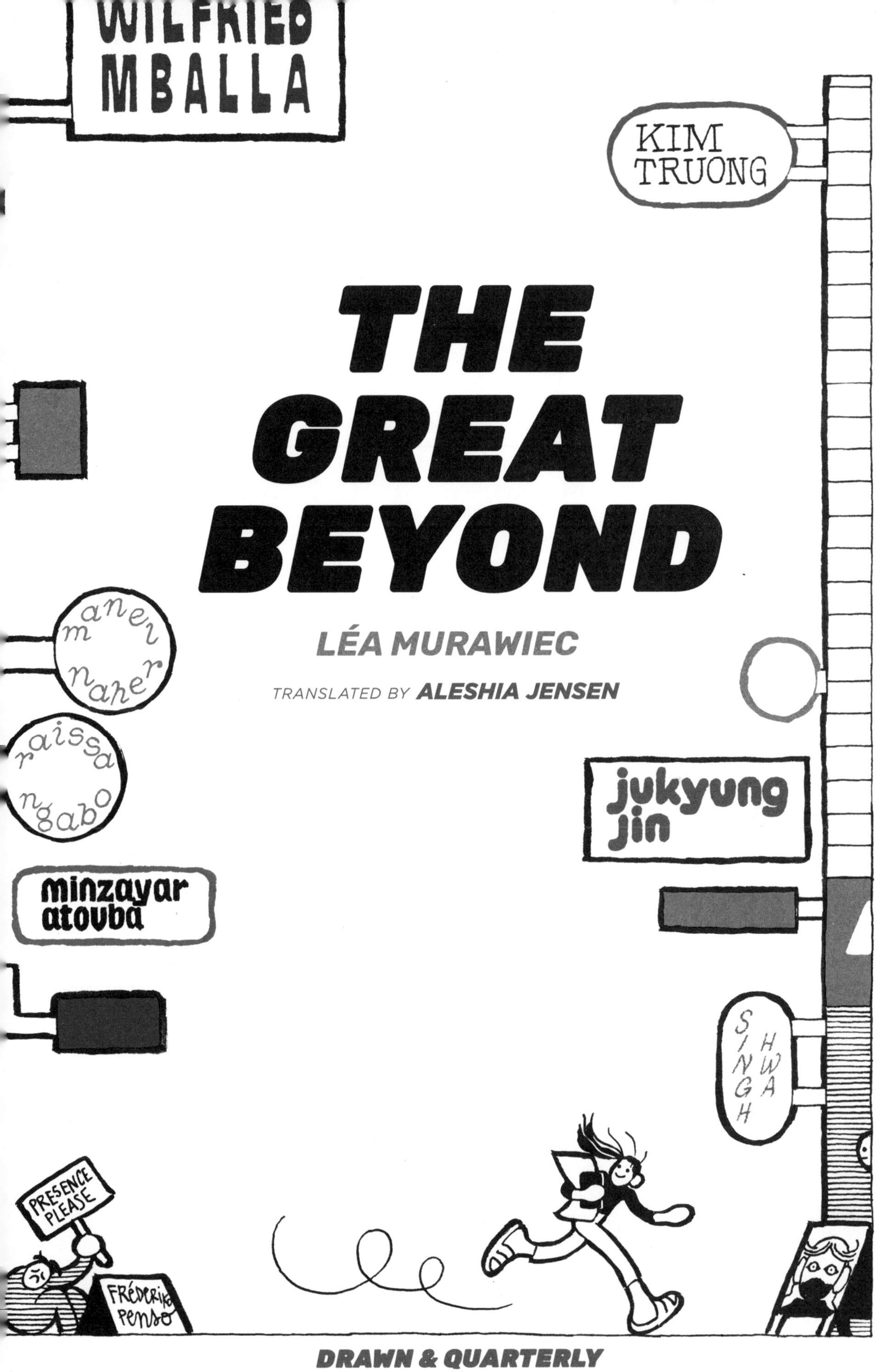
WILFRIED
MBALLA
KIM
TRUONG
manel
naher
raissa
ngabo
jukyung
jin
minzayar
atouba
SINGH
HWA
PRESENCE
PLEASE
FRÉDERIKA
PENSO

DRAWN & QUARTERLY

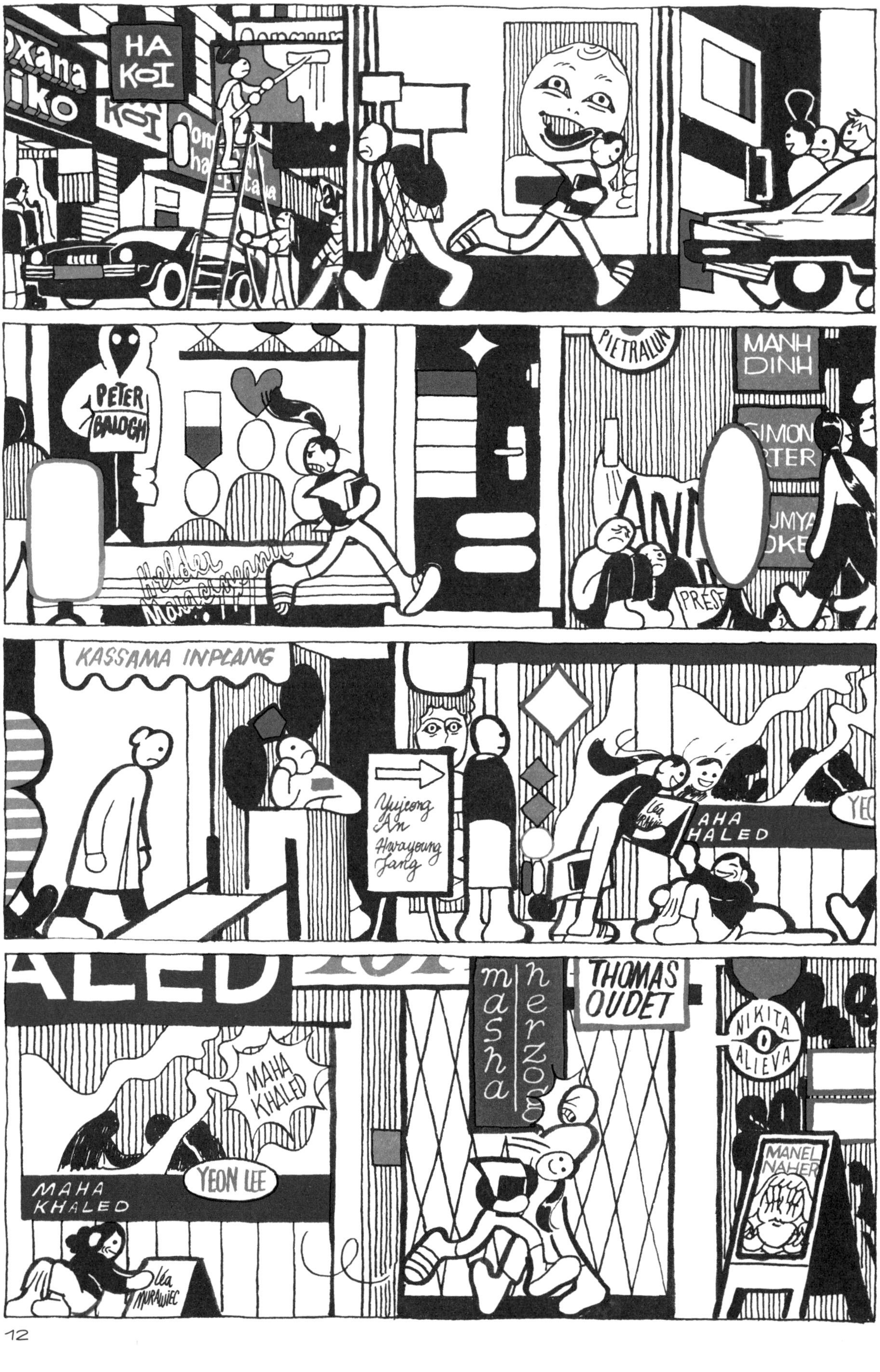
Oxana
iko
HA KOI
PETER BALOGH
Helder Mazzaggiani
MANH DINH
KASSAMA INPLANG
Yujeong An
Hwayoung Jang
MAHA KHALED
YEON LEE
MAHA KHALED
Léa Murawiec
masha herzog
THOMAS OUDET
NIKITA ALIEVA
MANEL NAHER

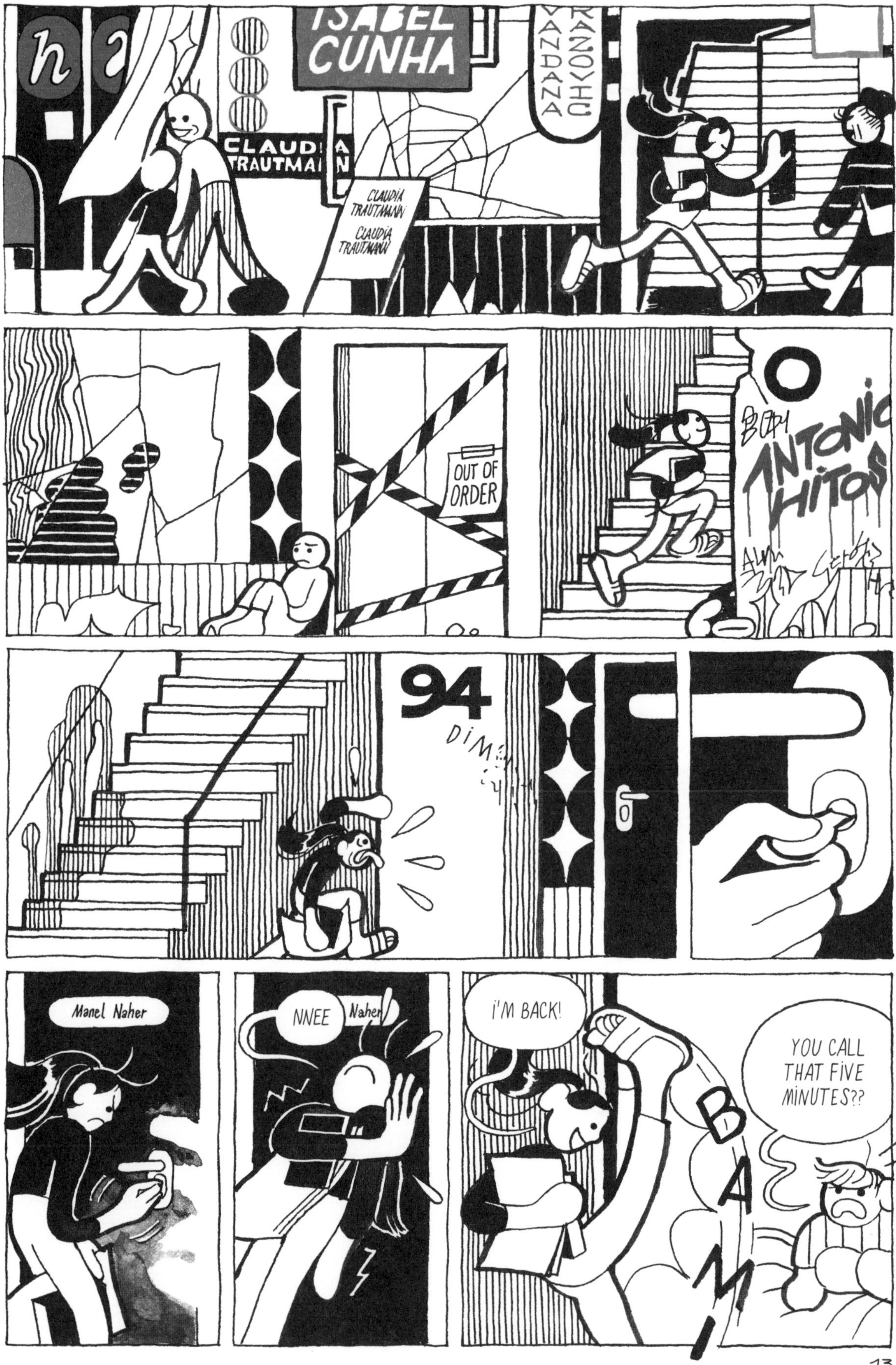
ISABEL CUNHA
CLAUDIA TRAUTMANN
VANDANA RAZOVIC
CLAUDIA TRAUTMANN CLAUDIA TRAUTMANN
OUT OF ORDER
HITOS
94
Manel Naher
NNEE
Naher
I'M BACK!
BAM!
YOU CALL THAT FIVE MINUTES??

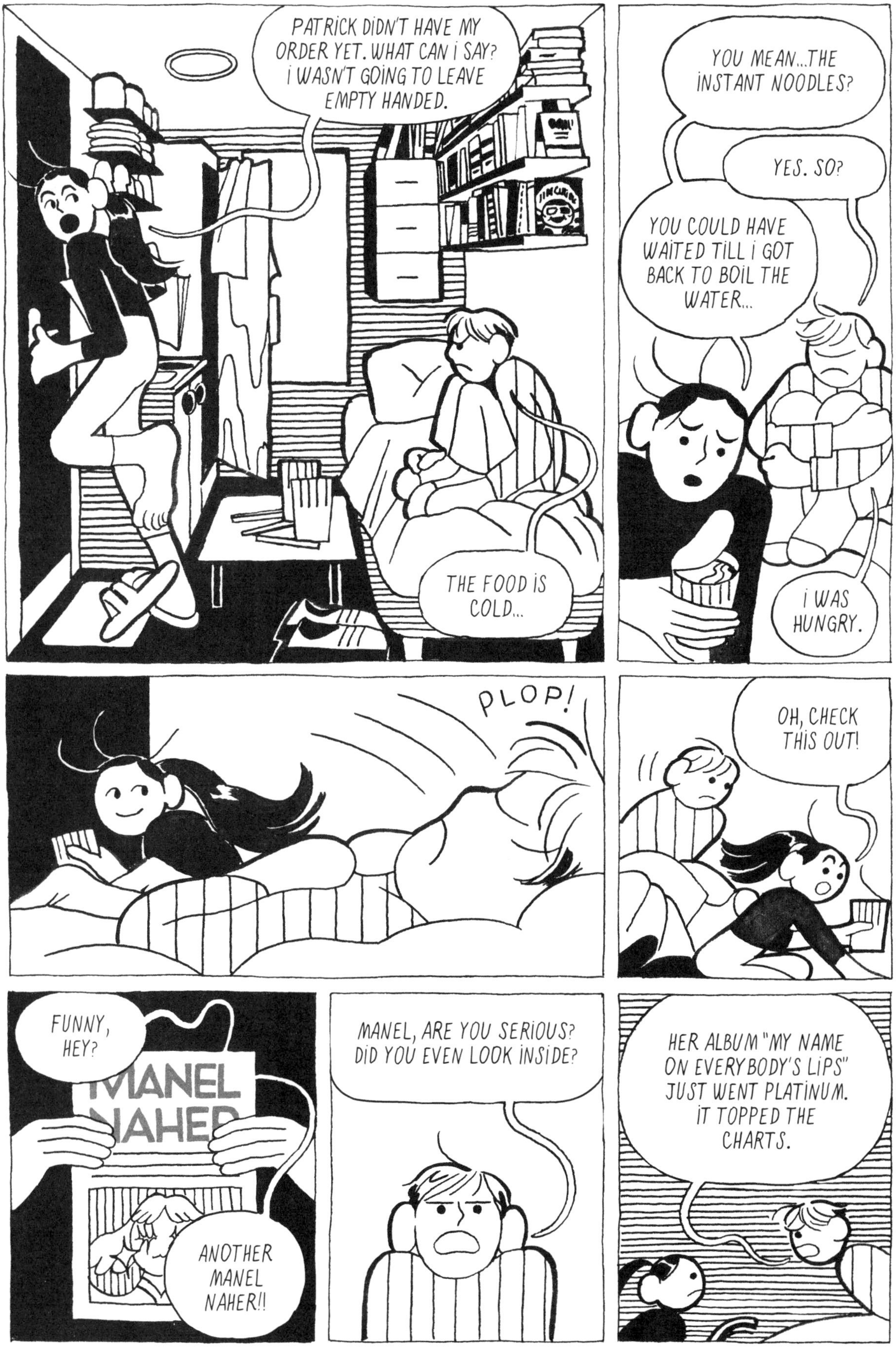
PATRICK DIDN'T HAVE MY ORDER YET. WHAT CAN I SAY? I WASN'T GOING TO LEAVE EMPTY HANDED.
THE FOOD IS COLD...
YOU MEAN...THE INSTANT NOODLES?
YES. SO?
YOU COULD HAVE WAITED TILL I GOT BACK TO BOIL THE WATER...
I WAS HUNGRY.
PLOP!
OH, CHECK THIS OUT!
FUNNY, HEY?
MANEL NAHER
ANOTHER MANEL NAHER!!
MANEL, ARE YOU SERIOUS? DID YOU EVEN LOOK INSIDE?
HER ALBUM "MY NAME ON EVERYBODY'S LIPS" JUST WENT PLATINUM. IT TOPPED THE CHARTS.

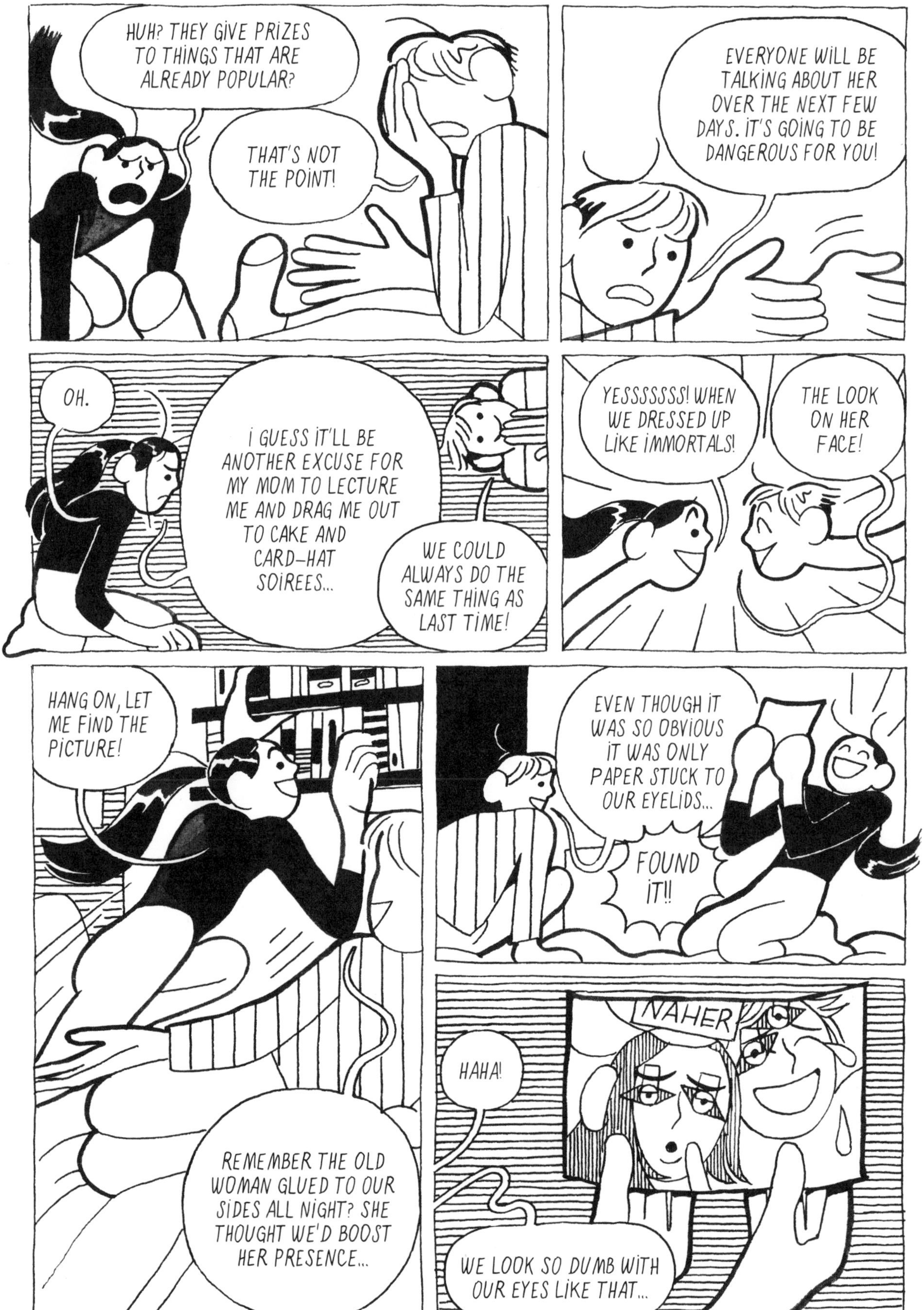
HUH? THEY GIVE PRIZES TO THINGS THAT ARE ALREADY POPULAR?
THAT'S NOT THE POINT!
EVERYONE WILL BE TALKING ABOUT HER OVER THE NEXT FEW DAYS. IT'S GOING TO BE DANGEROUS FOR YOU!
OH.
I GUESS IT'LL BE ANOTHER EXCUSE FOR MY MOM TO LECTURE ME AND DRAG ME OUT TO CAKE AND CARD-HAT SOIREES...
WE COULD ALWAYS DO THE SAME THING AS LAST TIME!
YESSSSSSS! WHEN WE DRESSED UP LIKE IMMORTALS!
THE LOOK ON HER FACE!
HANG ON, LET ME FIND THE PICTURE!
REMEMBER THE OLD WOMAN GLUED TO OUR SIDES ALL NIGHT? SHE THOUGHT WE'D BOOST HER PRESENCE...
EVEN THOUGH IT WAS SO OBVIOUS IT WAS ONLY PAPER STUCK TO OUR EYELIDS...
FOUND IT!!
NAHER
HAHA!
WE LOOK SO DUMB WITH OUR EYES LIKE THAT...

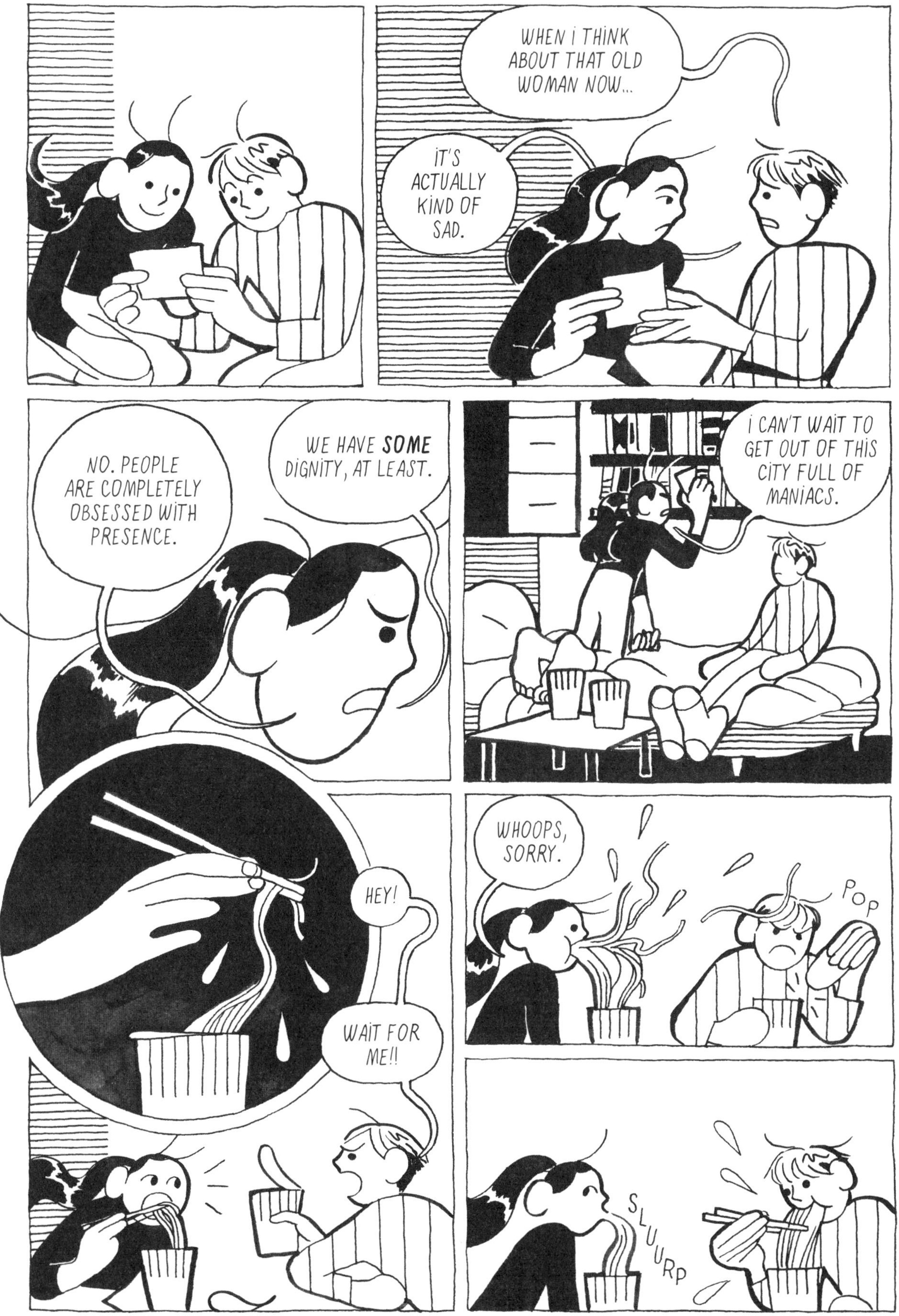
WHEN I THINK ABOUT THAT OLD WOMAN NOW...
IT'S ACTUALLY KIND OF SAD.
WE HAVE **SOME** DIGNITY, AT LEAST.
NO. PEOPLE ARE COMPLETELY OBSESSED WITH PRESENCE.
I CAN'T WAIT TO GET OUT OF THIS CITY FULL OF MANIACS.
HEY!
WAIT FOR ME!!
WHOOPS, SORRY.
POP
SLUURP

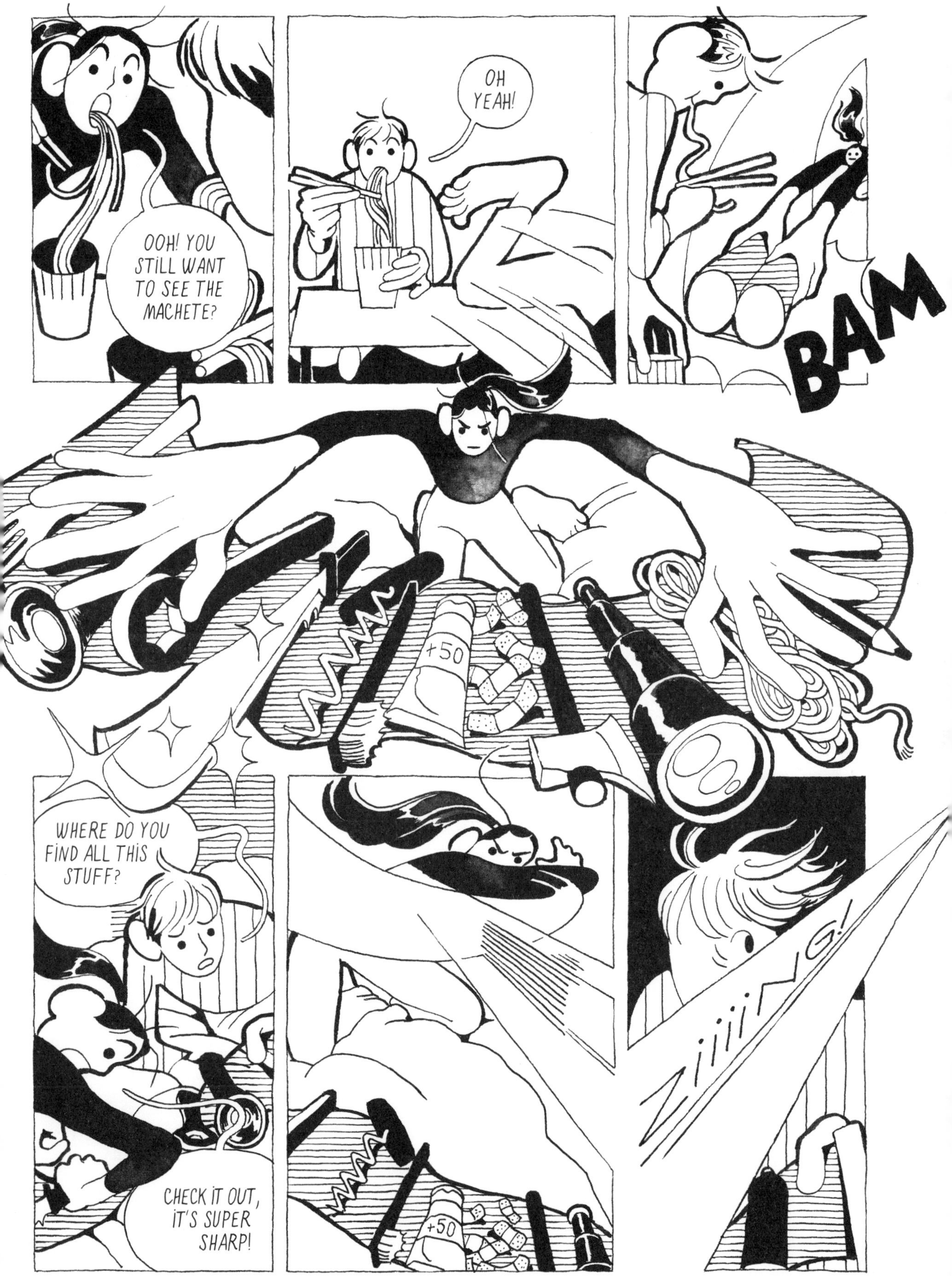
OOH! YOU STILL WANT TO SEE THE MACHETE?
OH YEAH!
BAM
+50
WHERE DO YOU FIND ALL THIS STUFF?
CHECK IT OUT, IT'S SUPER SHARP!
+50
ZIIIIING!

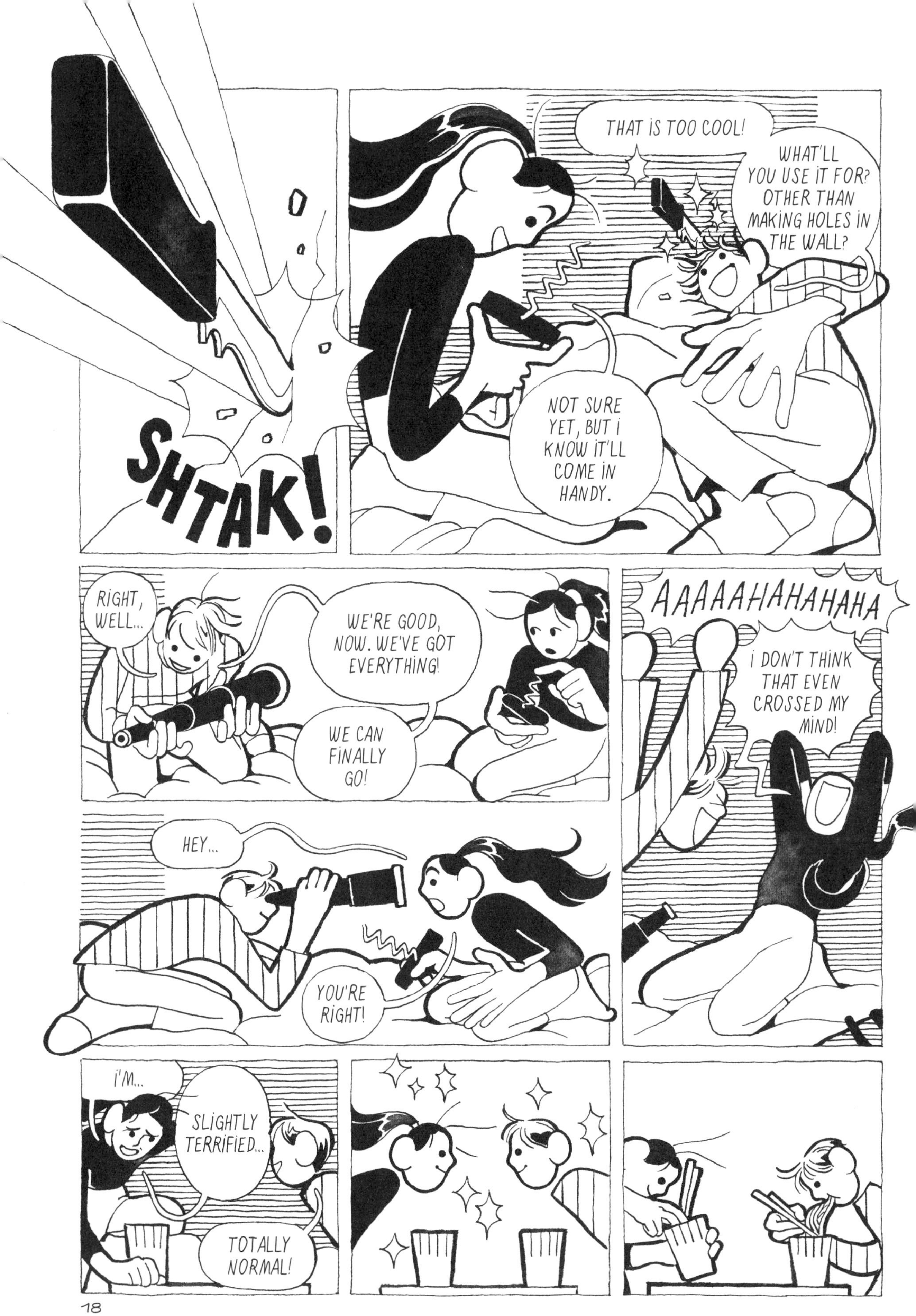
SHTAK!
THAT IS TOO COOL!
WHAT'LL YOU USE IT FOR? OTHER THAN MAKING HOLES IN THE WALL?
NOT SURE YET, BUT I KNOW IT'LL COME IN HANDY.
RIGHT, WELL...
WE'RE GOOD, NOW. WE'VE GOT EVERYTHING!
WE CAN FINALLY GO!
HEY...
YOU'RE RIGHT!
AAAAAHAHAHAHA
I DON'T THINK THAT EVEN CROSSED MY MIND!
I'M...
SLIGHTLY TERRIFIED...
TOTALLY NORMAL!

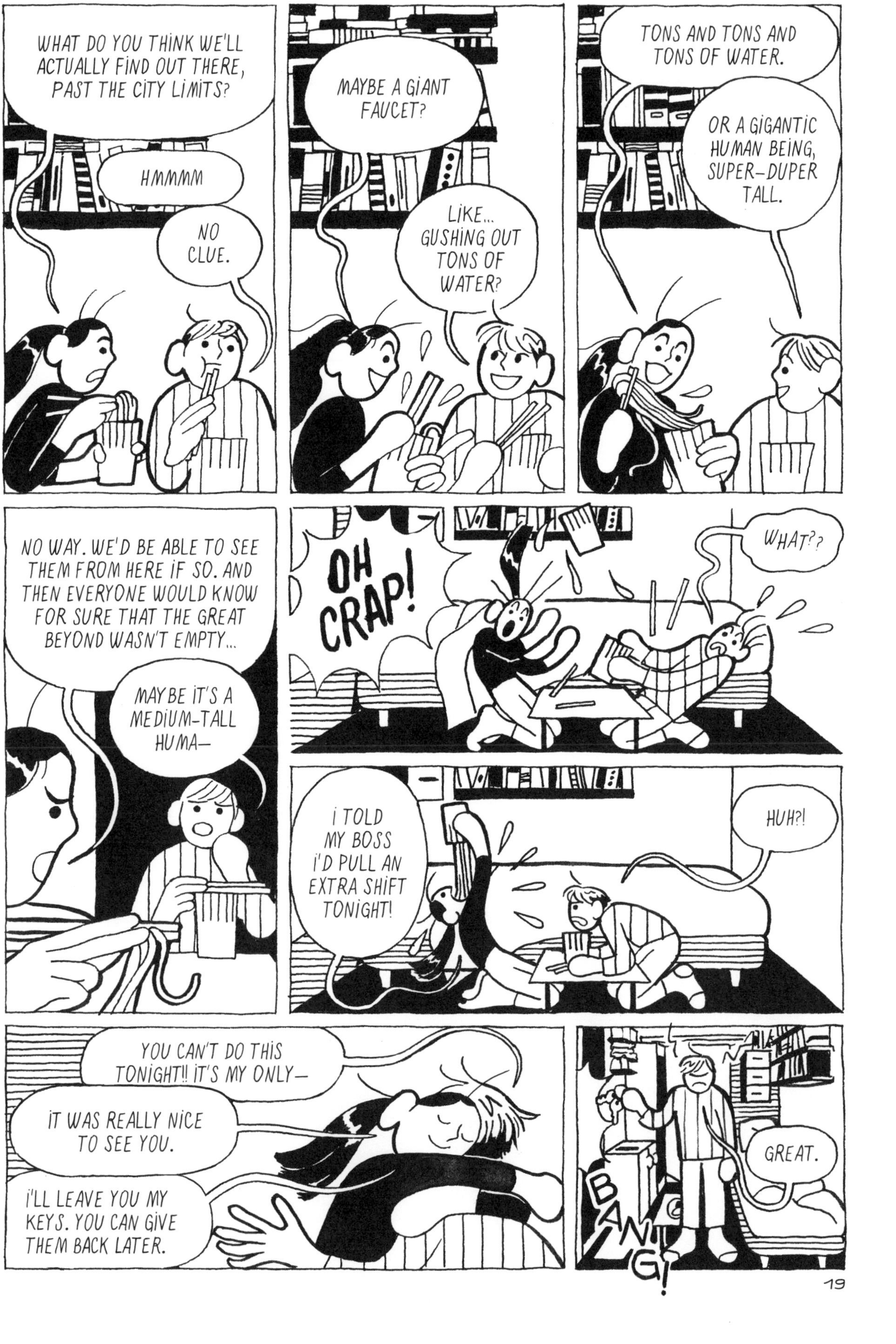
WHAT DO YOU THINK WE'LL ACTUALLY FIND OUT THERE, PAST THE CITY LIMITS?
HMMMM
NO CLUE.
MAYBE A GIANT FAUCET?
LIKE... GUSHING OUT TONS OF WATER?
TONS AND TONS AND TONS OF WATER.
OR A GIGANTIC HUMAN BEING, SUPER-DUPER TALL.
NO WAY. WE'D BE ABLE TO SEE THEM FROM HERE IF SO. AND THEN EVERYONE WOULD KNOW FOR SURE THAT THE GREAT BEYOND WASN'T EMPTY...
MAYBE IT'S A MEDIUM-TALL HUMA—
OH CRAP!
WHAT??
I TOLD MY BOSS I'D PULL AN EXTRA SHIFT TONIGHT!
HUH?!
YOU CAN'T DO THIS TONIGHT!! IT'S MY ONLY—
IT WAS REALLY NICE TO SEE YOU.
I'LL LEAVE YOU MY KEYS. YOU CAN GIVE THEM BACK LATER.
BANG!
GREAT.

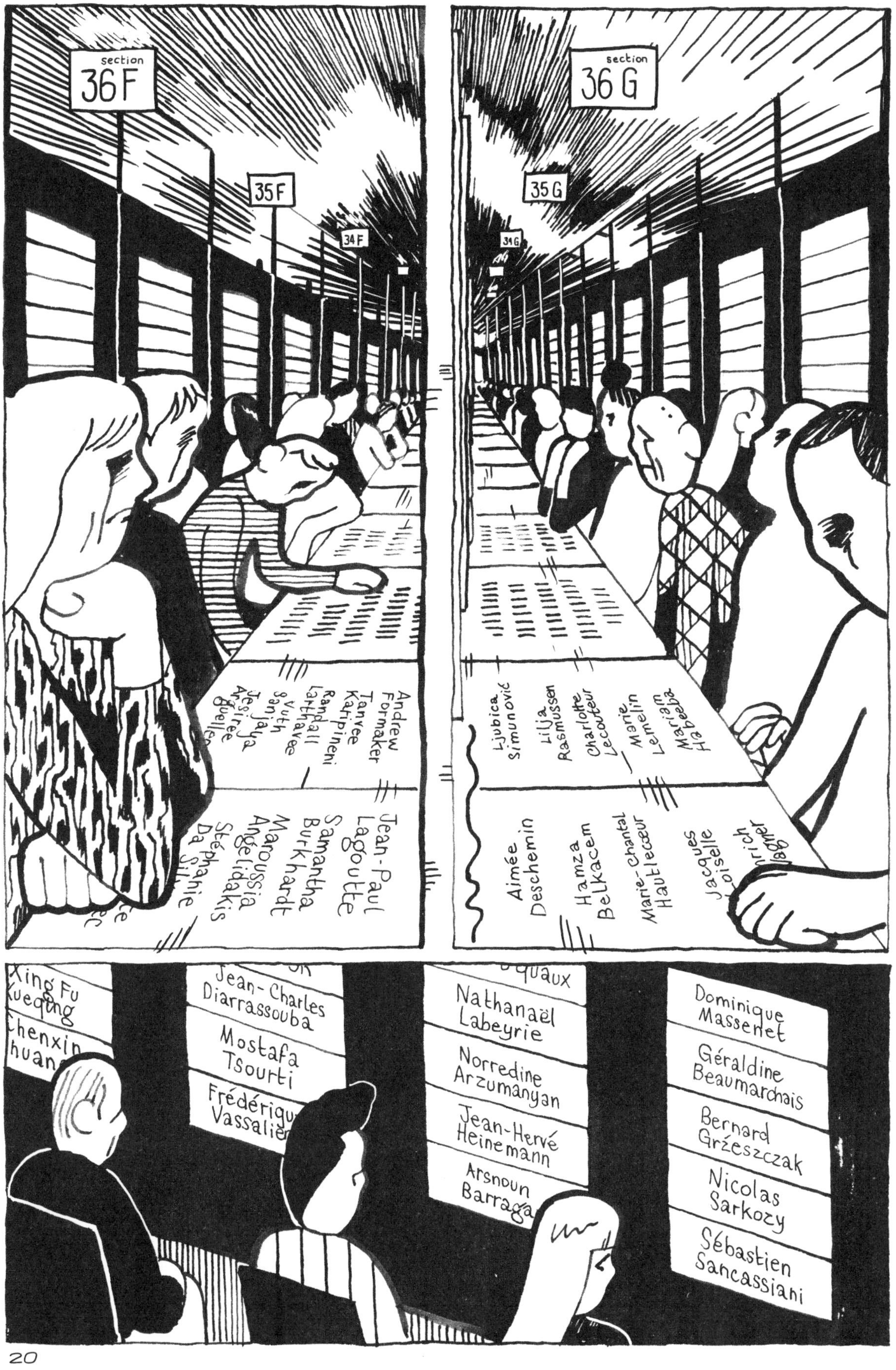
section
36F
35F
34F
Andrew Formaker
Jean-Paul Lagoutte
Samantha Burkhardt
Maroussia Angelidakis
section
36G
35G
34G
Lilja Rasmussen
Charlotte Lecouteur
Marie Lemelin
Aimée Deschemin
Hamza Belkacem
Marie-Chantal Hautlecoeur
Jacques Loiselle
Jean-Charles Diarrassouba
Mostafa Tsourti
Nathanaël Labeyrie
Norredine Arzumanyan
Jean-Hervé Heinemann
Dominique Massenet
Géraldine Beaumarchais
Bernard Grźeszczak
Nicolas Sarkozy
Sébastien Sancassiani

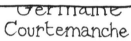
Germaine
Courtemanche

Capitolina
Kazantseva

Steingrimura
Baldursdot

Louis-Honoré
Karamazovitch

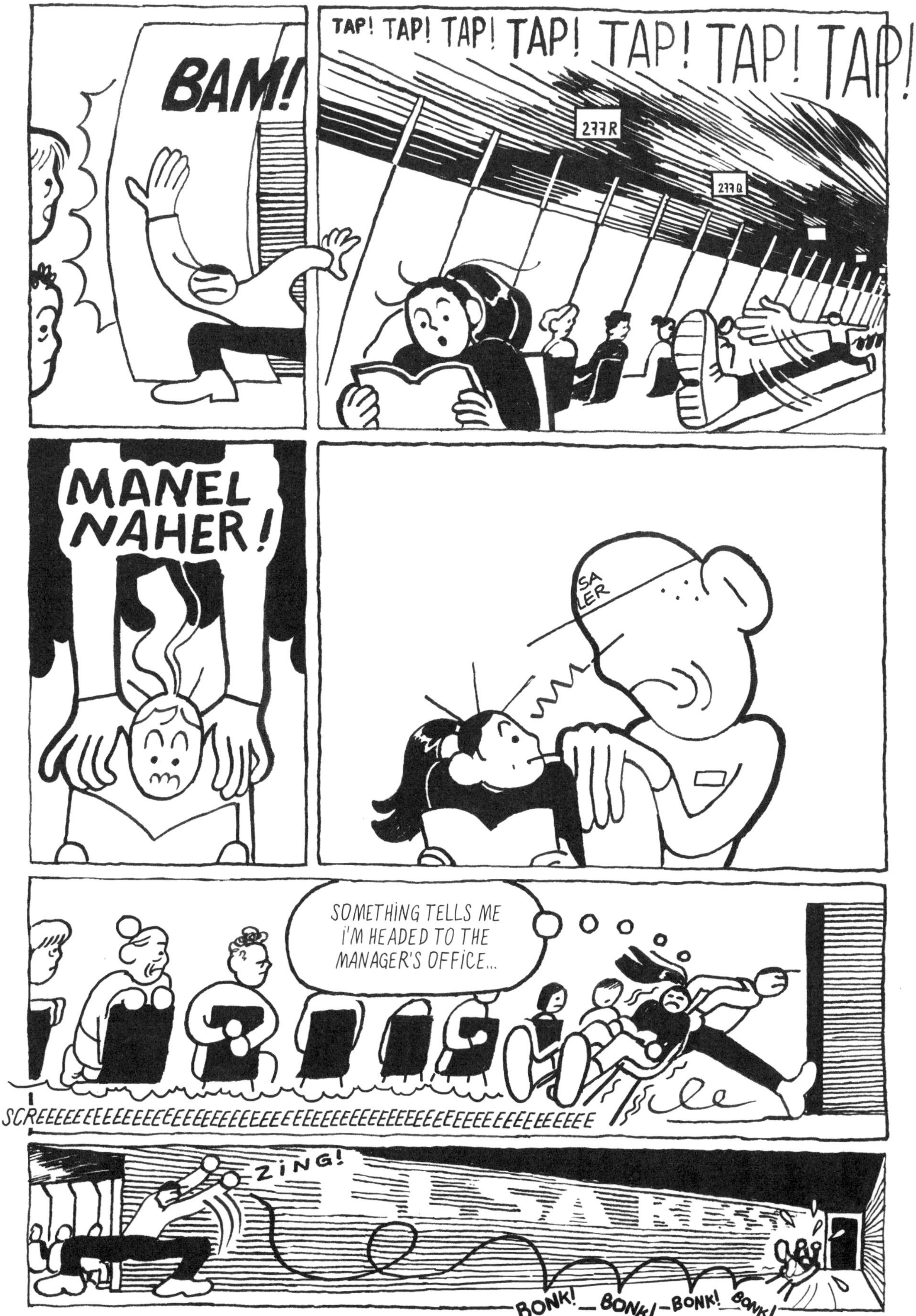
BAM!
TAP! TAP! TAP! TAP! TAP! TAP! TAP!
277R
277Q
MANEL NAHER!
SALER
SOMETHING TELLS ME I'M HEADED TO THE MANAGER'S OFFICE...
SCREEEEEEEEEEEEEEEEEEEEEEEEEEEEEEEEEEEEEEEEEEEEEEEEEEEEEEEEEE
ZING!
BONK! BONK! BONK! BONK!

MANEL NAHER.
YES?
I SUPPOSE YOU KNOW WHY YOU'VE BEEN SUMMONED. IT'S NOT EXACTLY THE FIRST TIME.
...
LISTEN, MANEL! JUST BECAUSE OUR CLIENTS DON'T PAY A LOT FOR OUR SERVICES DOESN'T MEAN YOU DON'T OWE THEM RESPECT!
THEIR LIVES ARE AT STAKE! IF YOU DON'T LOOK AT THEIR NAMES FOR TWO MINUTES, THEY'LL DIE!
THEY NEED YOU, MANEL NAHER.
THEY'RE ALONE IN THIS WORLD AND WE'RE THEIR ONLY CHANCE OF SURVIVAL.
KEEP A WARM PLACE FOR THEM IN YOUR THOUGHTS, AND WE'LL ALWAYS HAVE A PLACE FOR YOU HERE AT OUR COMPANY.

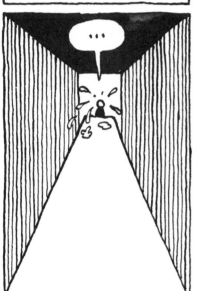

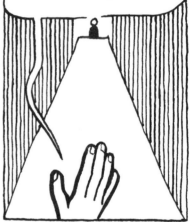

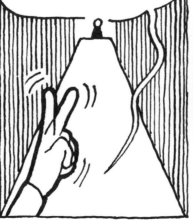

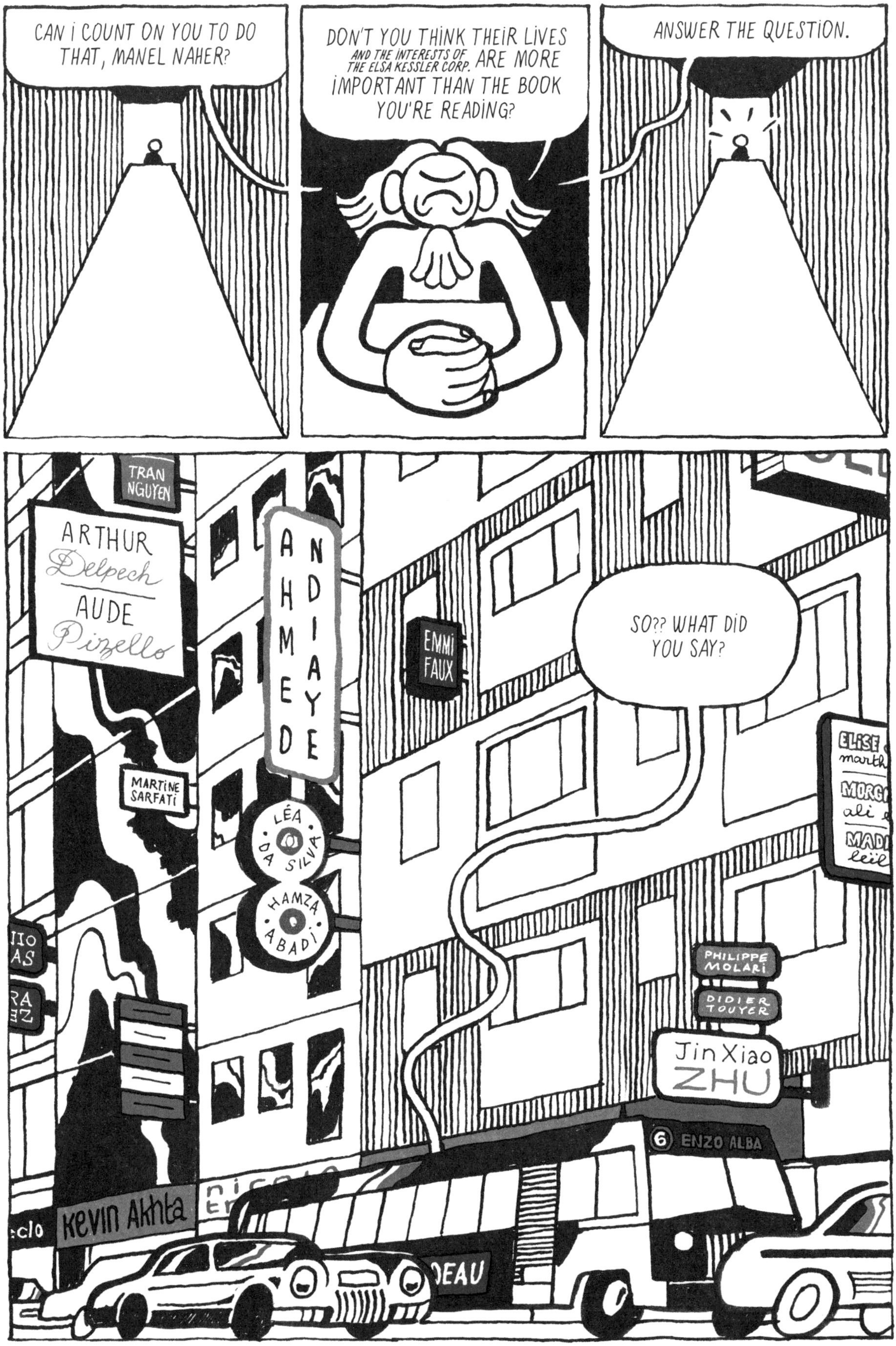
CAN I COUNT ON YOU TO DO THAT, MANEL NAHER?
DON'T YOU THINK THEIR LIVES AND THE INTERESTS OF THE ELSA KESSLER CORP. ARE MORE IMPORTANT THAN THE BOOK YOU'RE READING?
ANSWER THE QUESTION.
TRAN NGUYEN
ARTHUR Delpech
AUDE Pizello
AHMED
NDIAYE
EMMI FAUX
SO?? WHAT DID YOU SAY?
MARTINE SARFATI
LÉA DA SILVA
HAMZA ABADI
PHILIPPE MOLARI
DIDIER TOUYER
Jin Xiao ZHU
6 ENZO ALBA
Kevin Akhta

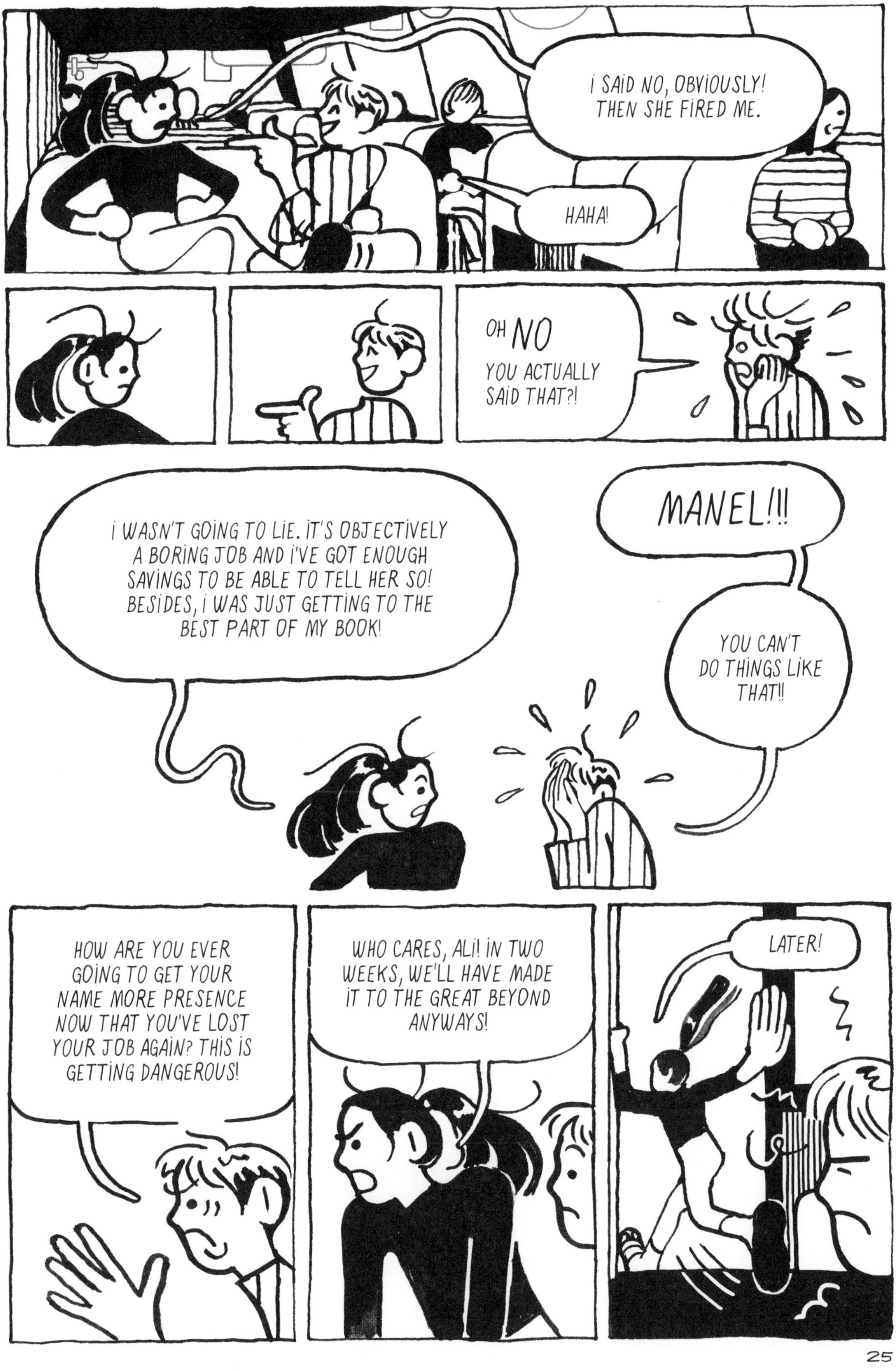

I SAID NO, OBVIOUSLY! THEN SHE FIRED ME.
HAHA!
OH NO YOU ACTUALLY SAID THAT?!
I WASN'T GOING TO LIE. IT'S OBJECTIVELY A BORING JOB AND I'VE GOT ENOUGH SAVINGS TO BE ABLE TO TELL HER SO! BESIDES, I WAS JUST GETTING TO THE BEST PART OF MY BOOK!
MANEL!!!
YOU CAN'T DO THINGS LIKE THAT!!
HOW ARE YOU EVER GOING TO GET YOUR NAME MORE PRESENCE NOW THAT YOU'VE LOST YOUR JOB AGAIN? THIS IS GETTING DANGEROUS!
WHO CARES, ALI! IN TWO WEEKS, WE'LL HAVE MADE IT TO THE GREAT BEYOND ANYWAYS!
LATER!

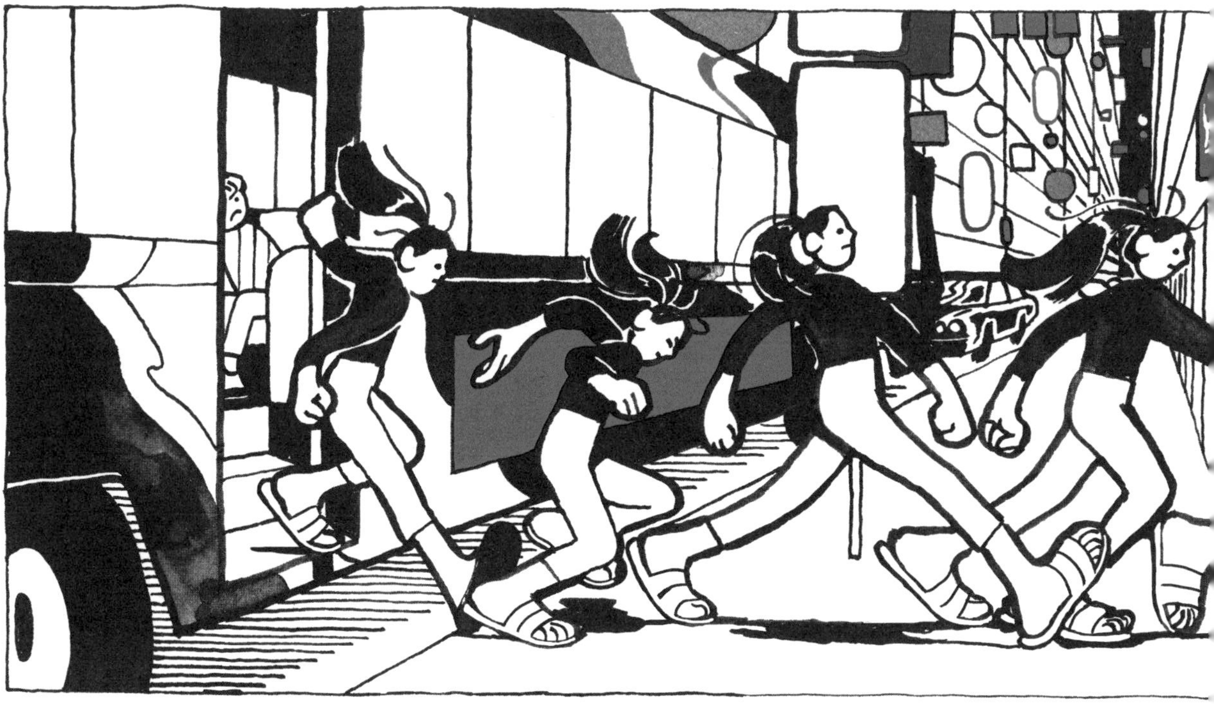

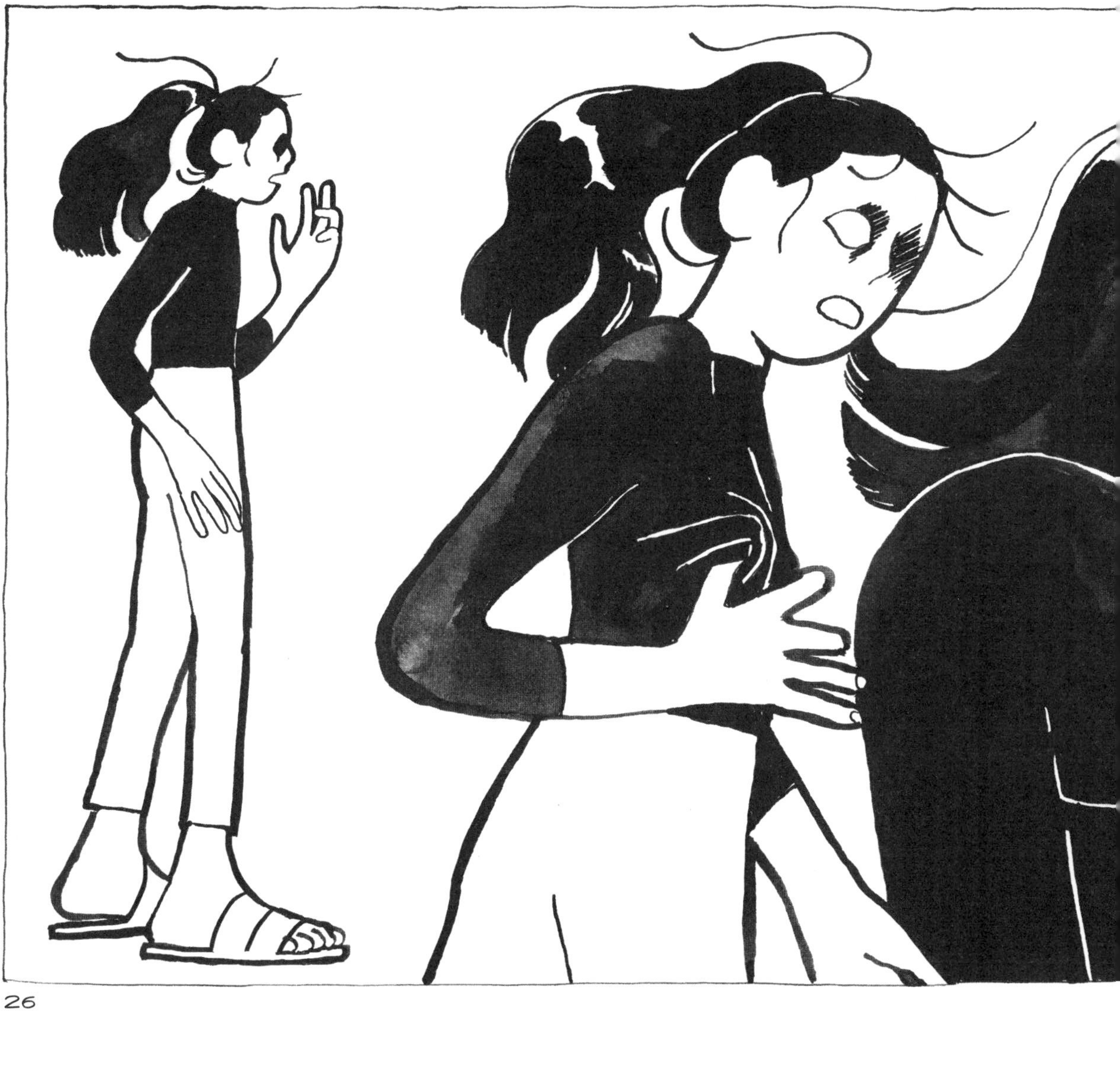

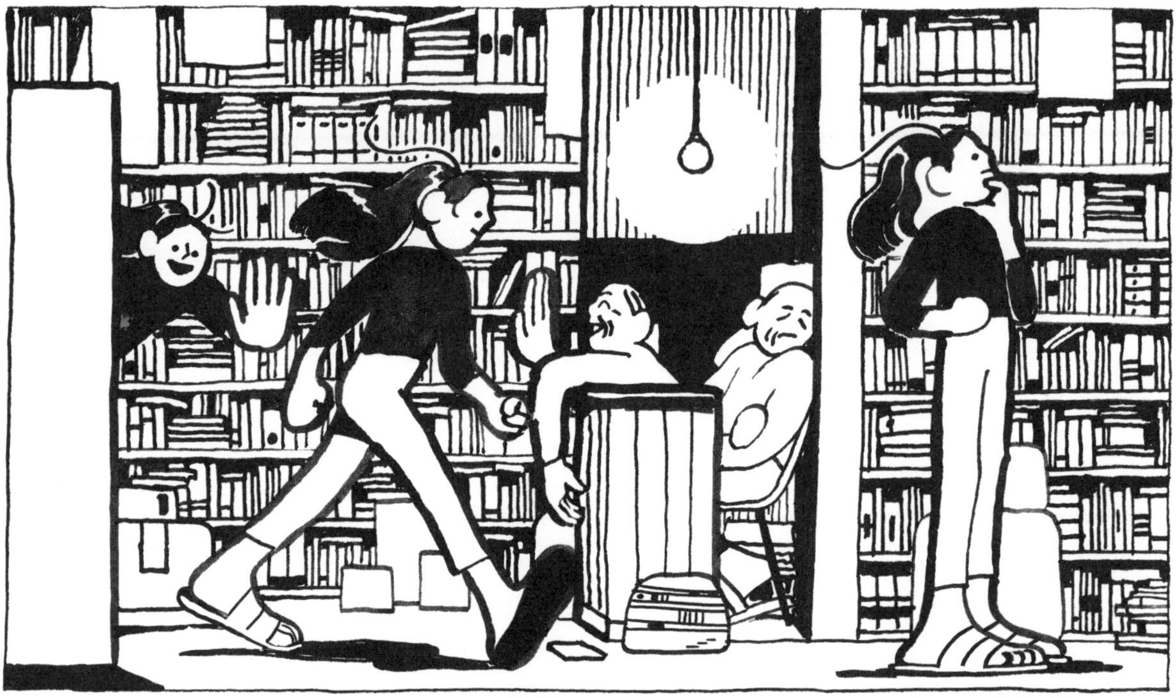

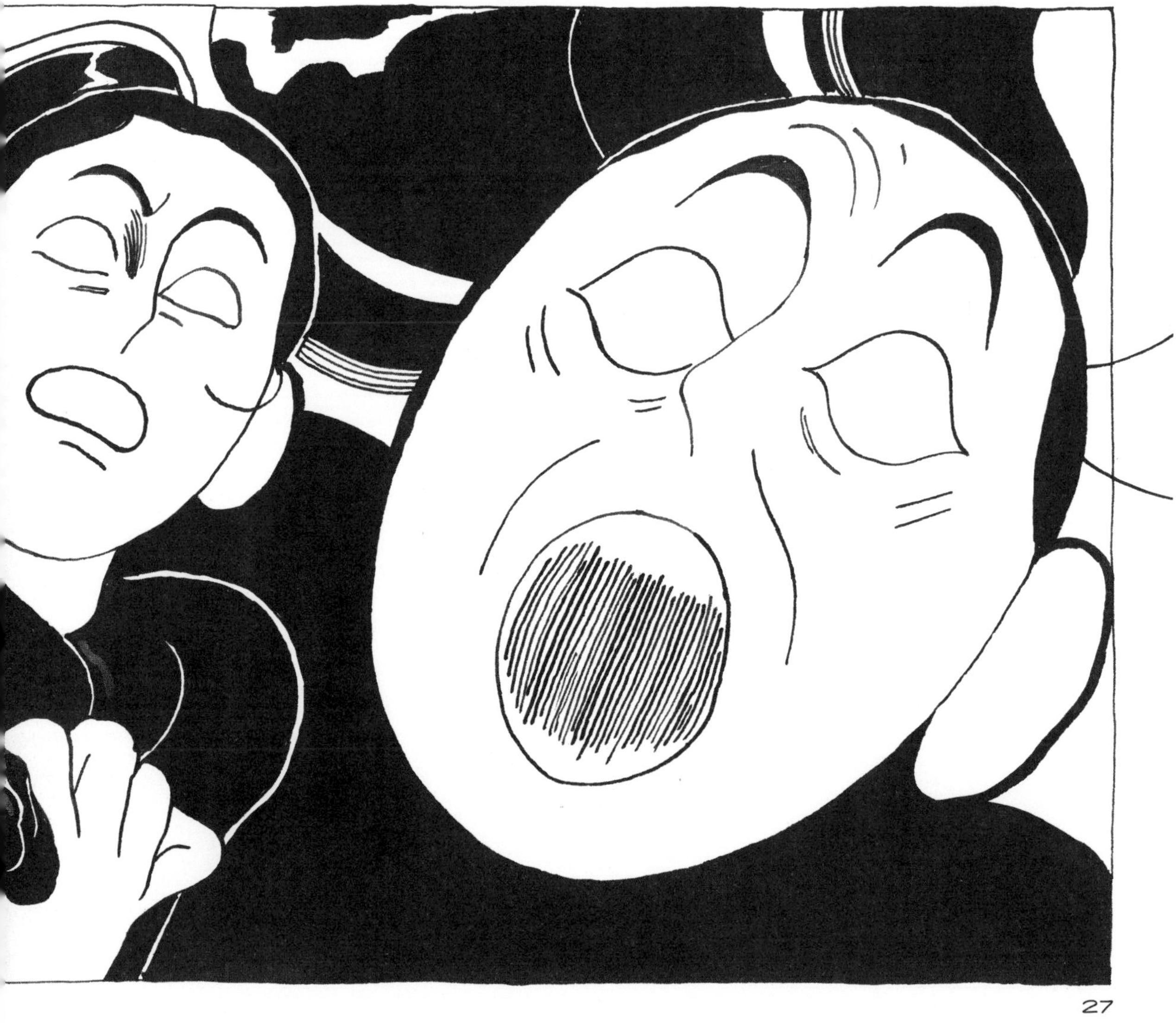

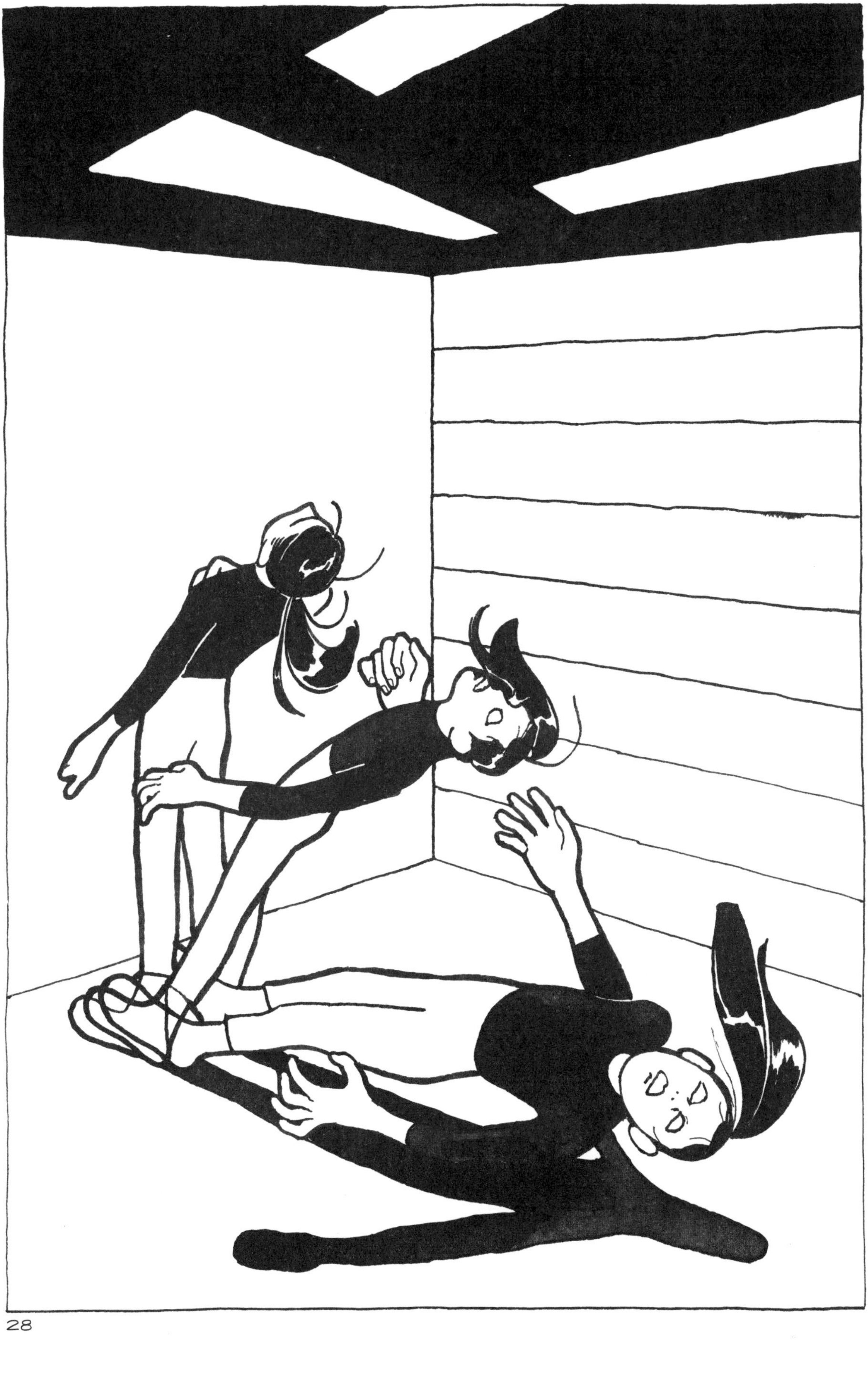

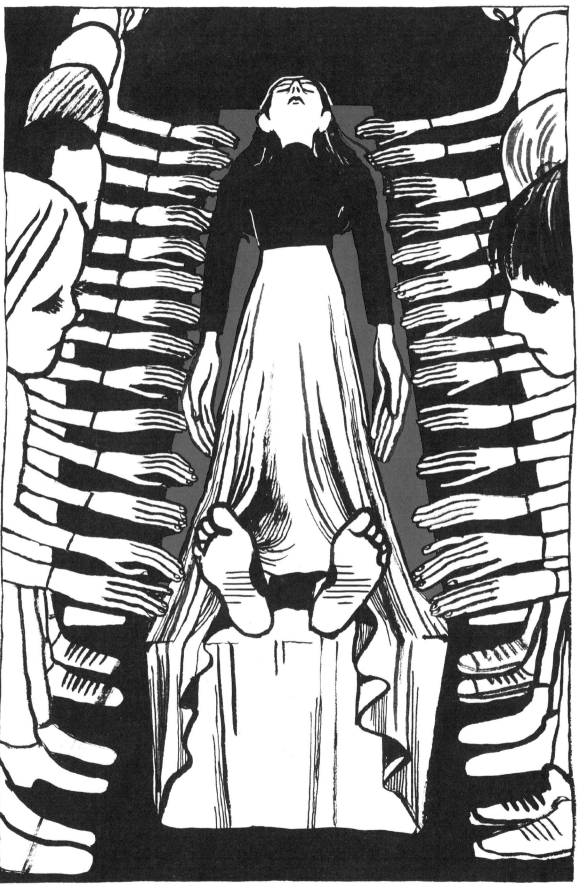

AIAN
NAL

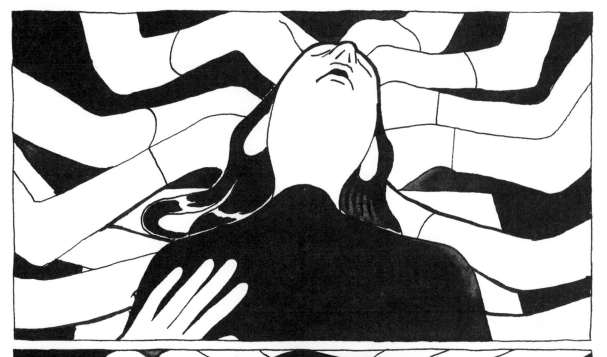

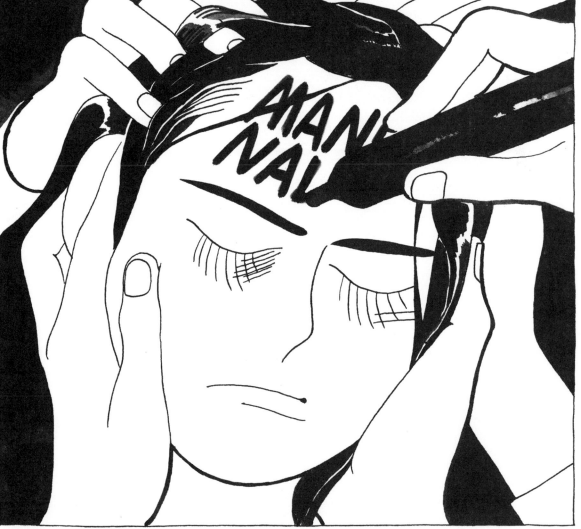

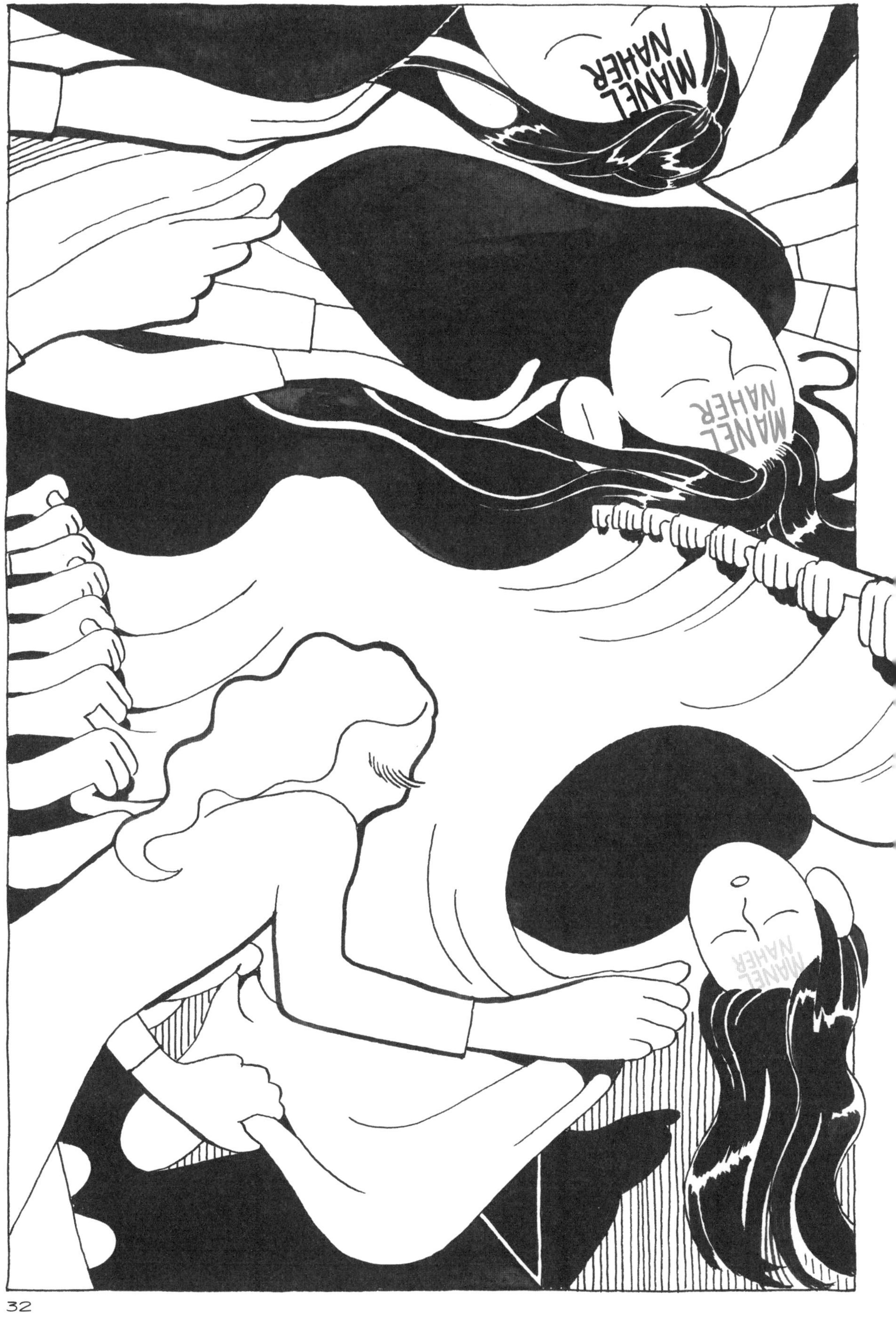
MANEL NAHER
MANEL NAHER
MANEL NAHER

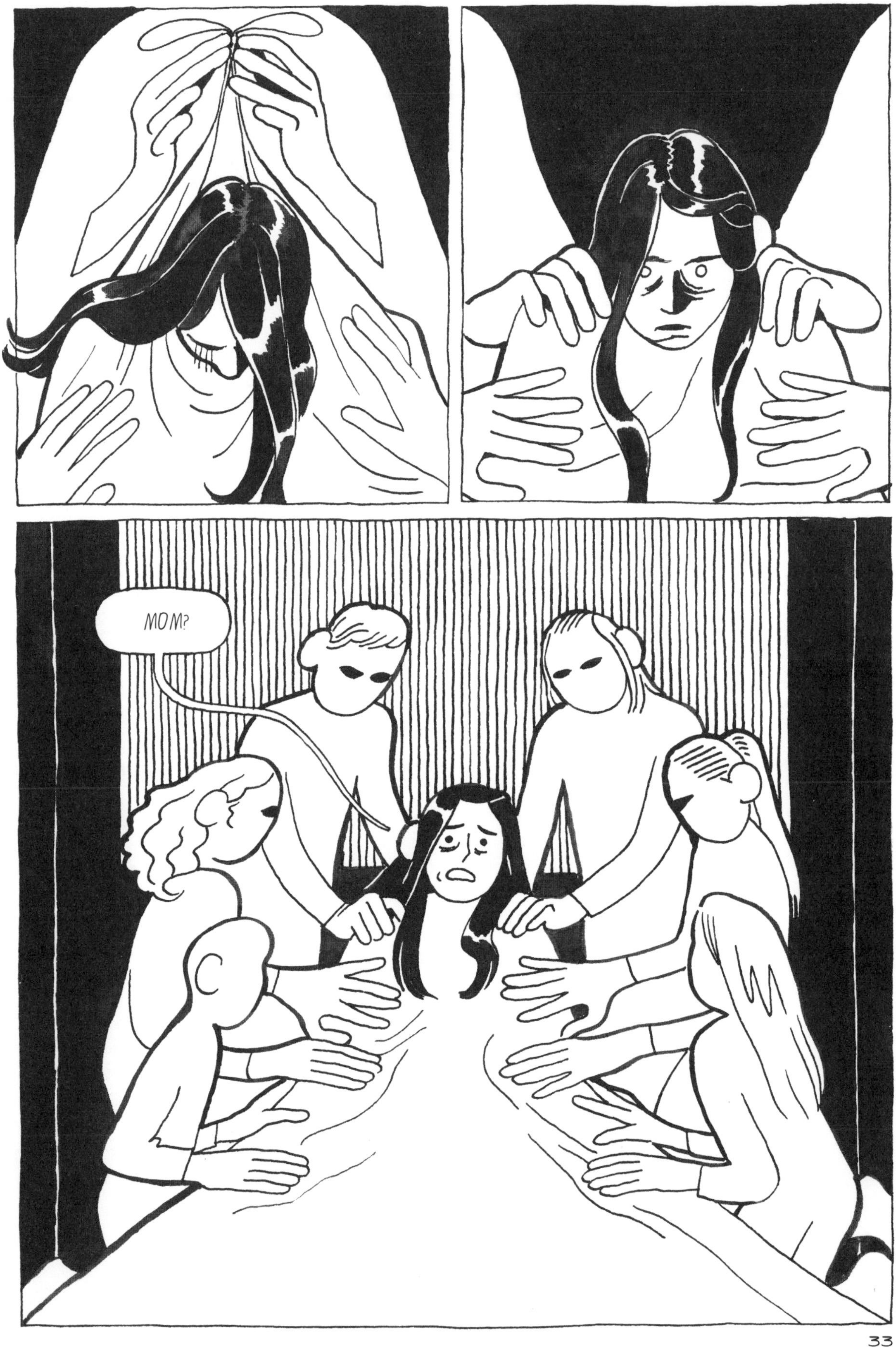
MOM?

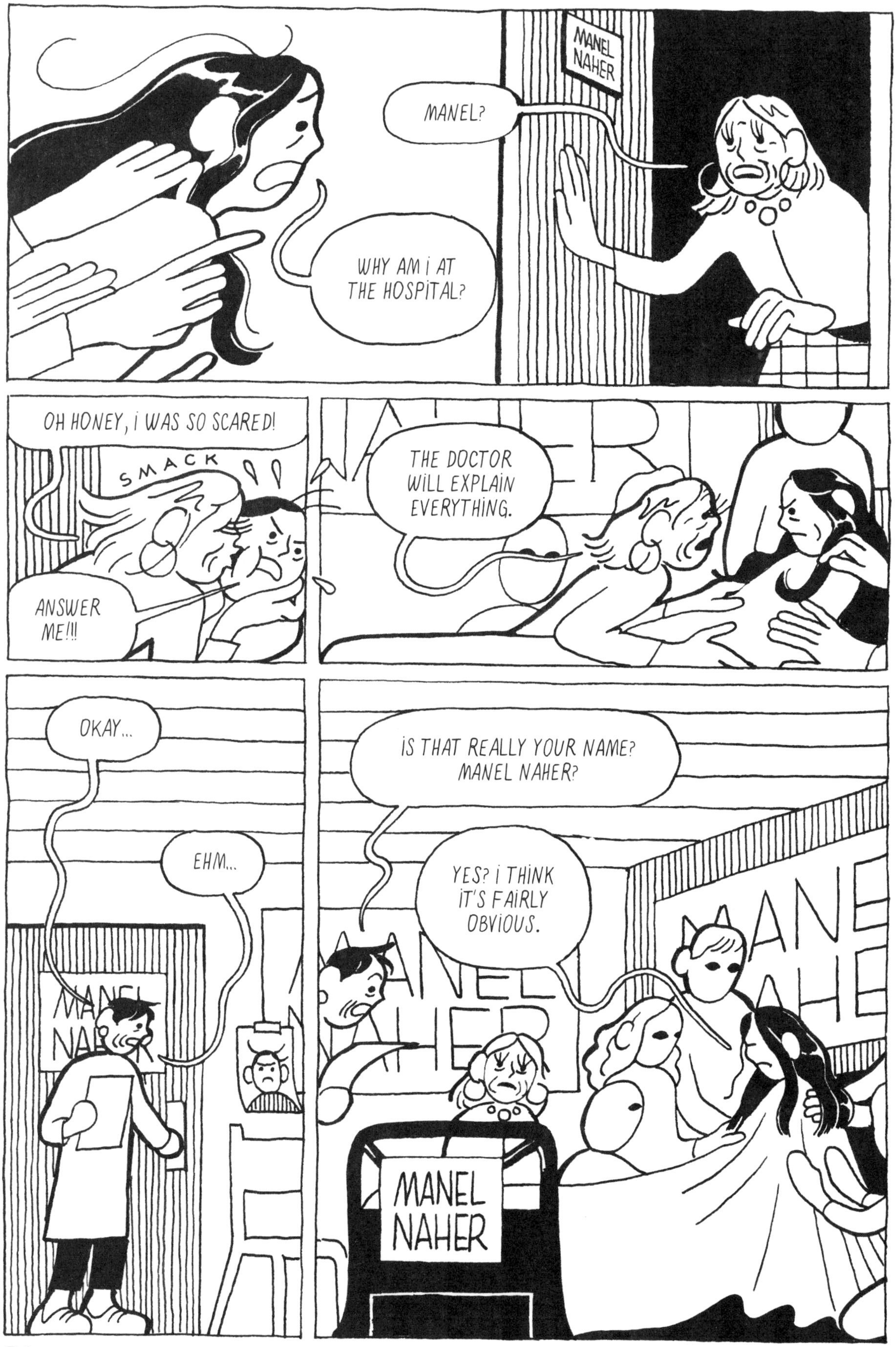
MANEL NAHER
MANEL?
WHY AM I AT THE HOSPITAL?
OH HONEY, I WAS SO SCARED!
SMACK
ANSWER ME!!!
THE DOCTOR WILL EXPLAIN EVERYTHING.
OKAY...
EHM...
MANEL NAHER
IS THAT REALLY YOUR NAME? MANEL NAHER?
YES? I THINK IT'S FAIRLY OBVIOUS.
MANEL NAHER

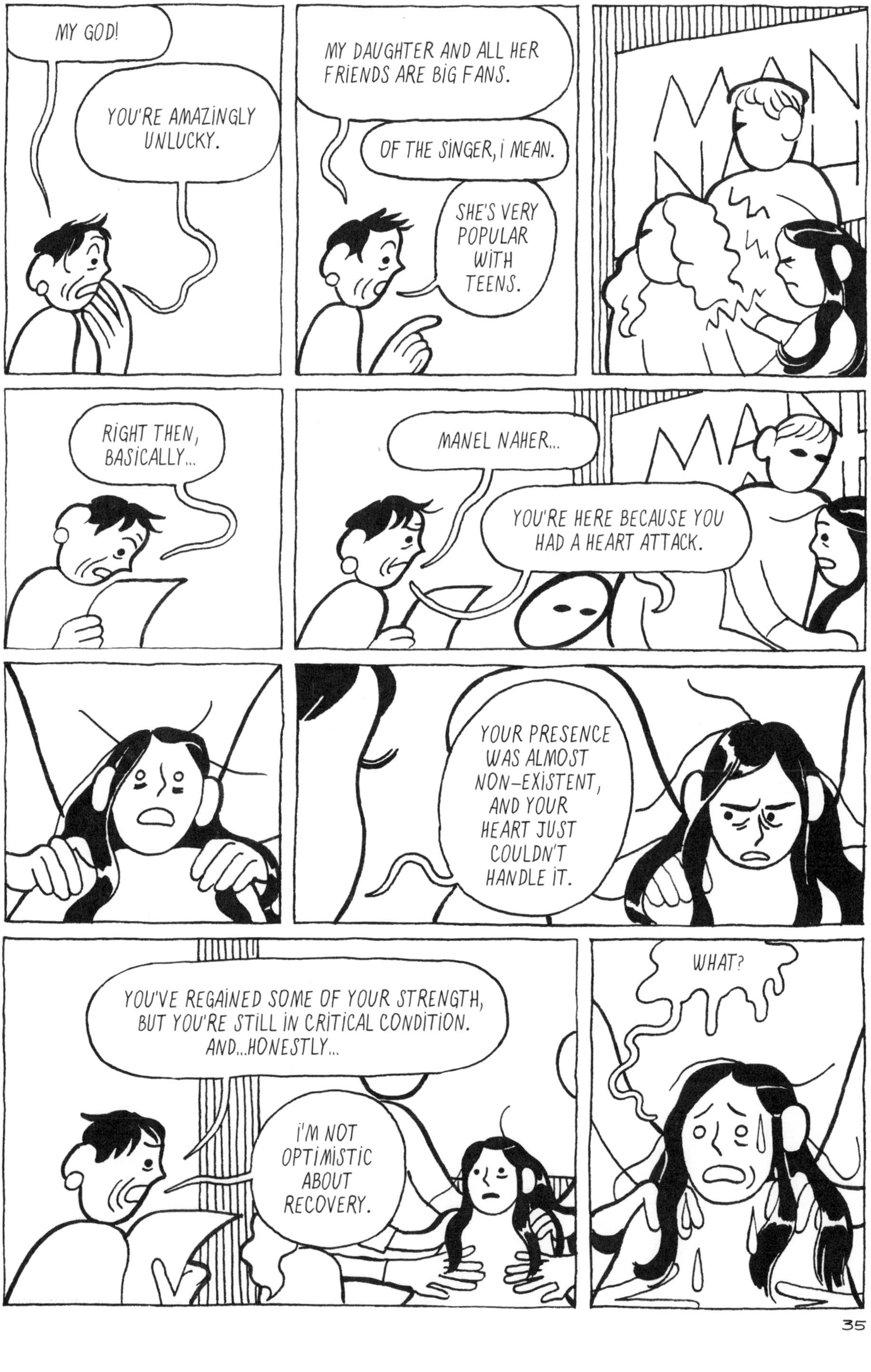
MY GOD!
YOU'RE AMAZINGLY UNLUCKY.
MY DAUGHTER AND ALL HER FRIENDS ARE BIG FANS.
OF THE SINGER, I MEAN.
SHE'S VERY POPULAR WITH TEENS.
MAN
RIGHT THEN, BASICALLY...
MANEL NAHER...
MA
YOU'RE HERE BECAUSE YOU HAD A HEART ATTACK.
YOUR PRESENCE WAS ALMOST NON-EXISTENT, AND YOUR HEART JUST COULDN'T HANDLE IT.
YOU'VE REGAINED SOME OF YOUR STRENGTH, BUT YOU'RE STILL IN CRITICAL CONDITION. AND...HONESTLY...
I'M NOT OPTIMISTIC ABOUT RECOVERY.
WHAT?

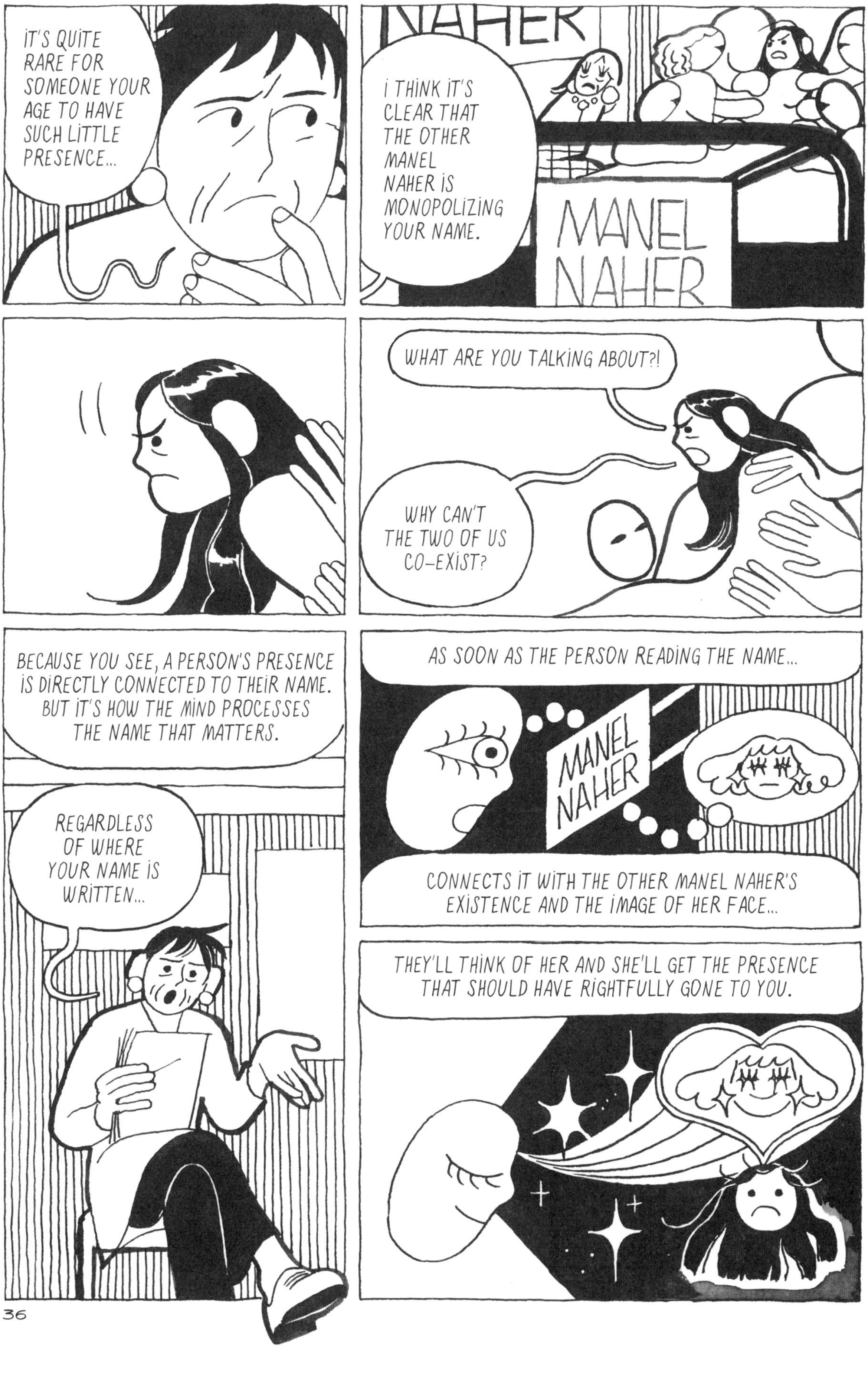
NAHER
IT'S QUITE RARE FOR SOMEONE YOUR AGE TO HAVE SUCH LITTLE PRESENCE...
I THINK IT'S CLEAR THAT THE OTHER MANEL NAHER IS MONOPOLIZING YOUR NAME.
MANEL NAHER
WHAT ARE YOU TALKING ABOUT?!
WHY CAN'T THE TWO OF US CO-EXIST?
BECAUSE YOU SEE, A PERSON'S PRESENCE IS DIRECTLY CONNECTED TO THEIR NAME. BUT IT'S HOW THE MIND PROCESSES THE NAME THAT MATTERS.
AS SOON AS THE PERSON READING THE NAME...
MANEL NAHER
CONNECTS IT WITH THE OTHER MANEL NAHER'S EXISTENCE AND THE IMAGE OF HER FACE...
REGARDLESS OF WHERE YOUR NAME IS WRITTEN...
THEY'LL THINK OF HER AND SHE'LL GET THE PRESENCE THAT SHOULD HAVE RIGHTFULLY GONE TO YOU.

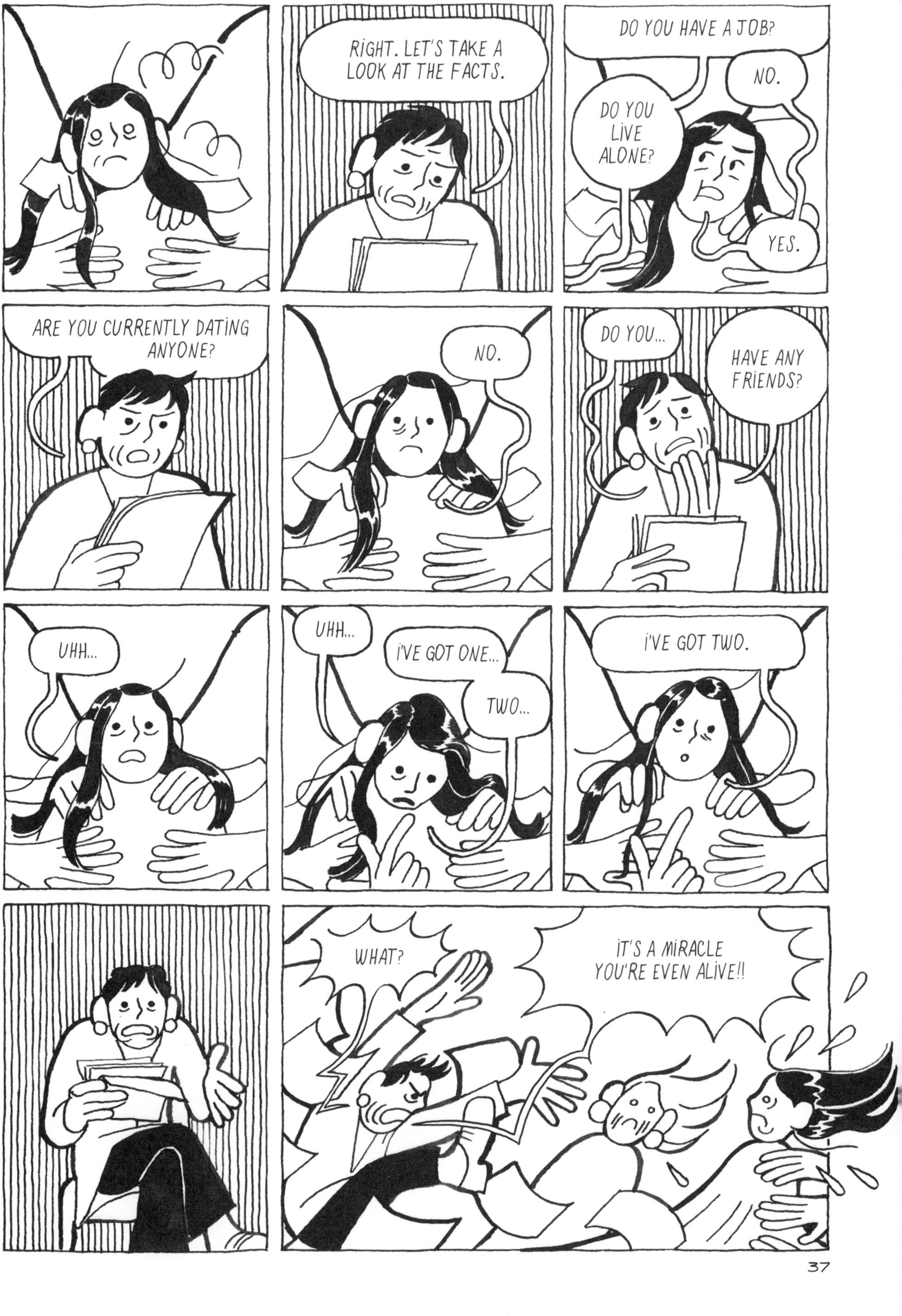
RIGHT. LET'S TAKE A LOOK AT THE FACTS.
DO YOU HAVE A JOB?
NO.
DO YOU LIVE ALONE?
YES.
ARE YOU CURRENTLY DATING ANYONE?
NO.
DO YOU...
HAVE ANY FRIENDS?
UHH...
UHH...
I'VE GOT ONE...
TWO...
I'VE GOT TWO.
WHAT?
IT'S A MIRACLE YOU'RE EVEN ALIVE!!

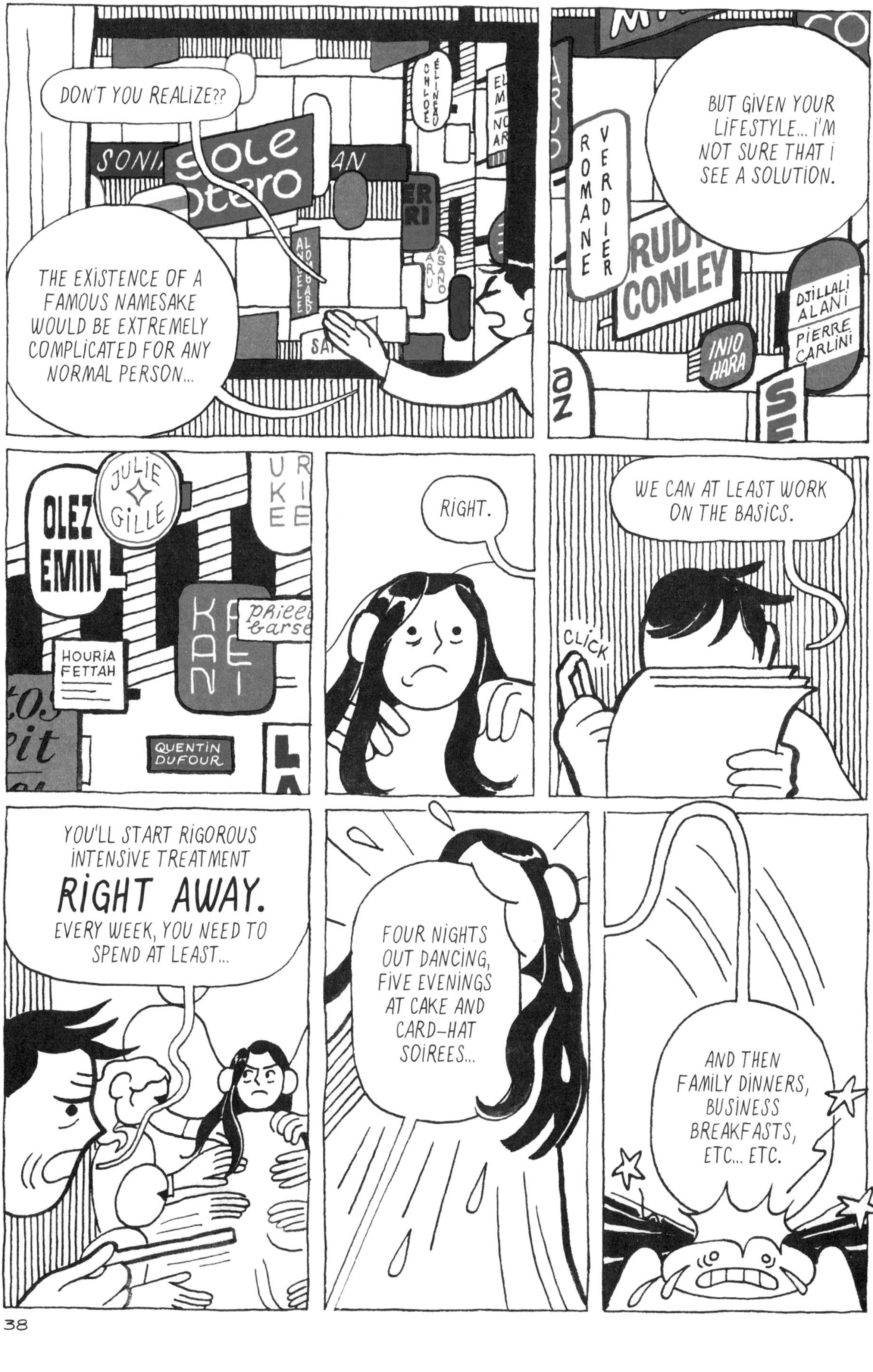
DON'T YOU REALIZE??
SOLE OTERO
THE EXISTENCE OF A FAMOUS NAMESAKE WOULD BE EXTREMELY COMPLICATED FOR ANY NORMAL PERSON...
ROMANE VERDIER
RUDY CONLEY
BUT GIVEN YOUR LIFESTYLE... I'M NOT SURE THAT I SEE A SOLUTION.
DJILLALI ALANI
PIERRE CARLINI
INIO HARA
OLEZ EMIN
JULIE GILLE
HOURIA FETTAH
QUENTIN DUFOUR
RIGHT.
WE CAN AT LEAST WORK ON THE BASICS.
CLICK
YOU'LL START RIGOROUS INTENSIVE TREATMENT RIGHT AWAY. EVERY WEEK, YOU NEED TO SPEND AT LEAST...
FOUR NIGHTS OUT DANCING, FIVE EVENINGS AT CAKE AND CARD-HAT SOIREES...
AND THEN FAMILY DINNERS, BUSINESS BREAKFASTS, ETC... ETC.

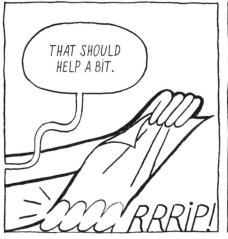

THAT SHOULD HELP A BIT.

RRRIP!

AND I'M GOING TO MAKE YOU AN APPOINTMENT RIGHT NOW FOR A PRESENCE TEST NEXT MONTH.

UMM...ABOUT THE PRESENCE TEST...

SCRITCHSCRUCRRRICRSSHCRCRITCHUCRRR

I'M NOT REALLY SURE WE CAN AFFORD IT.

I'LL LET YOU THINK ON IT THEN...

GOBERT

BUT WE'RE TALKING ABOUT YOUR DAUGHTER'S FUTURE, MA'AM.

CALL ME ONCE YOU'VE MADE A DECISION.

STAY STRONG, MANEL NAHER.

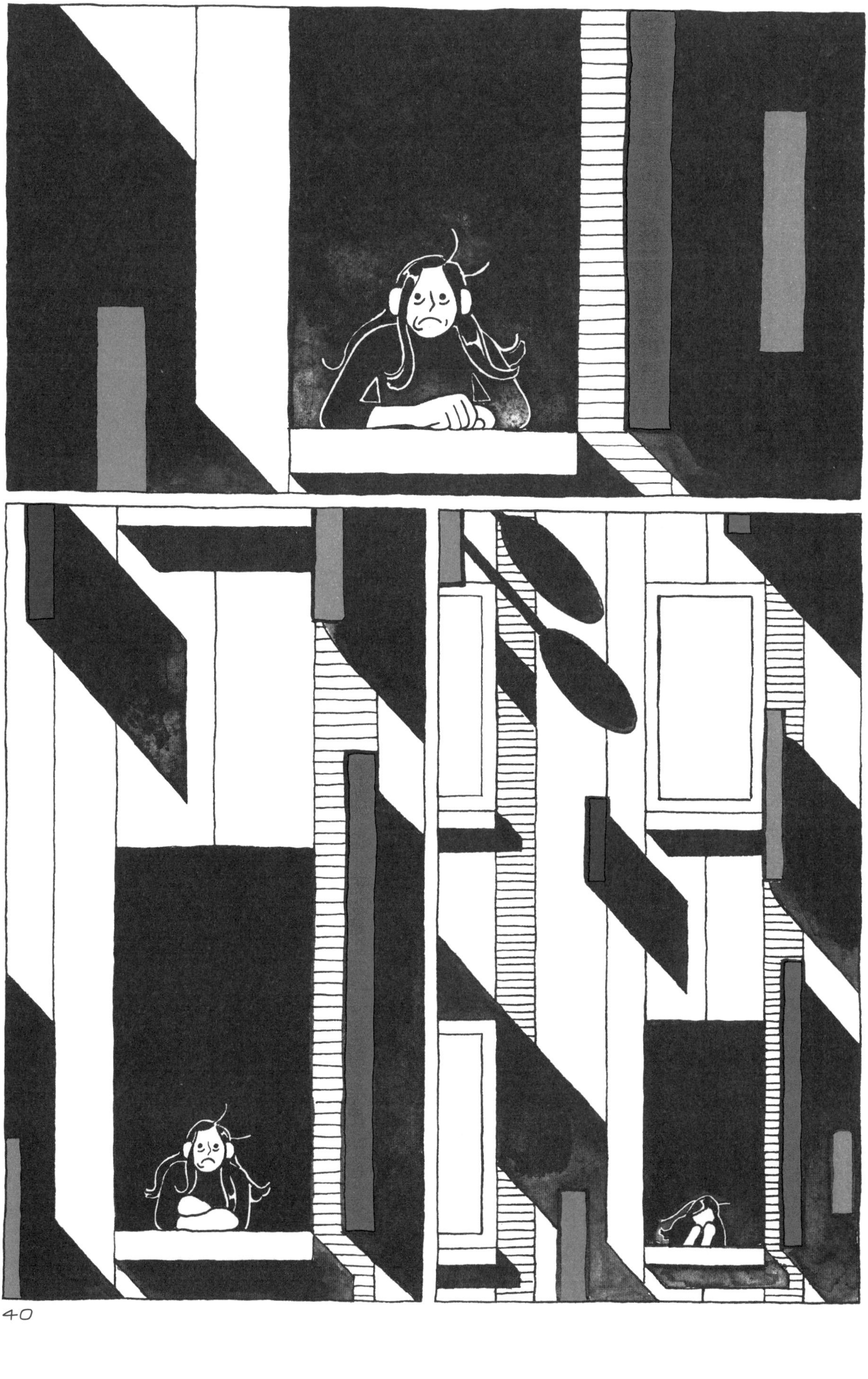

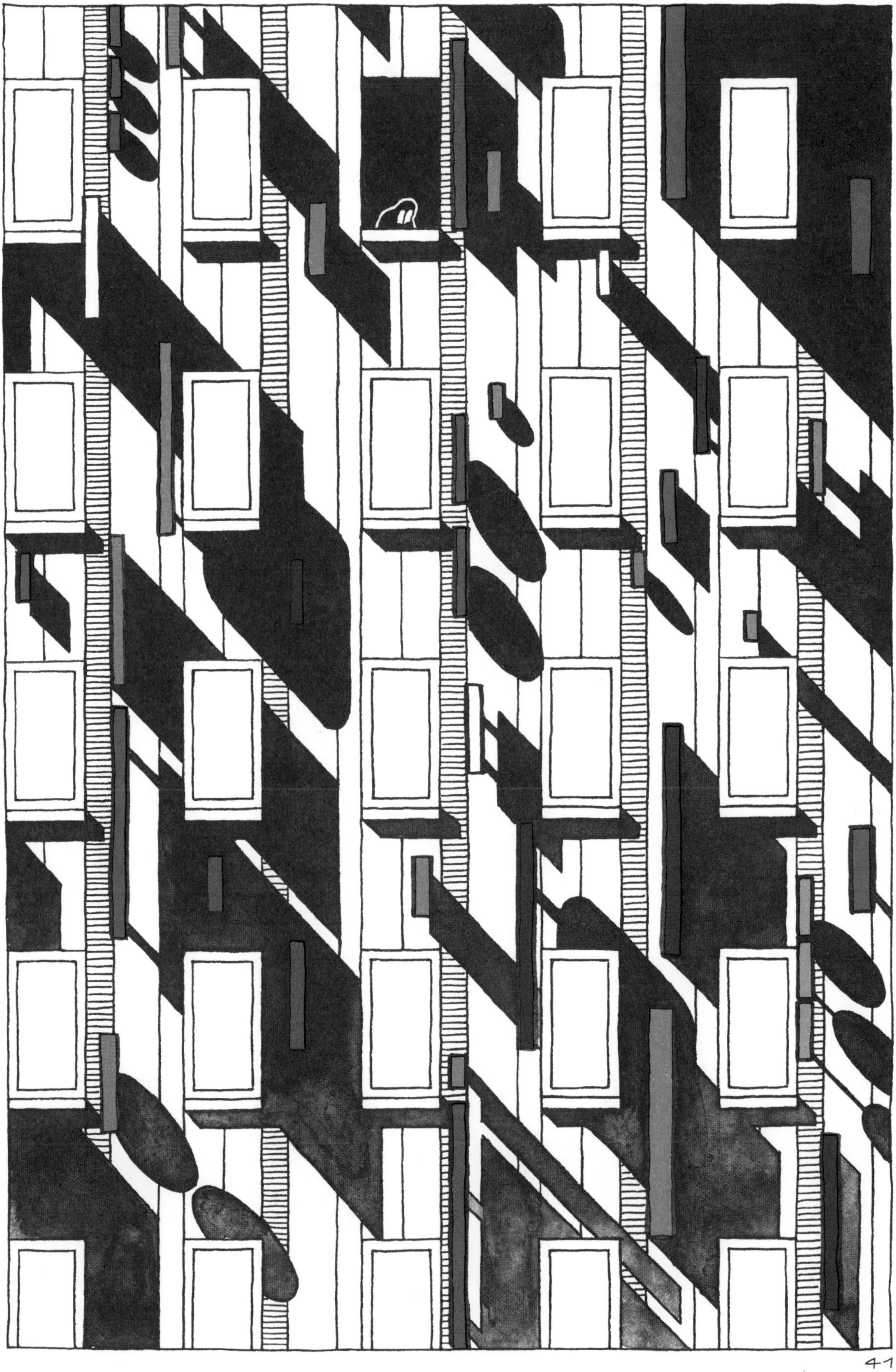

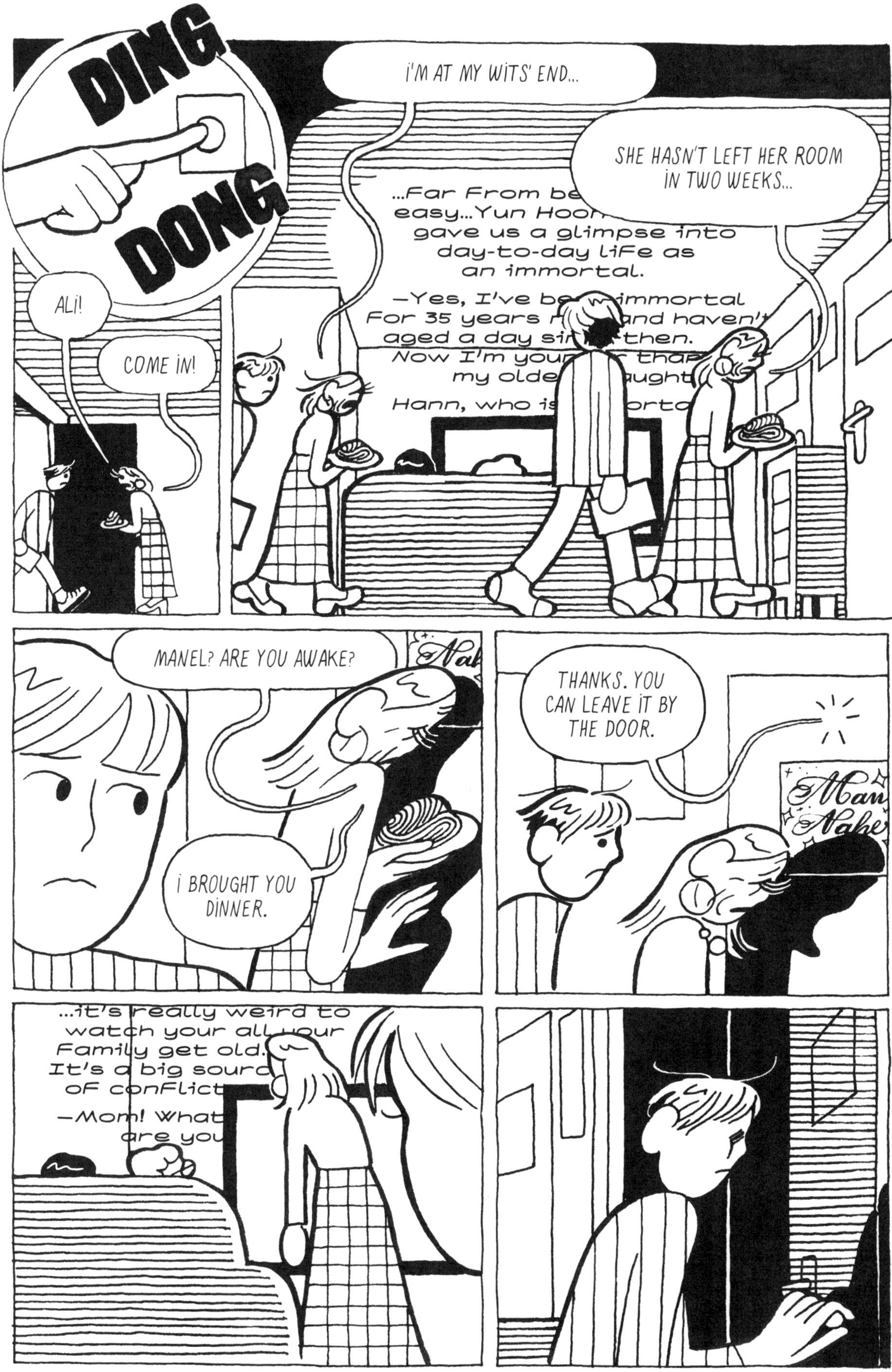
DING
DONG
ALI!
COME IN!
I'M AT MY WITS' END...
...Far From be
easy...Yun Hoon
gave us a glimpse into
day-to-day life as
an immortal.
SHE HASN'T LEFT HER ROOM IN TWO WEEKS...
MANEL? ARE YOU AWAKE?
I BROUGHT YOU DINNER.
THANKS. YOU CAN LEAVE IT BY THE DOOR.
...it's really weird to
watch your all your
Family get old.
It's a big sourc
of conflict
—Mom! What
are you

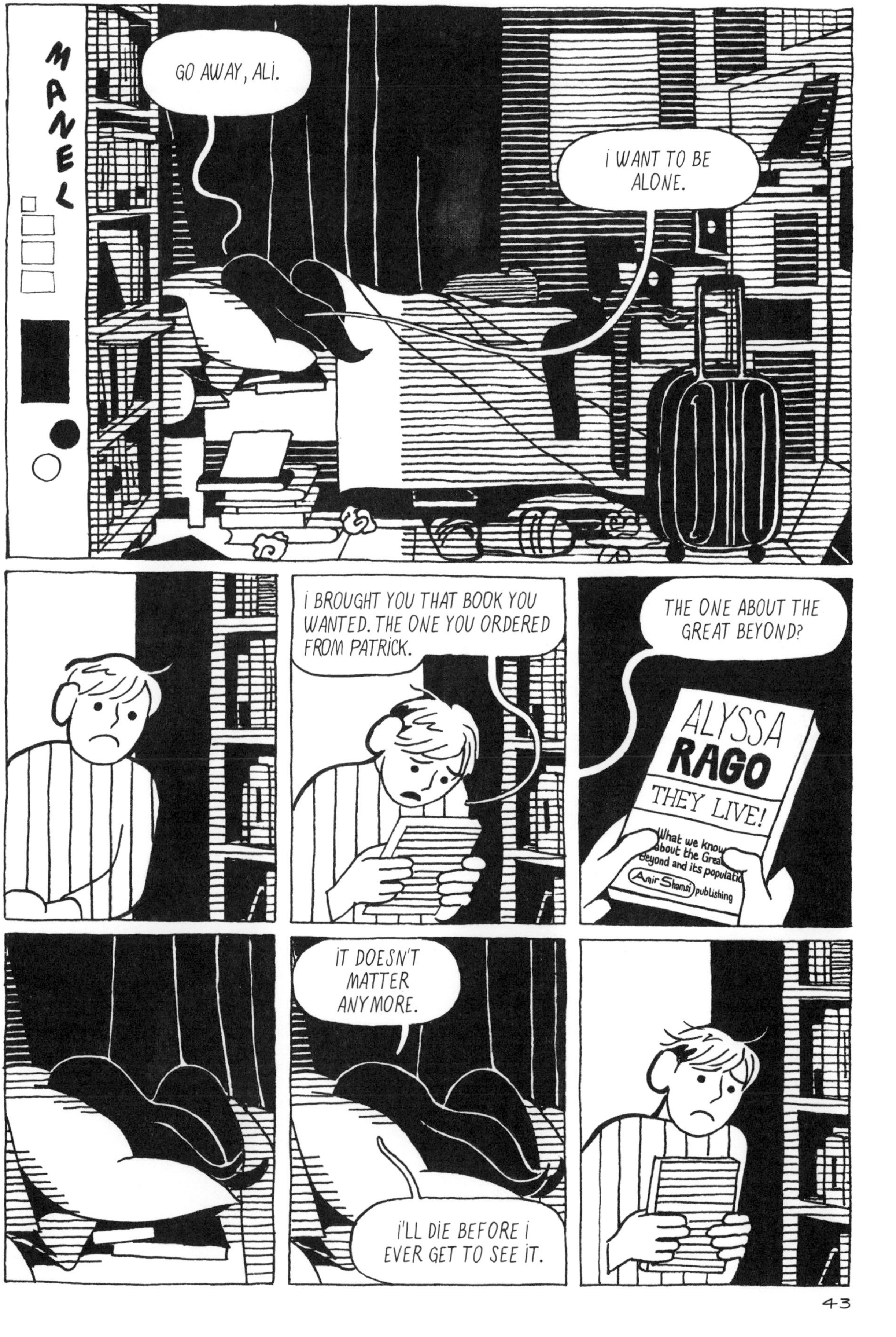
MANEL
GO AWAY, ALI.
I WANT TO BE ALONE.
I BROUGHT YOU THAT BOOK YOU WANTED. THE ONE YOU ORDERED FROM PATRICK.
THE ONE ABOUT THE GREAT BEYOND?
ALYSSA RAGO
THEY LIVE!
Amir Shamsi publishing
IT DOESN'T MATTER ANYMORE.
I'LL DIE BEFORE I EVER GET TO SEE IT.

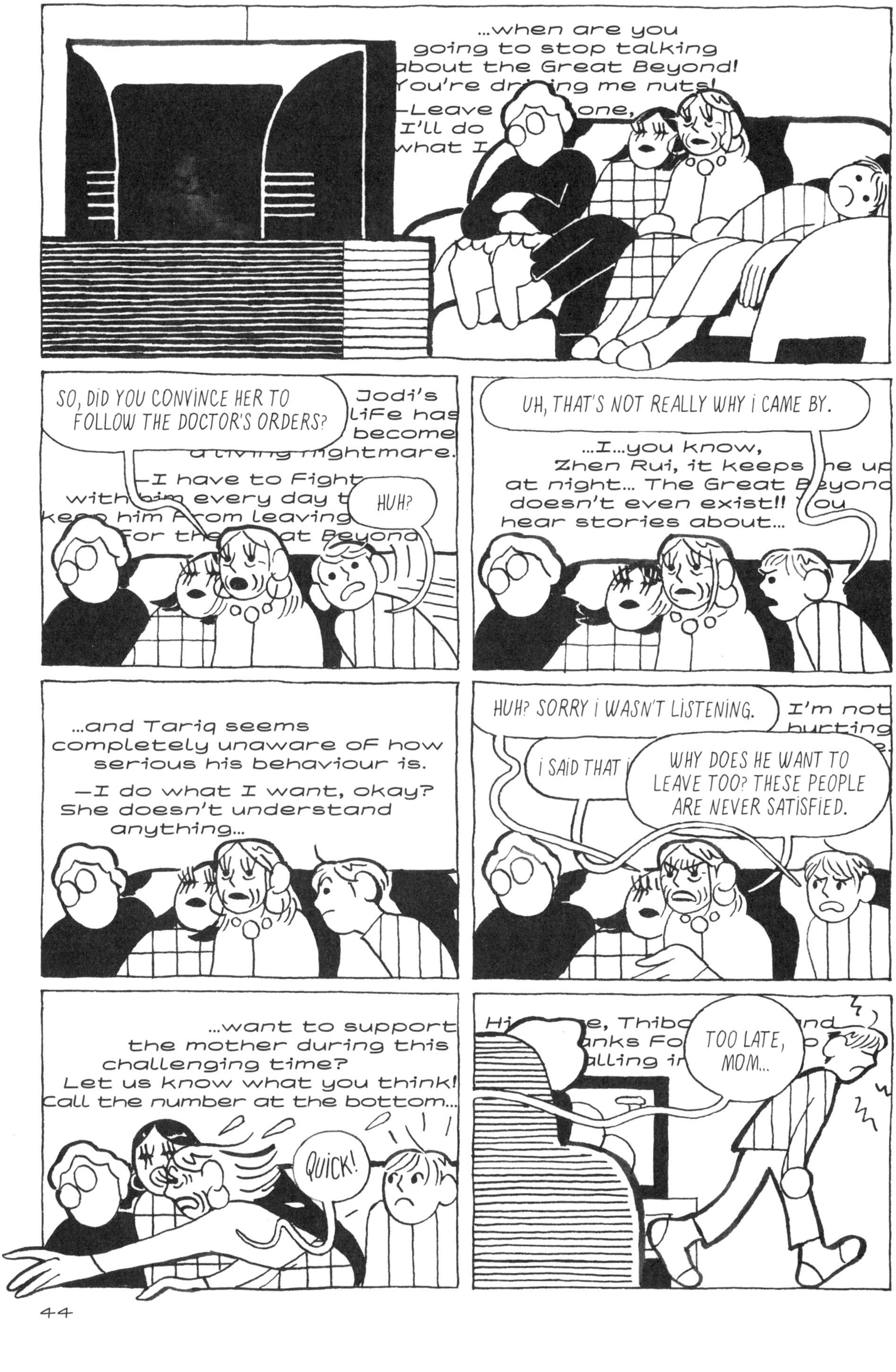

...when are you going to stop talking
about the Great Beyond!
You're dri ing me nuts!
—Leave one,
I'll do
what I
SO, DID YOU CONVINCE HER TO FOLLOW THE DOCTOR'S ORDERS?
Jodi's life has become
a living nightmare.
—I have to fight
with him every day t
keep him from leaving
for the at Beyond
HUH?
UH, THAT'S NOT REALLY WHY I CAME BY.
...I...you know,
Zhen Rui, it keeps e up
at night... The Great Beyond
doesn't even exist!! ou
hear stories about...
...and Tariq seems
completely unaware of how
serious his behaviour is.
—I do what I want, okay?
She doesn't understand
anything...
HUH? SORRY I WASN'T LISTENING.
I'm not
hurting
I SAID THAT I
WHY DOES HE WANT TO LEAVE TOO? THESE PEOPLE ARE NEVER SATISFIED.
...want to support
the mother during this
challenging time?
Let us know what you think!
Call the number at the bottom...
QUICK!
e, Thib nd
anks fo
alling in
TOO LATE, MOM...

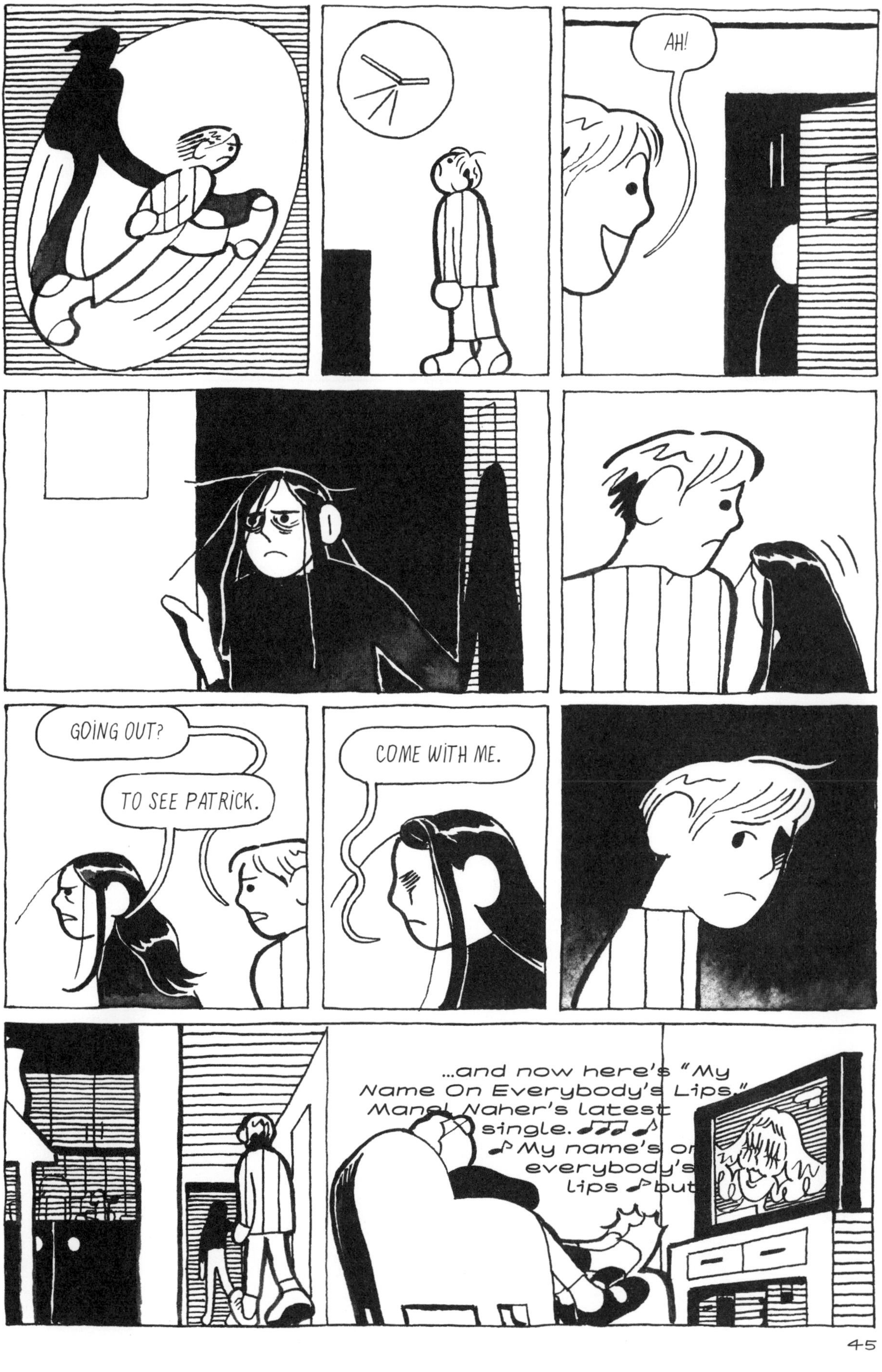
AH!
GOING OUT?
TO SEE PATRICK.
COME WITH ME.
...and now here's "My Name On Everybody's Lips." Manel Naher's latest single.
My name's on everybody's lips but

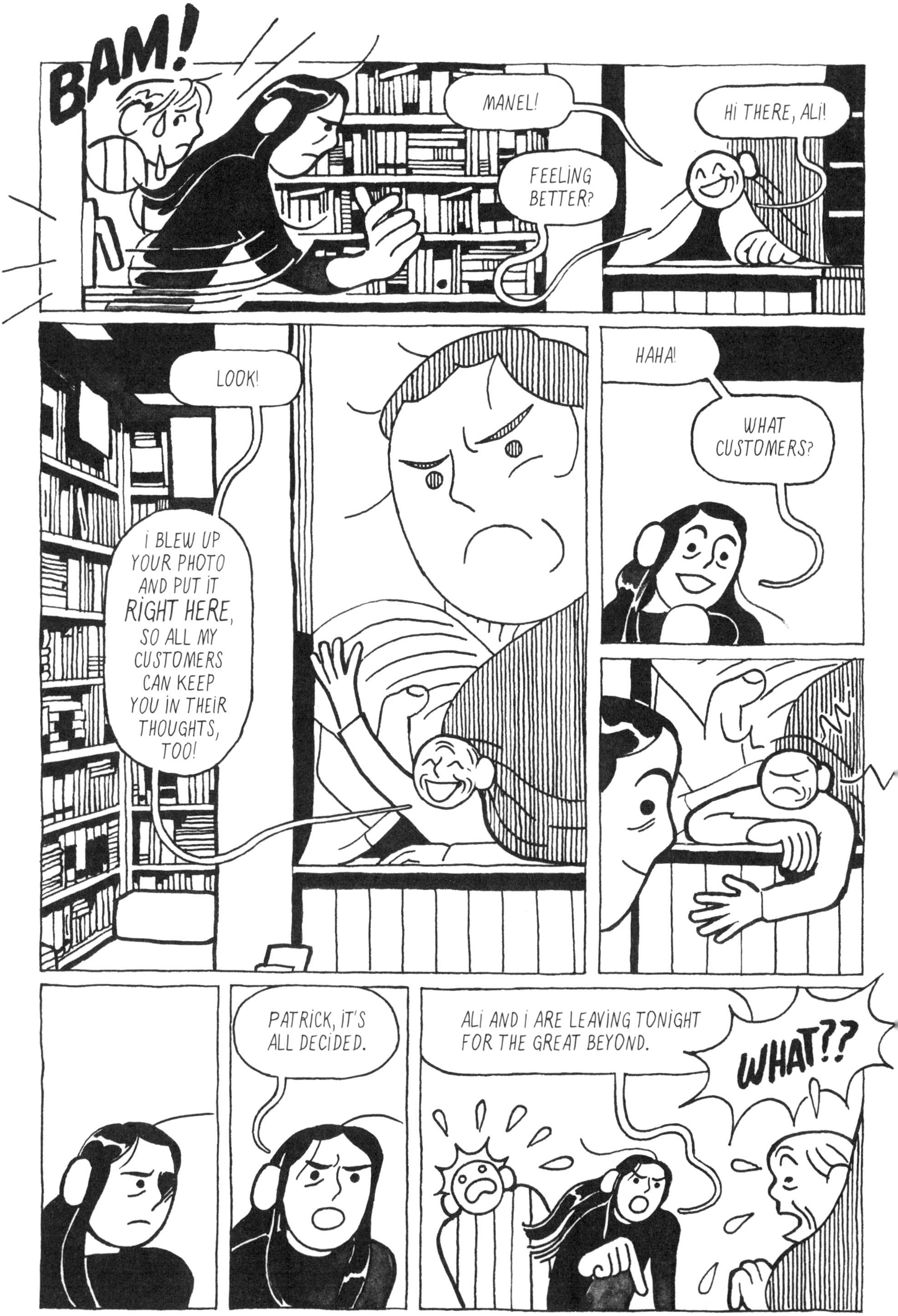
BAM!
MANEL!
FEELING BETTER?
HI THERE, ALI!
LOOK!
I BLEW UP YOUR PHOTO AND PUT IT RIGHT HERE, SO ALL MY CUSTOMERS CAN KEEP YOU IN THEIR THOUGHTS, TOO!
HAHA!
WHAT CUSTOMERS?
PATRICK, IT'S ALL DECIDED.
ALI AND I ARE LEAVING TONIGHT FOR THE GREAT BEYOND.
WHAT??

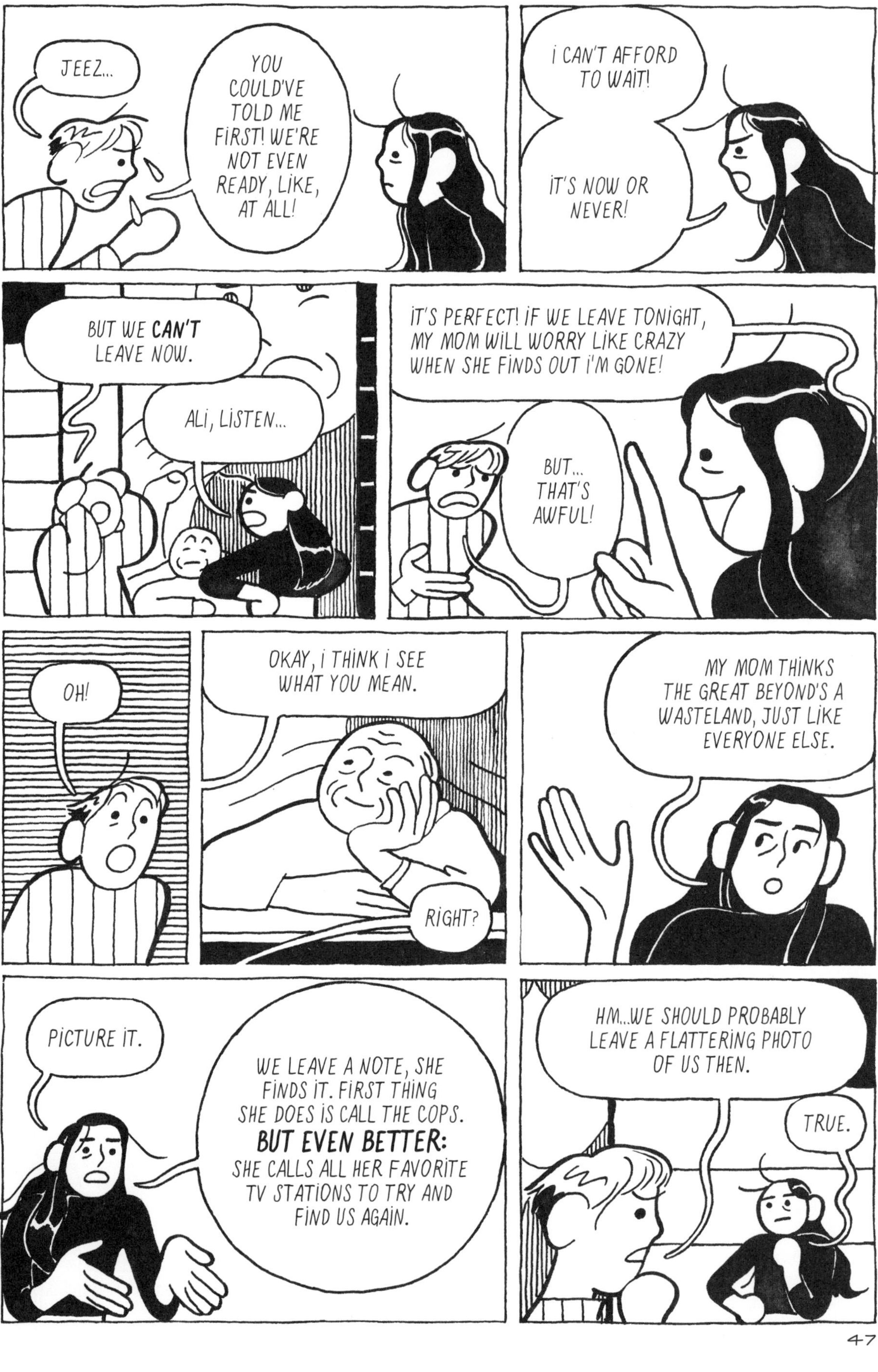
JEEZ...
YOU COULD'VE TOLD ME FIRST! WE'RE NOT EVEN READY, LIKE, AT ALL!
I CAN'T AFFORD TO WAIT!
IT'S NOW OR NEVER!
BUT WE **CAN'T** LEAVE NOW.
ALI, LISTEN...
IT'S PERFECT! IF WE LEAVE TONIGHT, MY MOM WILL WORRY LIKE CRAZY WHEN SHE FINDS OUT I'M GONE!
BUT... THAT'S AWFUL!
OH!
OKAY, I THINK I SEE WHAT YOU MEAN.
RIGHT?
MY MOM THINKS THE GREAT BEYOND'S A WASTELAND, JUST LIKE EVERYONE ELSE.
PICTURE IT.
WE LEAVE A NOTE, SHE FINDS IT. FIRST THING SHE DOES IS CALL THE COPS. **BUT EVEN BETTER:** SHE CALLS ALL HER FAVORITE TV STATIONS TO TRY AND FIND US AGAIN.
HM...WE SHOULD PROBABLY LEAVE A FLATTERING PHOTO OF US THEN.
TRUE.

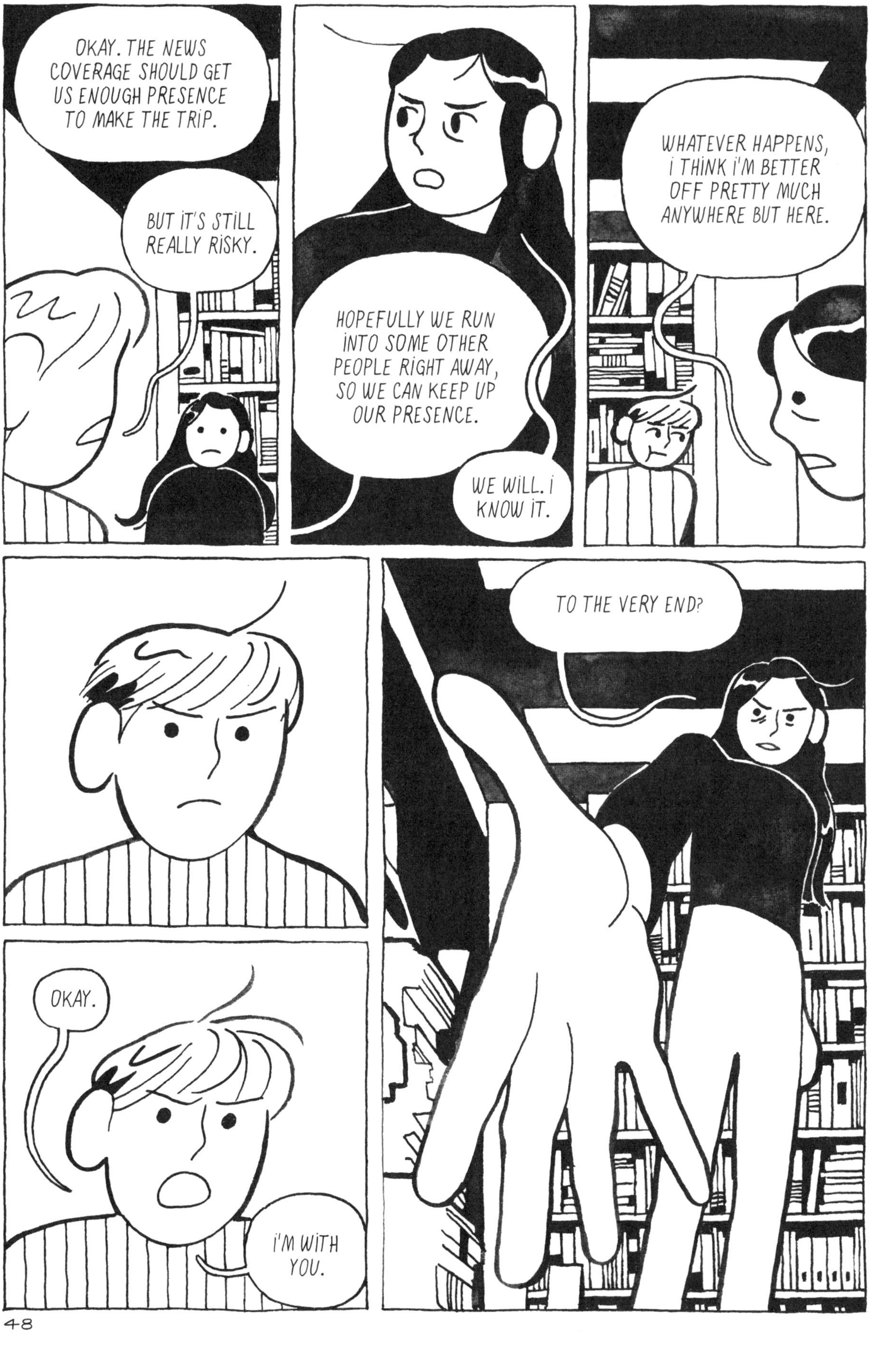
OKAY. THE NEWS COVERAGE SHOULD GET US ENOUGH PRESENCE TO MAKE THE TRIP.
BUT IT'S STILL REALLY RISKY.
HOPEFULLY WE RUN INTO SOME OTHER PEOPLE RIGHT AWAY, SO WE CAN KEEP UP OUR PRESENCE.
WE WILL. I KNOW IT.
WHATEVER HAPPENS, I THINK I'M BETTER OFF PRETTY MUCH ANYWHERE BUT HERE.
TO THE VERY END?
OKAY.
I'M WITH YOU.

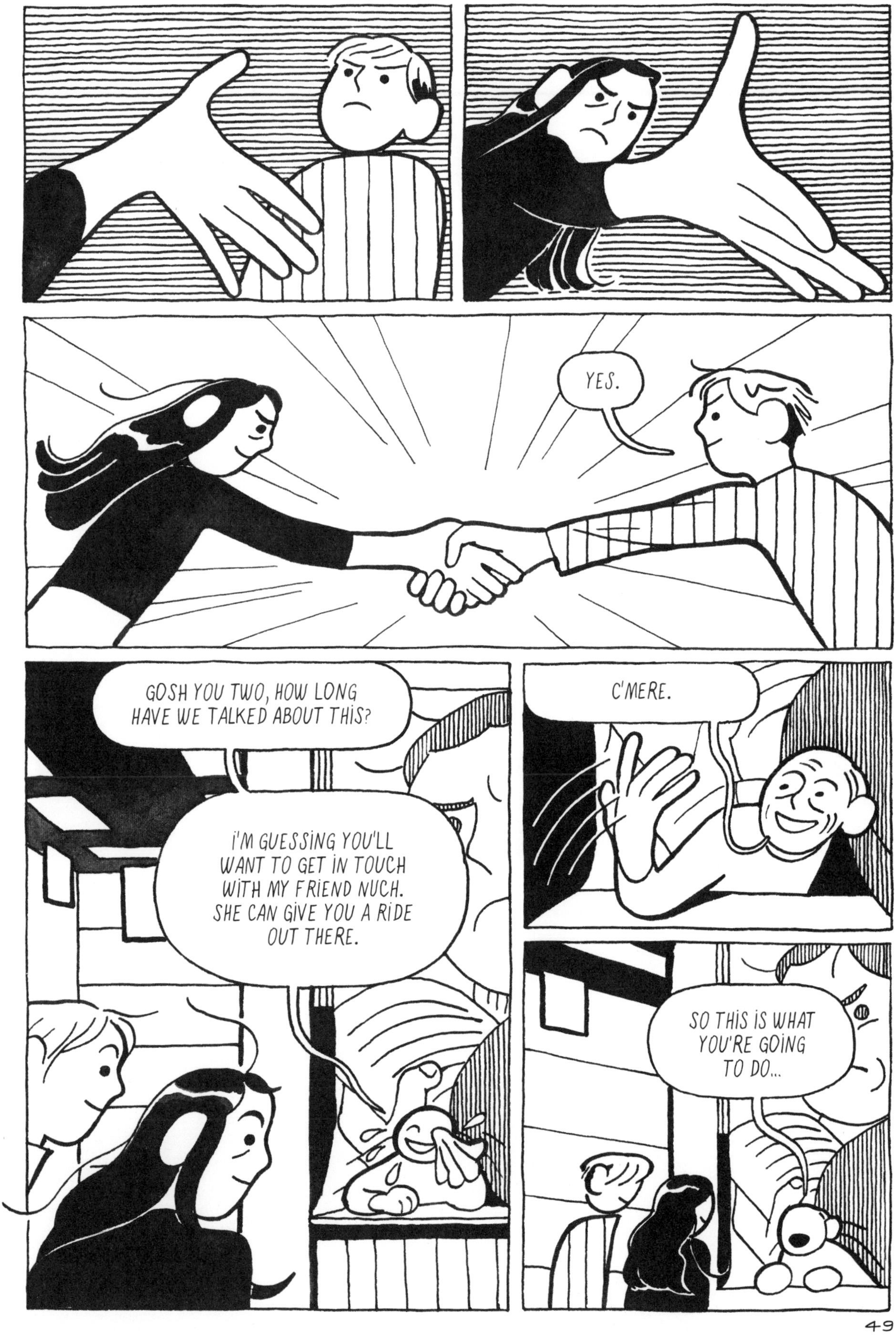
YES.
GOSH YOU TWO, HOW LONG HAVE WE TALKED ABOUT THIS?
I'M GUESSING YOU'LL WANT TO GET IN TOUCH WITH MY FRIEND NUCH. SHE CAN GIVE YOU A RIDE OUT THERE.
C'MERE.
SO THIS IS WHAT YOU'RE GOING TO DO...

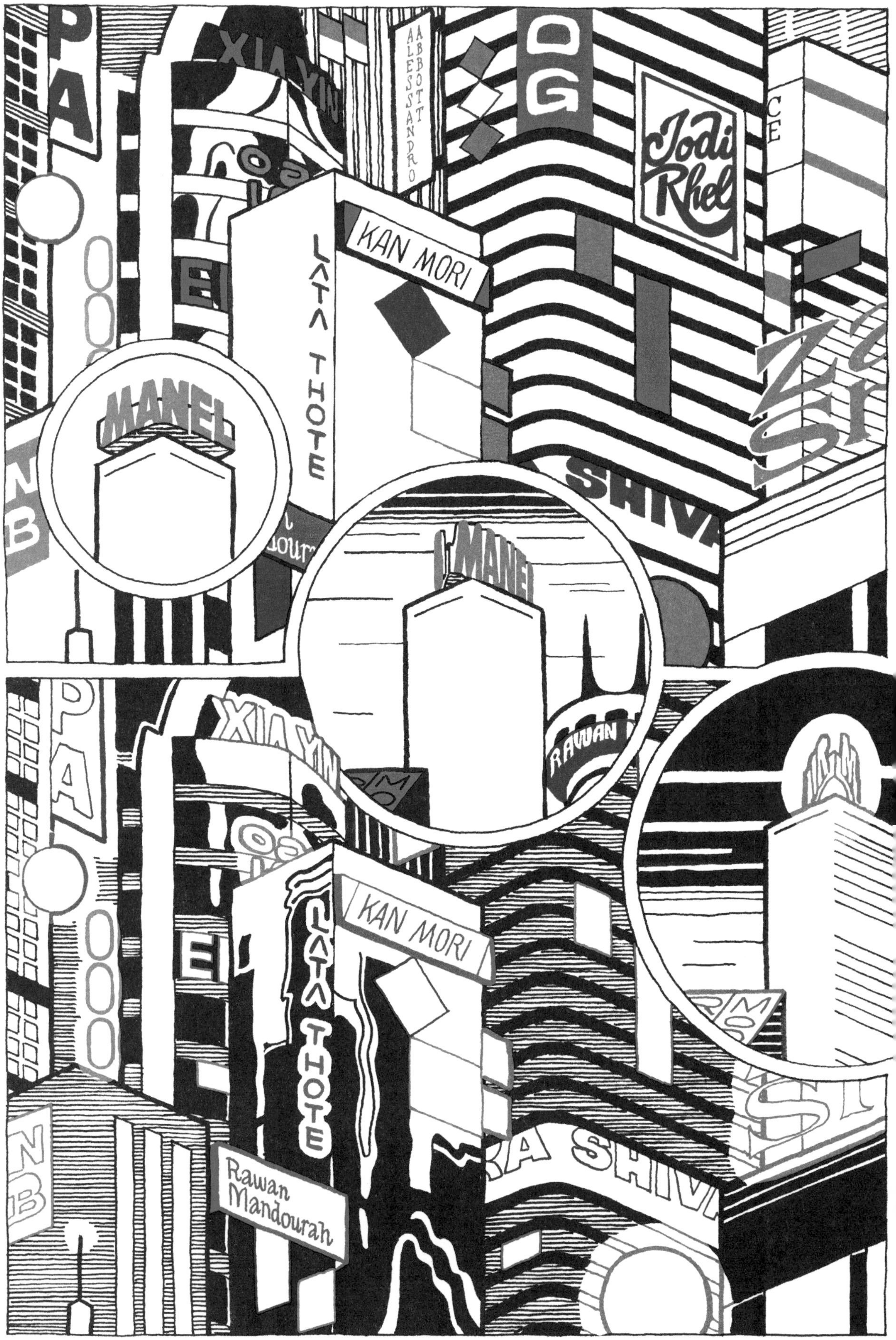
PA
XIA YIN
ALESSANDRO
ABBOTT
OG
Jodi Rhel
KAN MORI
LATA THOTE
MANEL
SHIVA
MANEL
RAWAN
PA
XIA YIN
KAN MORI
LATA THOTE
SHIVA
Rawan Mandourah

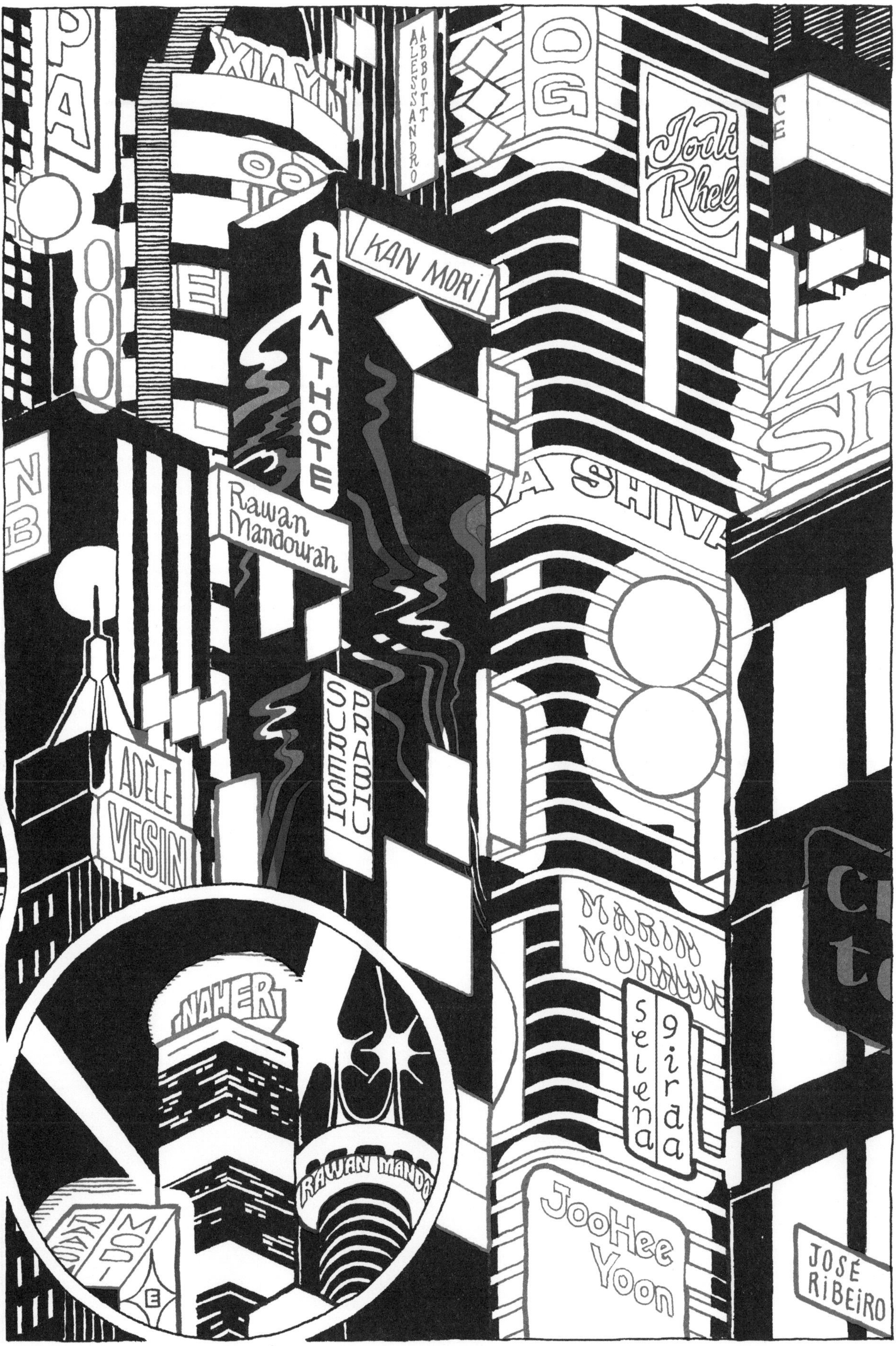
XIA YIN
ALESSANDRO ABBOTT
Jodi Rhel
KAN MORI
LATA THOTE
Rawan Mandourah
SURESH PRABHU
ADÈLE VESIN
NAHER
JooHee Yoon
JOSÉ RIBEIRO

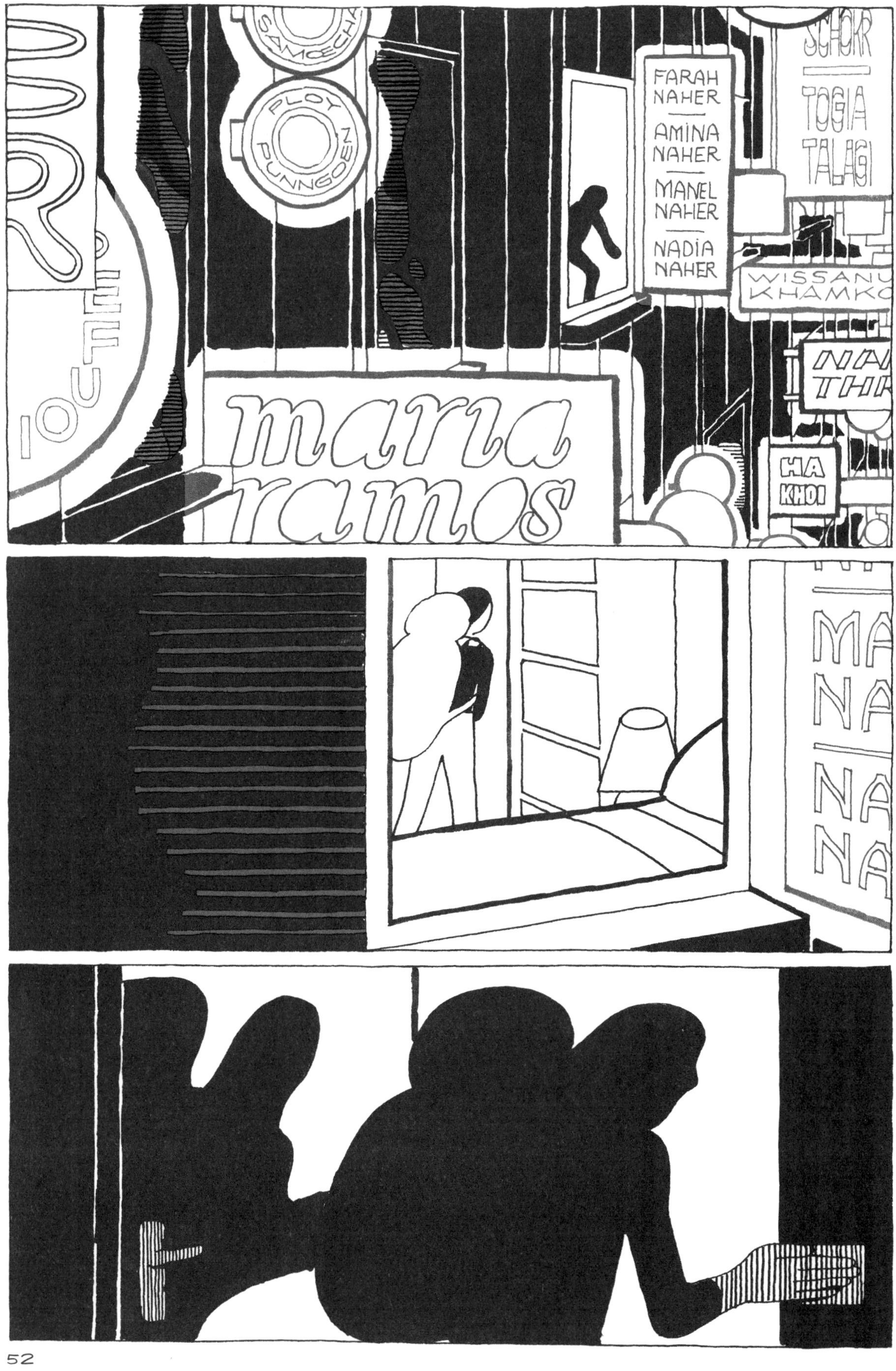
PLOY PUNNGOEN
FARAH NAHER
AMINA NAHER
MANEL NAHER
NADIA NAHER
TOGIA TALAGI
maria ramos
HA KHOI

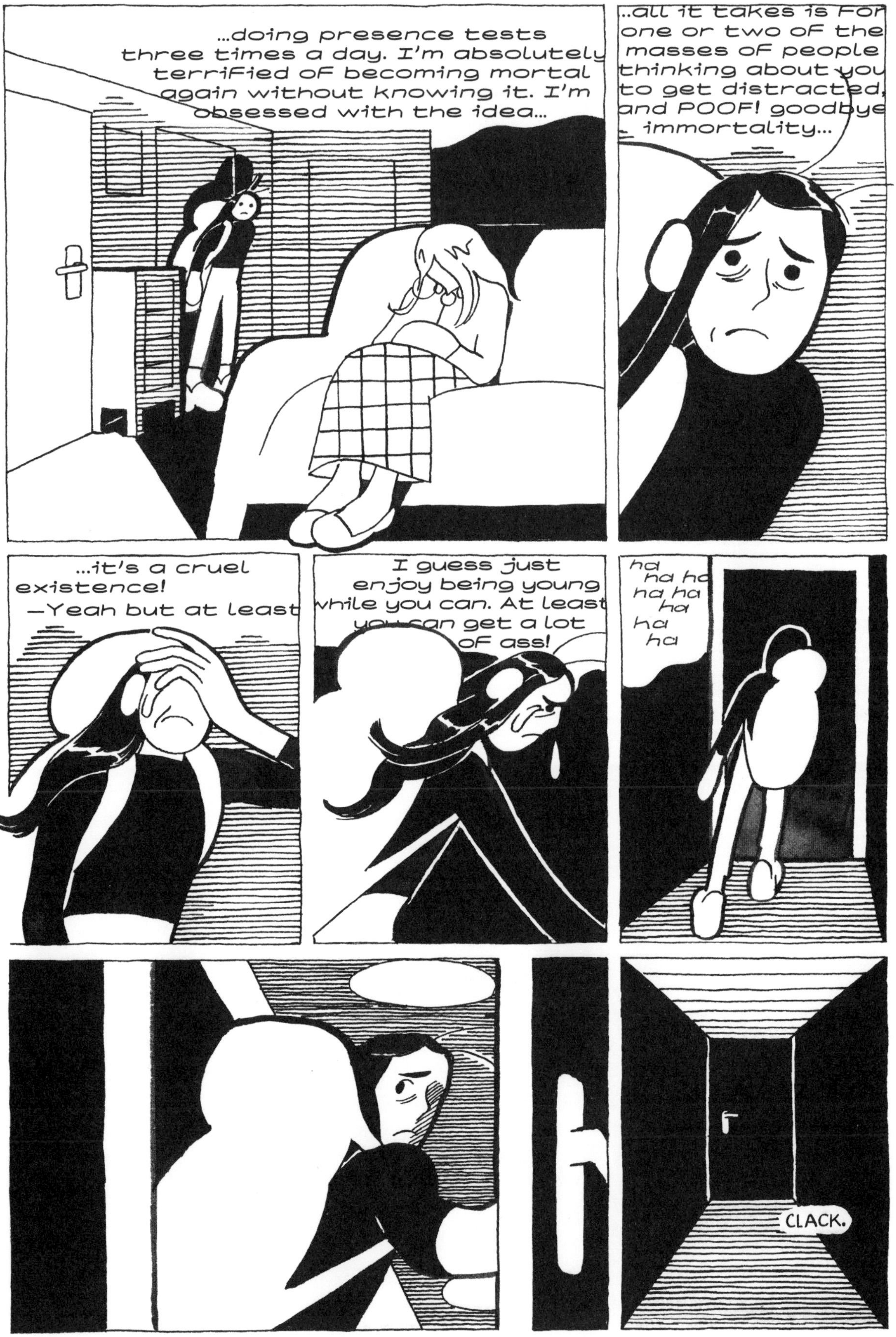
...doing presence tests three times a day. I'm absolutely terrified of becoming mortal again without knowing it. I'm obsessed with the idea...
...all it takes is for one or two of the masses of people thinking about you to get distracted, and POOF! goodbye immortality...
...it's a cruel existence!
—Yeah but at least
I guess just enjoy being young while you can. At least you can get a lot of ass!
ha ha ha ha ha ha ha ha
CLACK.

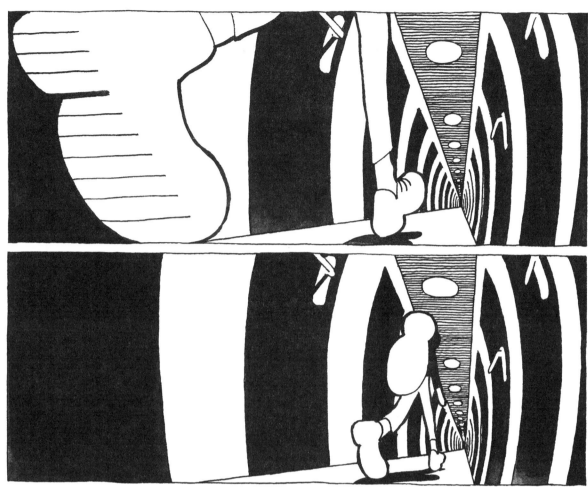

AH!

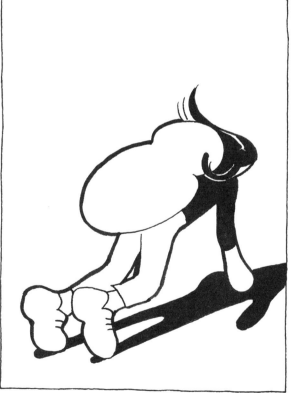

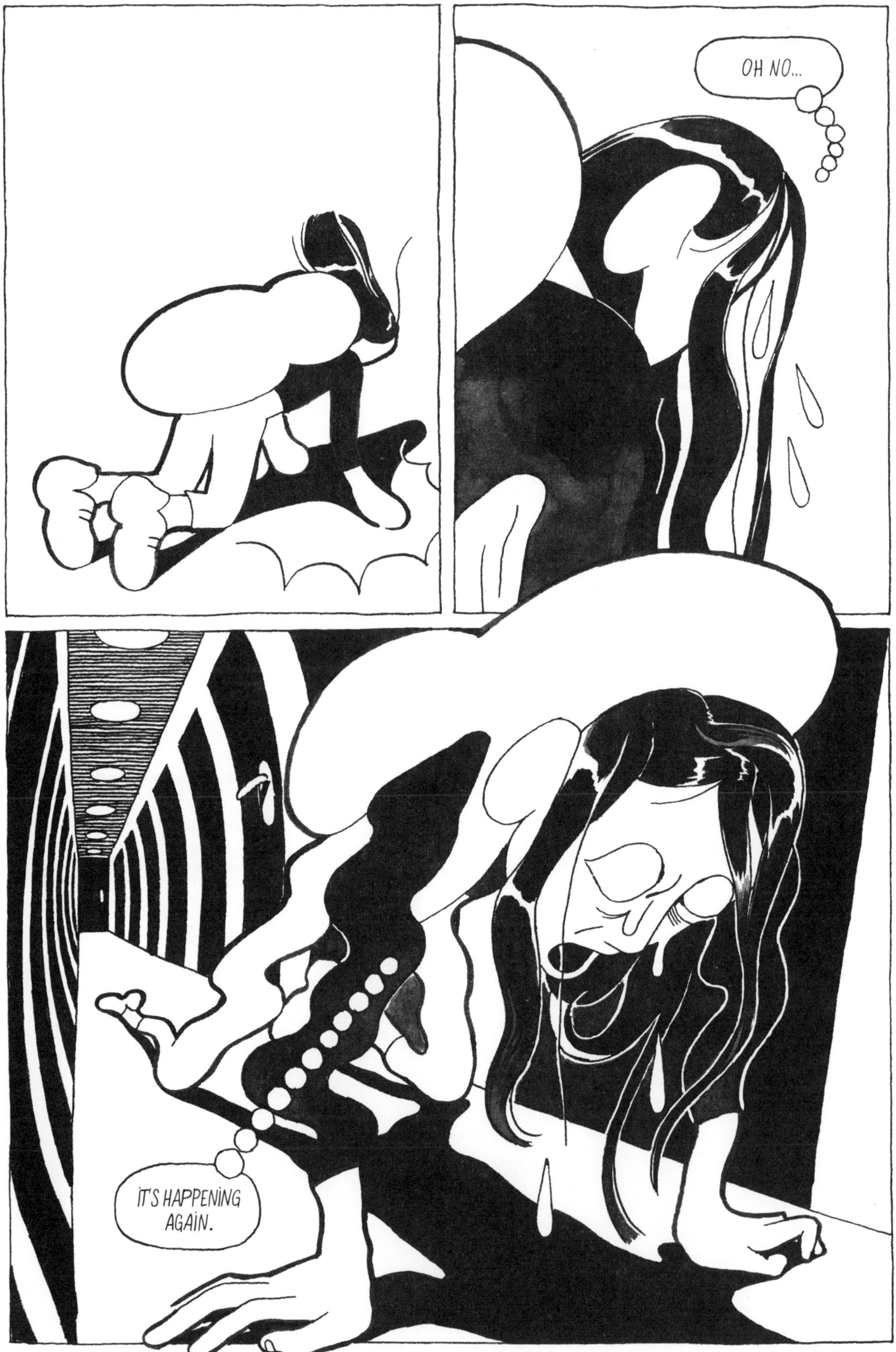
OH NO...
IT'S HAPPENING AGAIN.

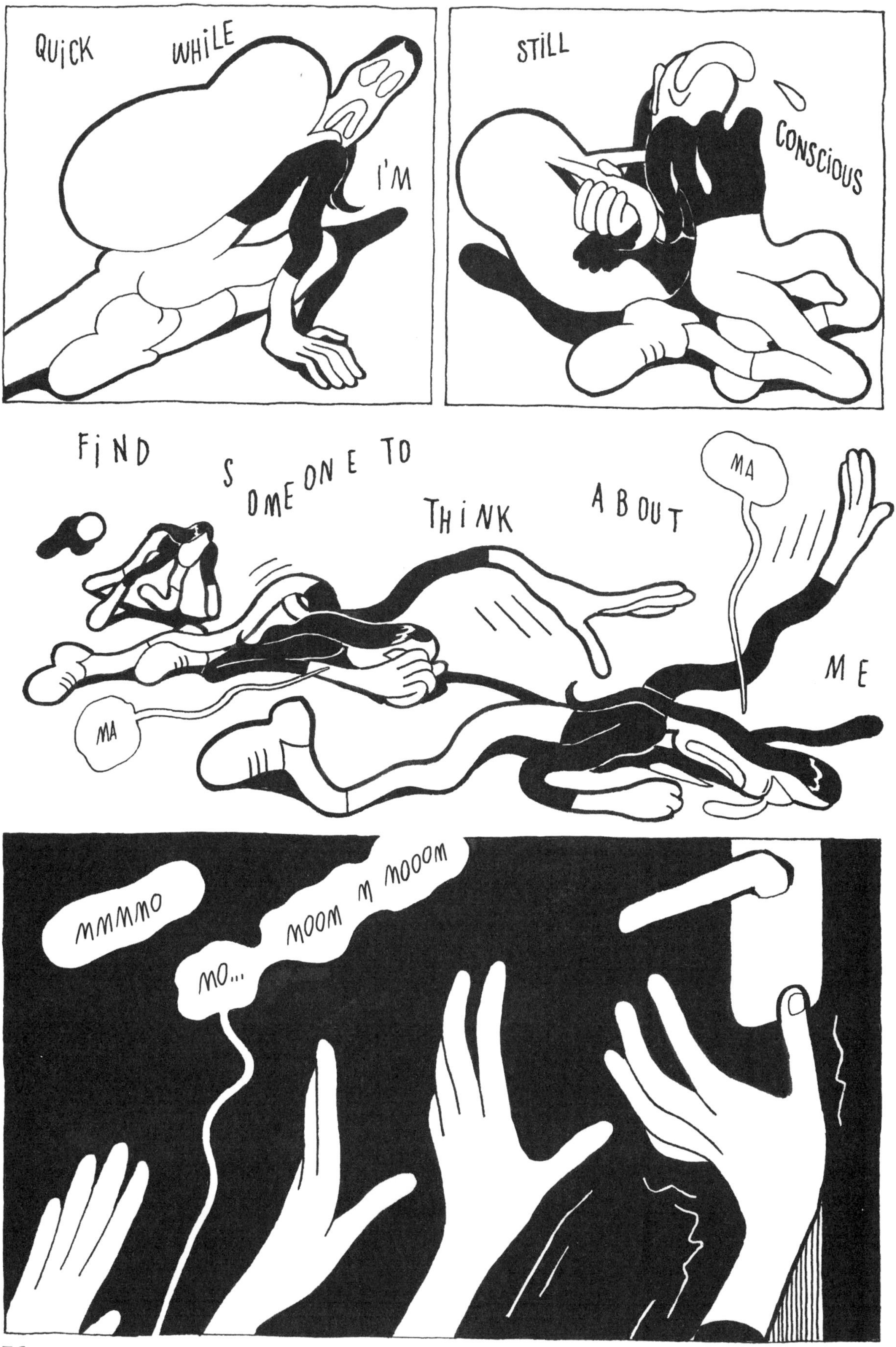
QUICK WHILE I'M
STILL CONSCIOUS
FIND SOMEONE TO THINK ABOUT ME
MA
MA
MMMMO
MO... MOOM M MOOOM

MOOOOM
MOO...
...OOMM
MO
MO...
...MMY
MANEL NAHER
NADIA NAHER

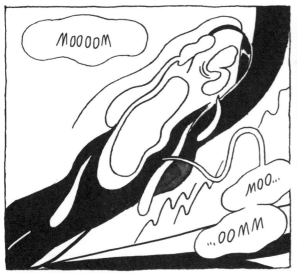

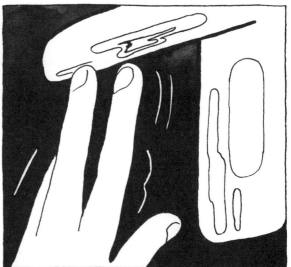

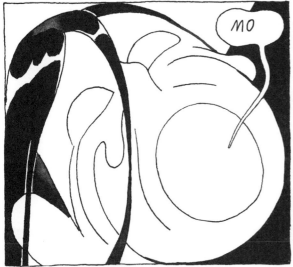

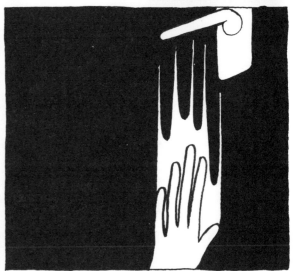

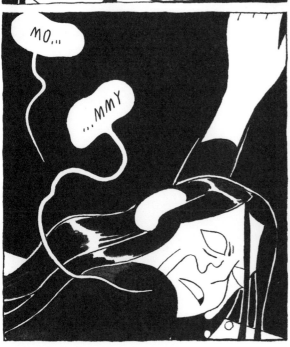

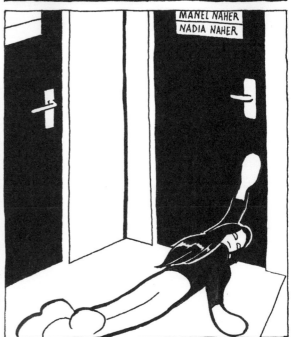

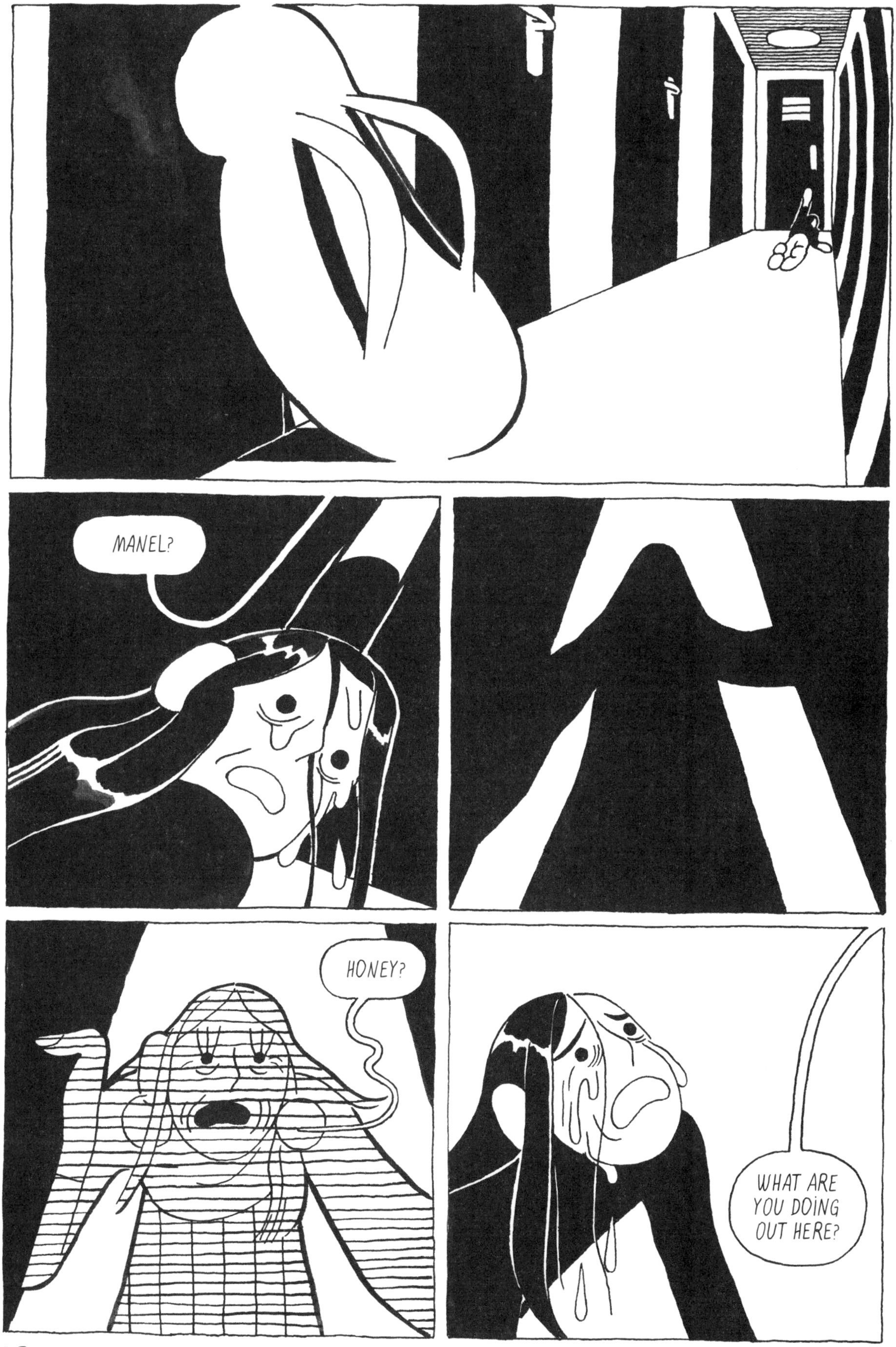
MANEL?
HONEY?
WHAT ARE YOU DOING OUT HERE?

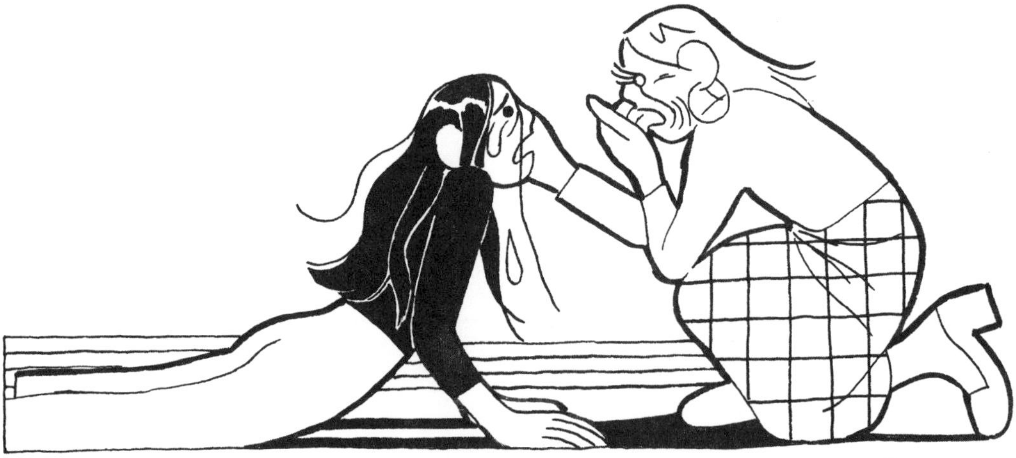

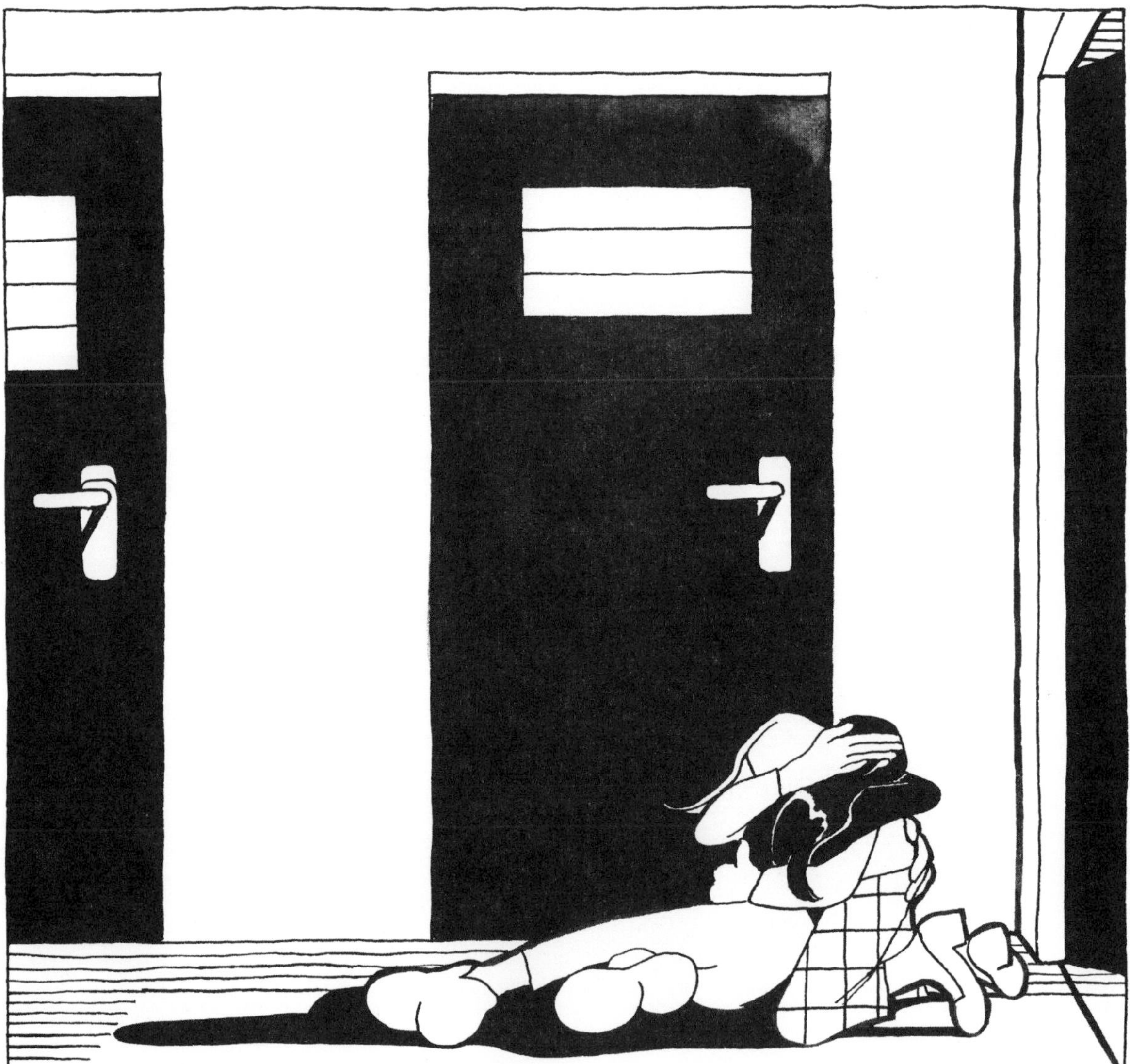

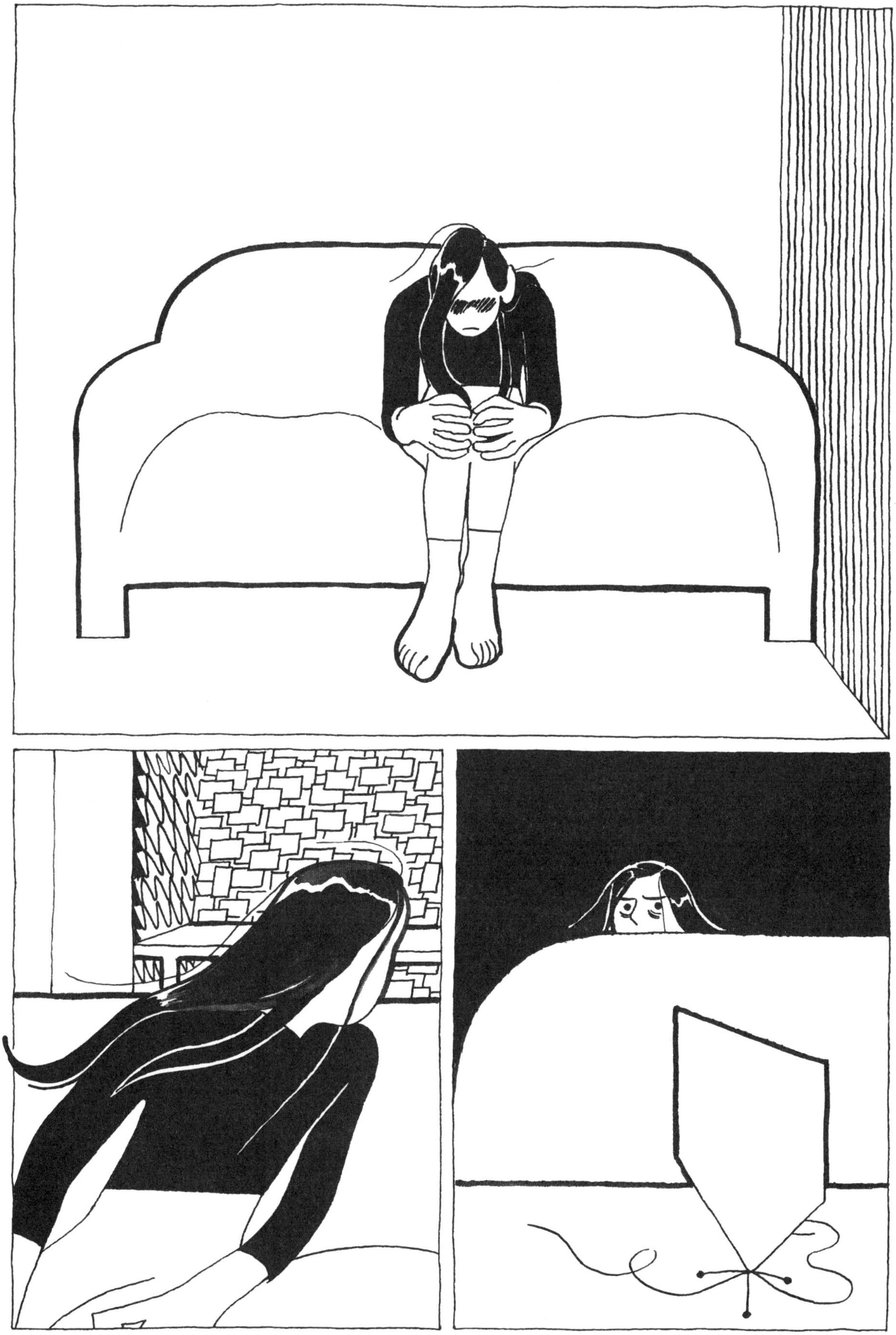

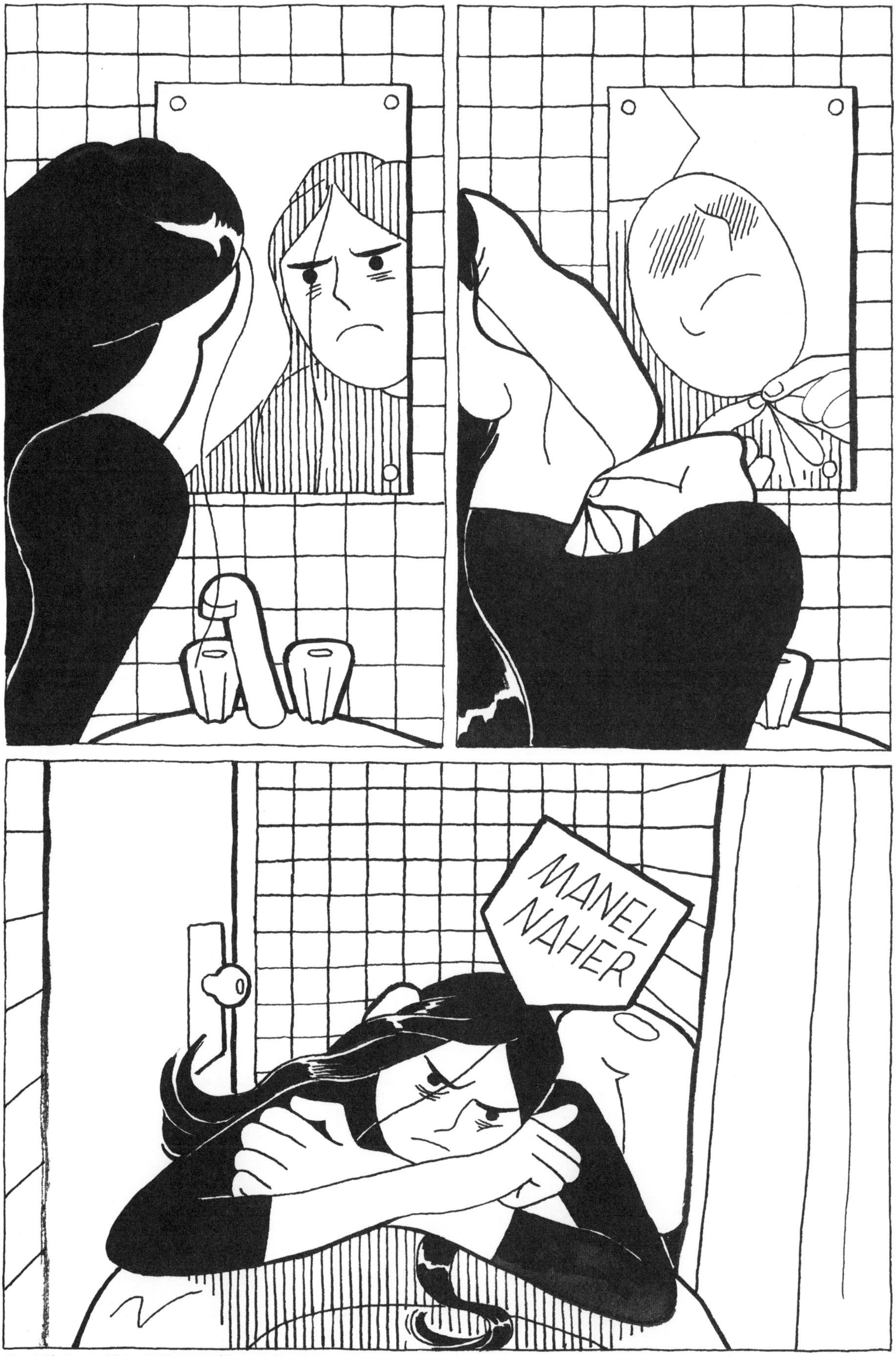
MANEL
NAHER

HEADPIECE: CARD-HAT MENTIONED ON PAGE 19

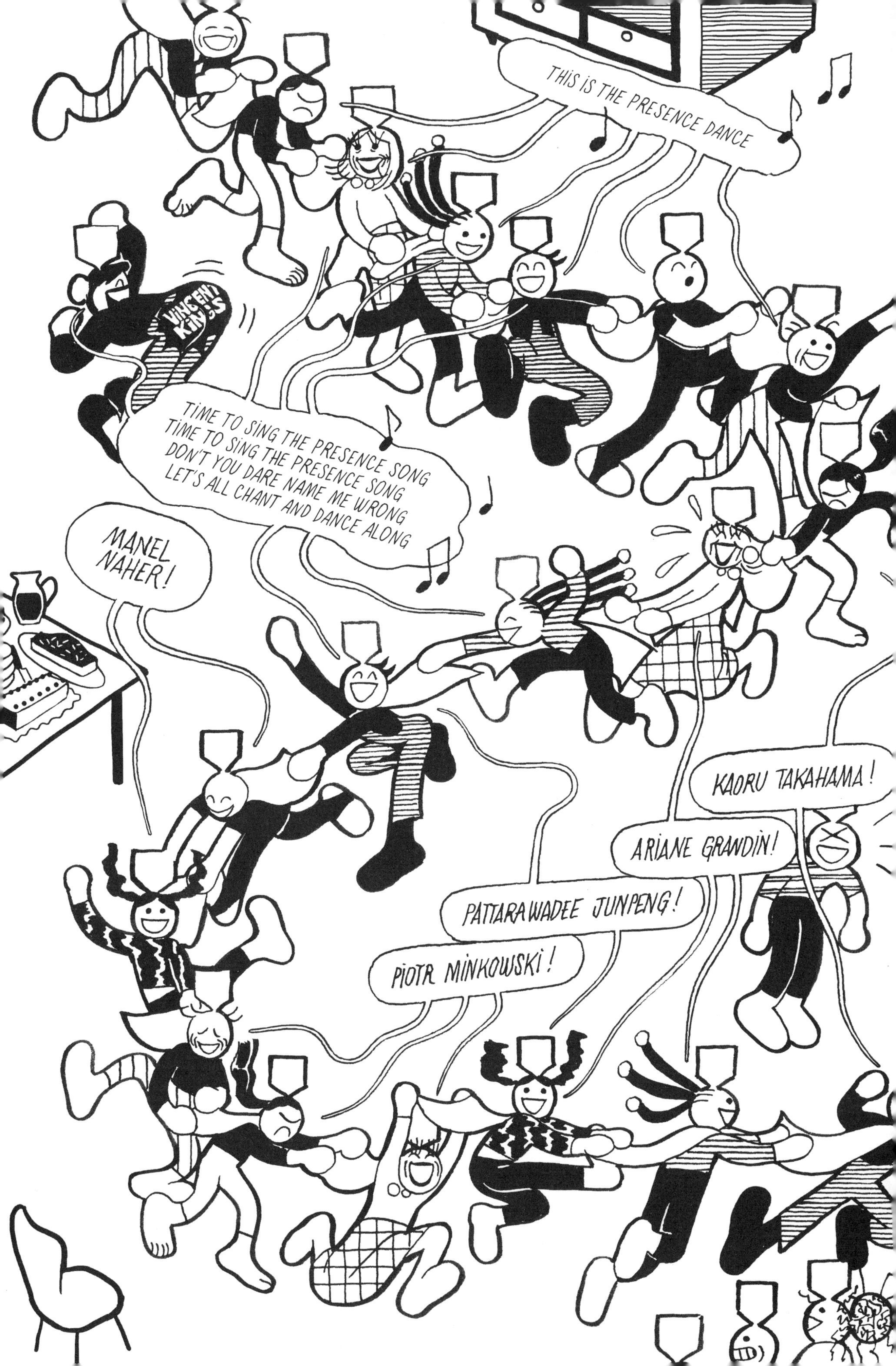
THIS IS THE PRESENCE DANCE
VINCENT KINGS
TIME TO SING THE PRESENCE SONG
TIME TO SING THE PRESENCE SONG
DON'T YOU DARE NAME ME WRONG
LET'S ALL CHANT AND DANCE ALONG
MANEL NAHER!
KAORU TAKAHAMA!
ARIANE GRANDIN!
PATTARAWADEE JUNPENG!
PIOTR MINKOWSKI!

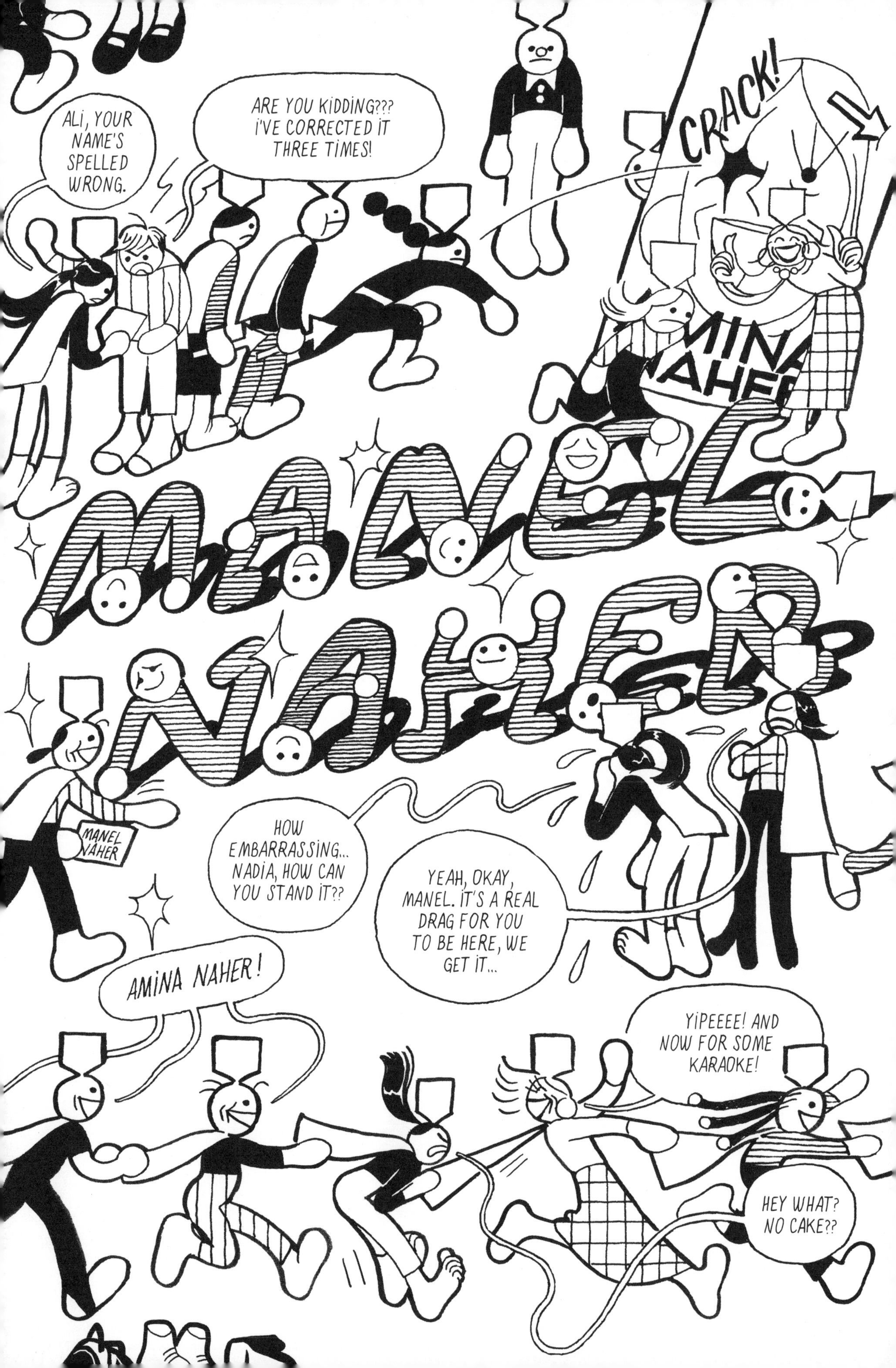
ALi, YOUR NAME'S SPELLED WRONG.
ARE YOU KiDDiNG??? i'VE CORRECTED iT THREE TiMES!
CRACK!
MINA NAHER
MANEL NAHER
MANEL NAHER
HOW EMBARRASSiNG... NADiA, HOW CAN YOU STAND iT??
YEAH, OKAY, MANEL. iT'S A REAL DRAG FOR YOU TO BE HERE, WE GET iT...
AMiNA NAHER!
YiPEEEE! AND NOW FOR SOME KARAOKE!
HEY WHAT? NO CAKE??

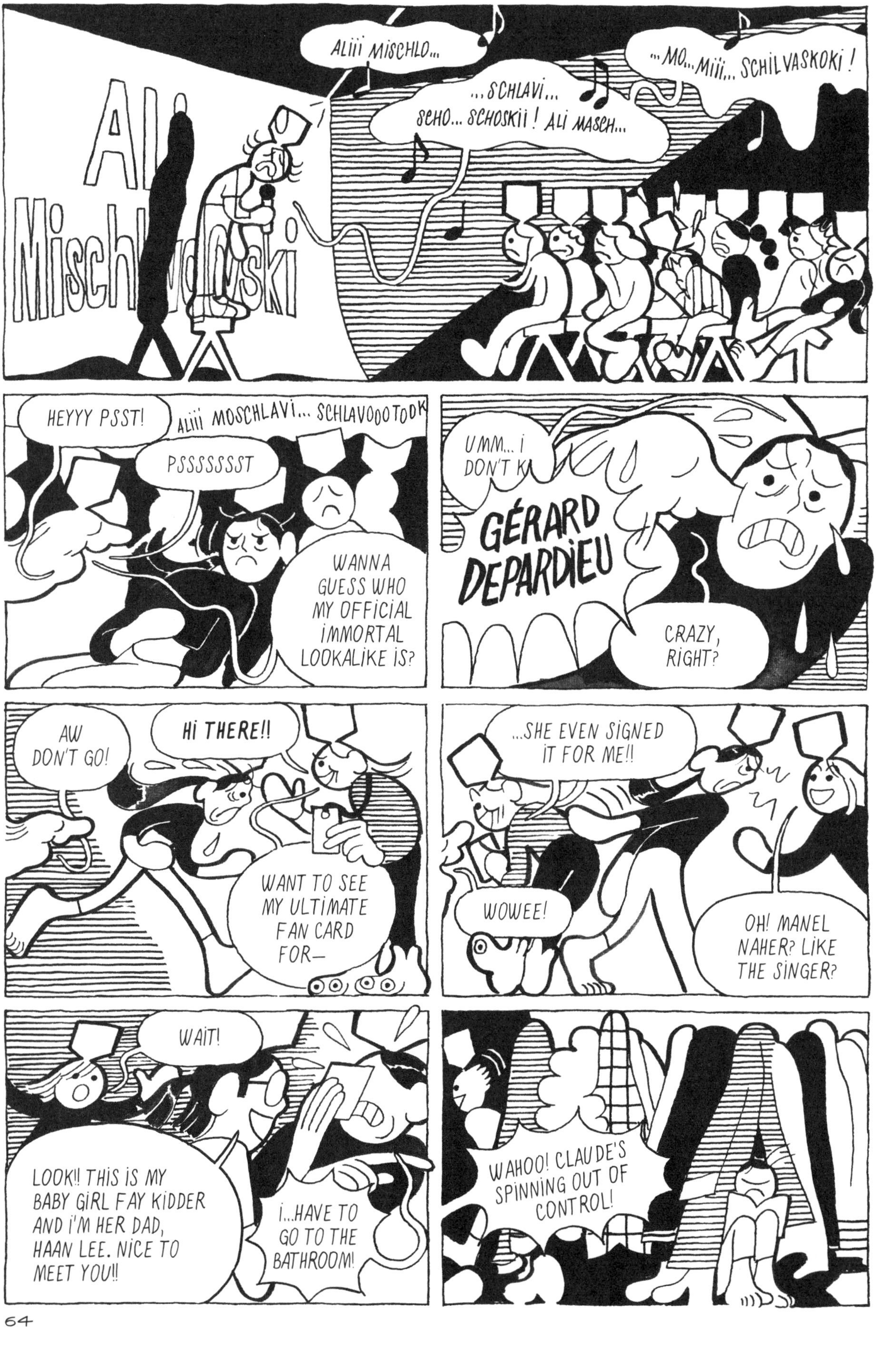
Aliii mischlo...
...schlavi...
scho... schoskii! Ali masch...
...mo...miii... schilvaskoki!
Ali Mischlowolowski
HEYYY PSST!
ALiii MOSCHLAVI... SCHLAVODOTOOK
PSSSSSSST
WANNA GUESS WHO MY OFFICIAL iMMORTAL LOOKALiKE iS?
UMM... i DON'T K
GÉRARD DEPARDiEU
CRAZY, RiGHT?
AW DON'T GO!
Hi THERE!!
WANT TO SEE MY ULTIMATE FAN CARD FOR—
...SHE EVEN SiGNED iT FOR ME!!
WOWEE!
OH! MANEL NAHER? LiKE THE SiNGER?
WAiT!
LOOK!! THiS iS MY BABY GiRL FAY KiDDER AND i'M HER DAD, HAAN LEE. NiCE TO MEET YOU!!
i...HAVE TO GO TO THE BATHROOM!
WAHOO! CLAUDE'S SPiNNiNG OUT OF CONTROL!

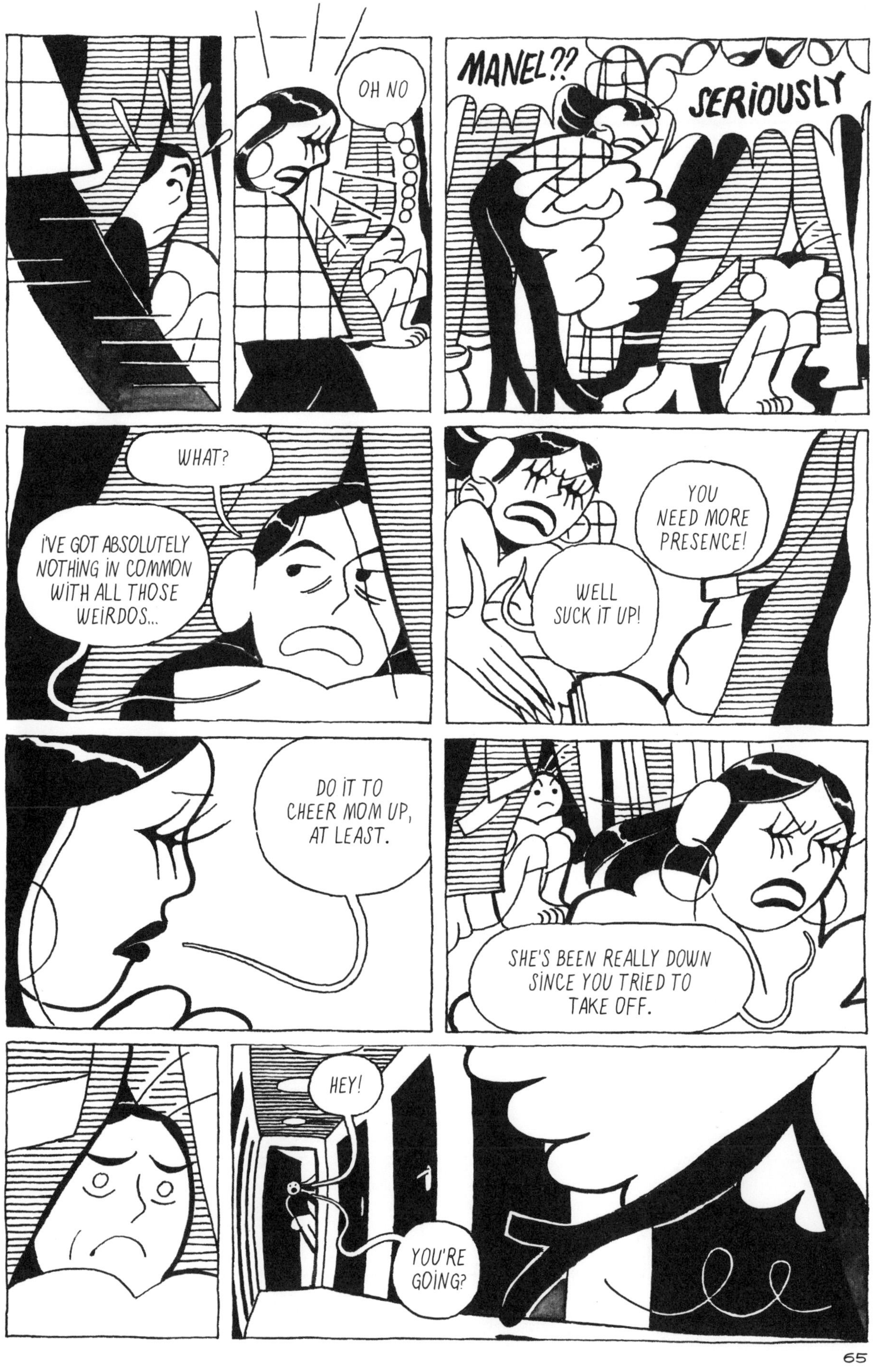
OH NO
MANEL??
SERIOUSLY
WHAT?
I'VE GOT ABSOLUTELY NOTHING IN COMMON WITH ALL THOSE WEIRDOS...
YOU NEED MORE PRESENCE!
WELL SUCK IT UP!
DO IT TO CHEER MOM UP, AT LEAST.
SHE'S BEEN REALLY DOWN SINCE YOU TRIED TO TAKE OFF.
HEY!
YOU'RE GOING?

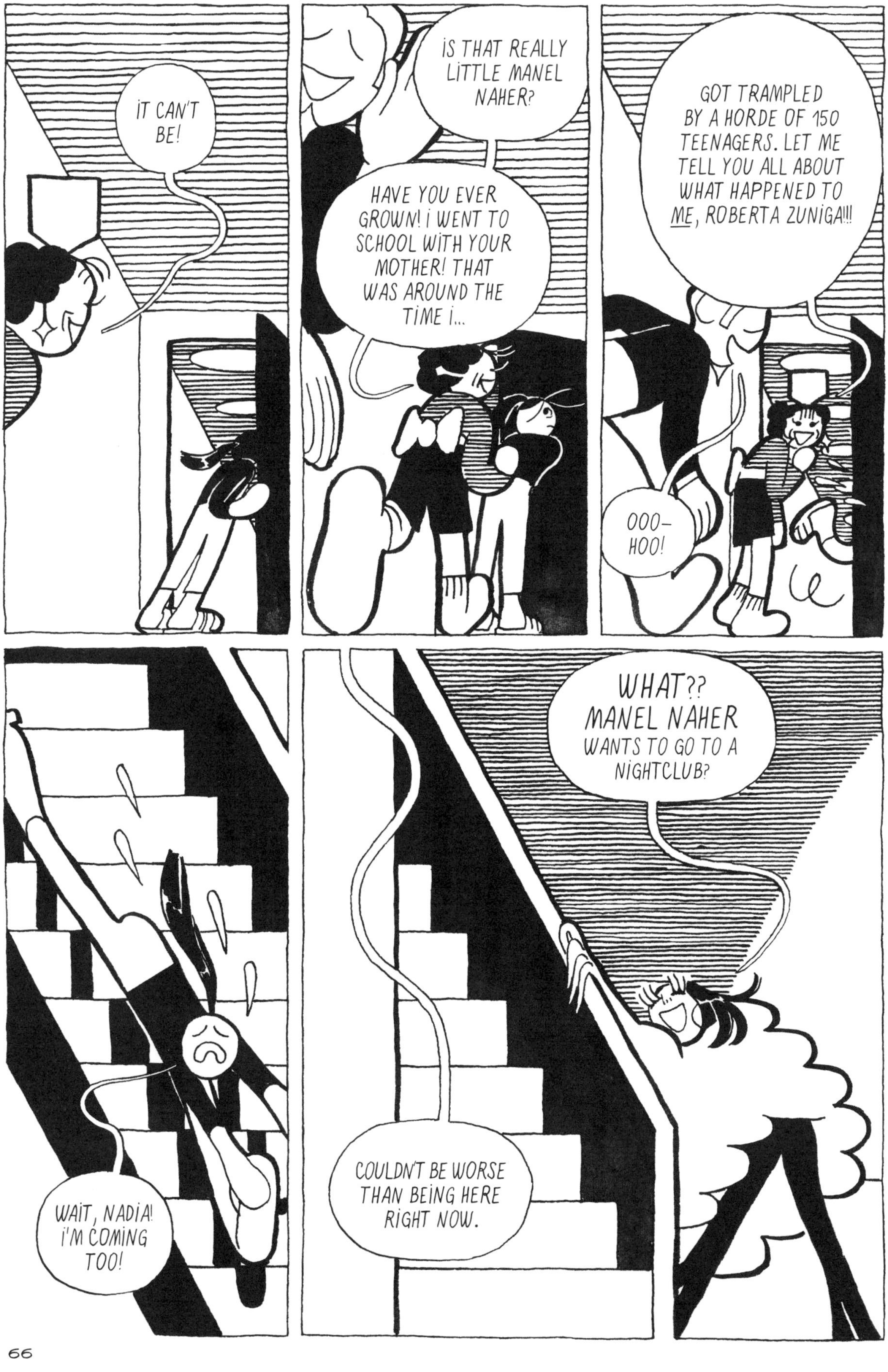
IT CAN'T BE!
IS THAT REALLY LITTLE MANEL NAHER?
HAVE YOU EVER GROWN! I WENT TO SCHOOL WITH YOUR MOTHER! THAT WAS AROUND THE TIME I...
GOT TRAMPLED BY A HORDE OF 150 TEENAGERS. LET ME TELL YOU ALL ABOUT WHAT HAPPENED TO ME, ROBERTA ZUNIGA!!!
OOO-HOO!
WAIT, NADIA! I'M COMING TOO!
COULDN'T BE WORSE THAN BEING HERE RIGHT NOW.
WHAT?? MANEL NAHER WANTS TO GO TO A NIGHTCLUB?

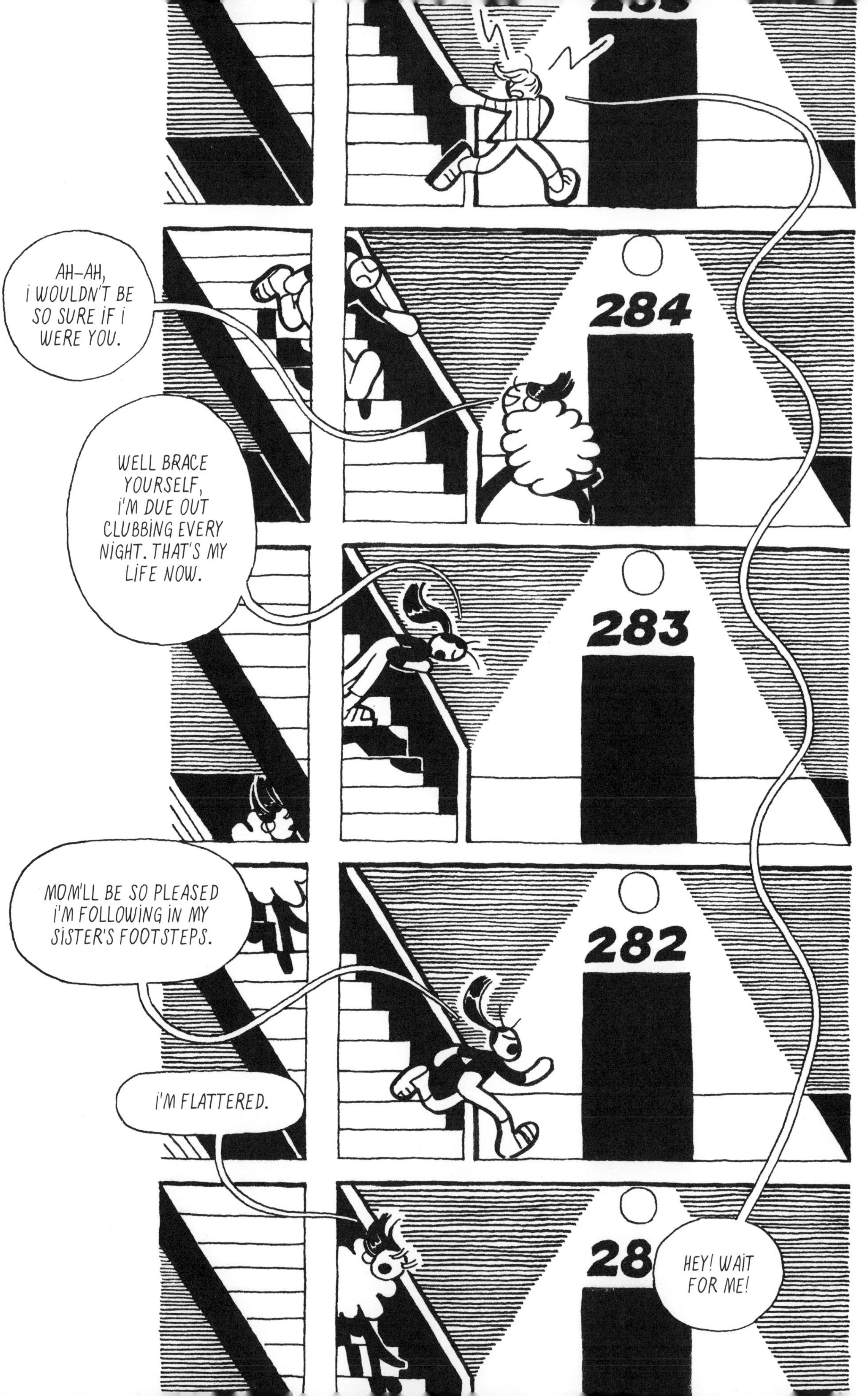
283
284
AH-AH, I WOULDN'T BE SO SURE IF I WERE YOU.
WELL BRACE YOURSELF, I'M DUE OUT CLUBBING EVERY NIGHT. THAT'S MY LIFE NOW.
283
MOM'LL BE SO PLEASED I'M FOLLOWING IN MY SISTER'S FOOTSTEPS.
282
I'M FLATTERED.
28
HEY! WAIT FOR ME!

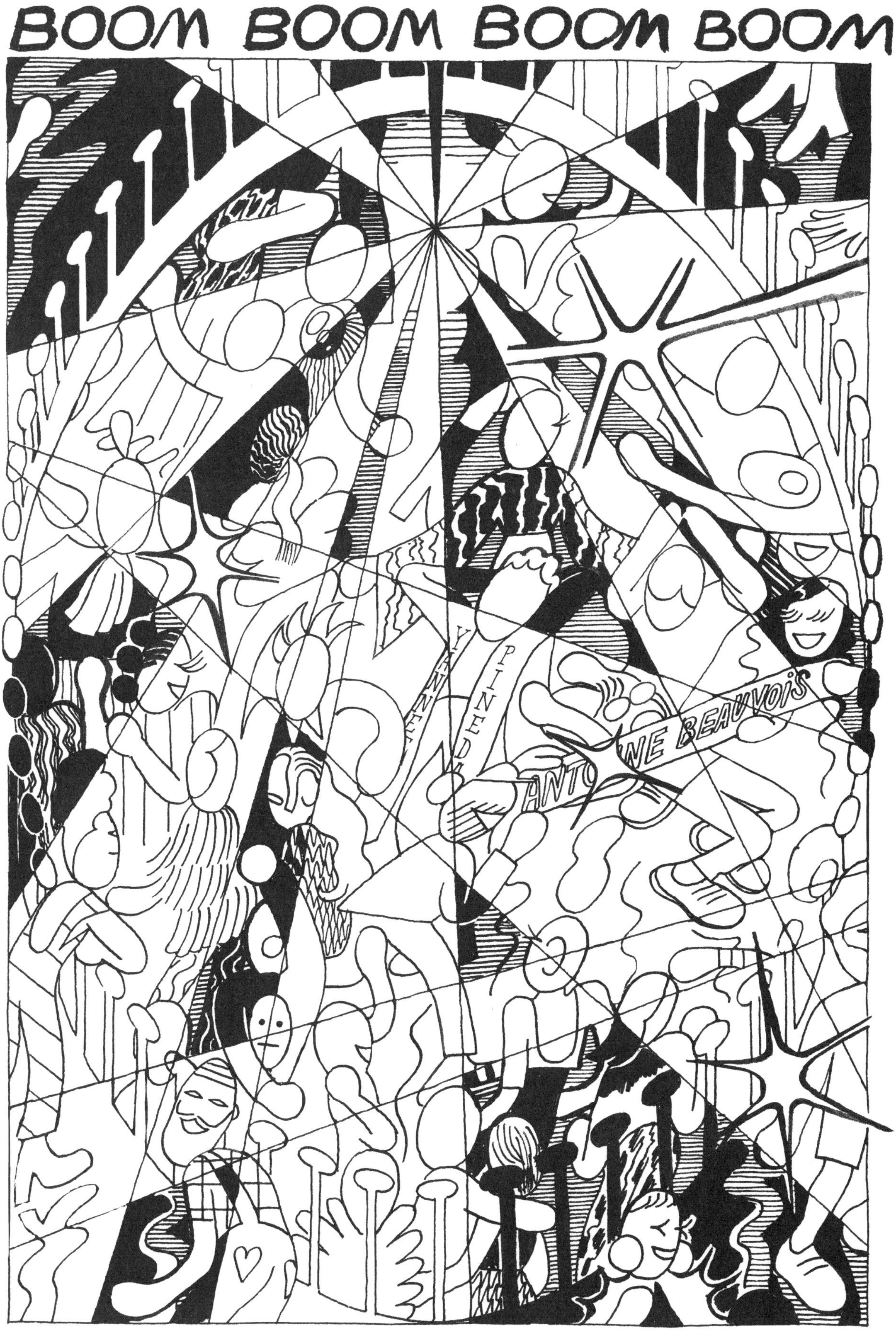
BOOM BOOM BOOM BOOM
YANNE
PINED
ANTO
NE BEAUVOIS

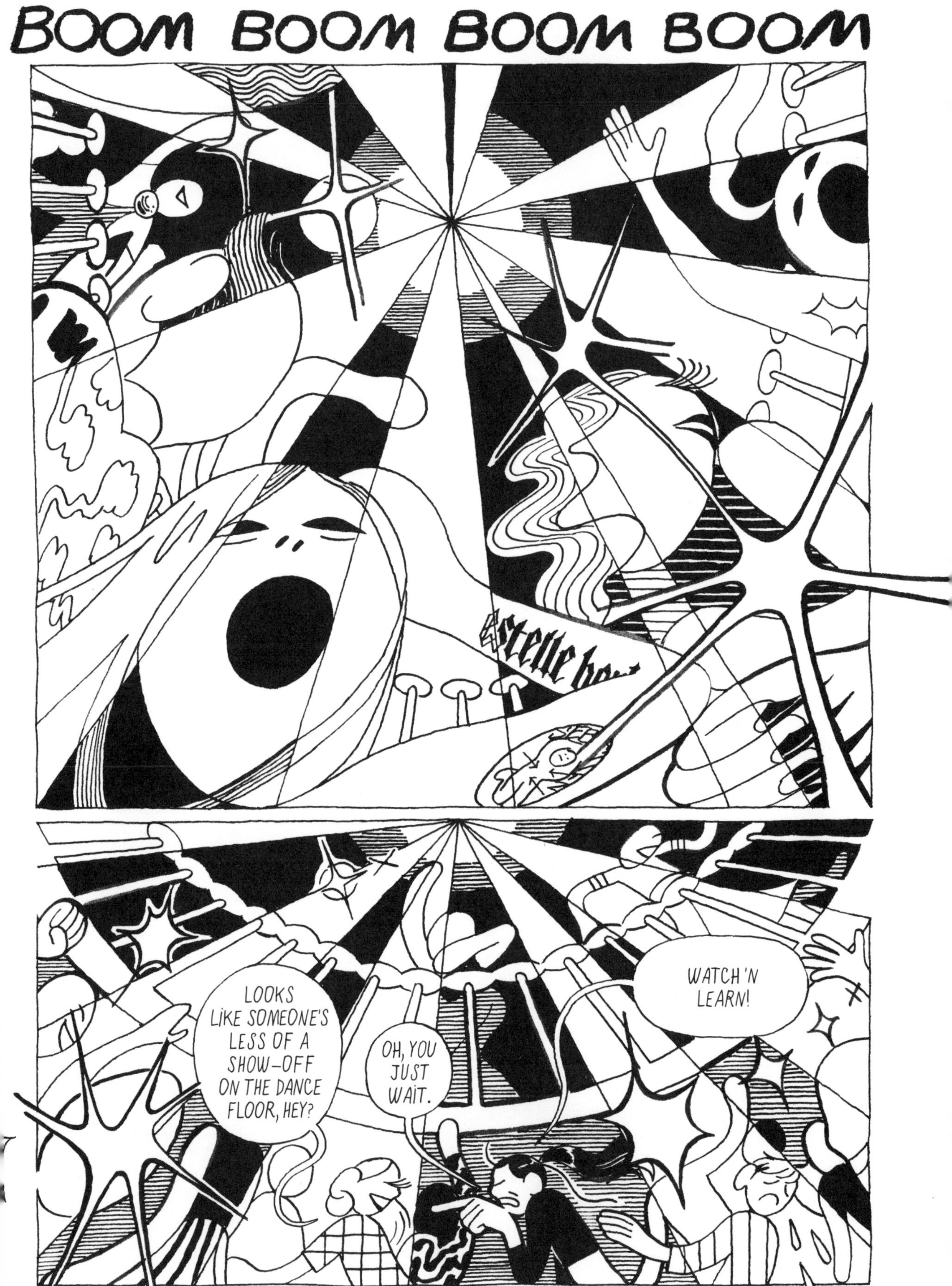

BOOM BOOM BOOM BOOM
LOOKS LIKE SOMEONE'S LESS OF A SHOW-OFF ON THE DANCE FLOOR, HEY?
OH, YOU JUST WAIT.
WATCH 'N LEARN!

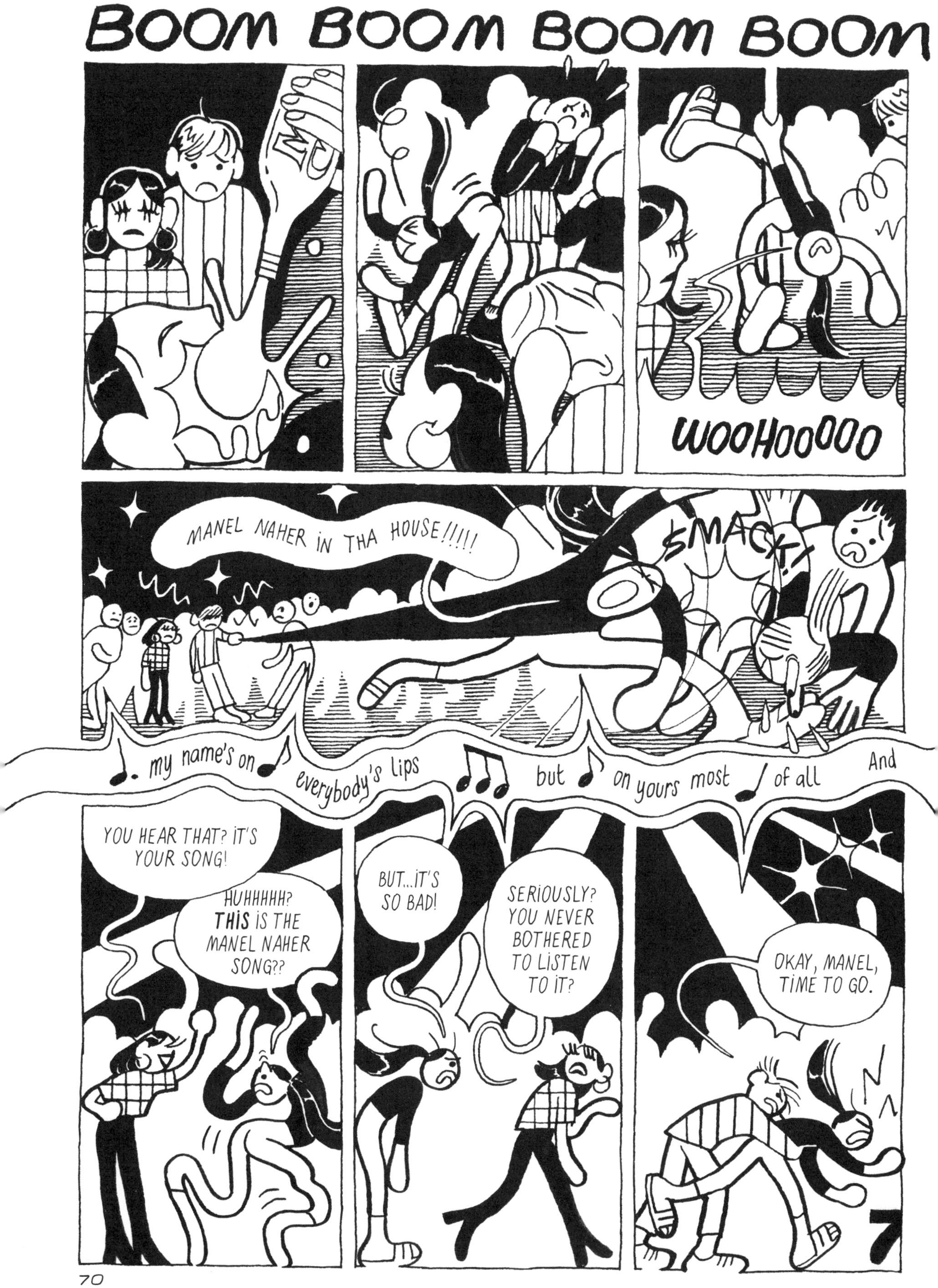

BOOM BOOM BOOM BOOM
WOOHOOOOO
MANEL NAHER IN THA HOUSE!!!!!
SMACK!
my name's on everybody's lips but on yours most of all And
YOU HEAR THAT? IT'S YOUR SONG!
HUHHHHH? THIS IS THE MANEL NAHER SONG??
BUT...IT'S SO BAD!
SERIOUSLY? YOU NEVER BOTHERED TO LISTEN TO IT?
OKAY, MANEL, TIME TO GO.
7

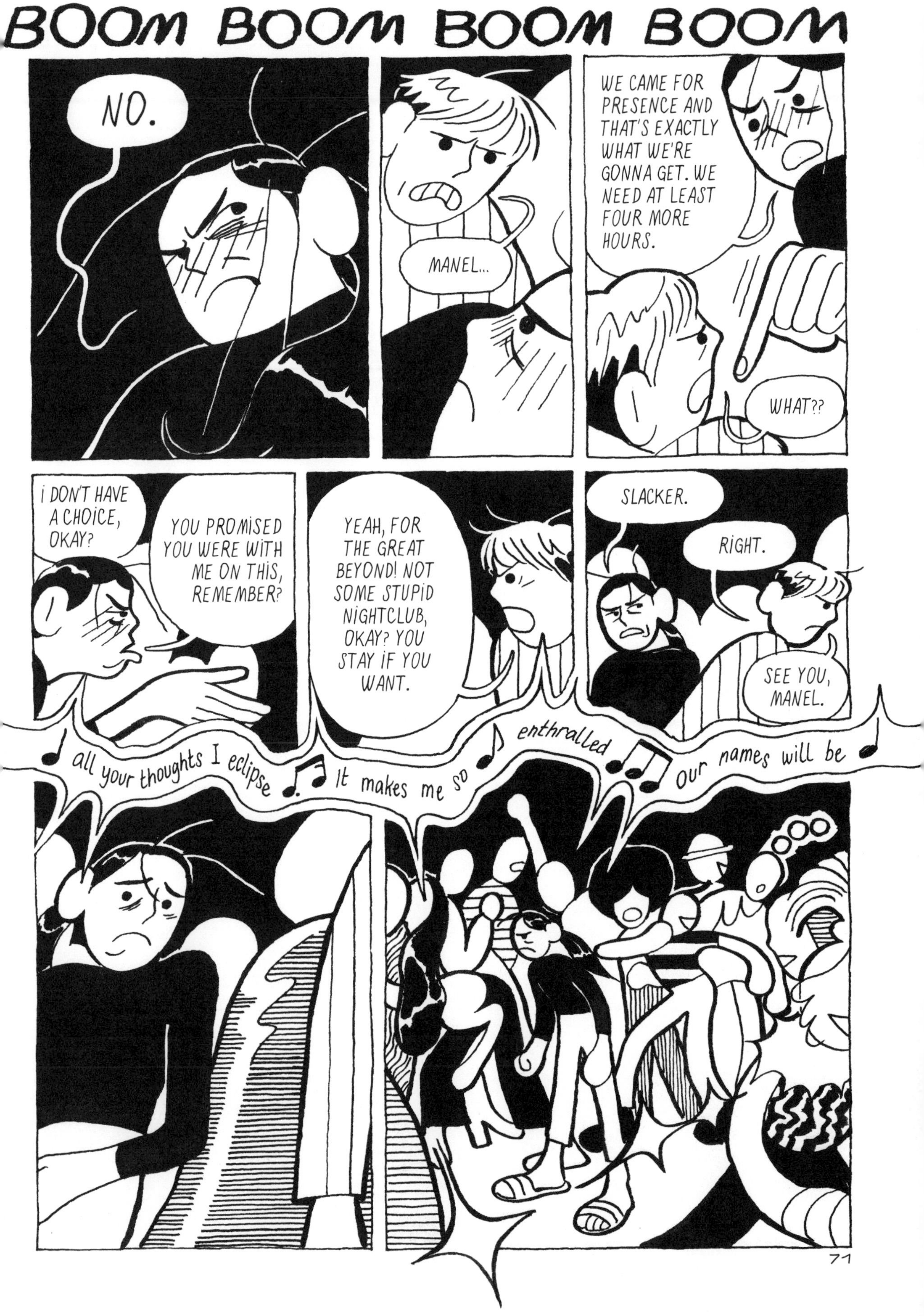

BOOM BOOM BOOM BOOM
NO.
MANEL...
WE CAME FOR PRESENCE AND THAT'S EXACTLY WHAT WE'RE GONNA GET. WE NEED AT LEAST FOUR MORE HOURS.
WHAT??
I DON'T HAVE A CHOICE, OKAY?
YOU PROMISED YOU WERE WITH ME ON THIS, REMEMBER?
YEAH, FOR THE GREAT BEYOND! NOT SOME STUPID NIGHTCLUB, OKAY? YOU STAY IF YOU WANT.
SLACKER.
RIGHT.
SEE YOU, MANEL.
all your thoughts I eclipse
It makes me so
enthralled
our names will be

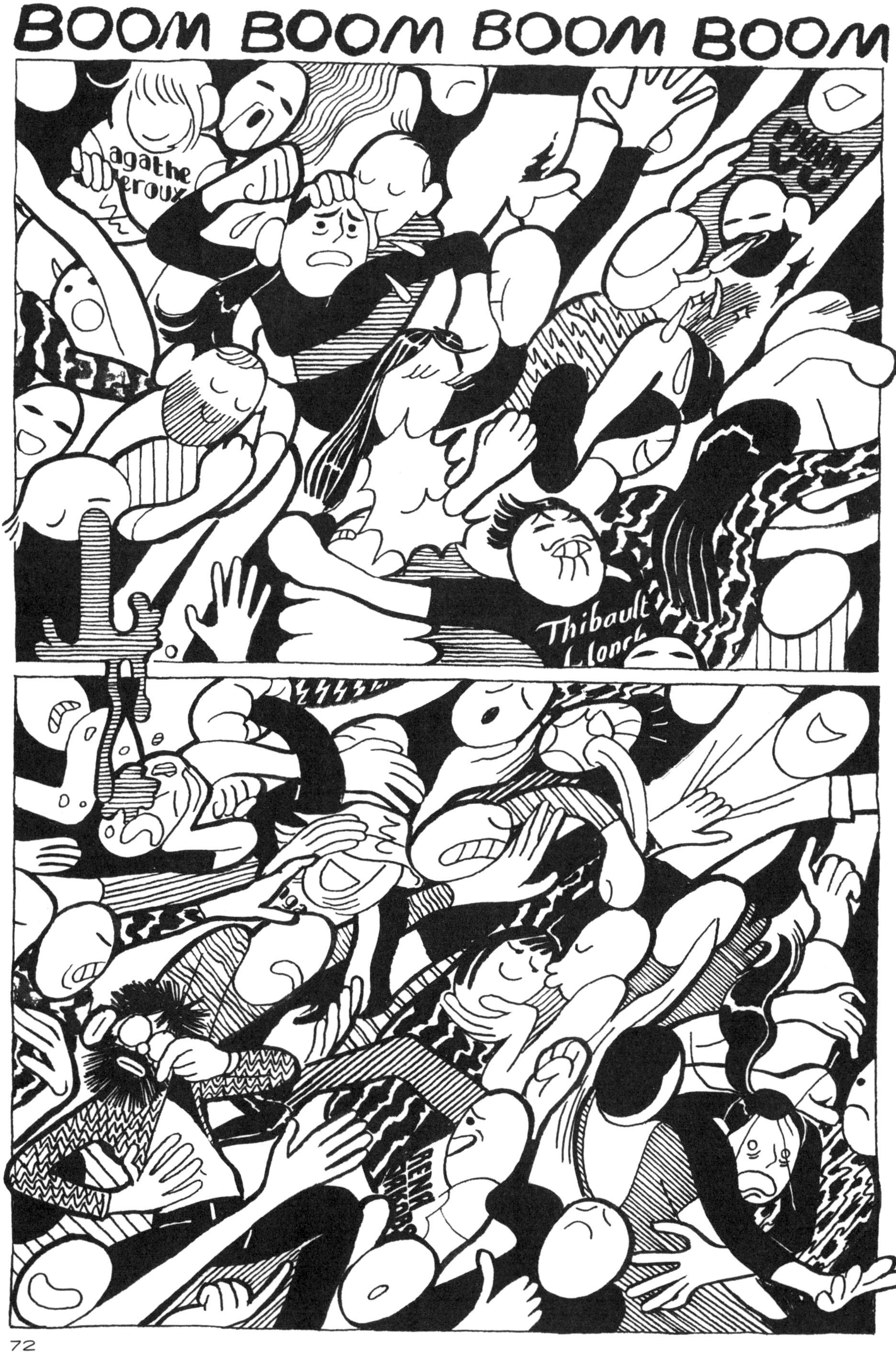
BOOM BOOM BOOM BOOM
agathe
Thibault

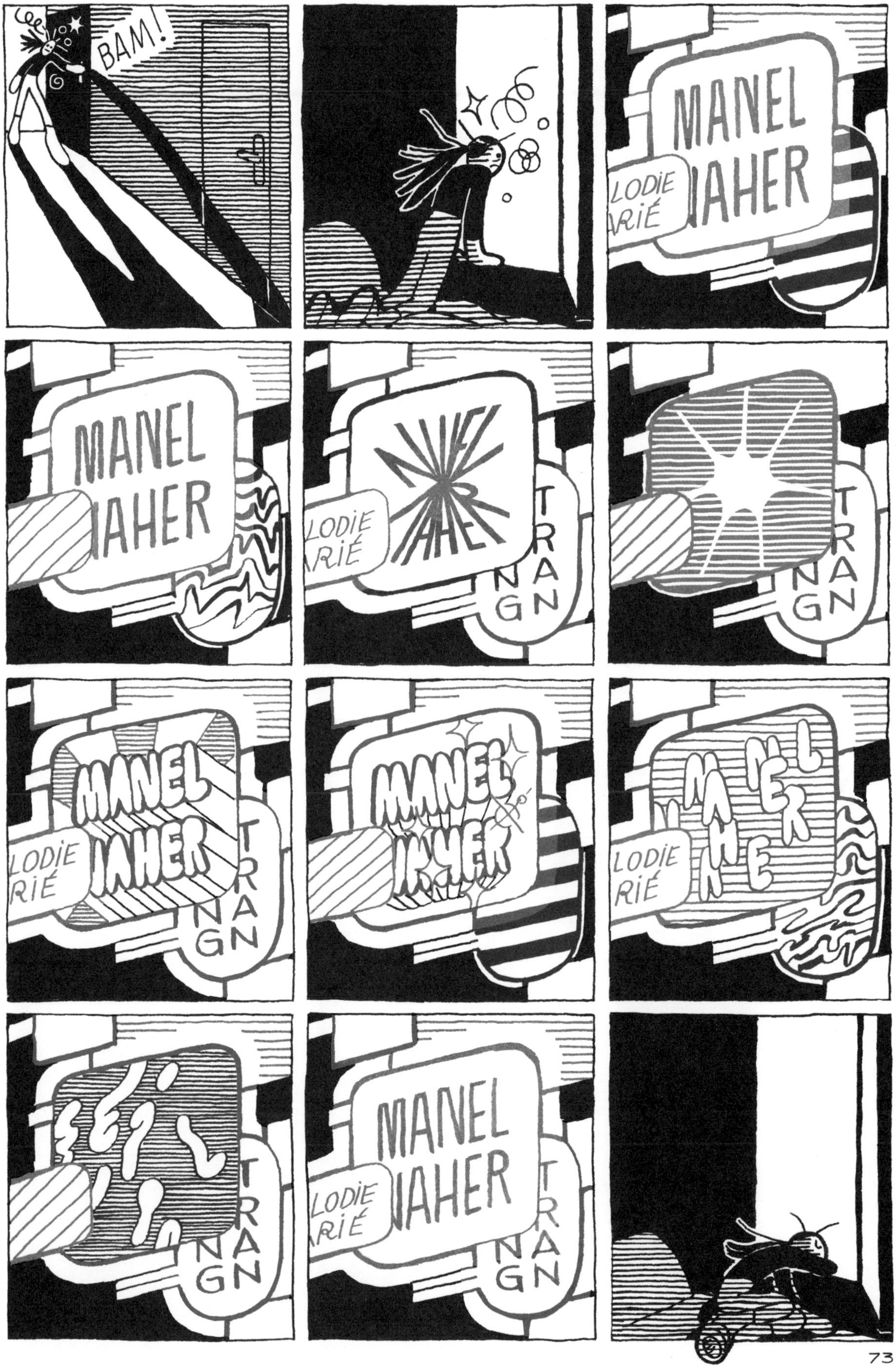
BAM!
MANEL
MAHER
LODIE
ARIÉ

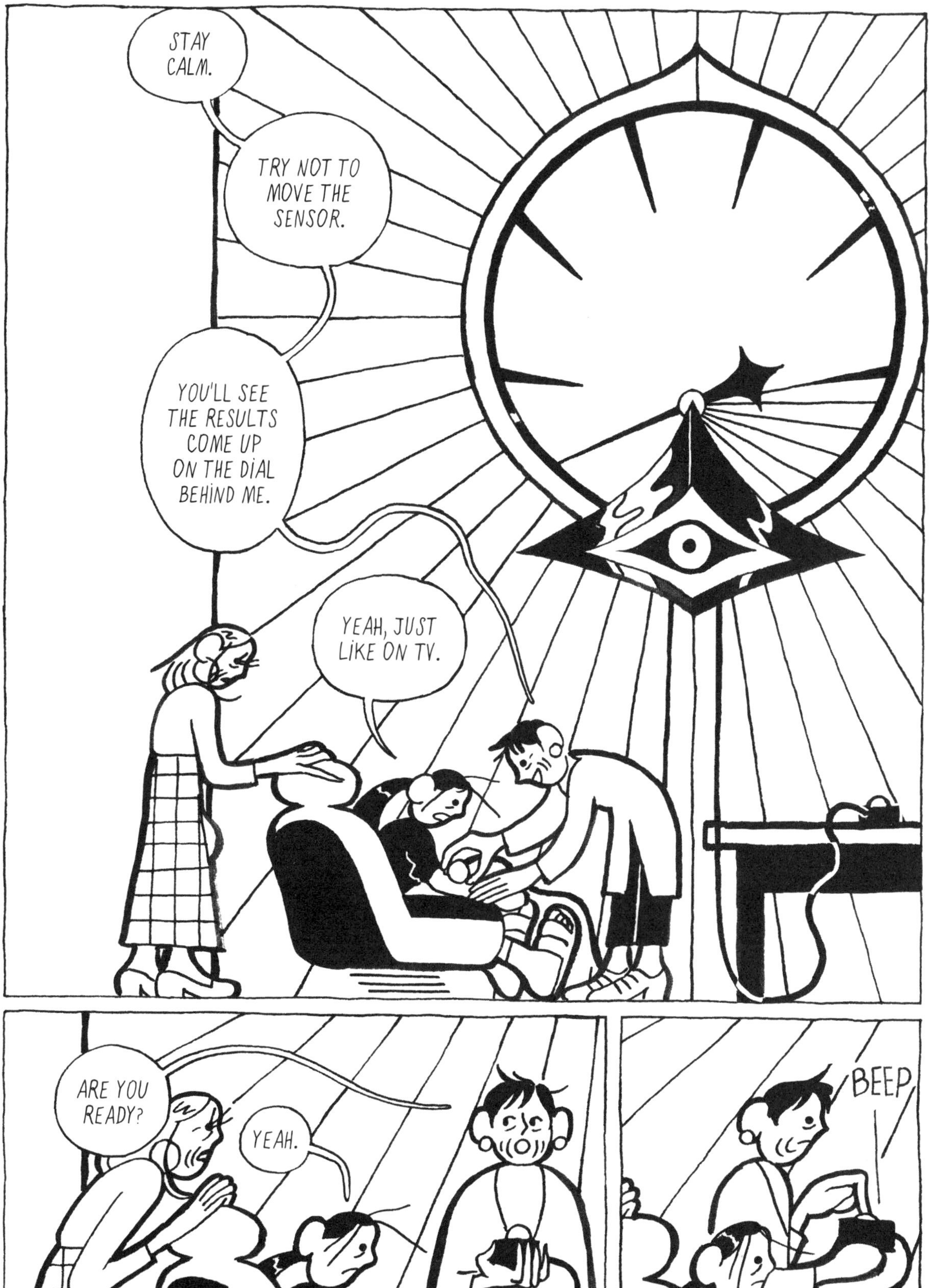
STAY CALM.
TRY NOT TO MOVE THE SENSOR.
YOU'LL SEE THE RESULTS COME UP ON THE DIAL BEHIND ME.
YEAH, JUST LIKE ON TV.
ARE YOU READY?
YEAH.
BEEP

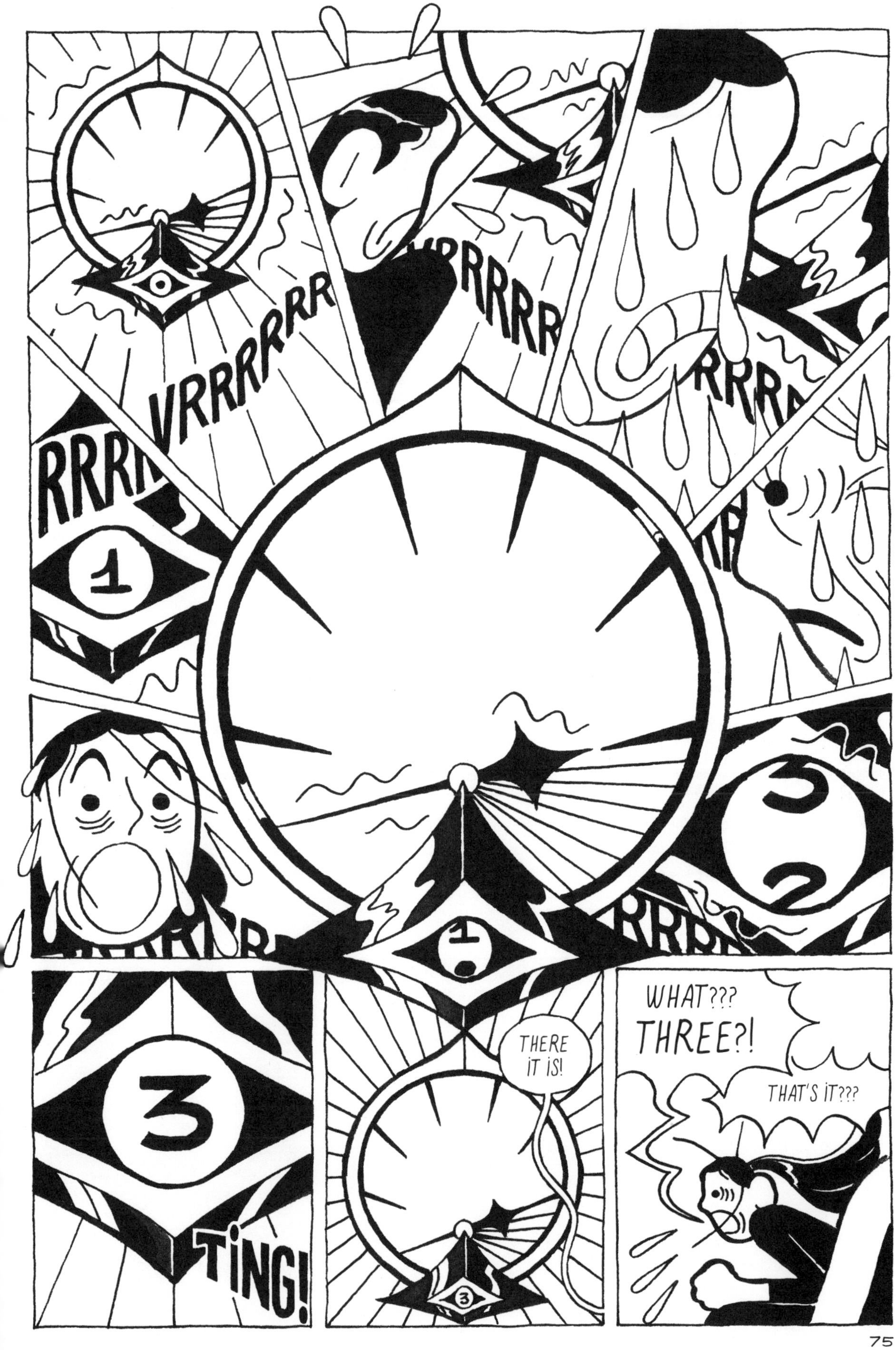
VRRRRRRR
VRRRRR
RRRR
RRRR
VRRRRRR
RR
1
3
RRRR
1
3
TING!
THERE IT IS!
3
WHAT???
THREE?!
THAT'S IT???

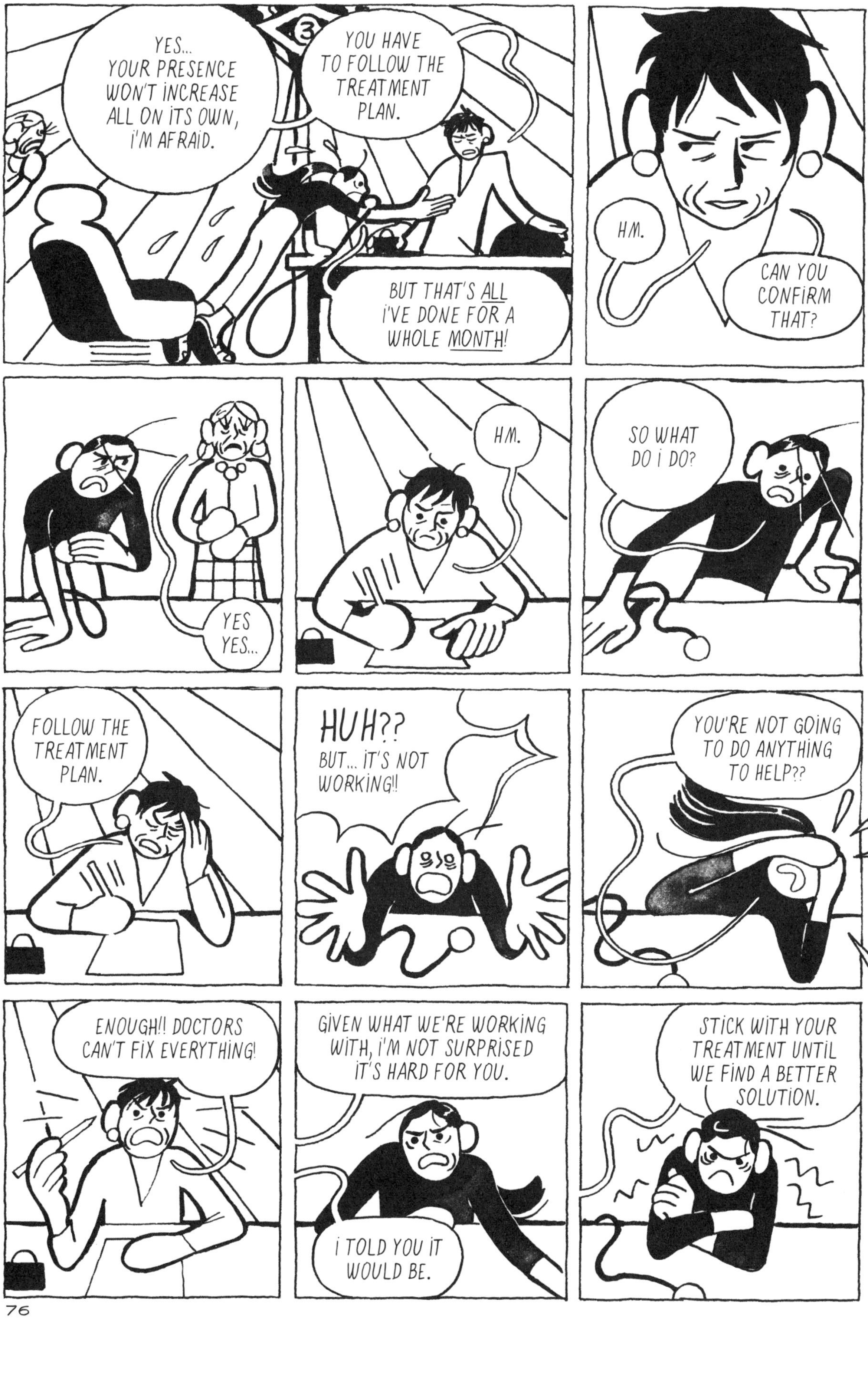
YES... YOUR PRESENCE WON'T INCREASE ALL ON ITS OWN, I'M AFRAID.
YOU HAVE TO FOLLOW THE TREATMENT PLAN.
BUT THAT'S ALL I'VE DONE FOR A WHOLE MONTH!
HM.
CAN YOU CONFIRM THAT?
YES YES...
HM.
SO WHAT DO I DO?
FOLLOW THE TREATMENT PLAN.
HUH?? BUT... IT'S NOT WORKING!!
YOU'RE NOT GOING TO DO ANYTHING TO HELP??
ENOUGH!! DOCTORS CAN'T FIX EVERYTHING!
GIVEN WHAT WE'RE WORKING WITH, I'M NOT SURPRISED IT'S HARD FOR YOU.
I TOLD YOU IT WOULD BE.
STICK WITH YOUR TREATMENT UNTIL WE FIND A BETTER SOLUTION.

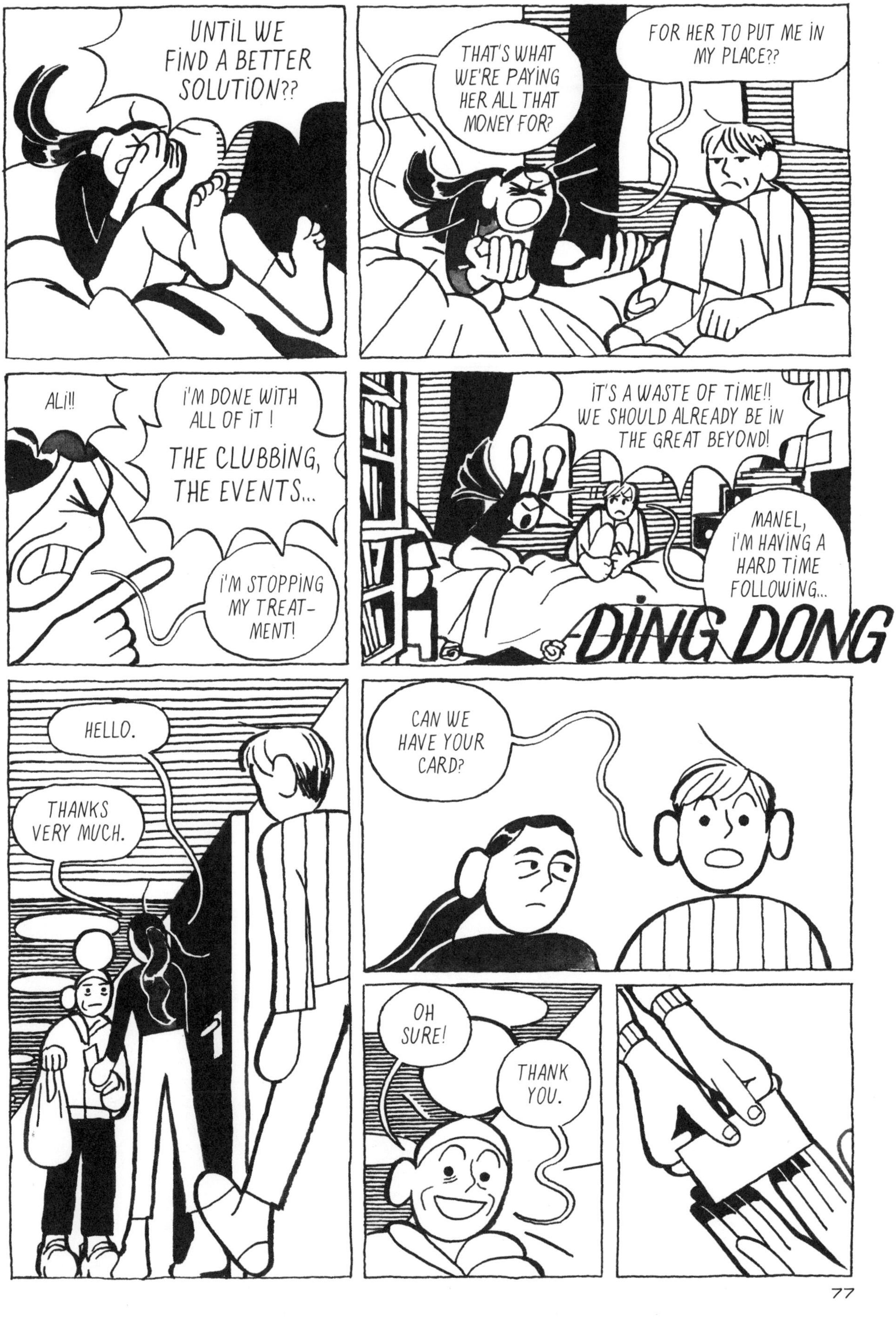
UNTIL WE FIND A BETTER SOLUTION??
THAT'S WHAT WE'RE PAYING HER ALL THAT MONEY FOR?
FOR HER TO PUT ME IN MY PLACE??
ALI!!
I'M DONE WITH ALL OF IT ! THE CLUBBING, THE EVENTS...
I'M STOPPING MY TREAT-MENT!
IT'S A WASTE OF TIME!! WE SHOULD ALREADY BE IN THE GREAT BEYOND!
MANEL, I'M HAVING A HARD TIME FOLLOWING...
DING DONG
HELLO.
THANKS VERY MUCH.
CAN WE HAVE YOUR CARD?
OH SURE!
THANK YOU.

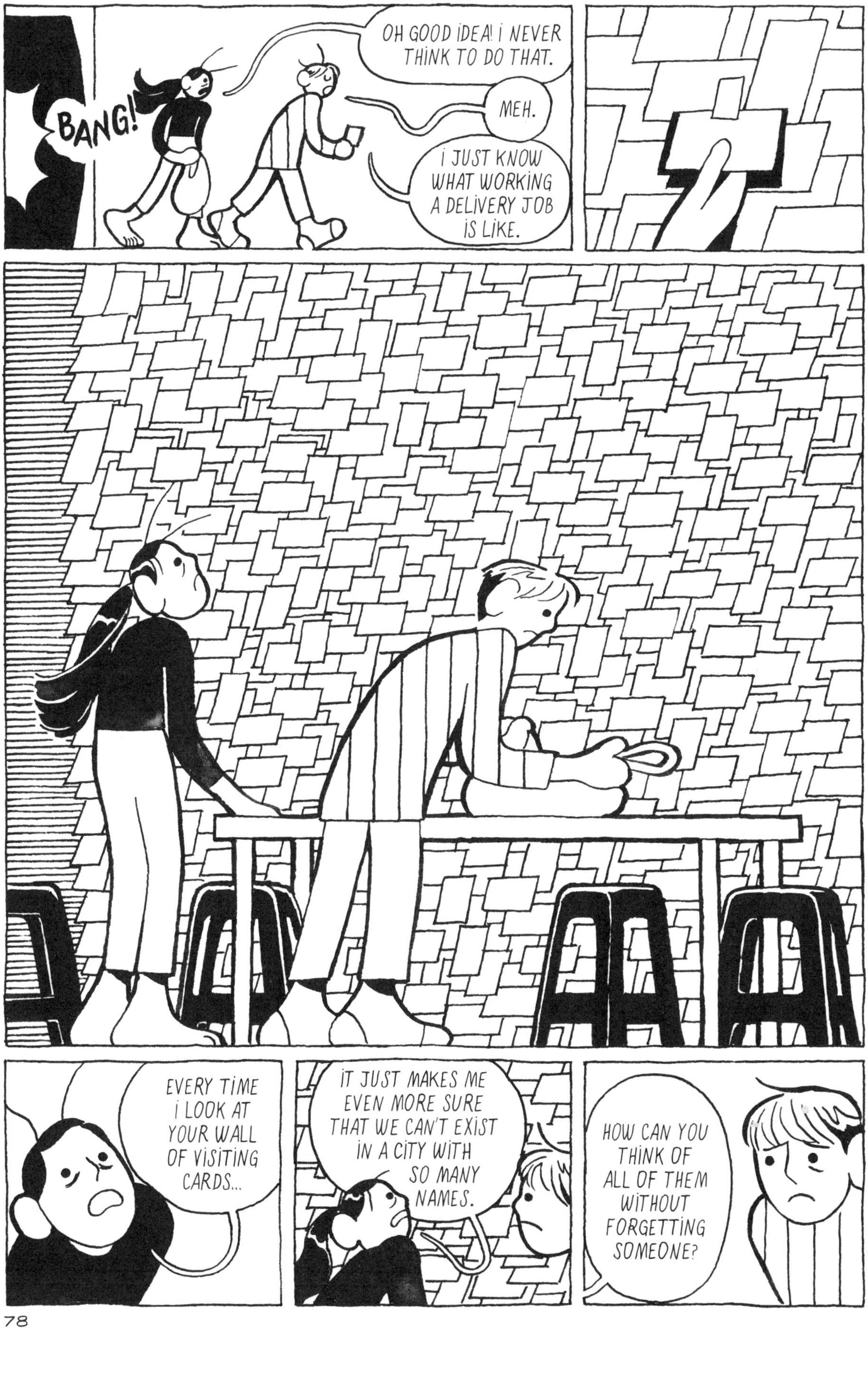
BANG!
OH GOOD IDEA! I NEVER THINK TO DO THAT.
MEH.
I JUST KNOW WHAT WORKING A DELIVERY JOB IS LIKE.
EVERY TIME I LOOK AT YOUR WALL OF VISITING CARDS...
IT JUST MAKES ME EVEN MORE SURE THAT WE CAN'T EXIST IN A CITY WITH SO MANY NAMES.
HOW CAN YOU THINK OF ALL OF THEM WITHOUT FORGETTING SOMEONE?

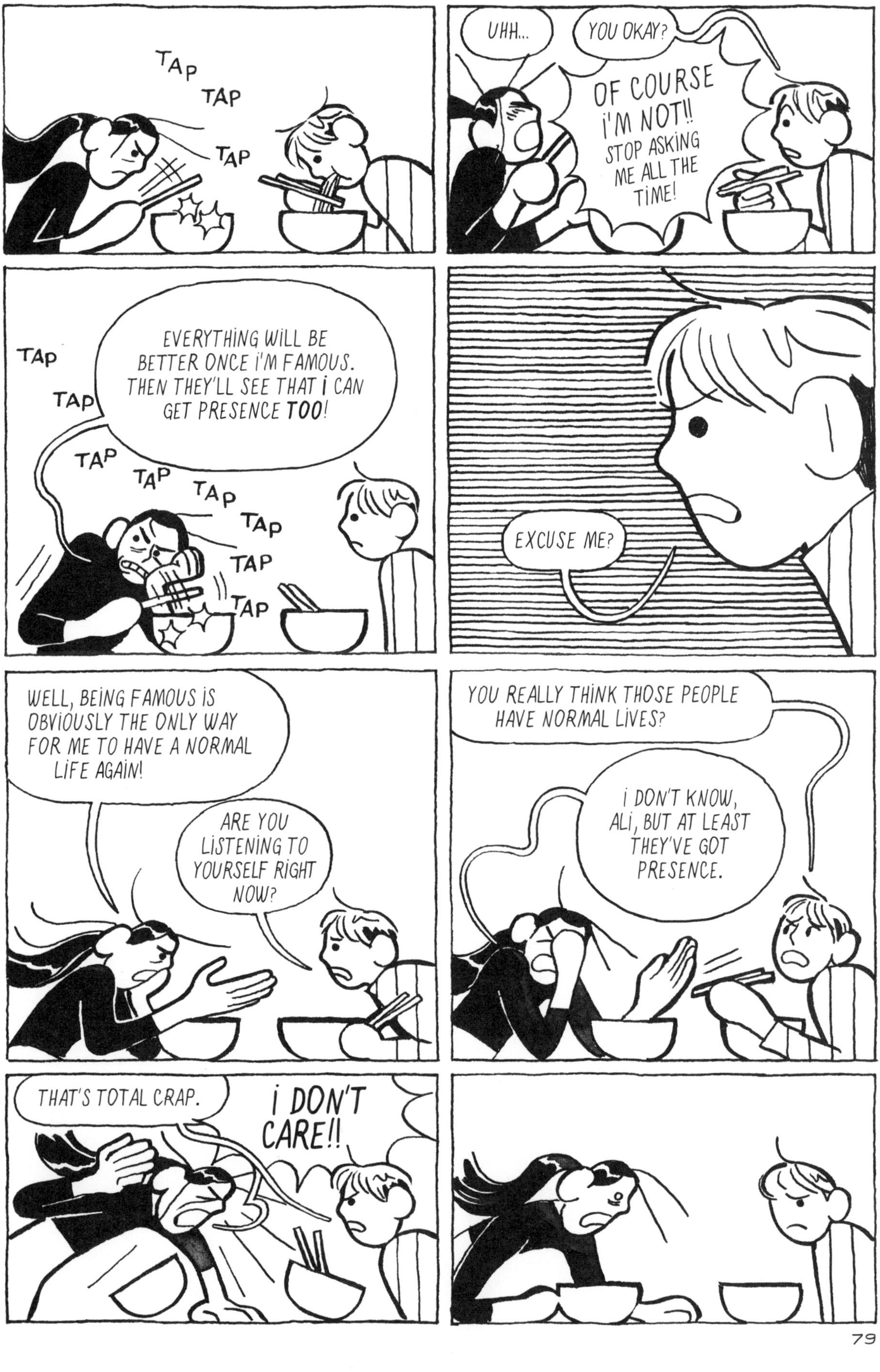
TAP
TAP
TAP
UHH...
YOU OKAY?
OF COURSE I'M NOT!! STOP ASKING ME ALL THE TIME!
EVERYTHING WILL BE BETTER ONCE I'M FAMOUS. THEN THEY'LL SEE THAT I CAN GET PRESENCE TOO!
TAP
TAP
TAP
TAP
TAP
TAP
TAP
TAP
EXCUSE ME?
WELL, BEING FAMOUS IS OBVIOUSLY THE ONLY WAY FOR ME TO HAVE A NORMAL LIFE AGAIN!
ARE YOU LISTENING TO YOURSELF RIGHT NOW?
YOU REALLY THINK THOSE PEOPLE HAVE NORMAL LIVES?
I DON'T KNOW, ALI, BUT AT LEAST THEY'VE GOT PRESENCE.
THAT'S TOTAL CRAP.
I DON'T CARE!!

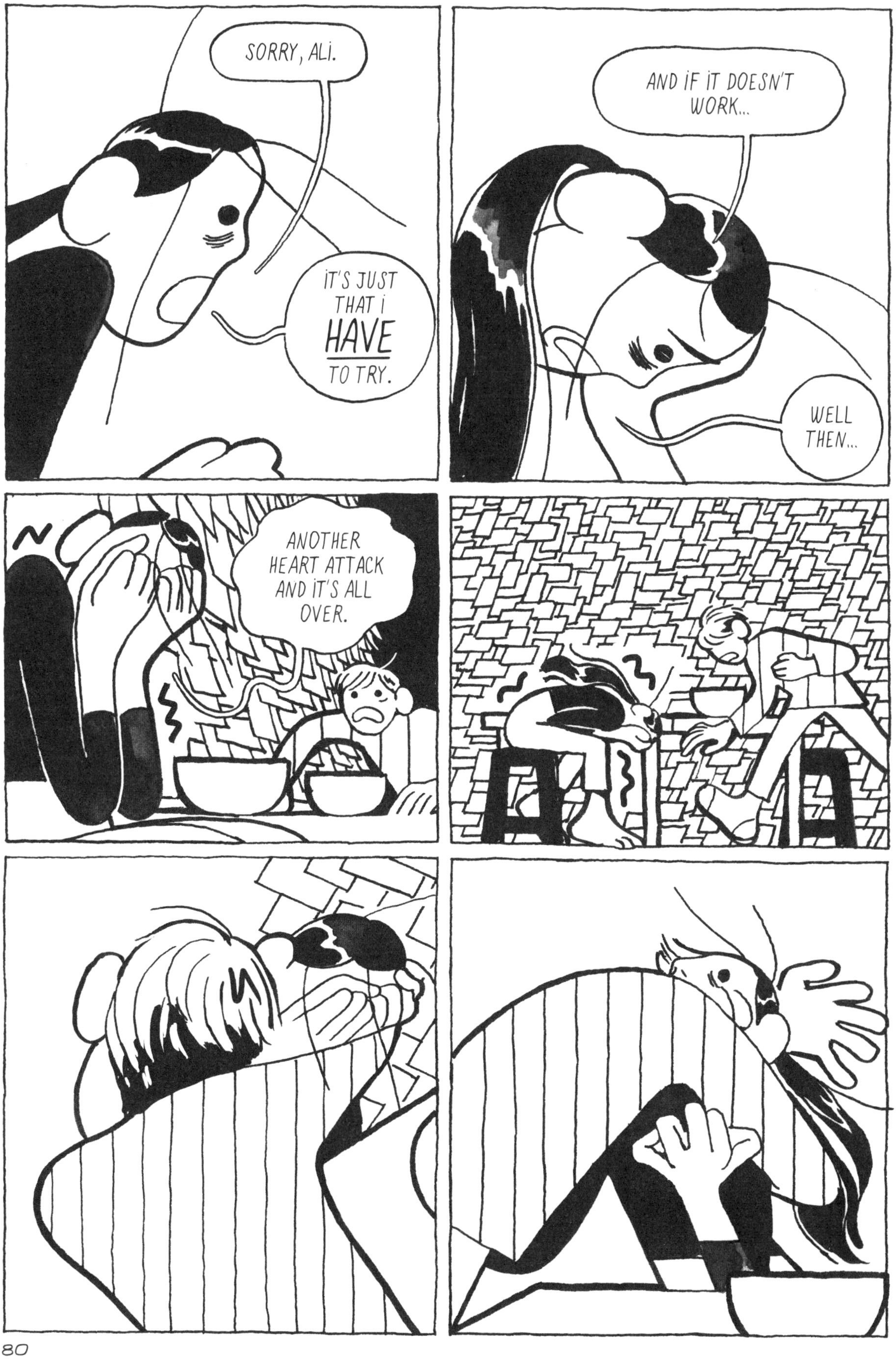
SORRY, ALi.
iT'S JUST THAT i HAVE TO TRY.
AND iF iT DOESN'T WORK...
WELL THEN...
ANOTHER HEART ATTACK AND iT'S ALL OVER.

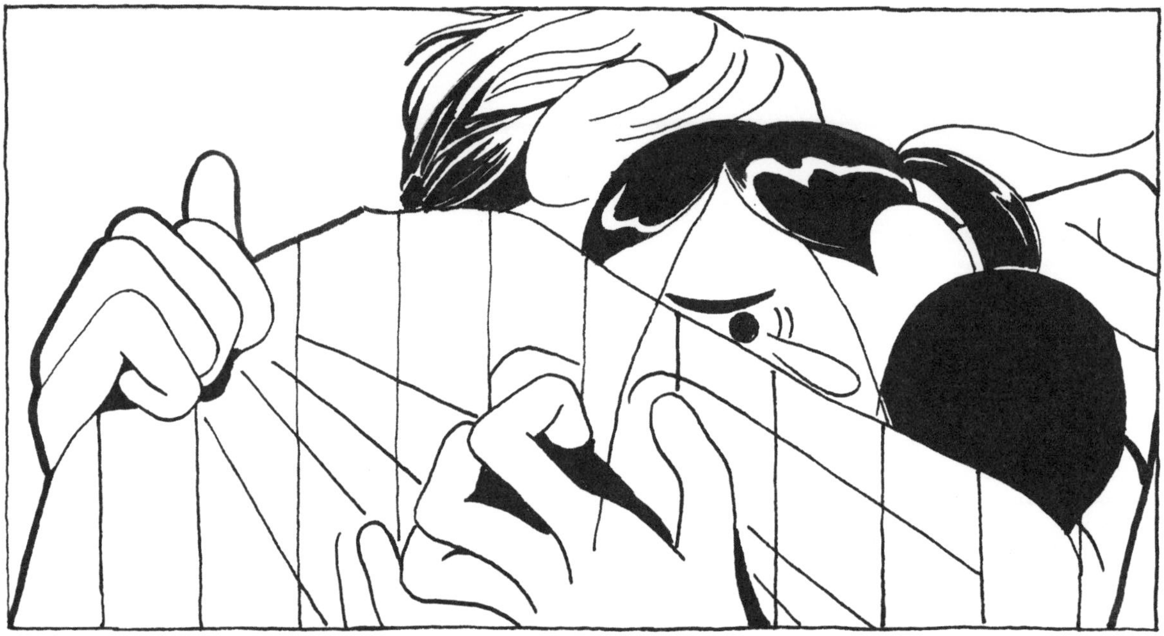

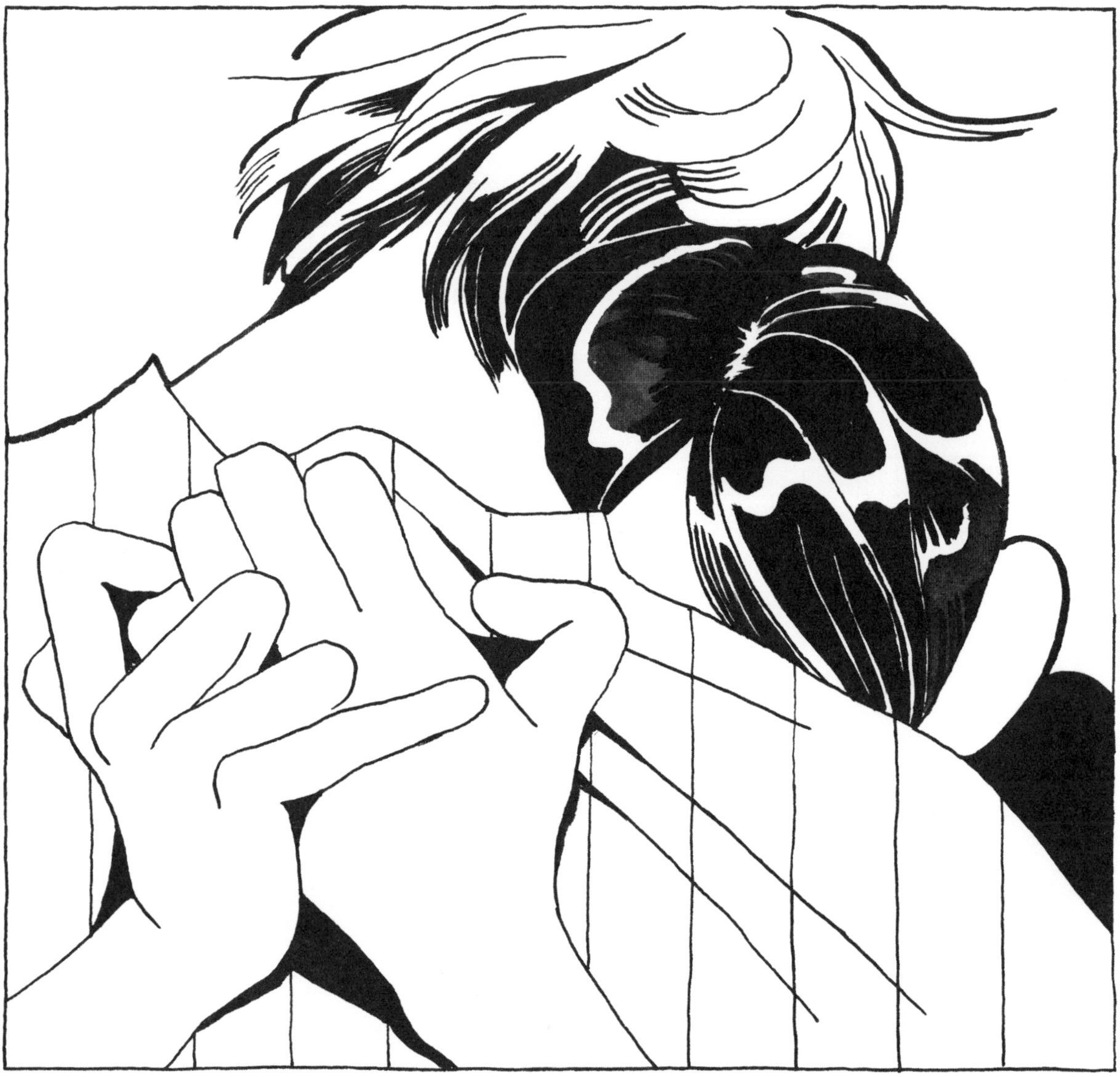

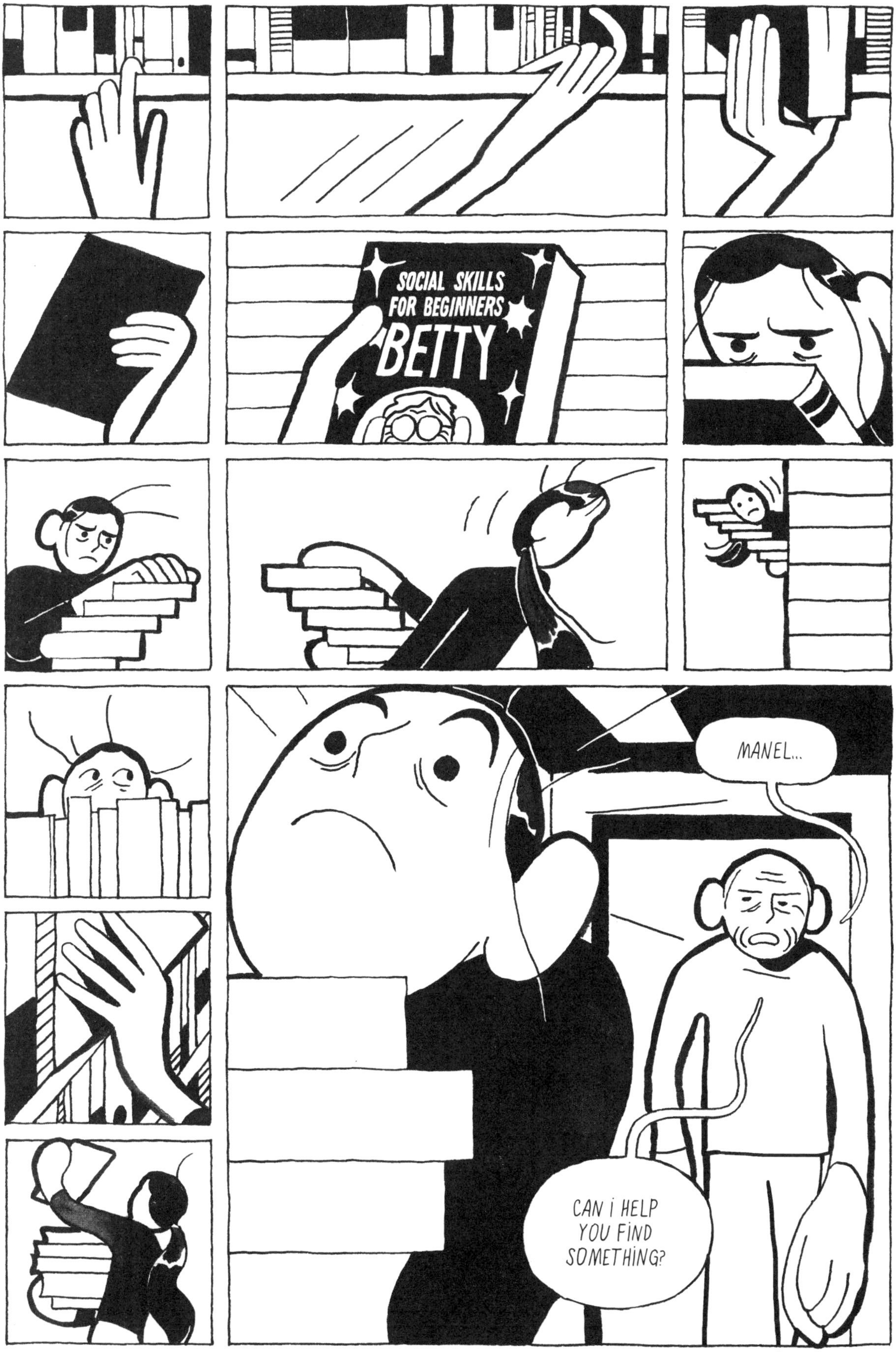
SOCIAL SKILLS FOR BEGINNERS
BETTY
MANEL...
CAN I HELP YOU FIND SOMETHING?

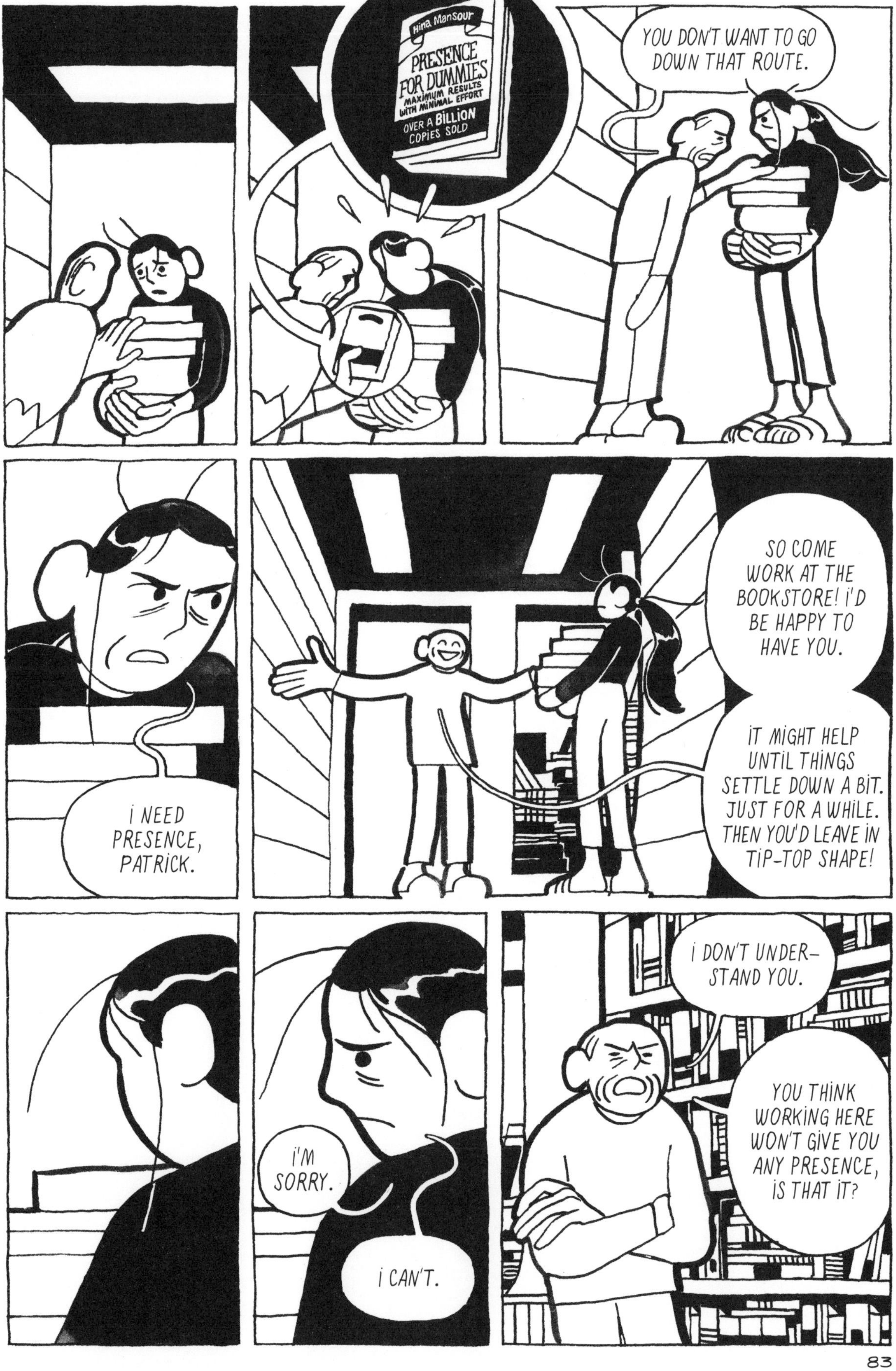
Hina Mansour
PRESENCE FOR DUMMIES
MAXIMUM RESULTS WITH MINIMAL EFFORT
OVER A BILLION COPIES SOLD
YOU DON'T WANT TO GO DOWN THAT ROUTE.
I NEED PRESENCE, PATRICK.
SO COME WORK AT THE BOOKSTORE! I'D BE HAPPY TO HAVE YOU.
IT MIGHT HELP UNTIL THINGS SETTLE DOWN A BIT. JUST FOR A WHILE. THEN YOU'D LEAVE IN TIP-TOP SHAPE!
I'M SORRY.
I CAN'T.
I DON'T UNDER-STAND YOU.
YOU THINK WORKING HERE WON'T GIVE YOU ANY PRESENCE, IS THAT IT?

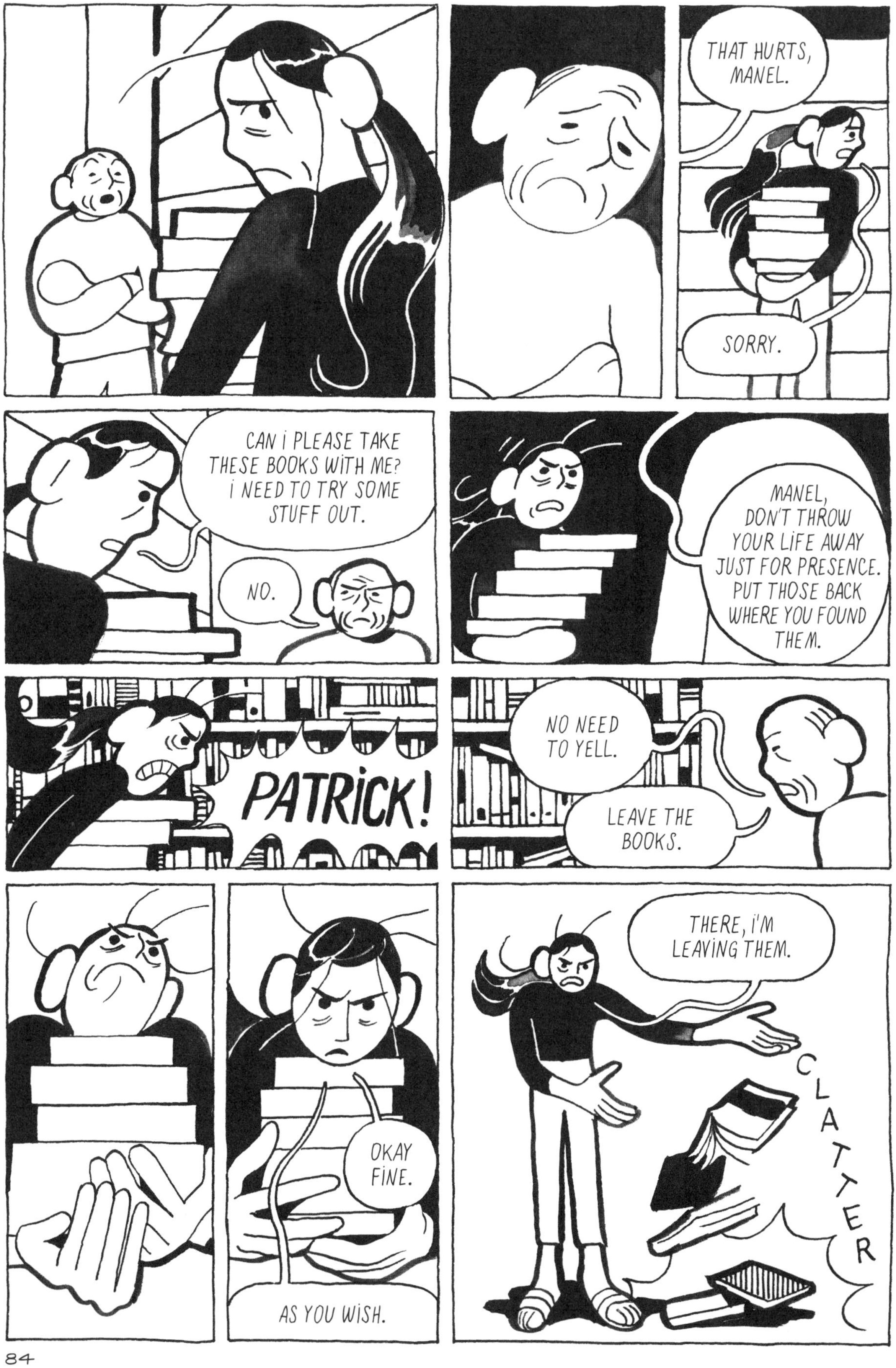
THAT HURTS, MANEL.
SORRY.
CAN I PLEASE TAKE THESE BOOKS WITH ME? I NEED TO TRY SOME STUFF OUT.
NO.
MANEL, DON'T THROW YOUR LIFE AWAY JUST FOR PRESENCE. PUT THOSE BACK WHERE YOU FOUND THEM.
PATRICK!
NO NEED TO YELL.
LEAVE THE BOOKS.
OKAY FINE.
AS YOU WISH.
THERE, I'M LEAVING THEM.
CLATTER

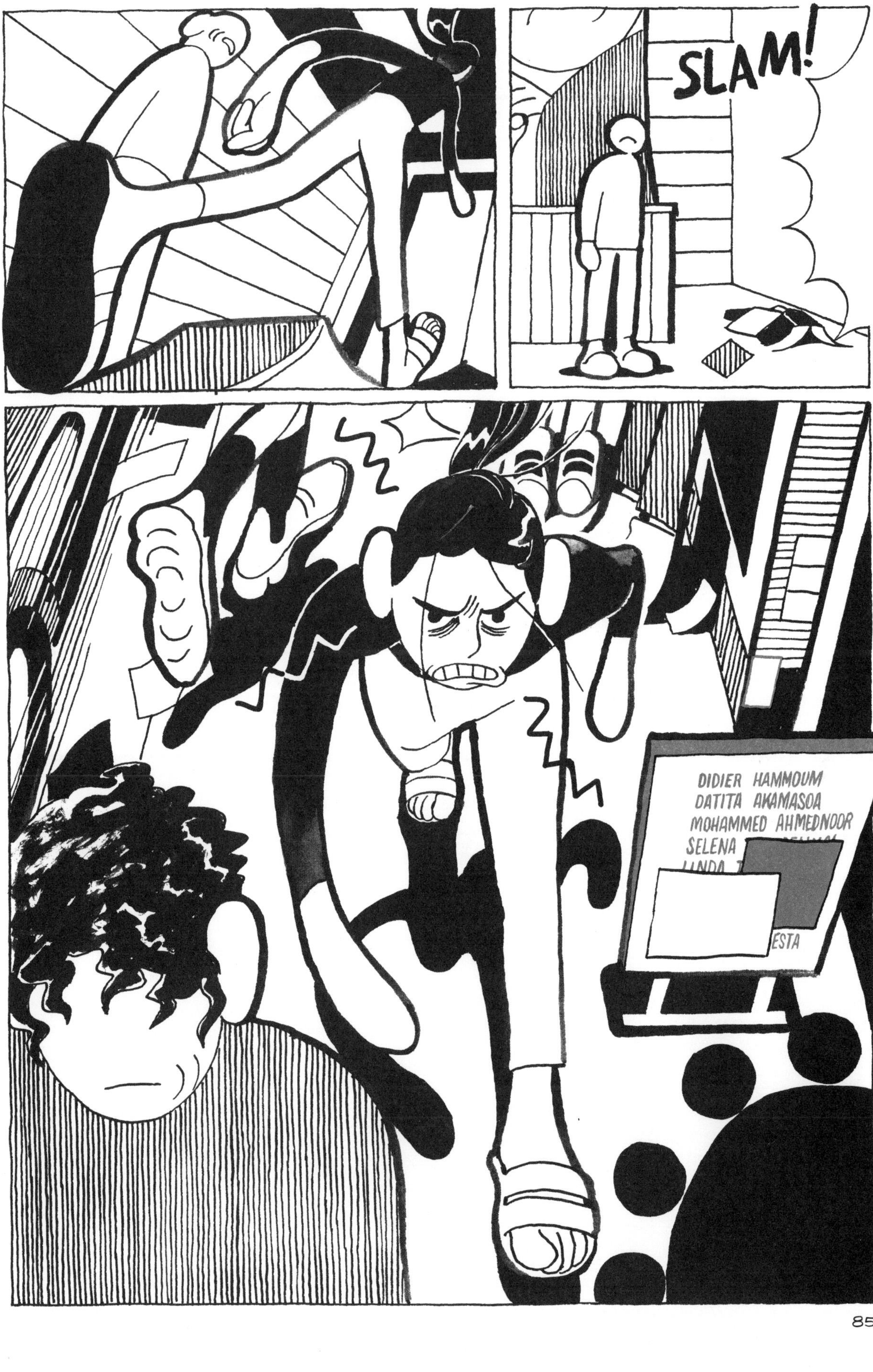
SLAM!
DIDIER HAMMOUM
DATITA AKAMASOA
MOHAMMED AHMEDNOOR
SELENA

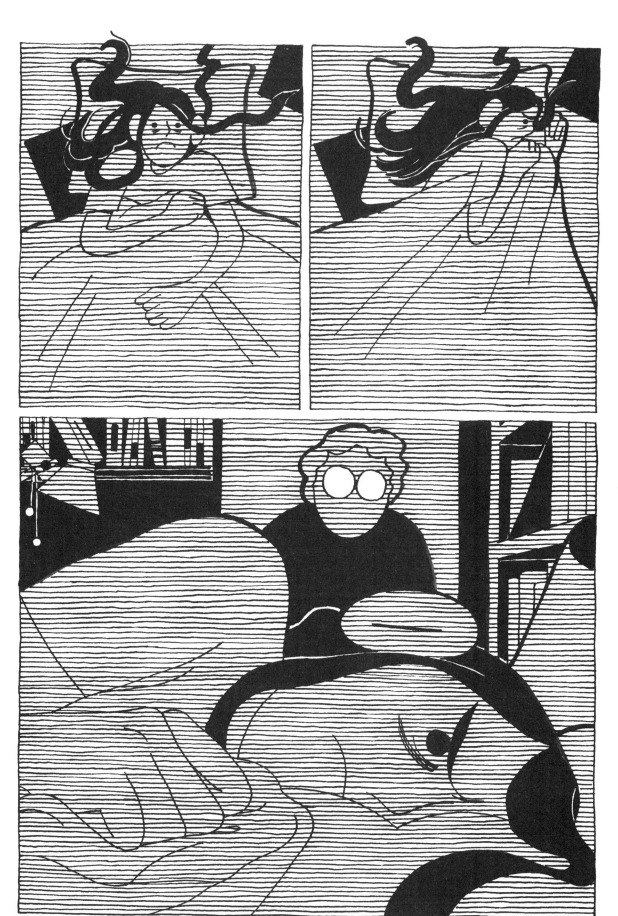

CAN'T YOU THINK OF ME WITHOUT STARING?
NO, MANEL. GO GET READY FOR DINNER WITH THE NEIGHBOURS.

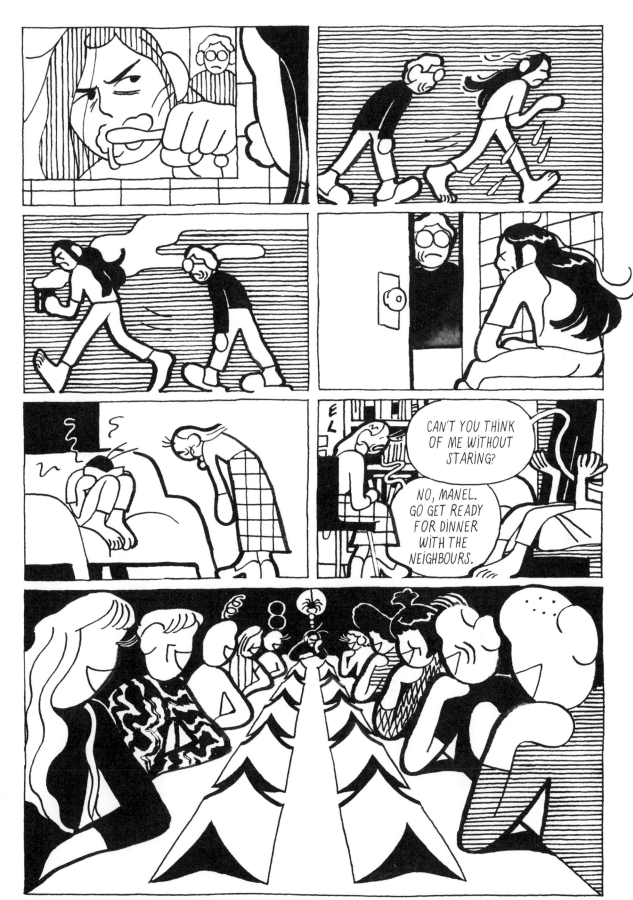

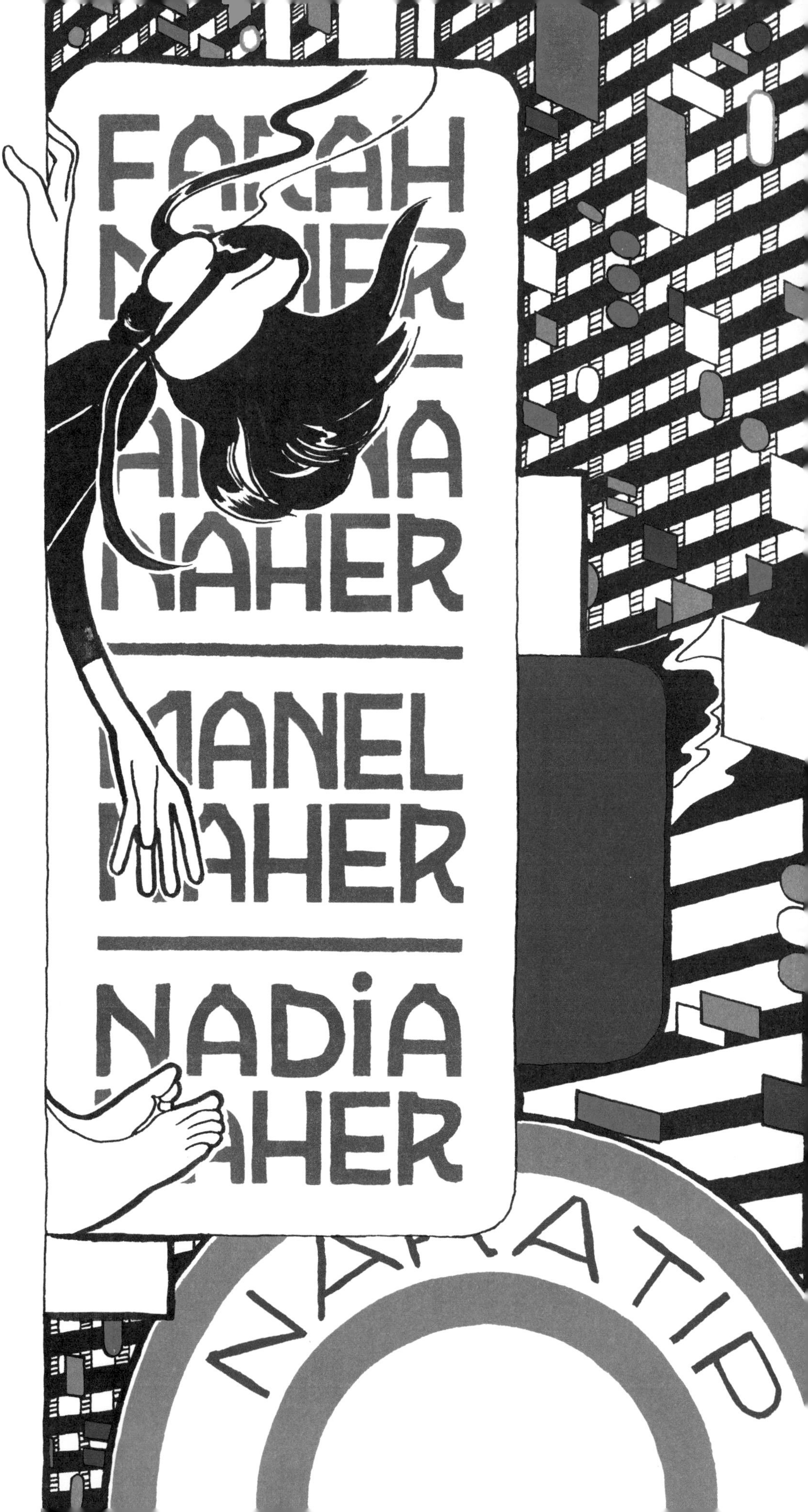
FARAH
NAHER
MANEL
NADIA

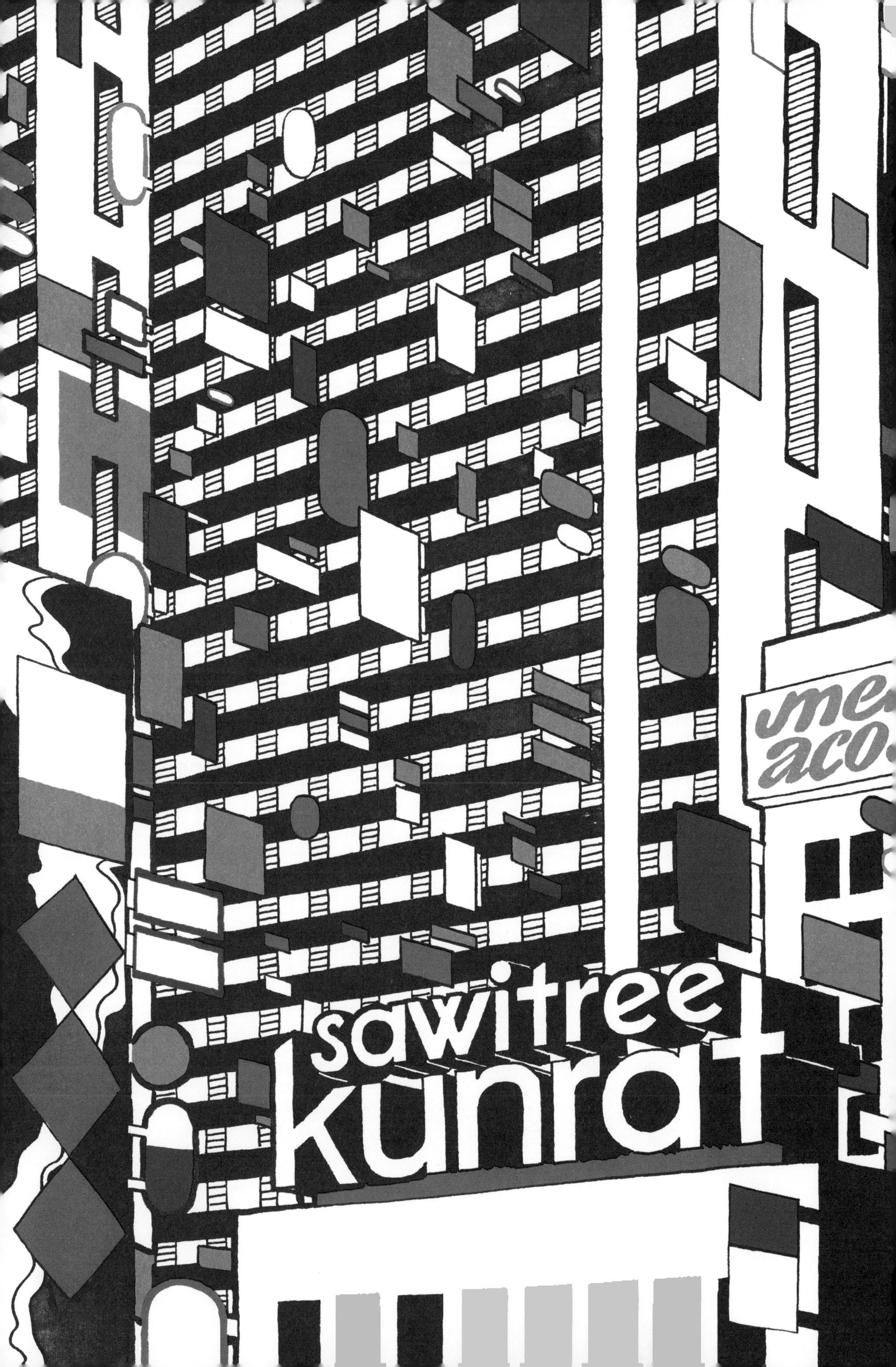
sawitree
kunrat

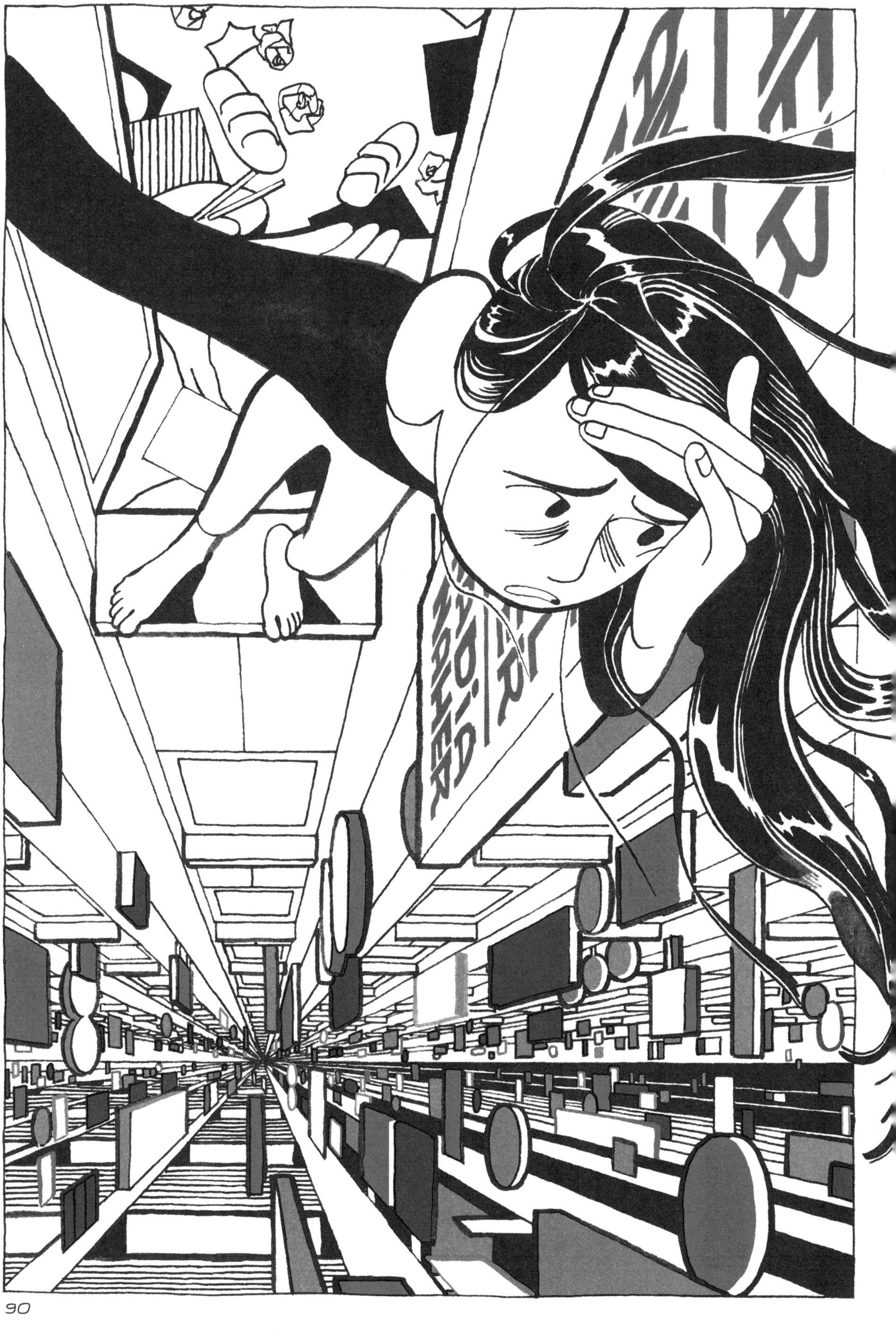

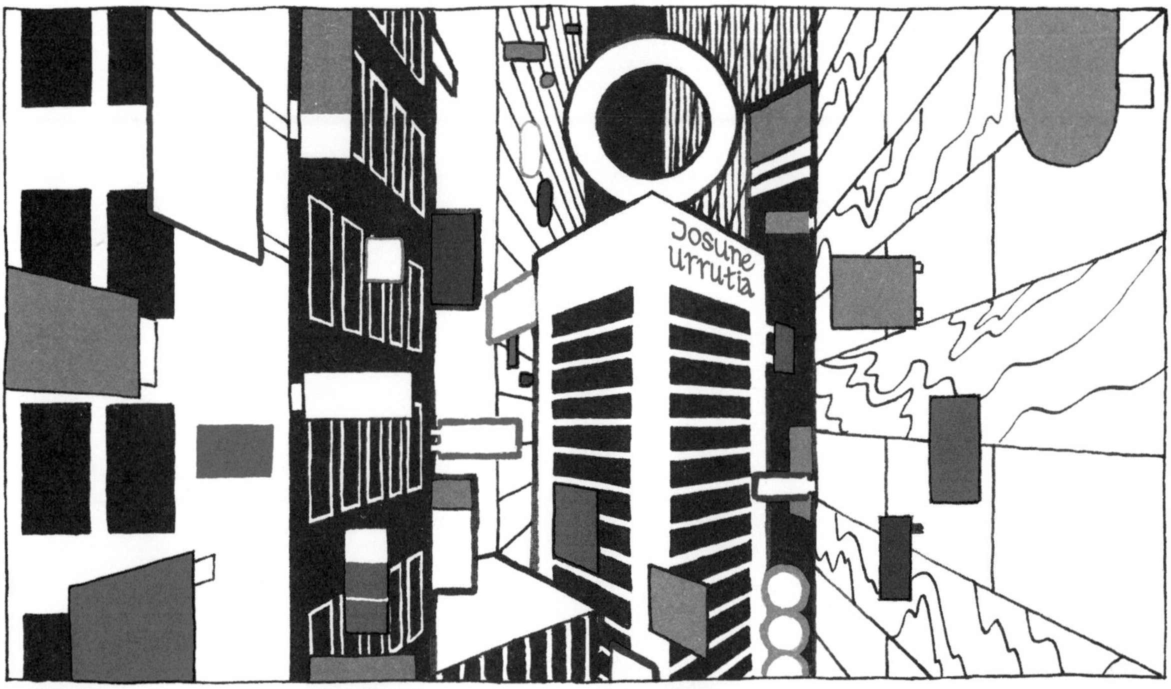
Josune
urrutia

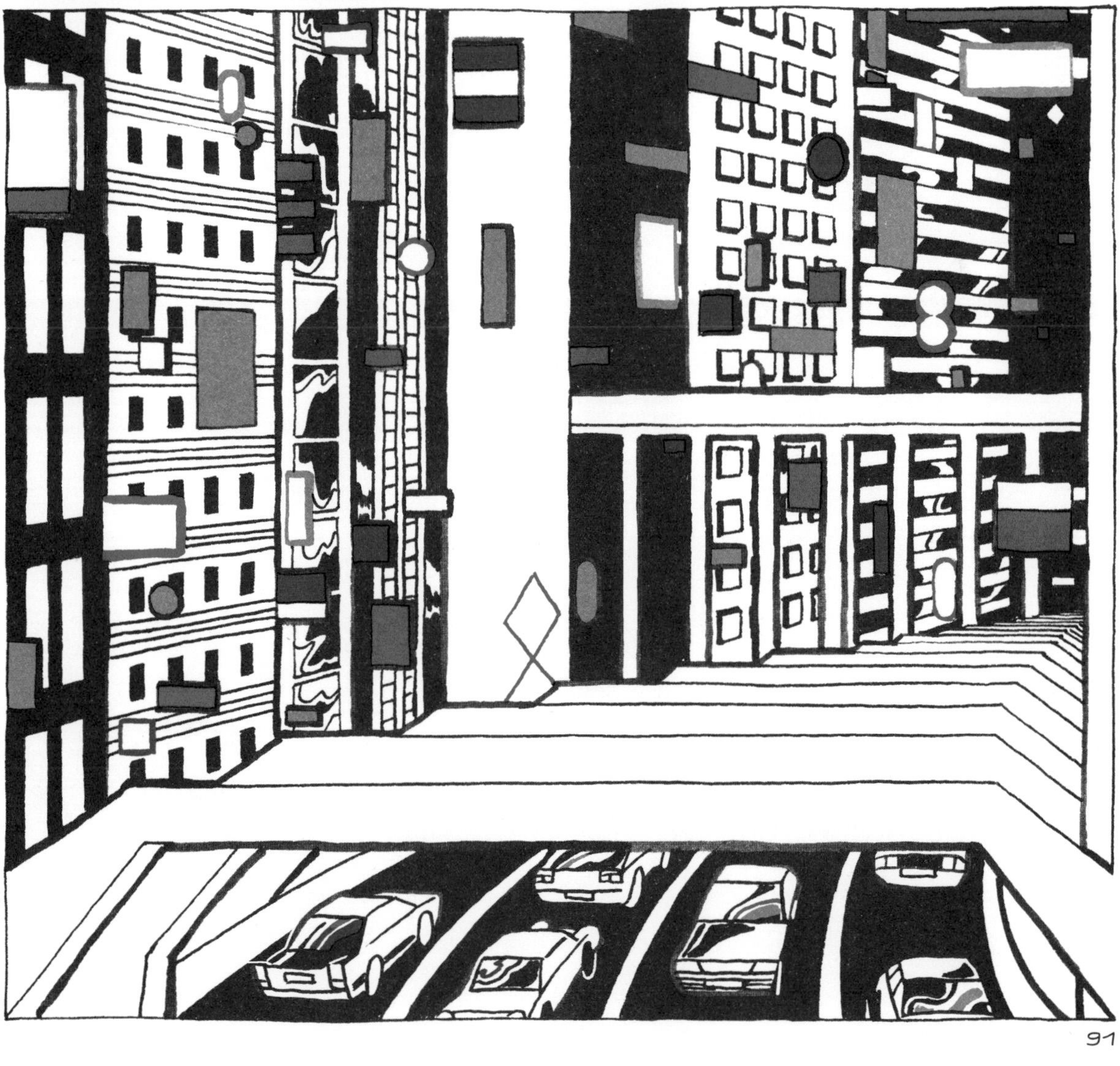

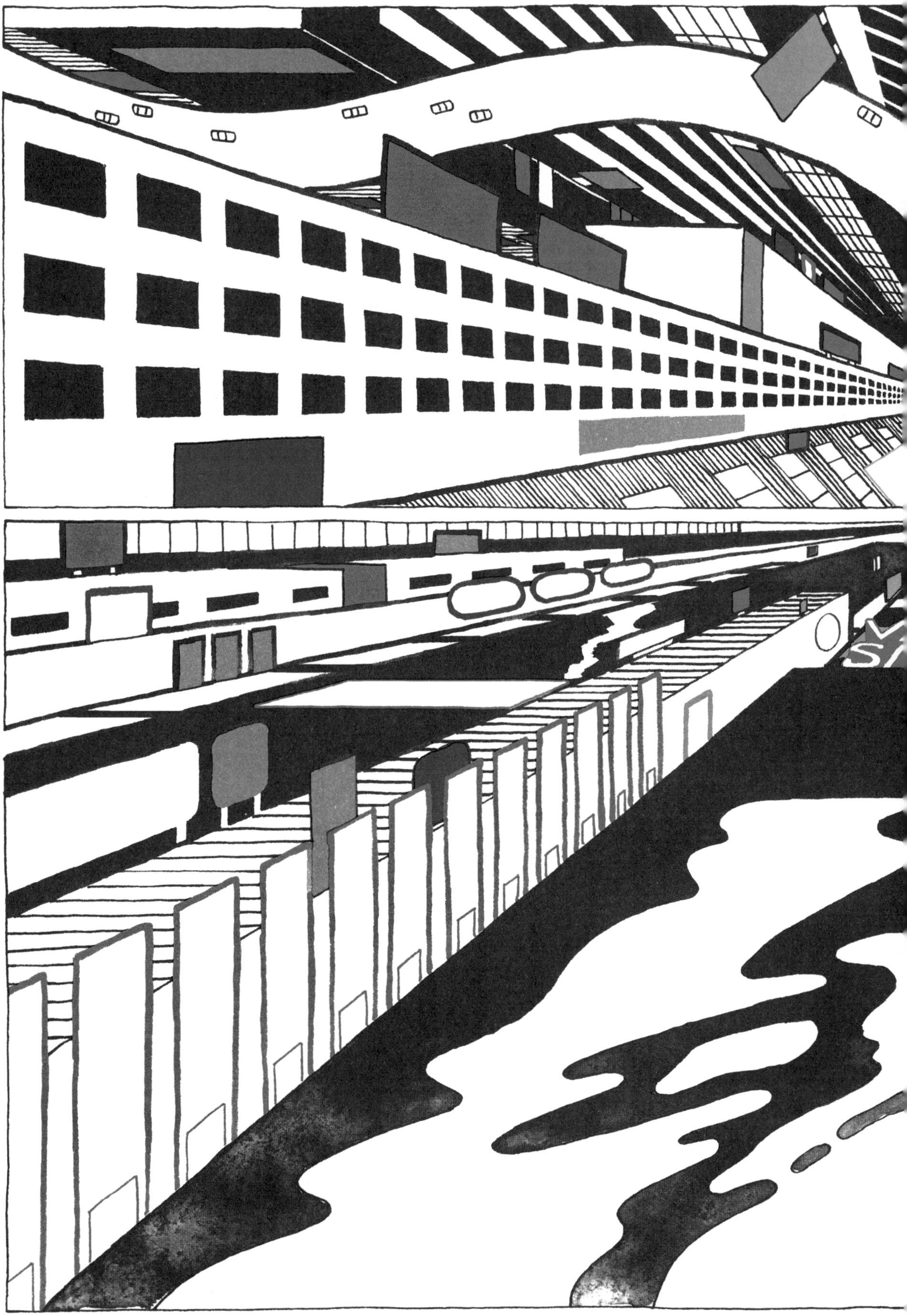

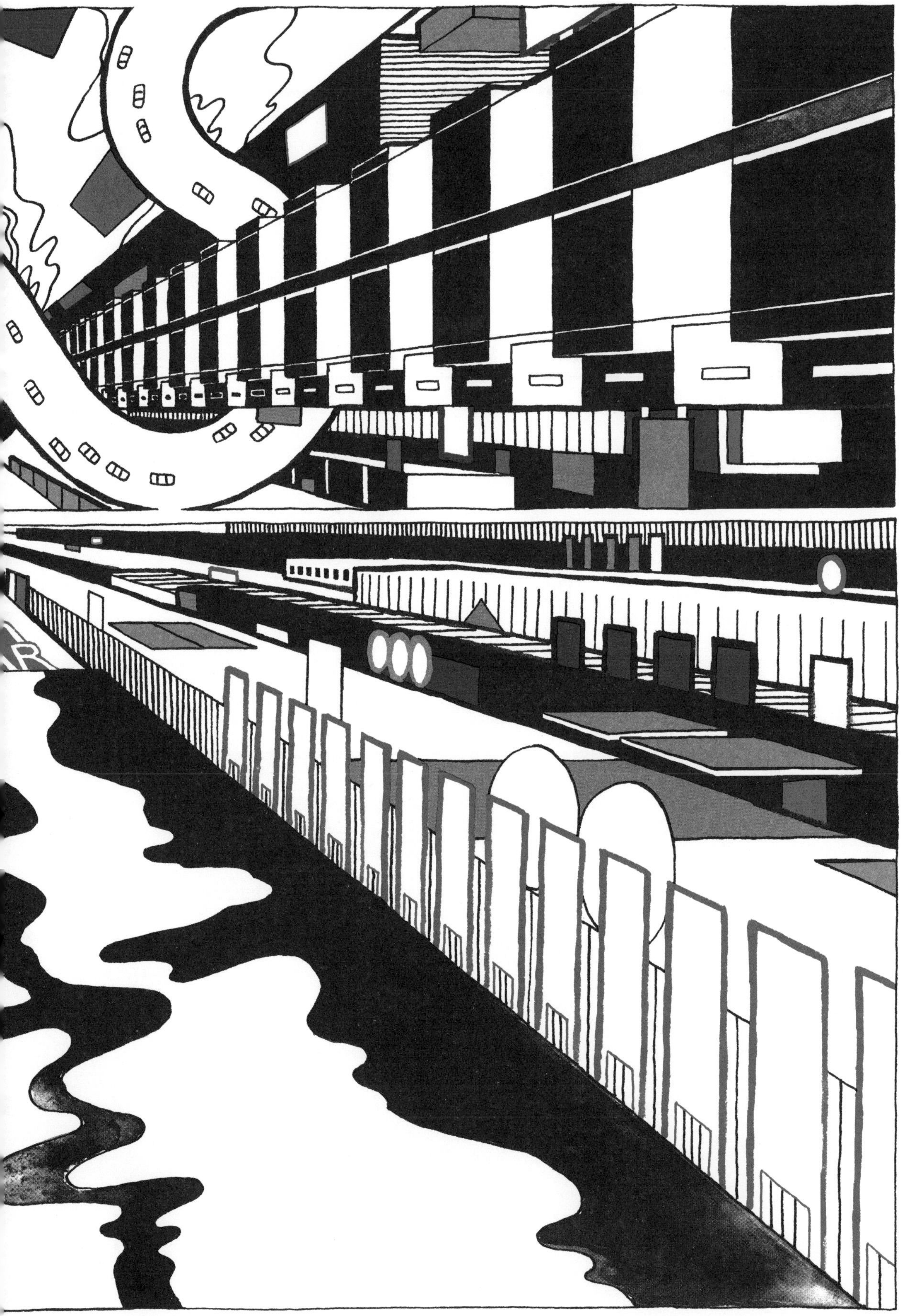

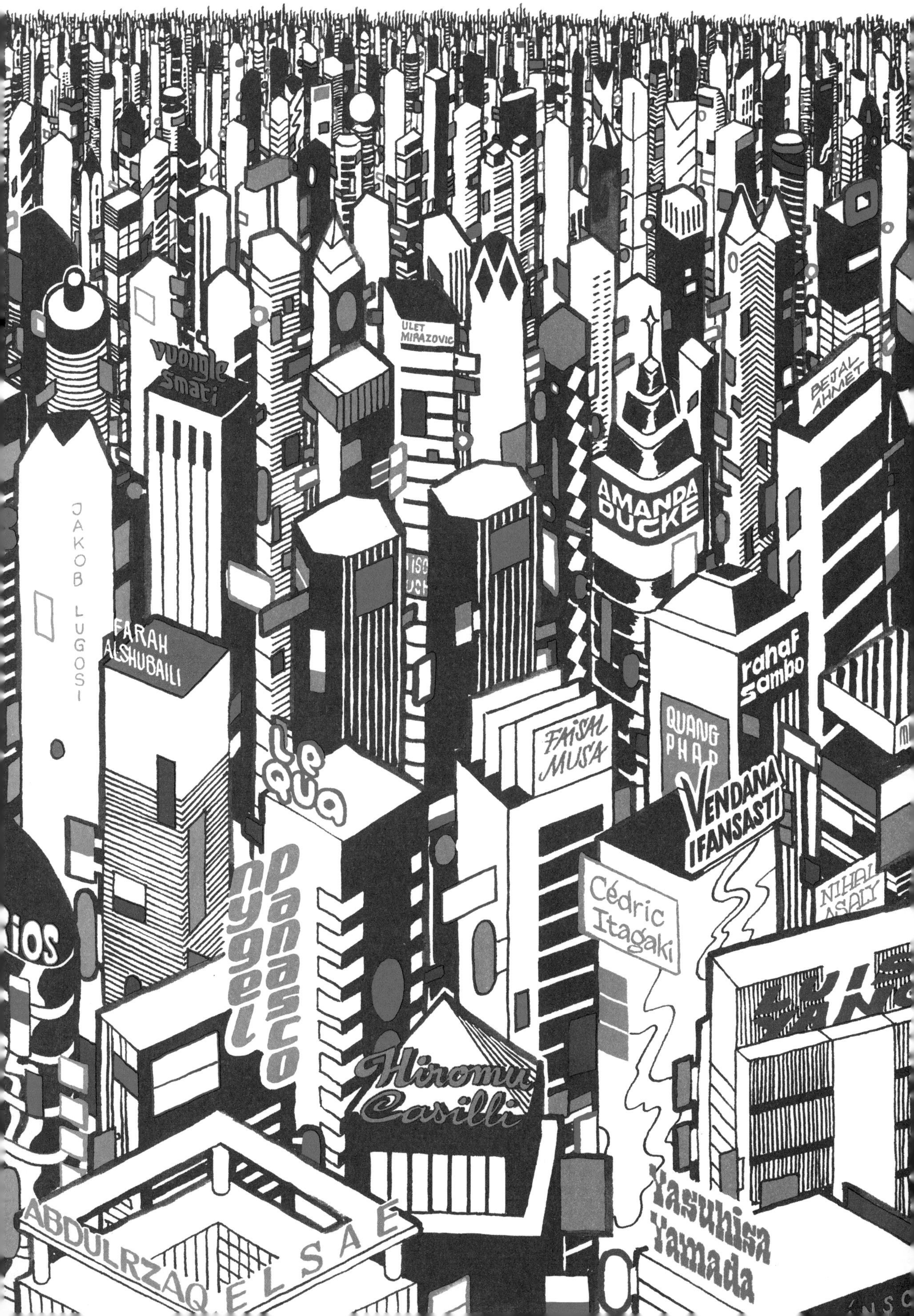
ULET MIRAZOVIC
vuongle smati
BEJAL AHMET
AMANDA DUCKE
JAKOB LUGOSI
FARAH ALSHUBAILI
rahaf sambo
QUANG
FAISAL MUSA
le qua
VENDANA IFANSASTI
NIHAL
Cédric Itagaki
nygel
panasco
Hiromu Casilli
Yasuhisa Yamada
ABDULRZAQ ELSAE

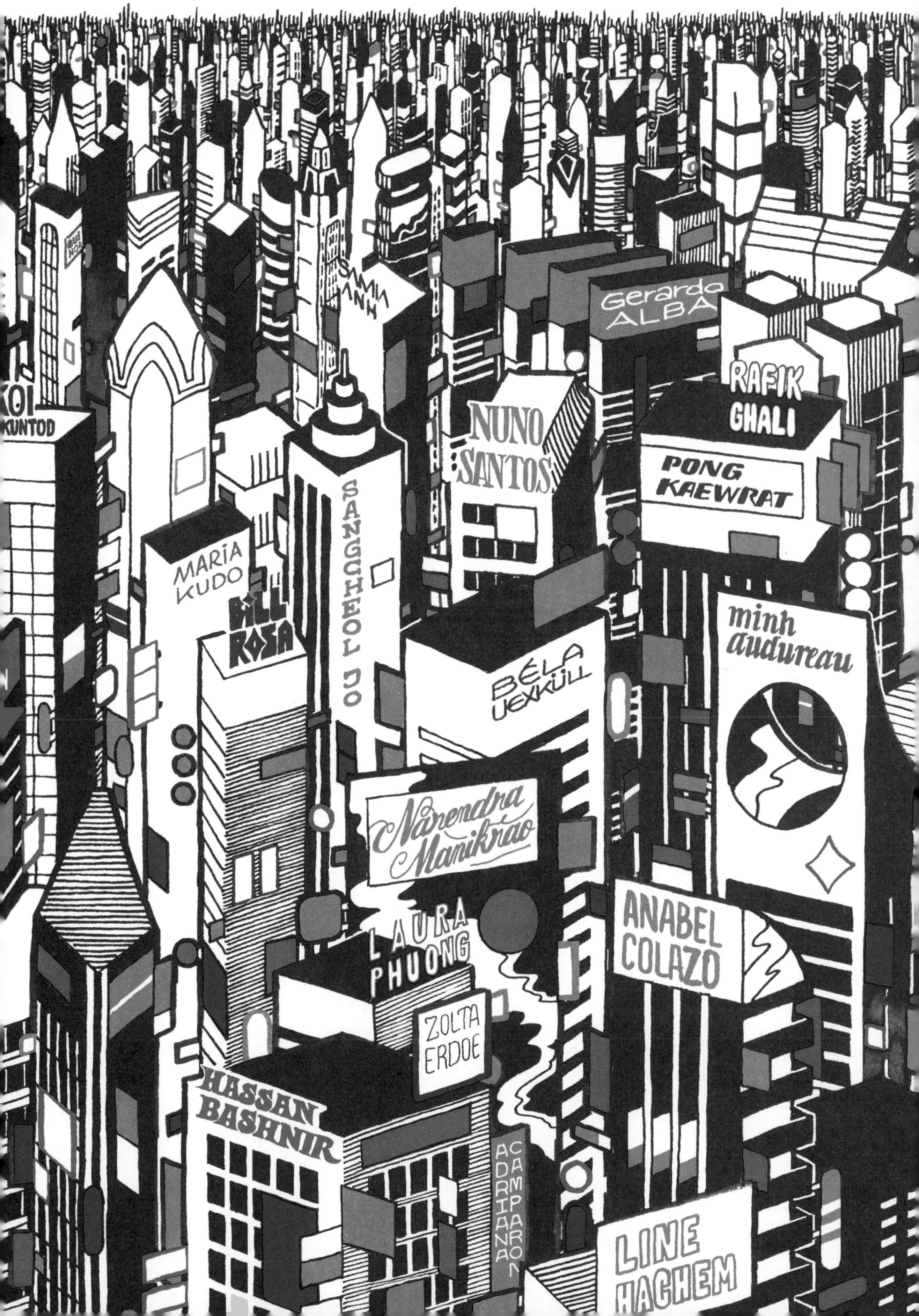
Gerardo ALBA
RAFIK GHALI
NUNO SANTOS
PONG KAEWRAT
MARIA KUDO
BILL ROSA
SANGCHEOL JO
BÉLA UEXKÜLL
minh audureau
Narendra Manikrao
ANABEL COLAZO
LAURA PHUONG
ZOLTA ERDOE
HASSAN BASHNIR
ADRIANA CAMPARON
LINE HACHEM

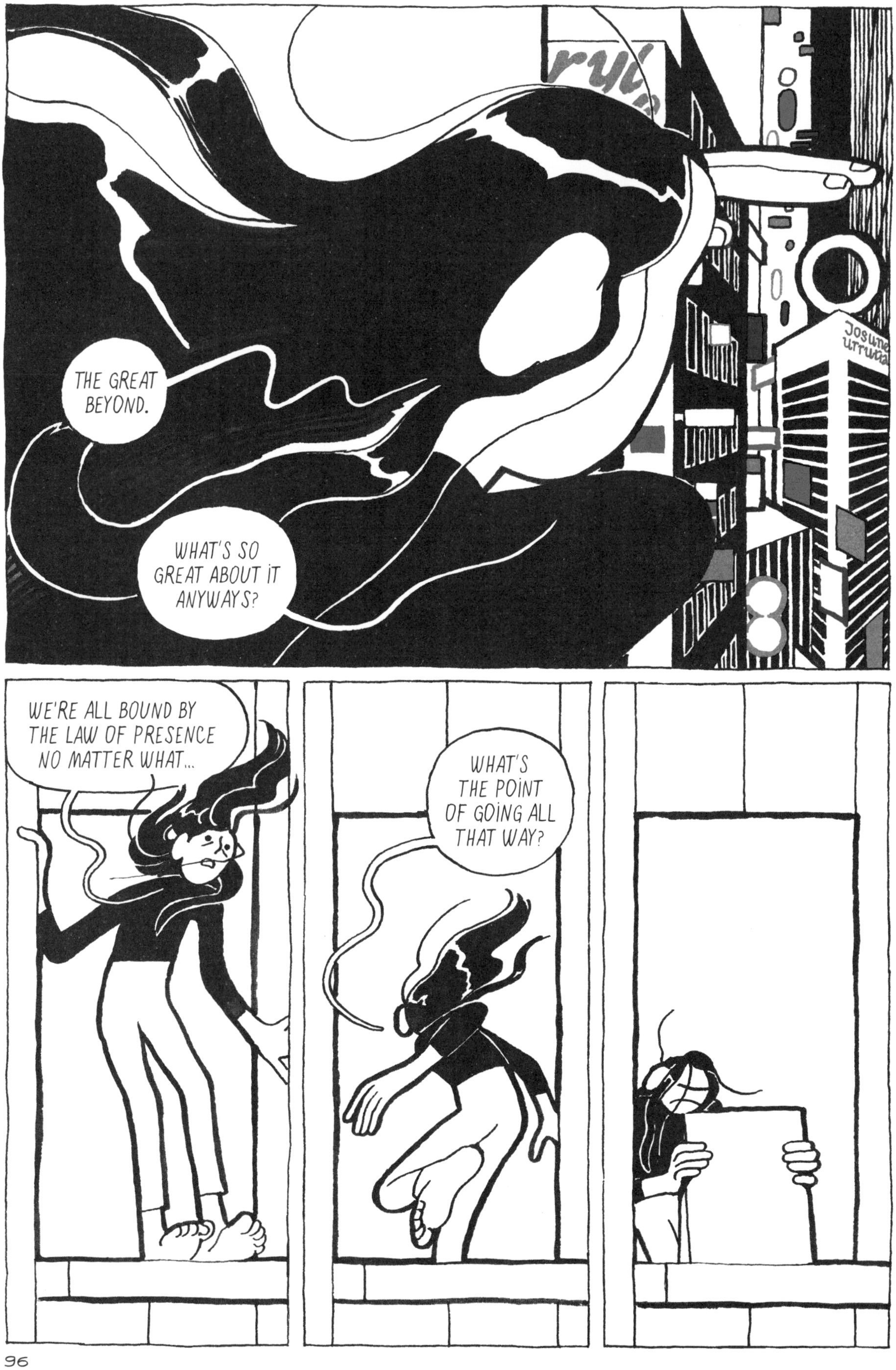
THE GREAT BEYOND.
WHAT'S SO GREAT ABOUT IT ANYWAYS?
Josune Urrutia
WE'RE ALL BOUND BY THE LAW OF PRESENCE NO MATTER WHAT...
WHAT'S THE POINT OF GOING ALL THAT WAY?

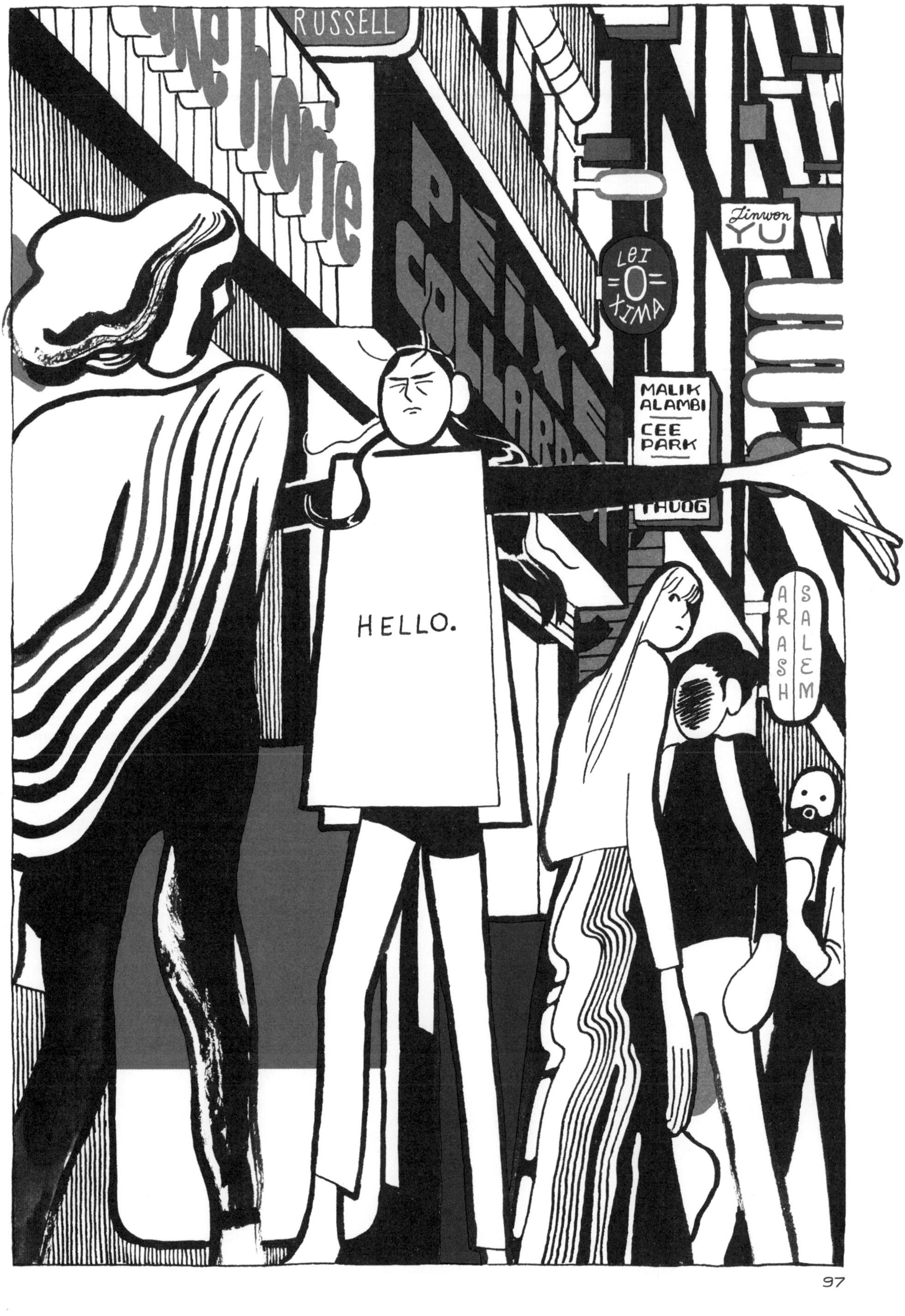
RUSSELL
PETITE
LEI O XIMA
Jinwon YU
MALIK ALAMBI
CEE PARK
HELLO.
ARASH
SALEM

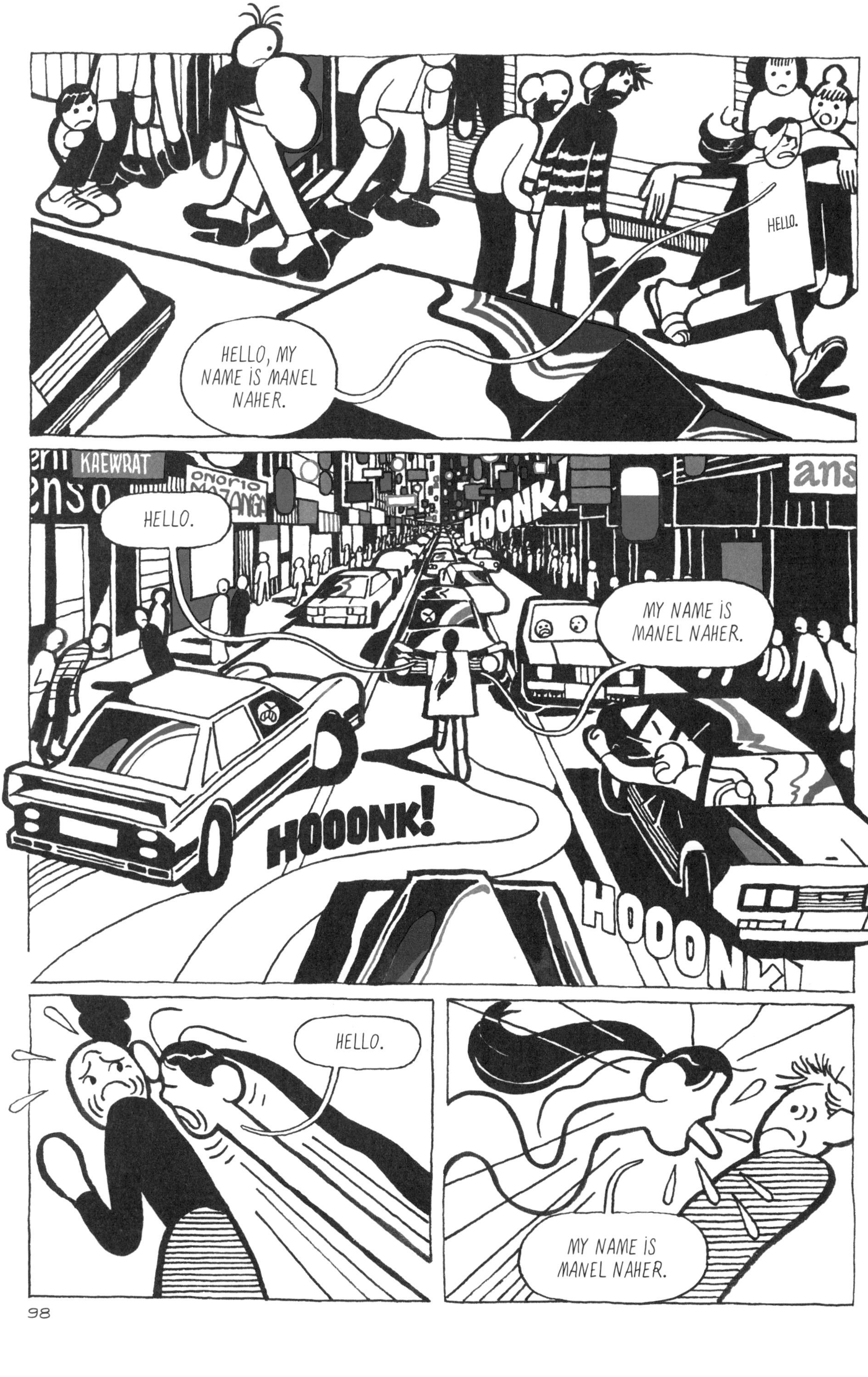
HELLO, MY NAME IS MANEL NAHER.
HELLO.
KAEWRAT
HELLO.
HOONK!
MY NAME IS MANEL NAHER.
HOOONK!
HELLO.
MY NAME IS MANEL NAHER.

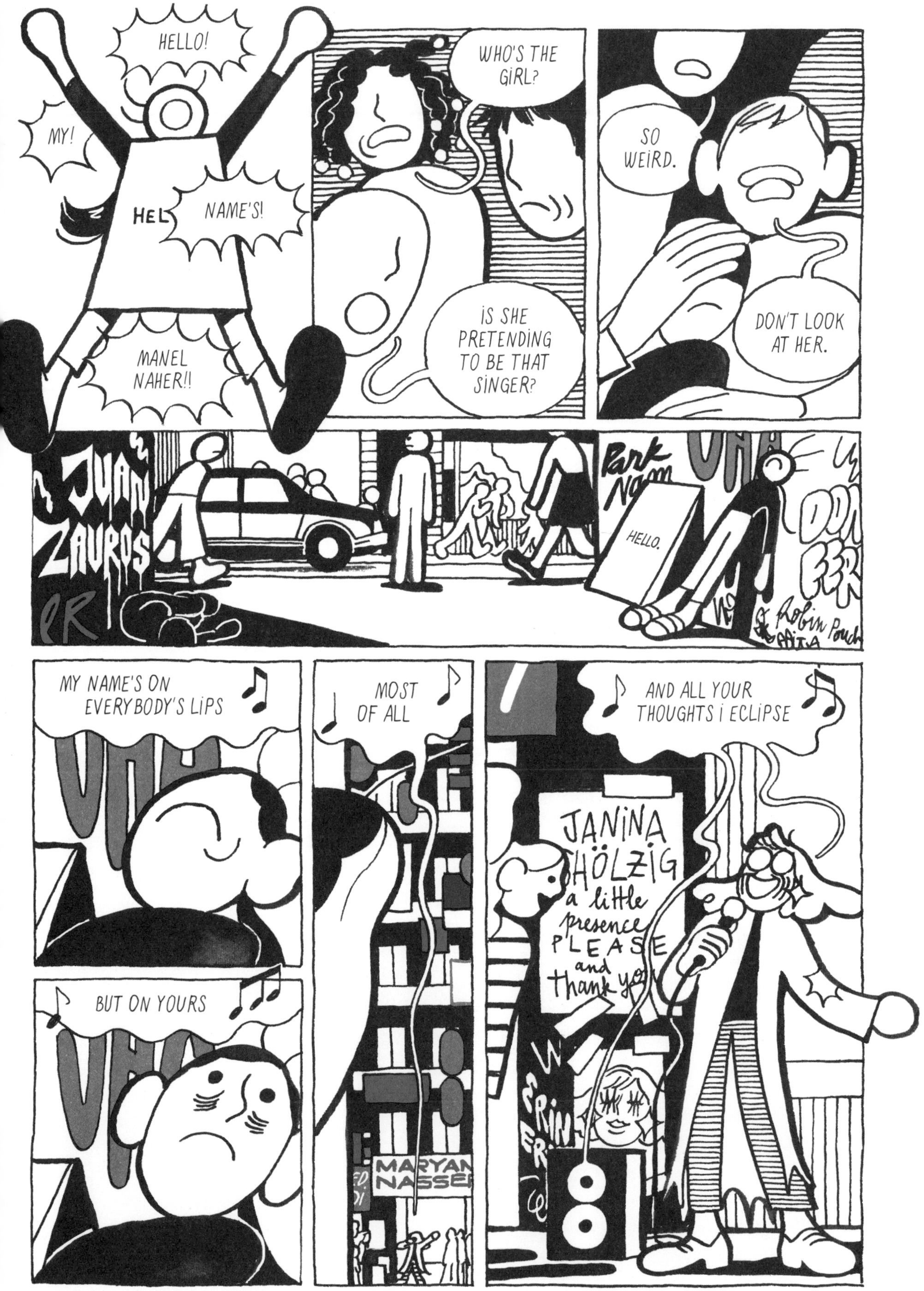

HELLO!
MY!
HEL
NAME'S!
MANEL NAHER!!
WHO'S THE GIRL?
IS SHE PRETENDING TO BE THAT SINGER?
SO WEIRD.
DON'T LOOK AT HER.
JUAN ZAUROS
HELLO.
MY NAME'S ON EVERYBODY'S LIPS
BUT ON YOURS
MOST OF ALL
MARYAM NASSER
AND ALL YOUR THOUGHTS I ECLIPSE
JANINA HÖLZIG a little presence PLEASE and Thank yo

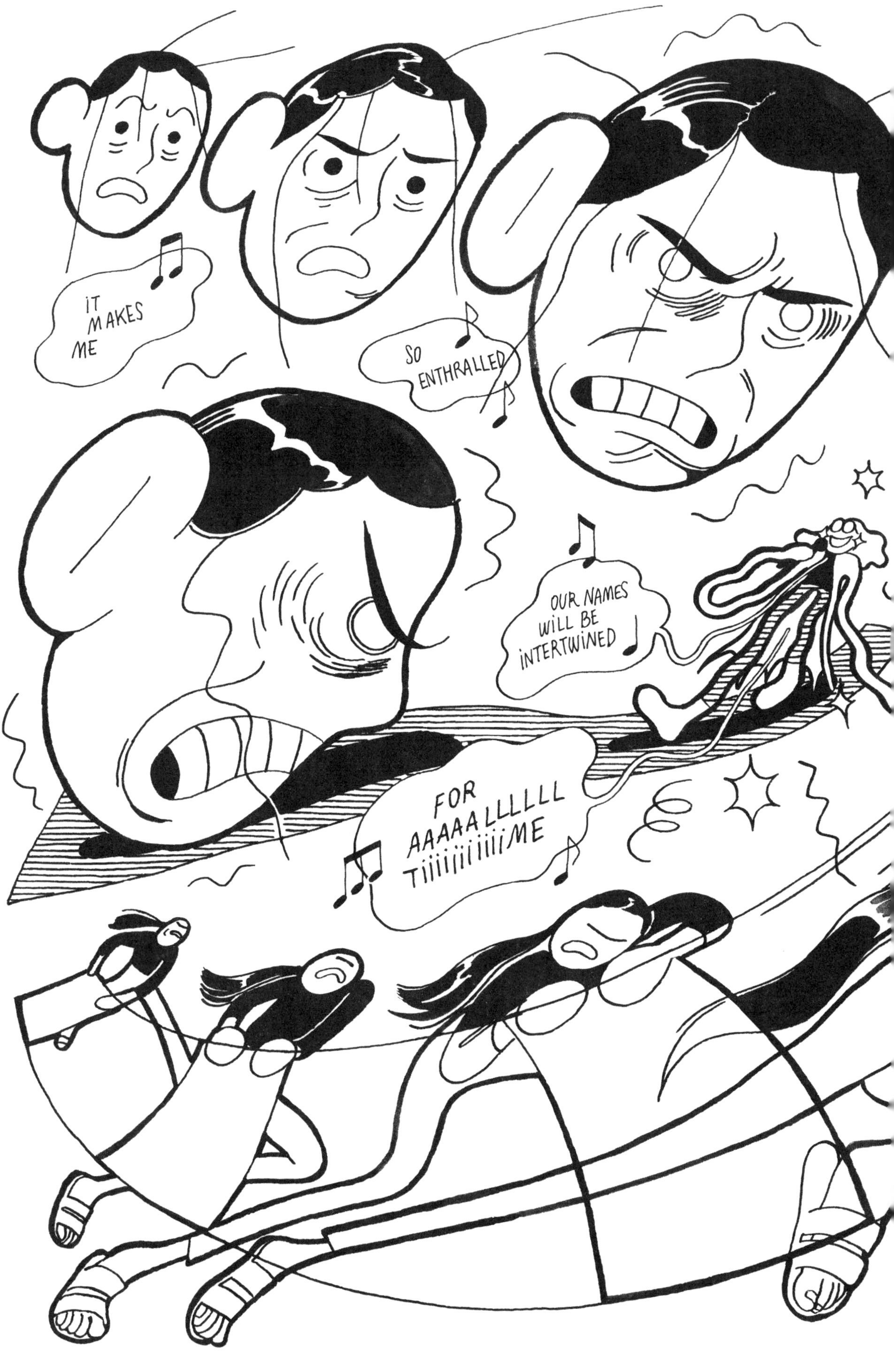
IT MAKES ME
SO ENTHRALLED
OUR NAMES WILL BE INTERTWINED
FOR AAAAALLLLLL TIIIIIIIIIIIME

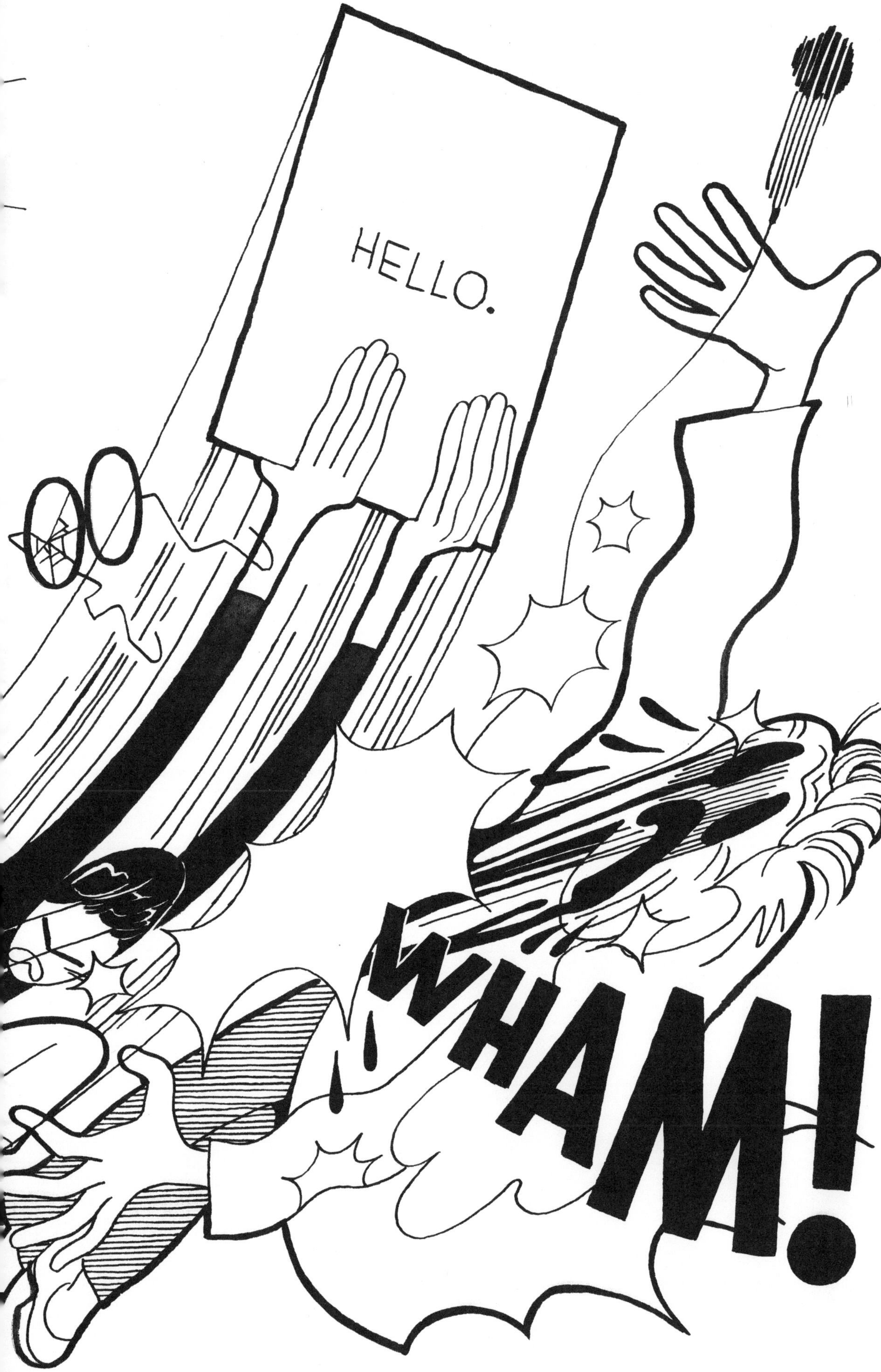
HELLO.
WHAM!

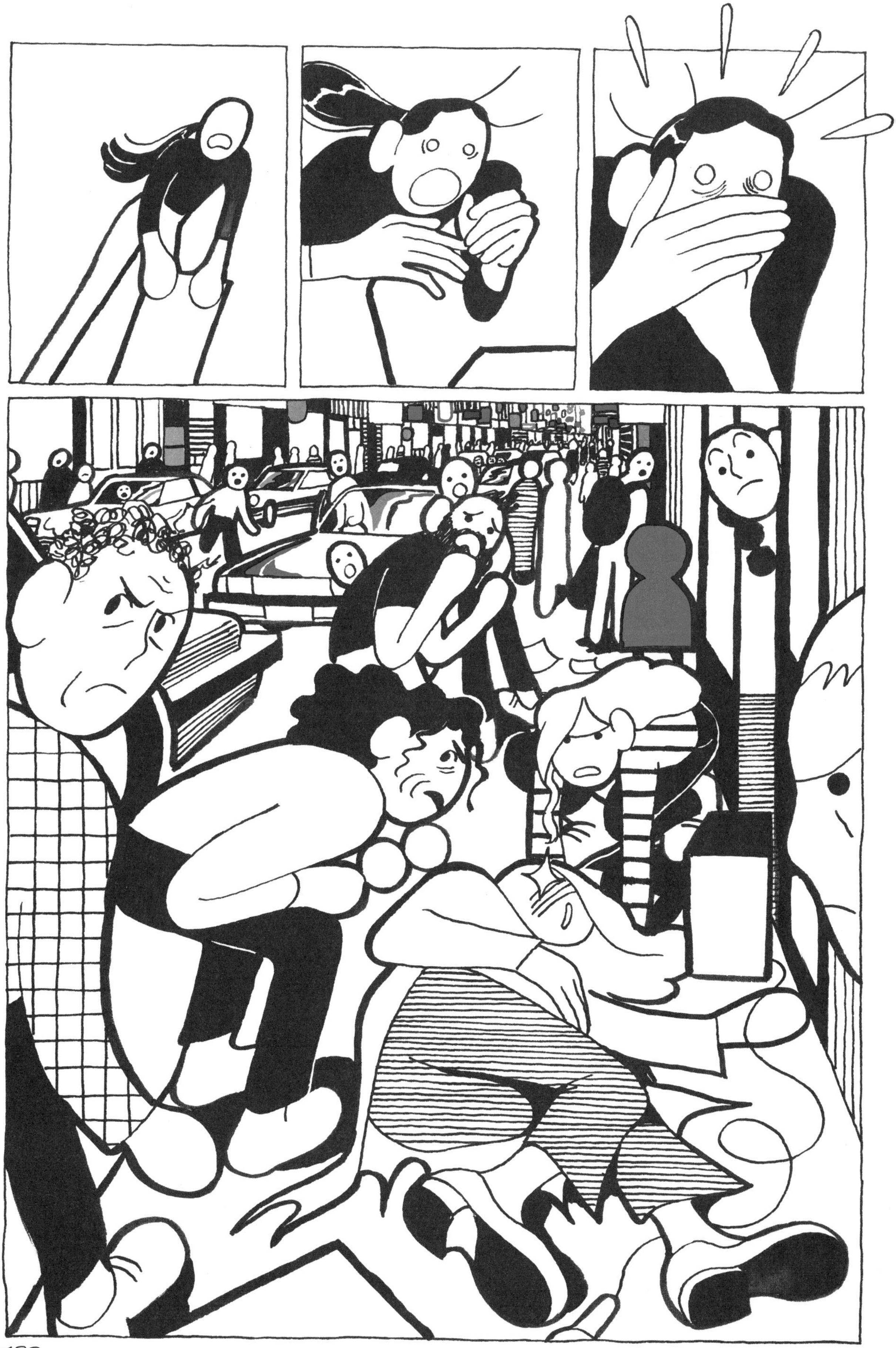

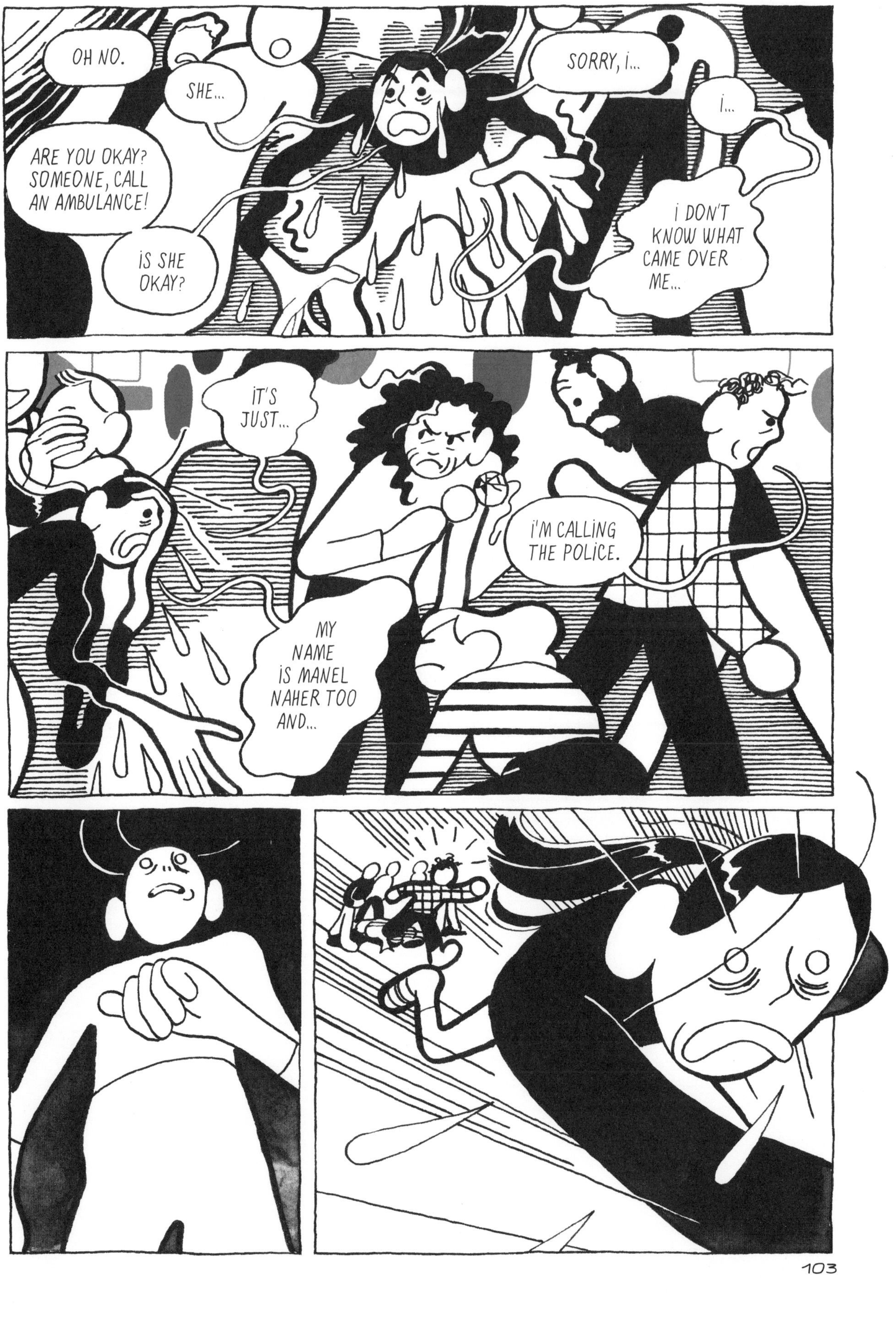
OH NO.
SHE...
ARE YOU OKAY? SOMEONE, CALL AN AMBULANCE!
IS SHE OKAY?
SORRY, I...
I...
I DON'T KNOW WHAT CAME OVER ME...
IT'S JUST...
I'M CALLING THE POLICE.
MY NAME IS MANEL NAHER TOO AND...

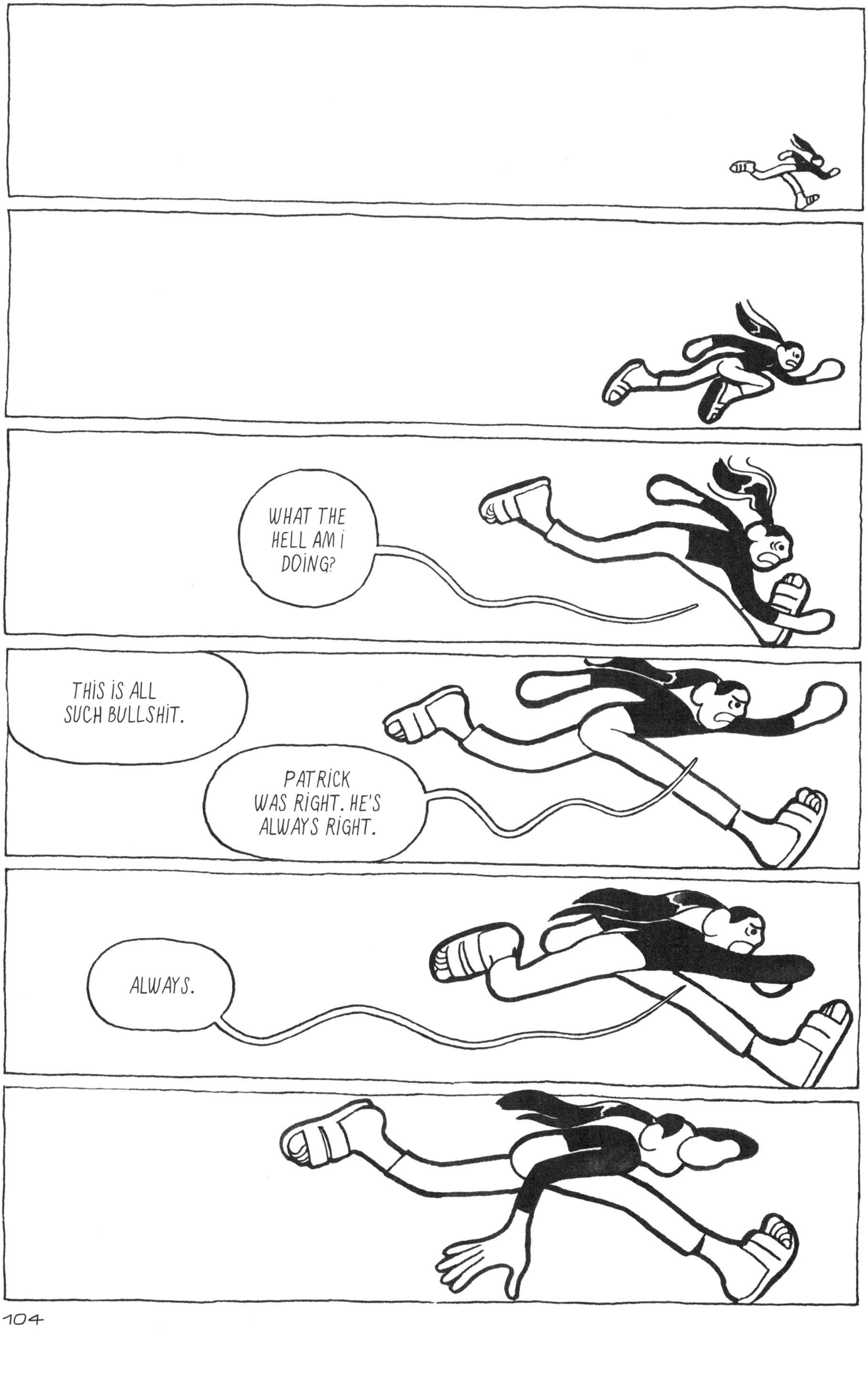
WHAT THE HELL AM I DOING?
THIS IS ALL SUCH BULLSHIT.
PATRICK WAS RIGHT. HE'S ALWAYS RIGHT.
ALWAYS.

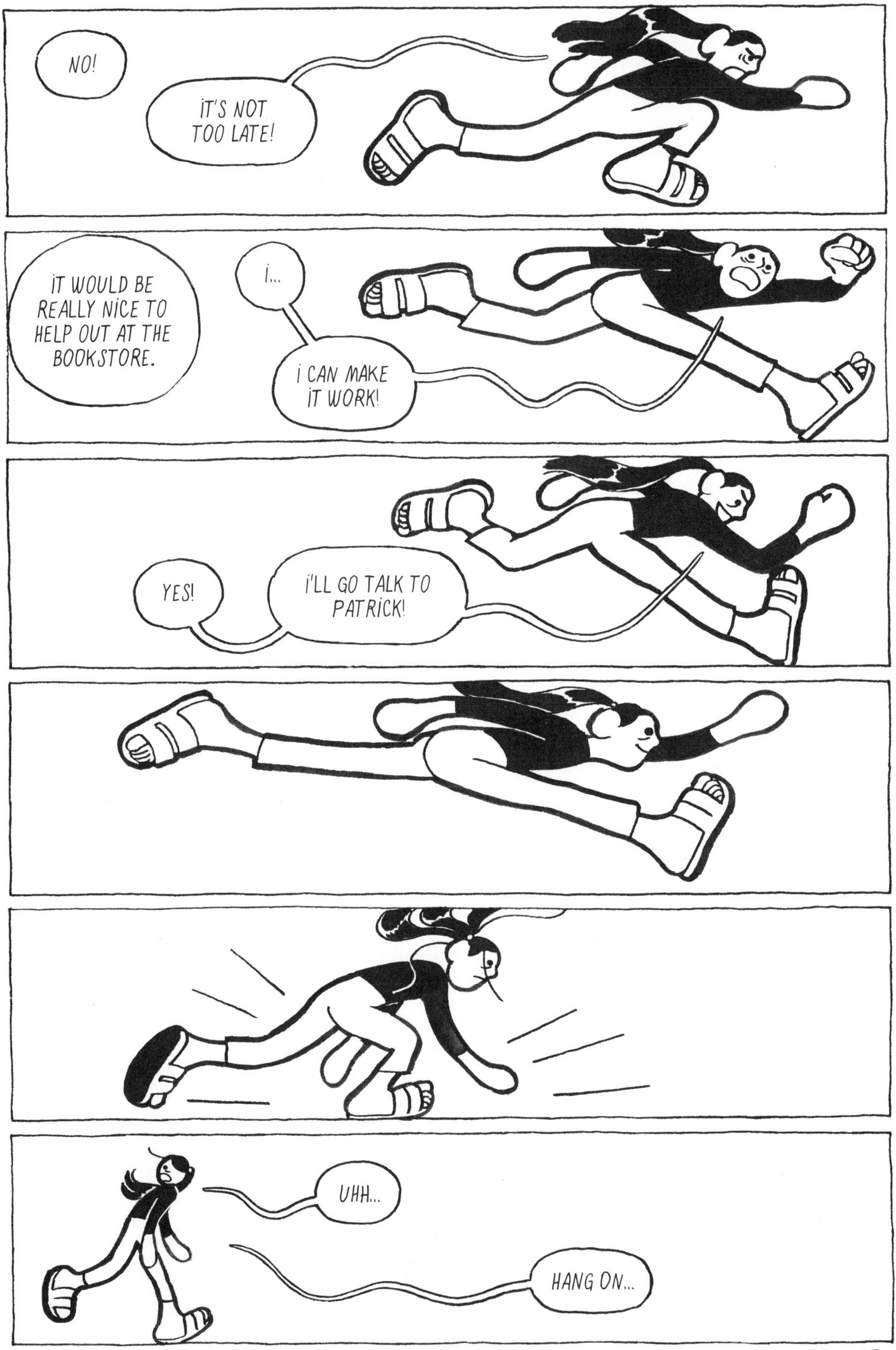
NO!
IT'S NOT TOO LATE!
IT WOULD BE REALLY NICE TO HELP OUT AT THE BOOKSTORE.
I...
I CAN MAKE IT WORK!
YES!
I'LL GO TALK TO PATRICK!
UHH...
HANG ON...

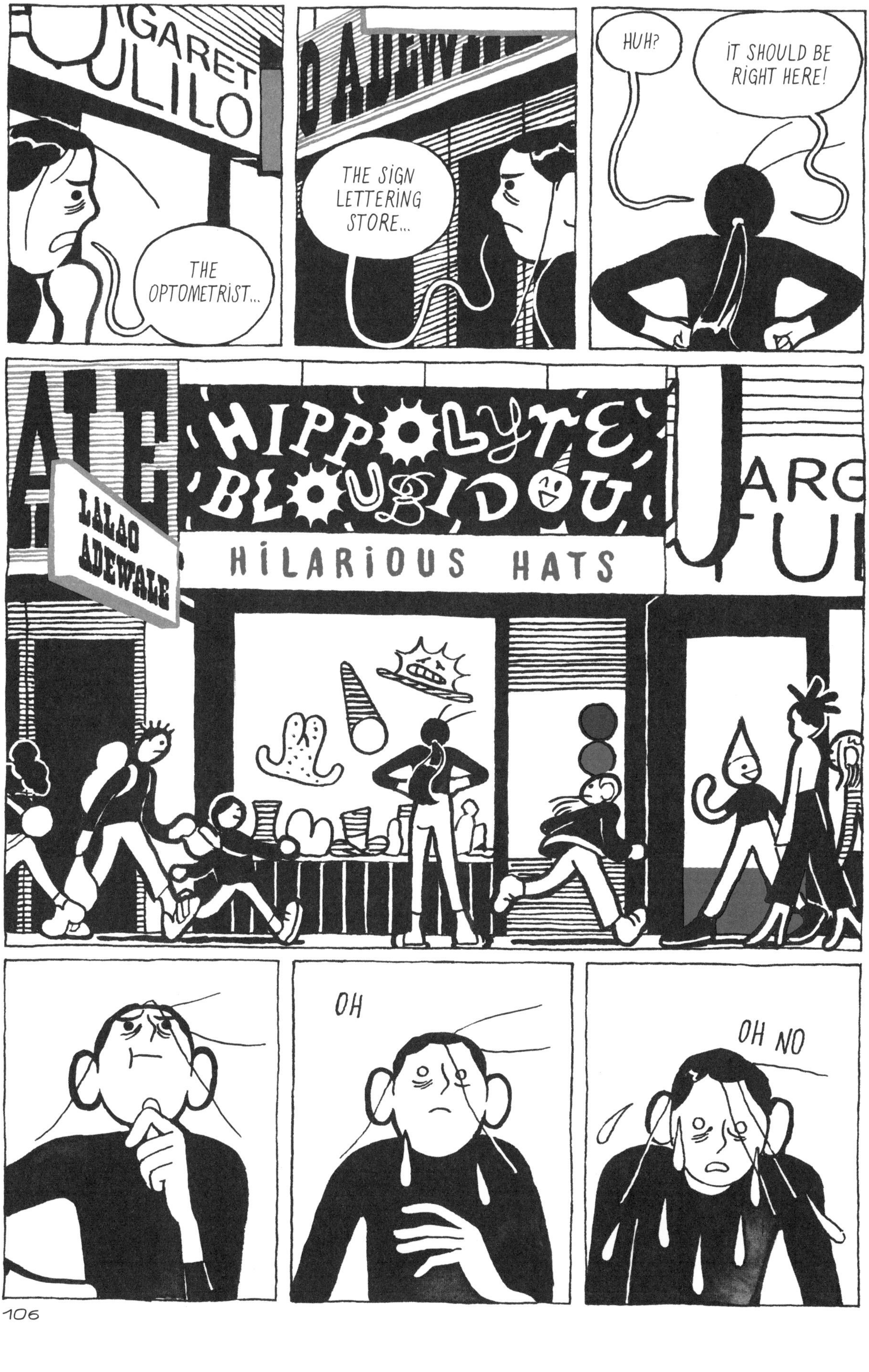
THE OPTOMETRIST...
THE SIGN LETTERING STORE...
HUH?
IT SHOULD BE RIGHT HERE!
LALAO ADEWALE
HIPPOLYTE BLOUBIDOU
HILARIOUS HATS
OH
OH NO

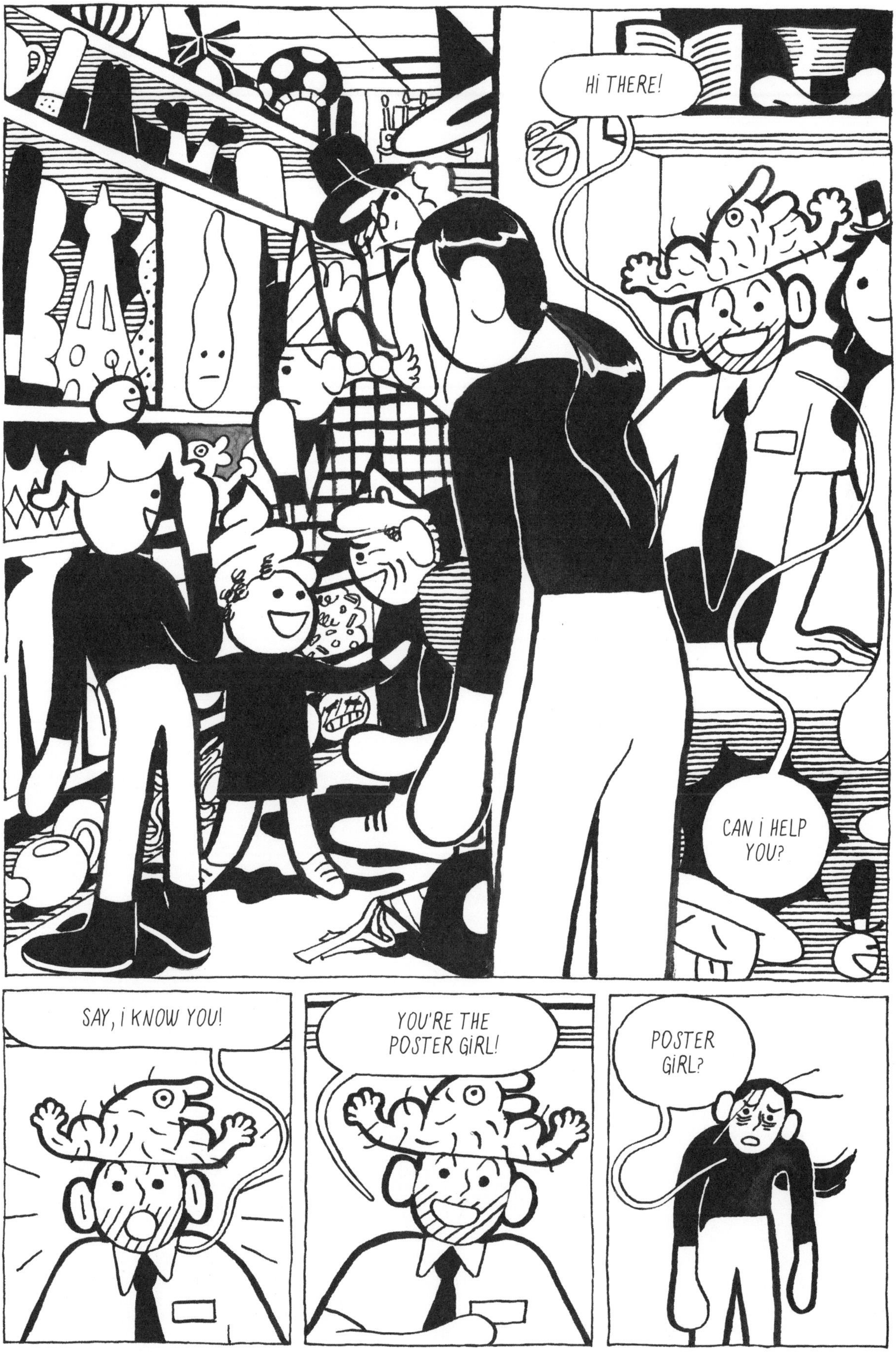
Hi THERE!
CAN i HELP YOU?
SAY, i KNOW YOU!
YOU'RE THE POSTER GiRL!
POSTER GiRL?

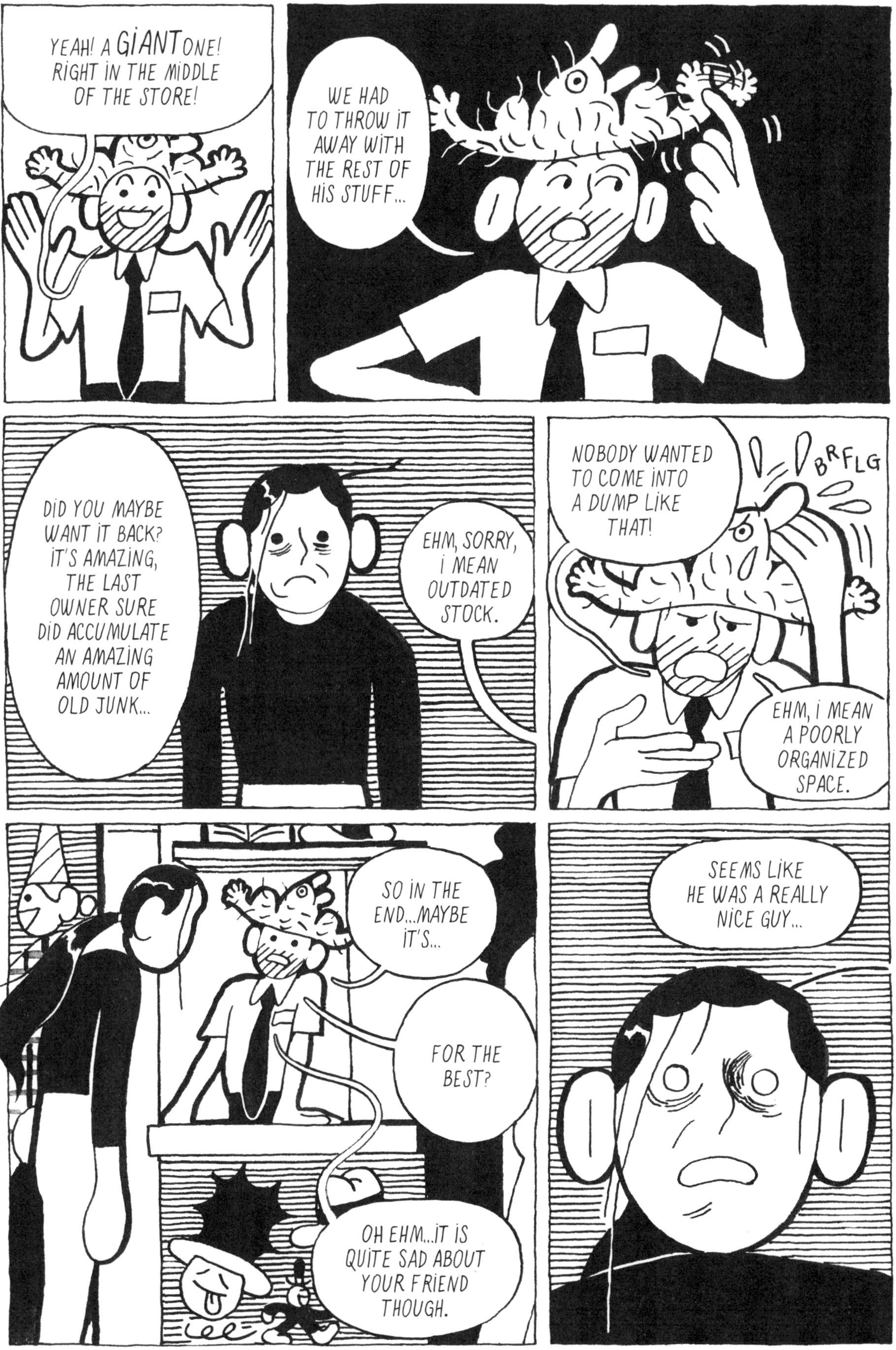
YEAH! A GIANT ONE! RIGHT IN THE MIDDLE OF THE STORE!
WE HAD TO THROW IT AWAY WITH THE REST OF HIS STUFF...
DID YOU MAYBE WANT IT BACK? IT'S AMAZING, THE LAST OWNER SURE DID ACCUMULATE AN AMAZING AMOUNT OF OLD JUNK...
EHM, SORRY, I MEAN OUTDATED STOCK.
NOBODY WANTED TO COME INTO A DUMP LIKE THAT!
BRFLG
EHM, I MEAN A POORLY ORGANIZED SPACE.
SO IN THE END...MAYBE IT'S...
FOR THE BEST?
OH EHM...IT IS QUITE SAD ABOUT YOUR FRIEND THOUGH.
SEEMS LIKE HE WAS A REALLY NICE GUY...

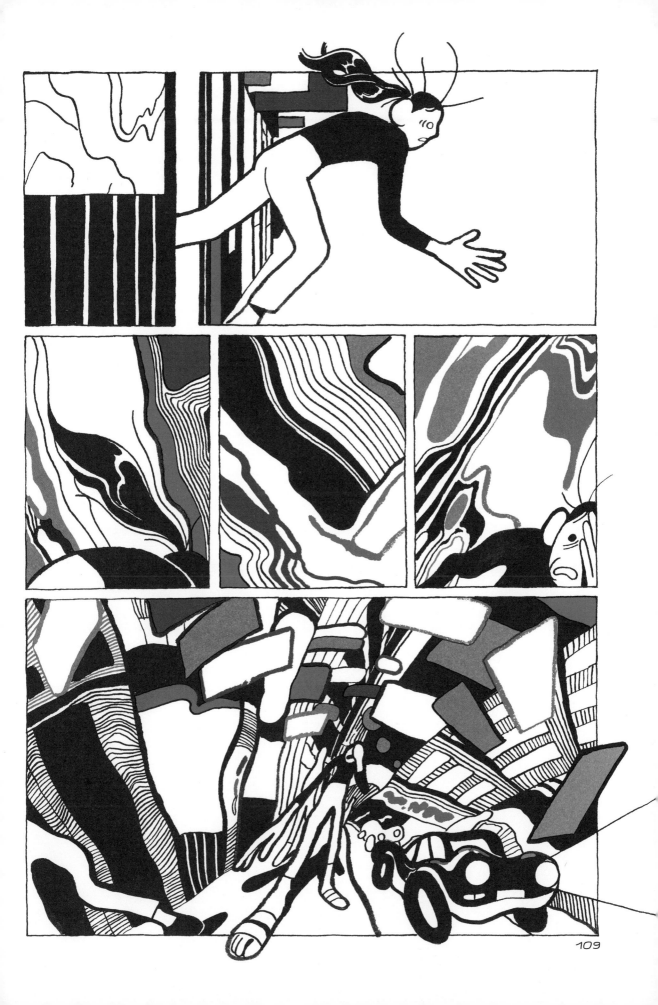

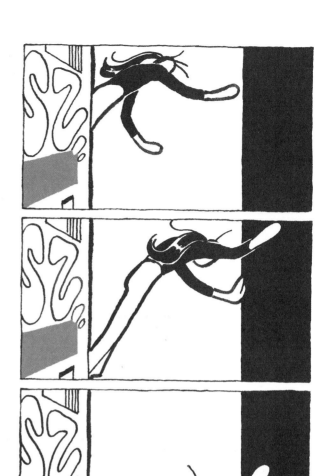

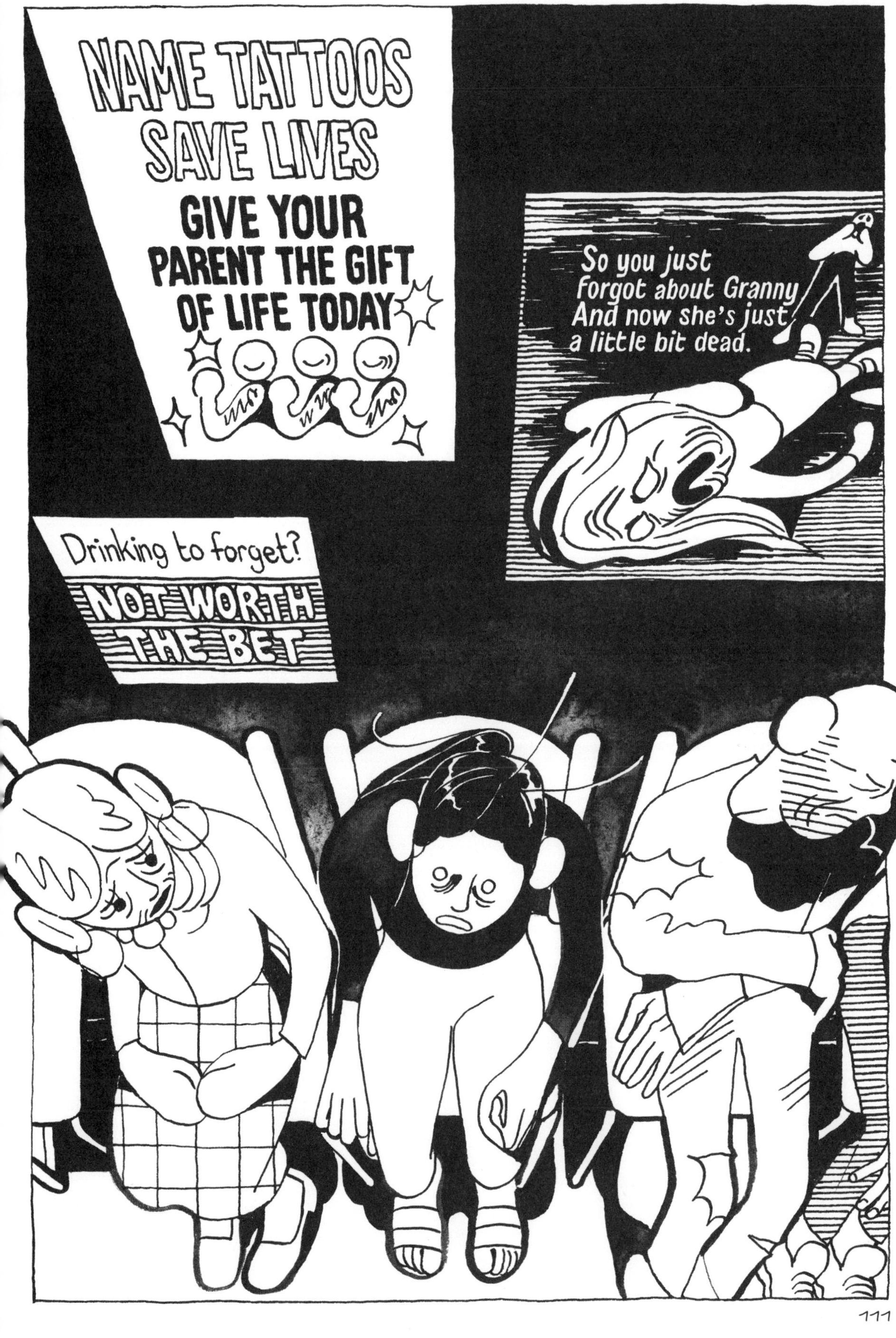
NAME TATTOOS SAVE LIVES
GIVE YOUR PARENT THE GIFT OF LIFE TODAY
So you just forgot about Granny And now she's just a little bit dead.
Drinking to forget?
NOT WORTH THE BET

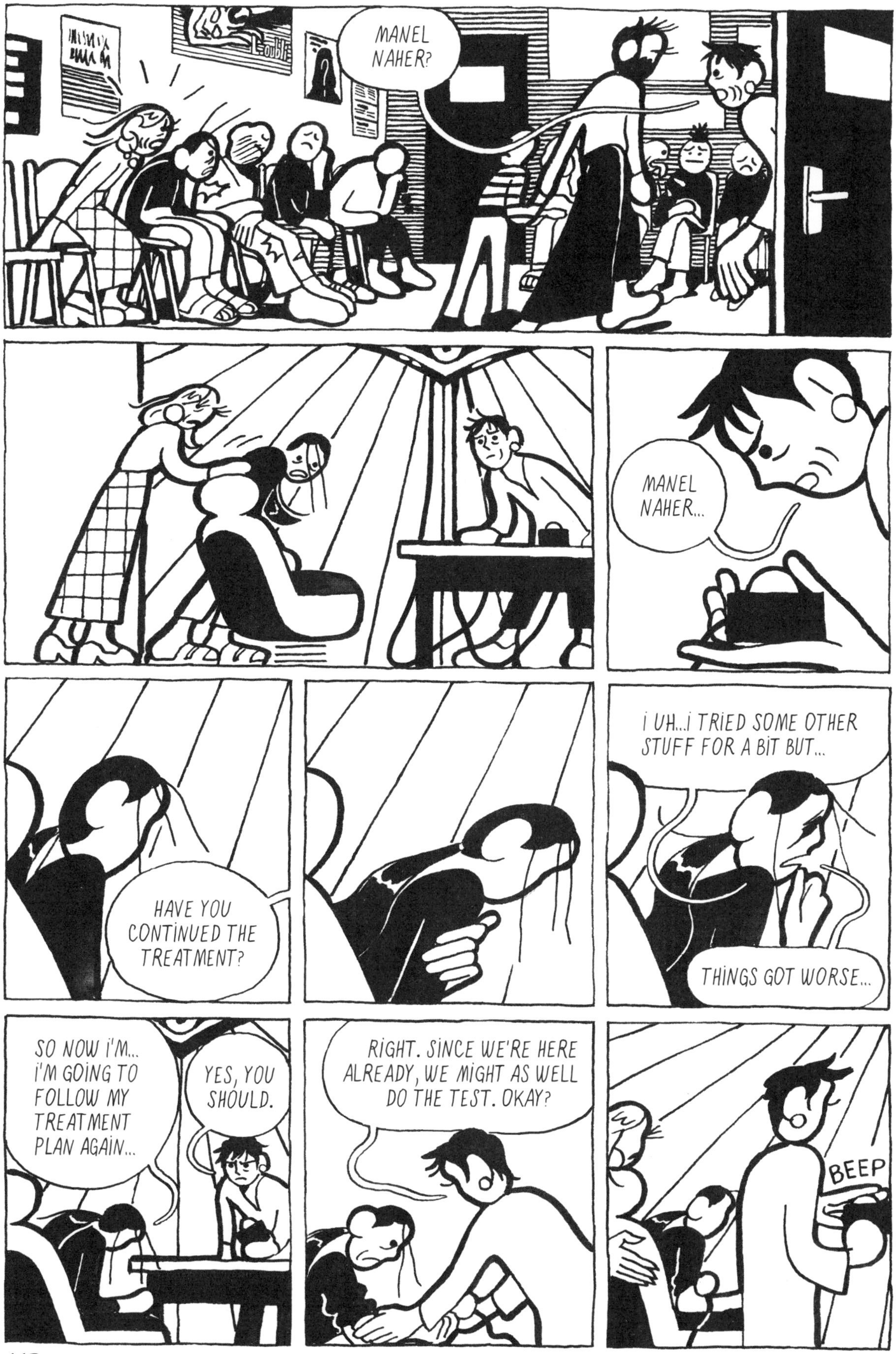
MANEL NAHER?
MANEL NAHER...
HAVE YOU CONTINUED THE TREATMENT?
I UH...I TRIED SOME OTHER STUFF FOR A BIT BUT...
THINGS GOT WORSE...
SO NOW I'M... I'M GOING TO FOLLOW MY TREATMENT PLAN AGAIN...
YES, YOU SHOULD.
RIGHT. SINCE WE'RE HERE ALREADY, WE MIGHT AS WELL DO THE TEST. OKAY?
BEEP

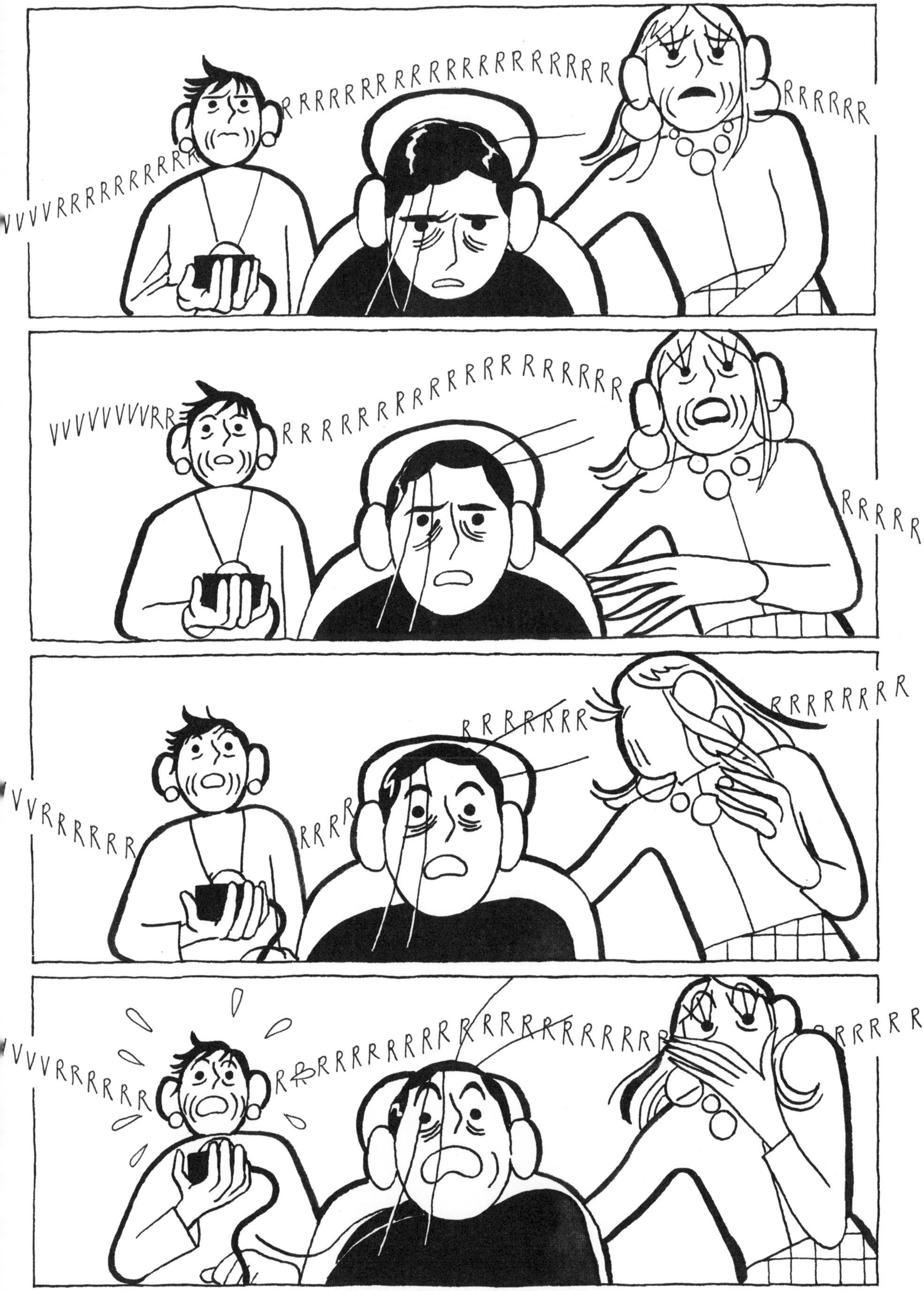
VVVVRRRRRRRRRRRRR
RRRRRRRRRRRRRRRRRR
RRRRRR
VVVVVVVVRR
RRRRRRRRRRRRRRRRRRRR
RRRRR
VVRRRRRRR
RRRR
RRRRRRRR
RRRRRRRR
VVVRRRRRRRR
RRRRRRRRRRRRRRRRRRRR
RRRRRR

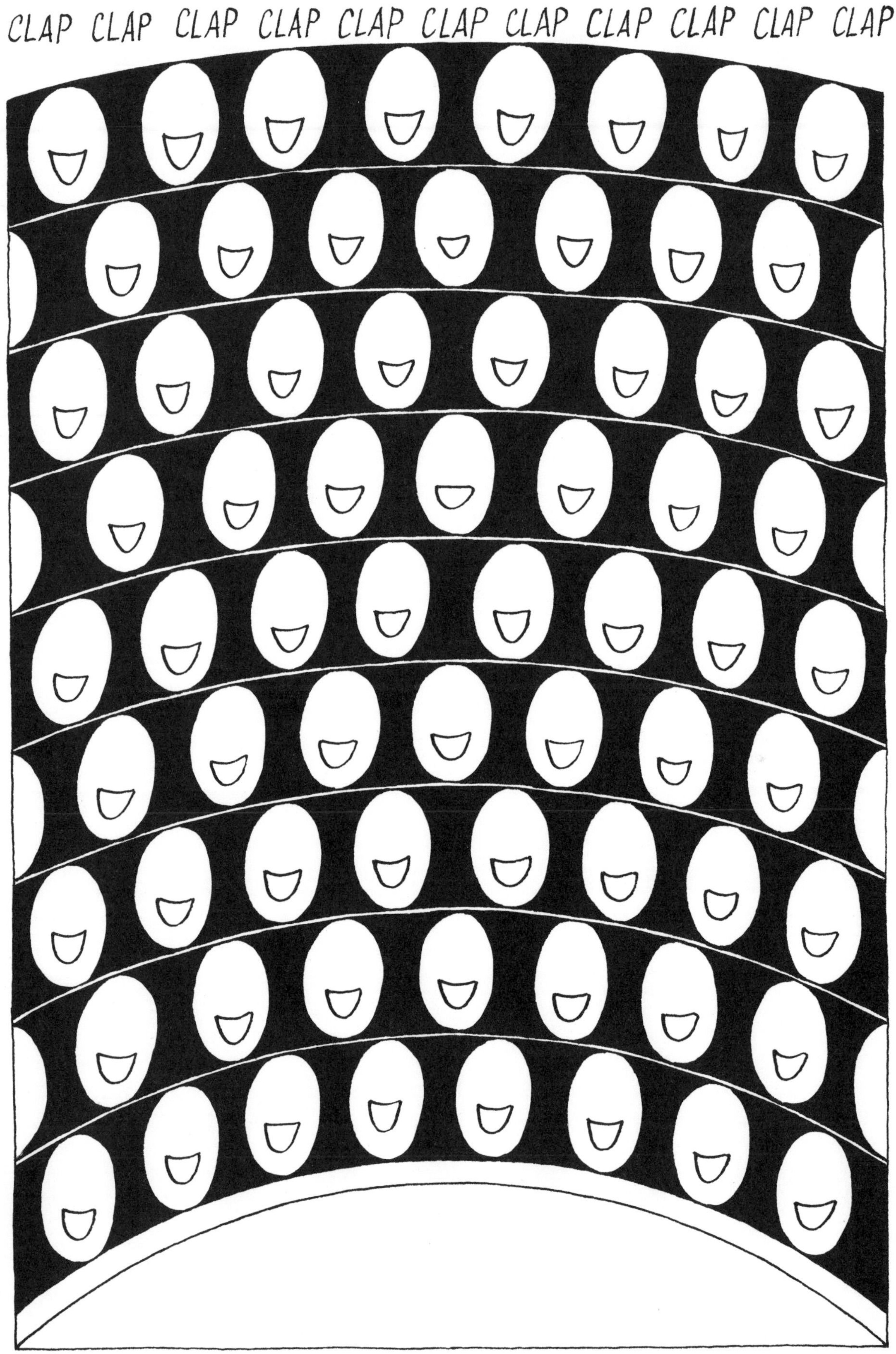
CLAP CLAP CLAP CLAP CLAP CLAP CLAP CLAP CLAP CLAP CLAP

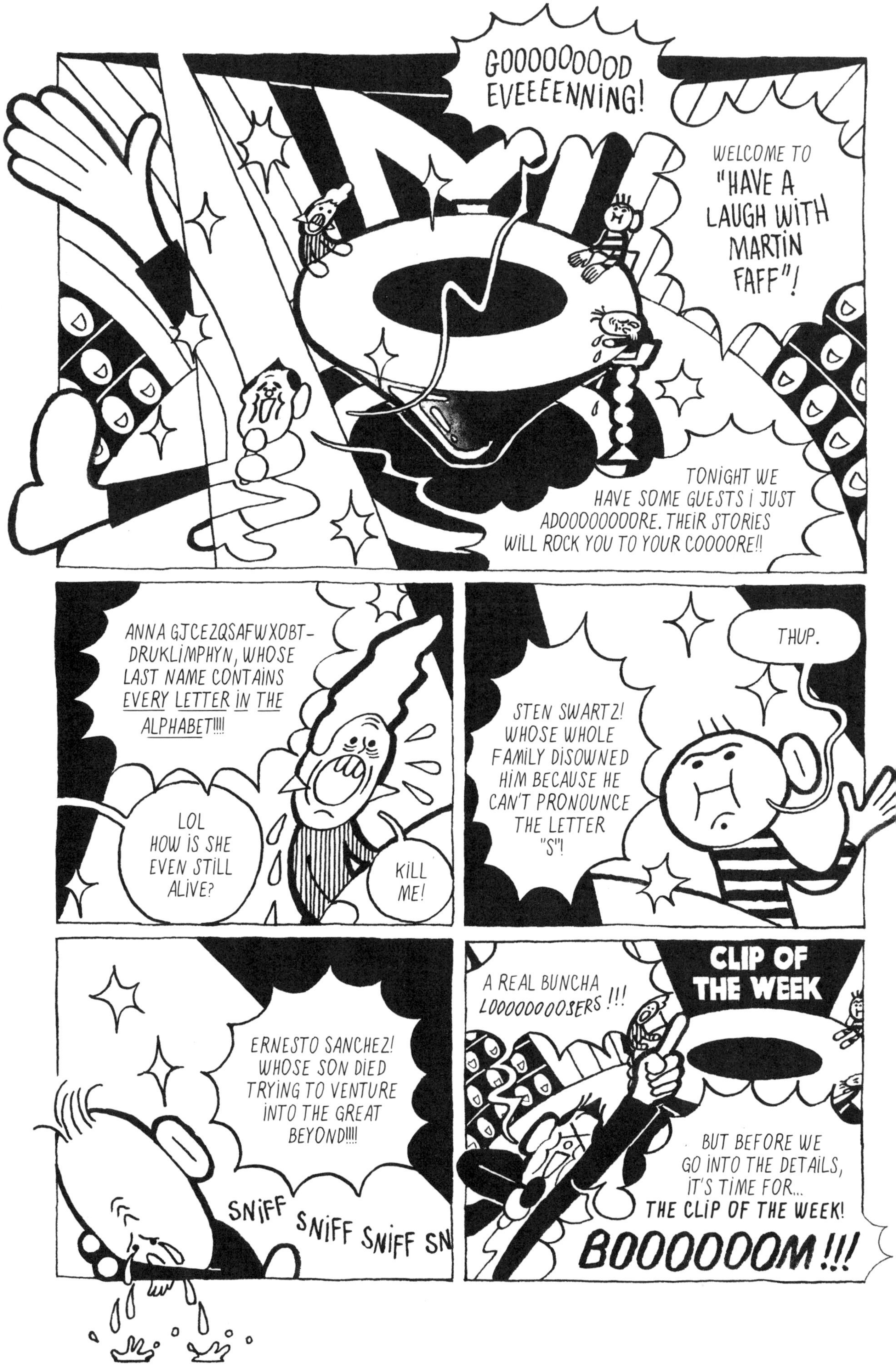
GOOOOOOOOOD EVEEEENNING!
WELCOME TO "HAVE A LAUGH WITH MARTIN FAFF"!
TONIGHT WE HAVE SOME GUESTS I JUST ADOOOOOOOORE. THEIR STORIES WILL ROCK YOU TO YOUR COOOORE!!
ANNA GJCEZQSAFWXOBT-DRUKLIMPHYN, WHOSE LAST NAME CONTAINS EVERY LETTER IN THE ALPHABET!!!!
LOL HOW IS SHE EVEN STILL ALIVE?
KILL ME!
STEN SWARTZ! WHOSE WHOLE FAMILY DISOWNED HIM BECAUSE HE CAN'T PRONOUNCE THE LETTER "S"!
THUP.
ERNESTO SANCHEZ! WHOSE SON DIED TRYING TO VENTURE INTO THE GREAT BEYOND!!!!
SNIFF SNIFF SNIFF SN
A REAL BUNCHA LOOOOOOOOSERS!!!
CLIP OF THE WEEK
BUT BEFORE WE GO INTO THE DETAILS, IT'S TIME FOR... THE CLIP OF THE WEEK!
BOOOOOOM!!!

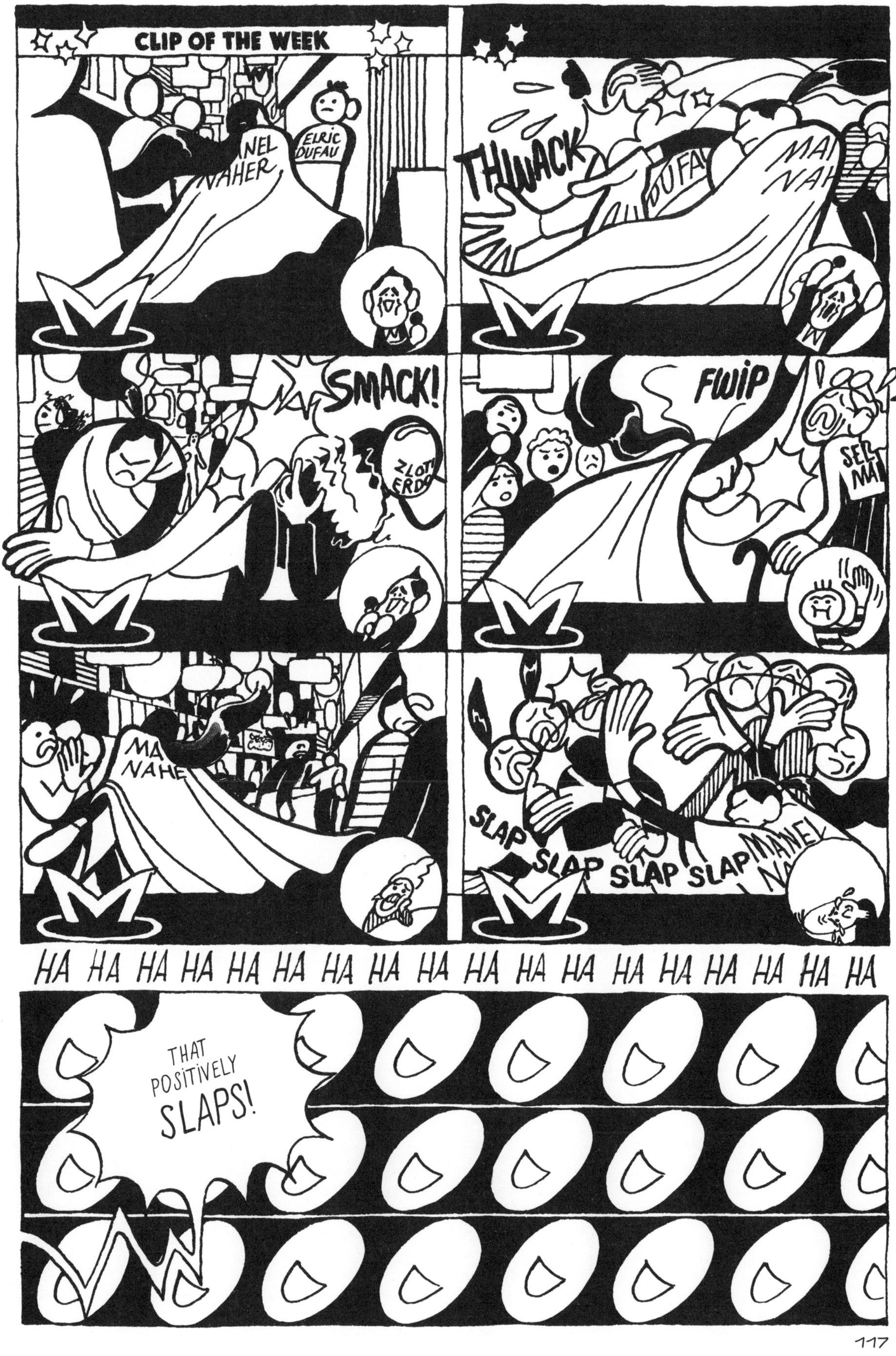
CLIP OF THE WEEK
NEL NAHER
ELRIC DUFAU
THWACK
DUFAU
MA NAH
SMACK!
ZLOT ERDO
FWIP
SEL MA
MA NAHE
SLAP SLAP SLAP SLAP
MANEL NA
HA HA HA HA HA HA HA HA HA HA HA HA HA HA HA HA HA HA
THAT POSITIVELY SLAPS!

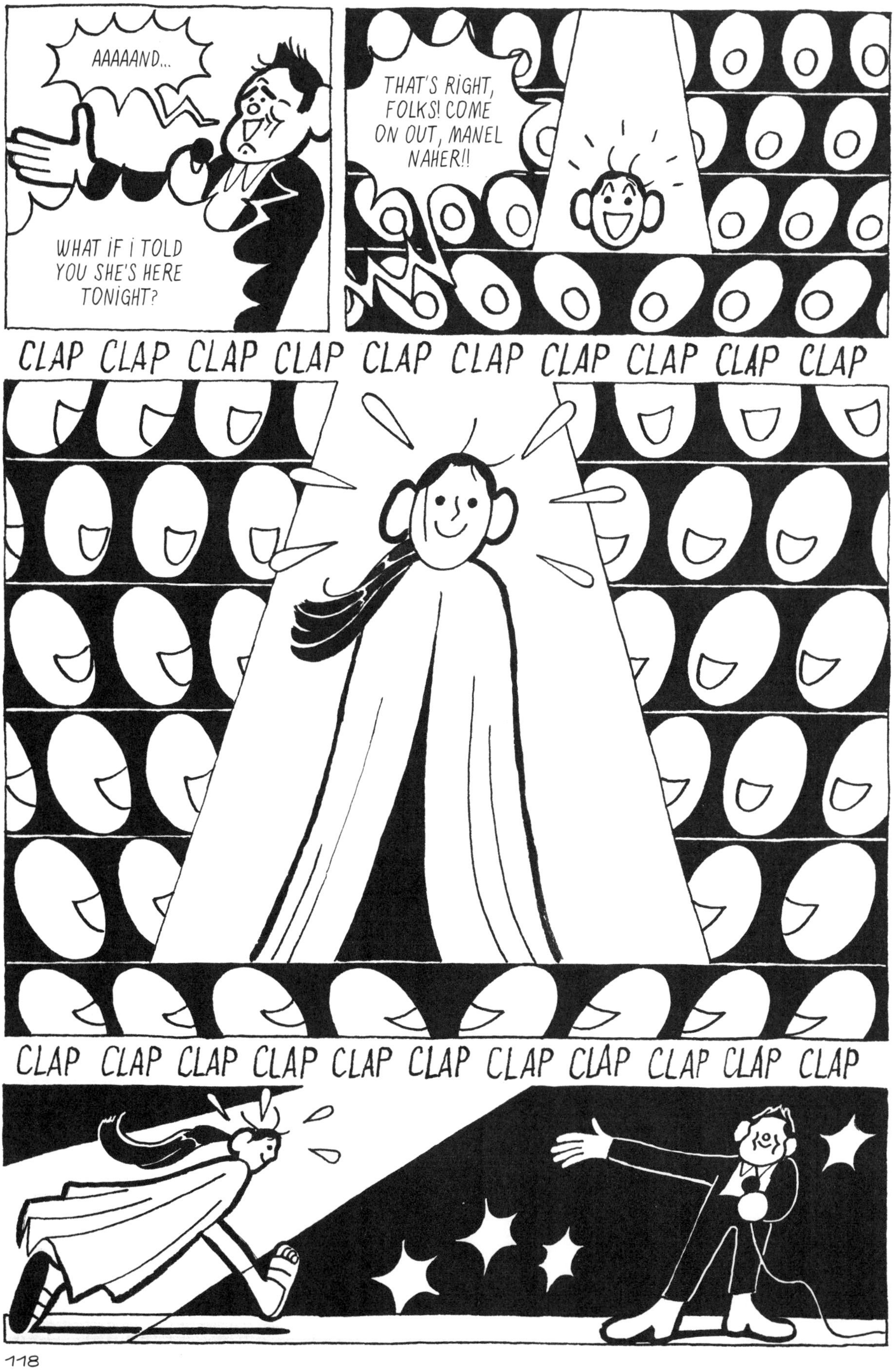
AAAAAND...
WHAT IF I TOLD YOU SHE'S HERE TONIGHT?
THAT'S RIGHT, FOLKS! COME ON OUT, MANEL NAHER!!
CLAP CLAP CLAP CLAP CLAP CLAP CLAP CLAP CLAP CLAP
CLAP CLAP CLAP CLAP CLAP CLAP CLAP CLAP CLAP CLAP CLAP

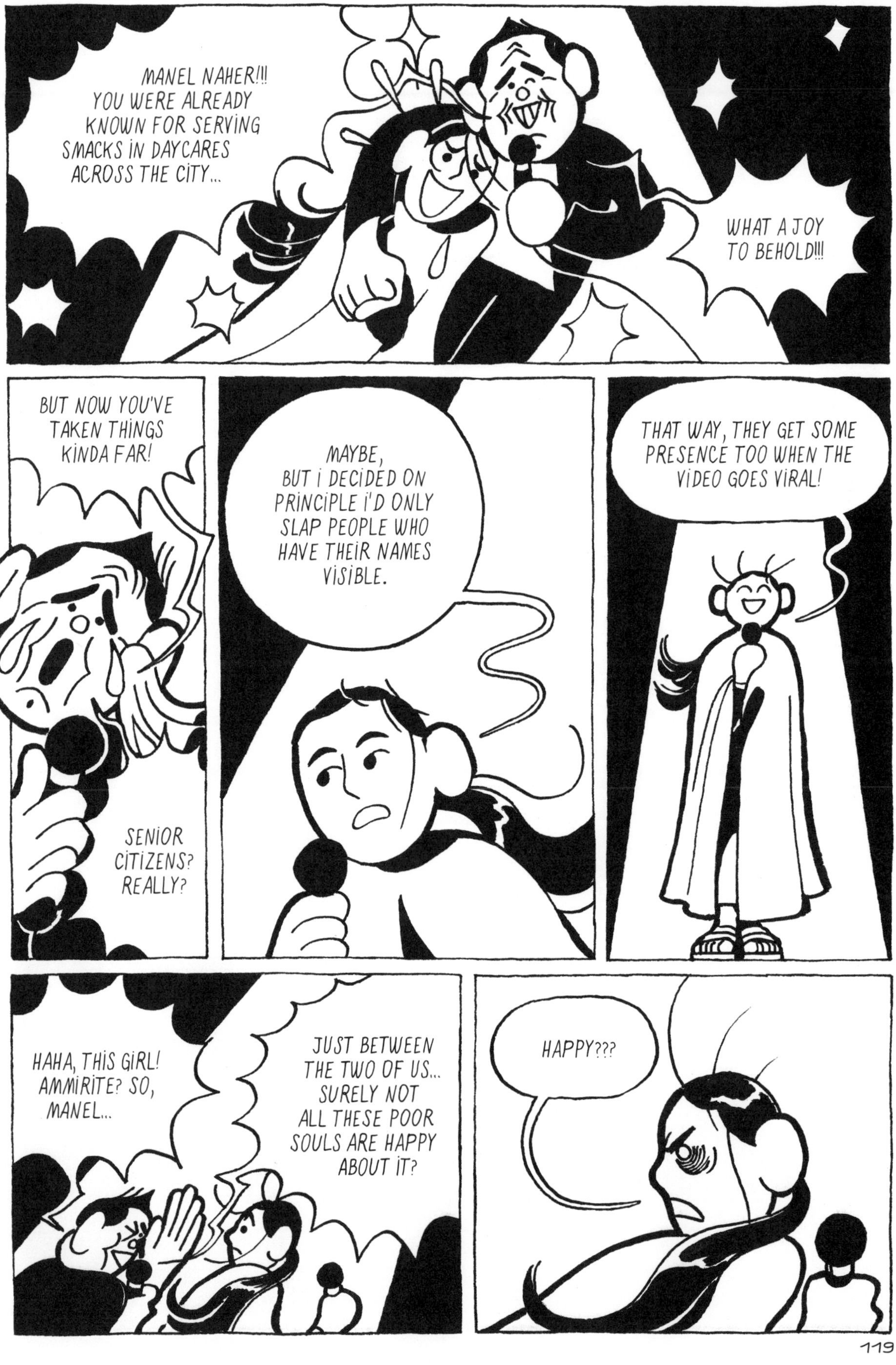
MANEL NAHER!!! YOU WERE ALREADY KNOWN FOR SERVING SMACKS IN DAYCARES ACROSS THE CITY...
WHAT A JOY TO BEHOLD!!!
BUT NOW YOU'VE TAKEN THINGS KINDA FAR!
SENIOR CITIZENS? REALLY?
MAYBE, BUT I DECIDED ON PRINCIPLE I'D ONLY SLAP PEOPLE WHO HAVE THEIR NAMES VISIBLE.
THAT WAY, THEY GET SOME PRESENCE TOO WHEN THE VIDEO GOES VIRAL!
HAHA, THIS GIRL! AMMIRITE? SO, MANEL...
JUST BETWEEN THE TWO OF US... SURELY NOT ALL THESE POOR SOULS ARE HAPPY ABOUT IT?
HAPPY???

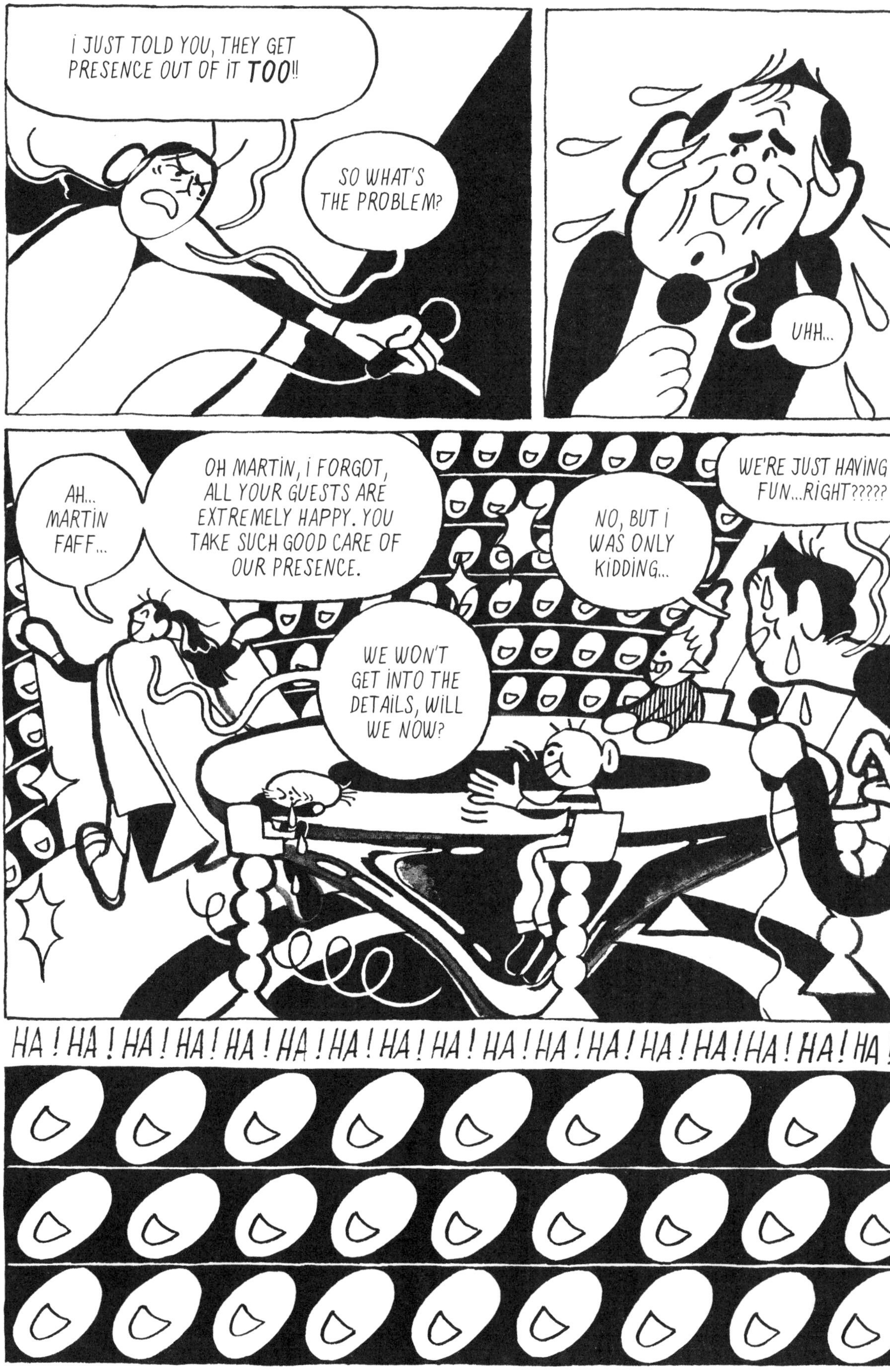
I JUST TOLD YOU, THEY GET PRESENCE OUT OF IT TOO!!
SO WHAT'S THE PROBLEM?
UHH...
AH... MARTIN FAFF...
OH MARTIN, I FORGOT, ALL YOUR GUESTS ARE EXTREMELY HAPPY. YOU TAKE SUCH GOOD CARE OF OUR PRESENCE.
NO, BUT I WAS ONLY KIDDING...
WE'RE JUST HAVING FUN...RIGHT?????
WE WON'T GET INTO THE DETAILS, WILL WE NOW?
HA! HA! HA! HA! HA! HA! HA! HA! HA! HA! HA! HA! HA! HA! HA! HA! HA!

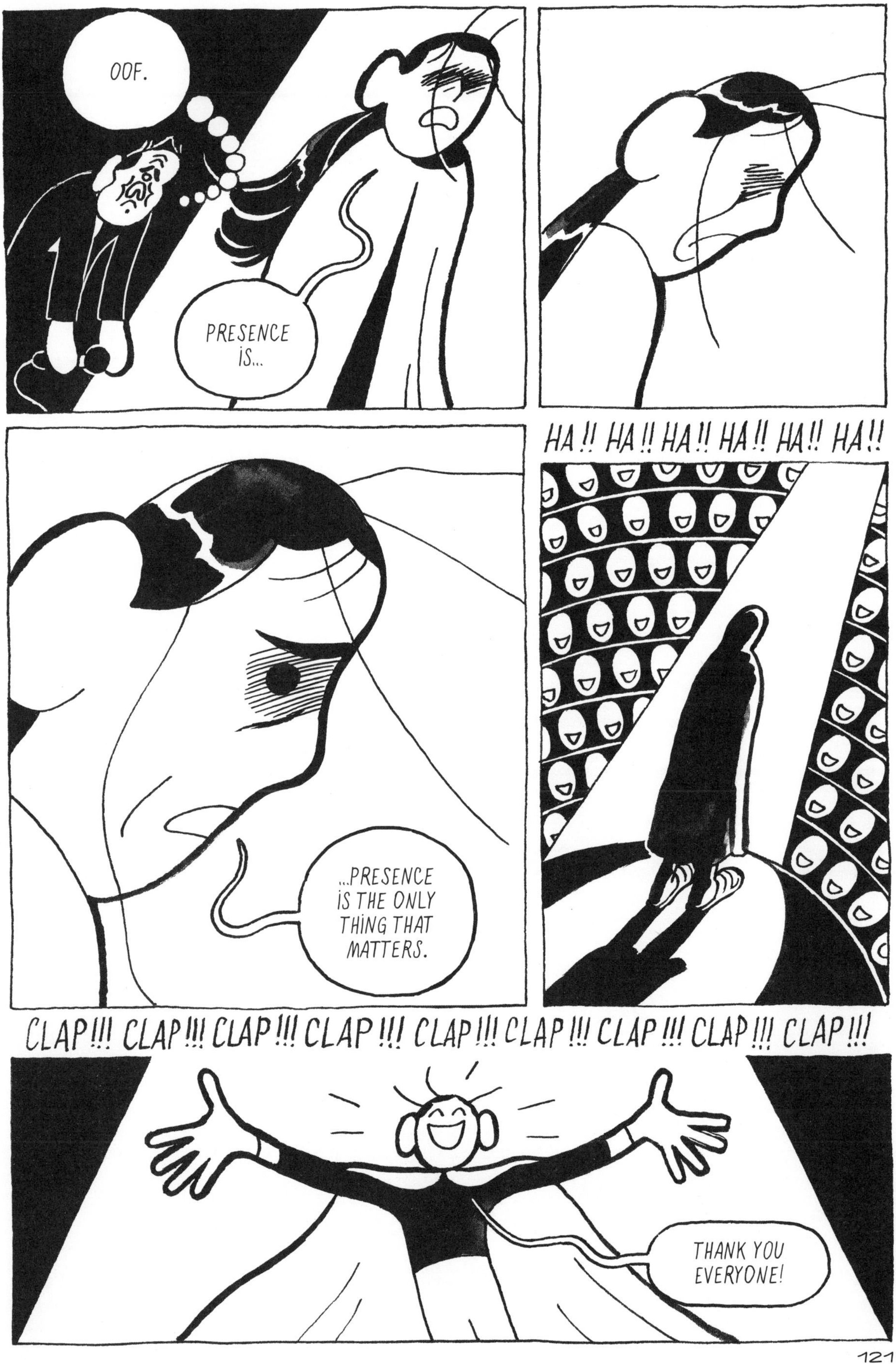
OOF.
PRESENCE IS...
HA!! HA!! HA!! HA!! HA!! HA!!
...PRESENCE IS THE ONLY THING THAT MATTERS.
CLAP!!! CLAP!!! CLAP!!! CLAP!!! CLAP!!! CLAP!!! CLAP!!! CLAP!!! CLAP!!!
THANK YOU EVERYONE!

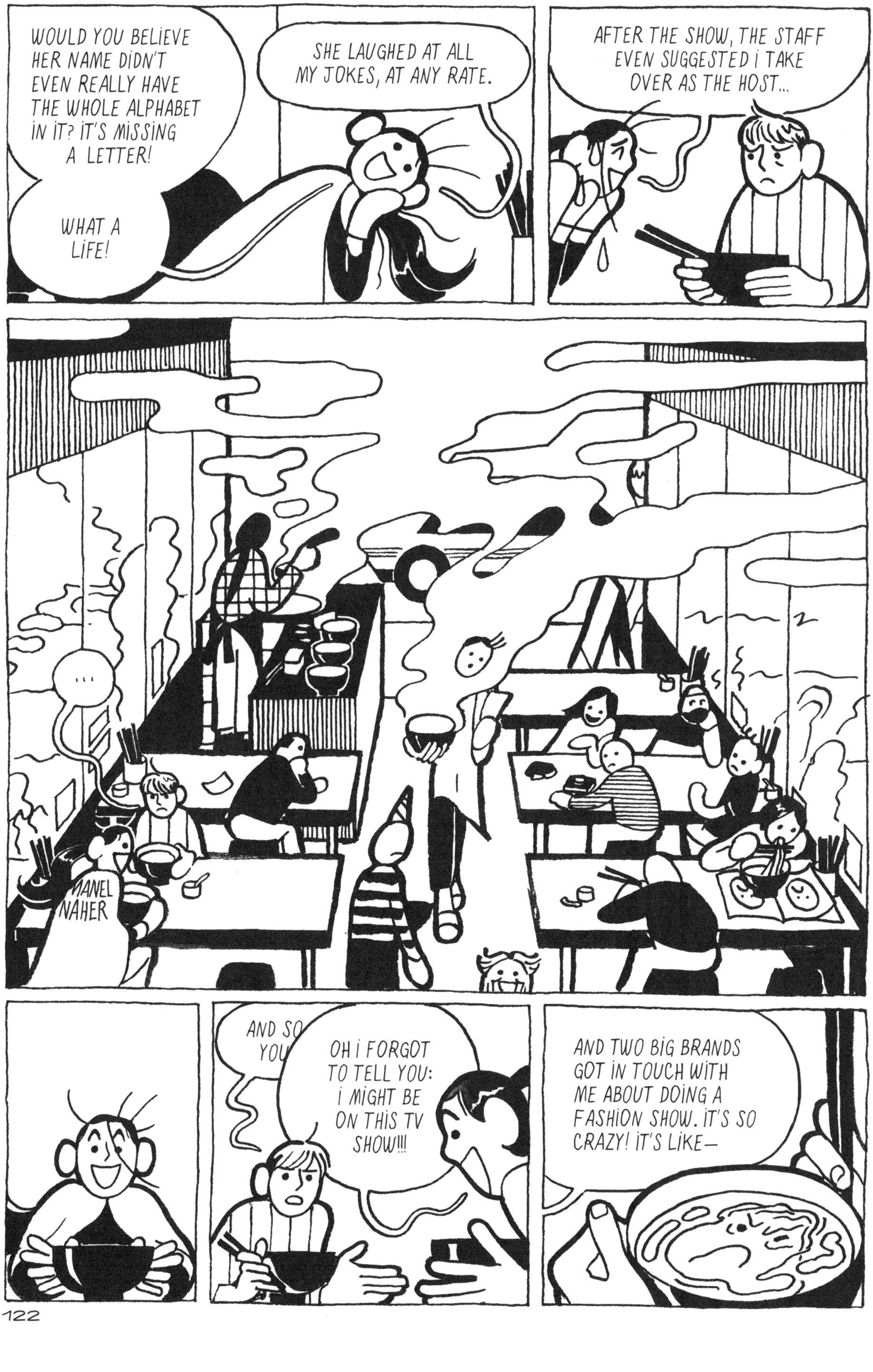
WOULD YOU BELIEVE HER NAME DIDN'T EVEN REALLY HAVE THE WHOLE ALPHABET IN IT? IT'S MISSING A LETTER!
WHAT A LIFE!
SHE LAUGHED AT ALL MY JOKES, AT ANY RATE.
AFTER THE SHOW, THE STAFF EVEN SUGGESTED I TAKE OVER AS THE HOST...
...
MANEL NAHER
OH I FORGOT TO TELL YOU: I MIGHT BE ON THIS TV SHOW!!!
AND TWO BIG BRANDS GOT IN TOUCH WITH ME ABOUT DOING A FASHION SHOW. IT'S SO CRAZY! IT'S LIKE—

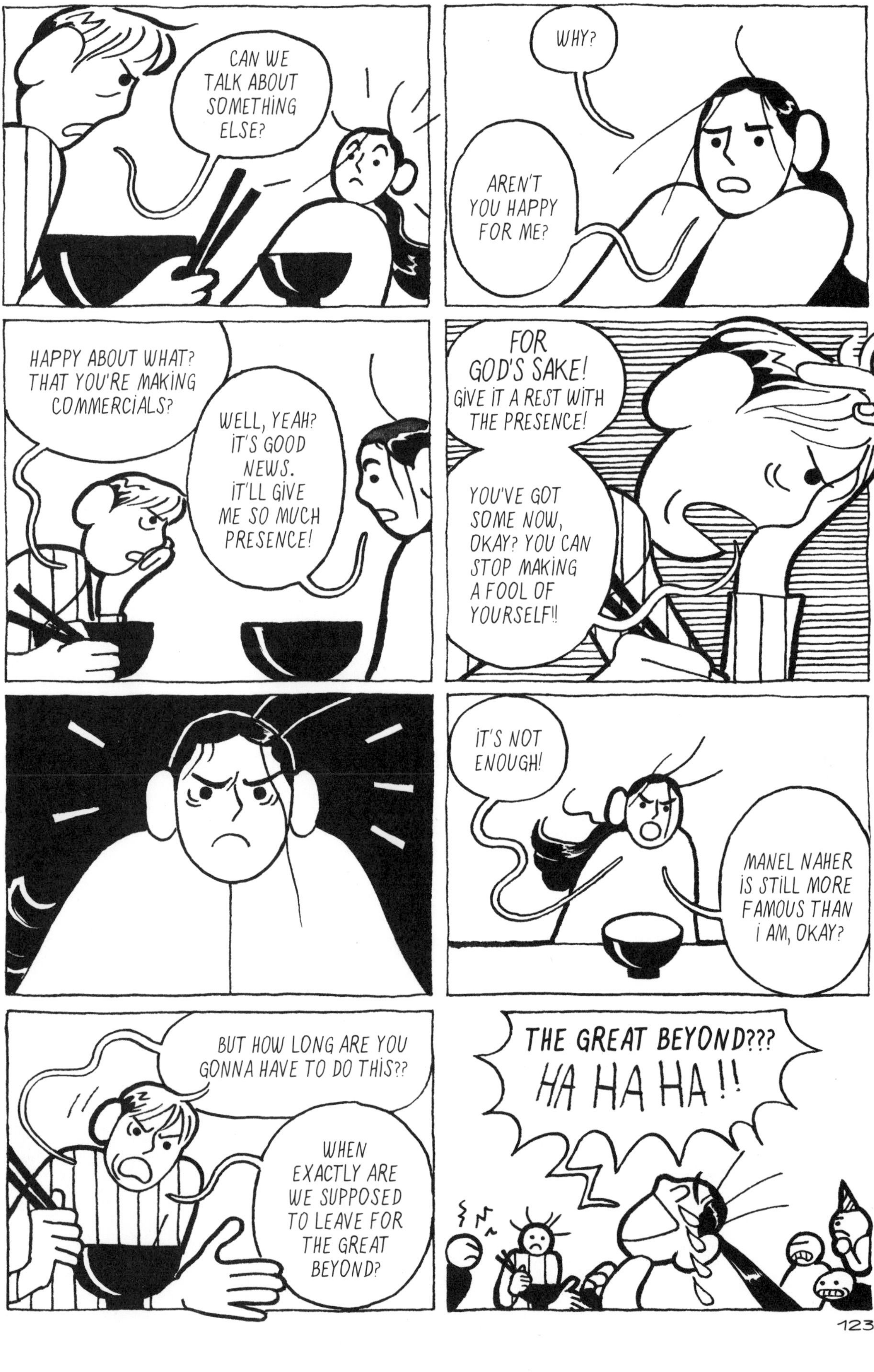
CAN WE TALK ABOUT SOMETHING ELSE?
WHY?
AREN'T YOU HAPPY FOR ME?
HAPPY ABOUT WHAT? THAT YOU'RE MAKING COMMERCIALS?
WELL, YEAH? IT'S GOOD NEWS. IT'LL GIVE ME SO MUCH PRESENCE!
FOR GOD'S SAKE! GIVE IT A REST WITH THE PRESENCE!
YOU'VE GOT SOME NOW, OKAY? YOU CAN STOP MAKING A FOOL OF YOURSELF!!
IT'S NOT ENOUGH!
MANEL NAHER IS STILL MORE FAMOUS THAN I AM, OKAY?
BUT HOW LONG ARE YOU GONNA HAVE TO DO THIS??
WHEN EXACTLY ARE WE SUPPOSED TO LEAVE FOR THE GREAT BEYOND?
THE GREAT BEYOND??? HA HA HA!!

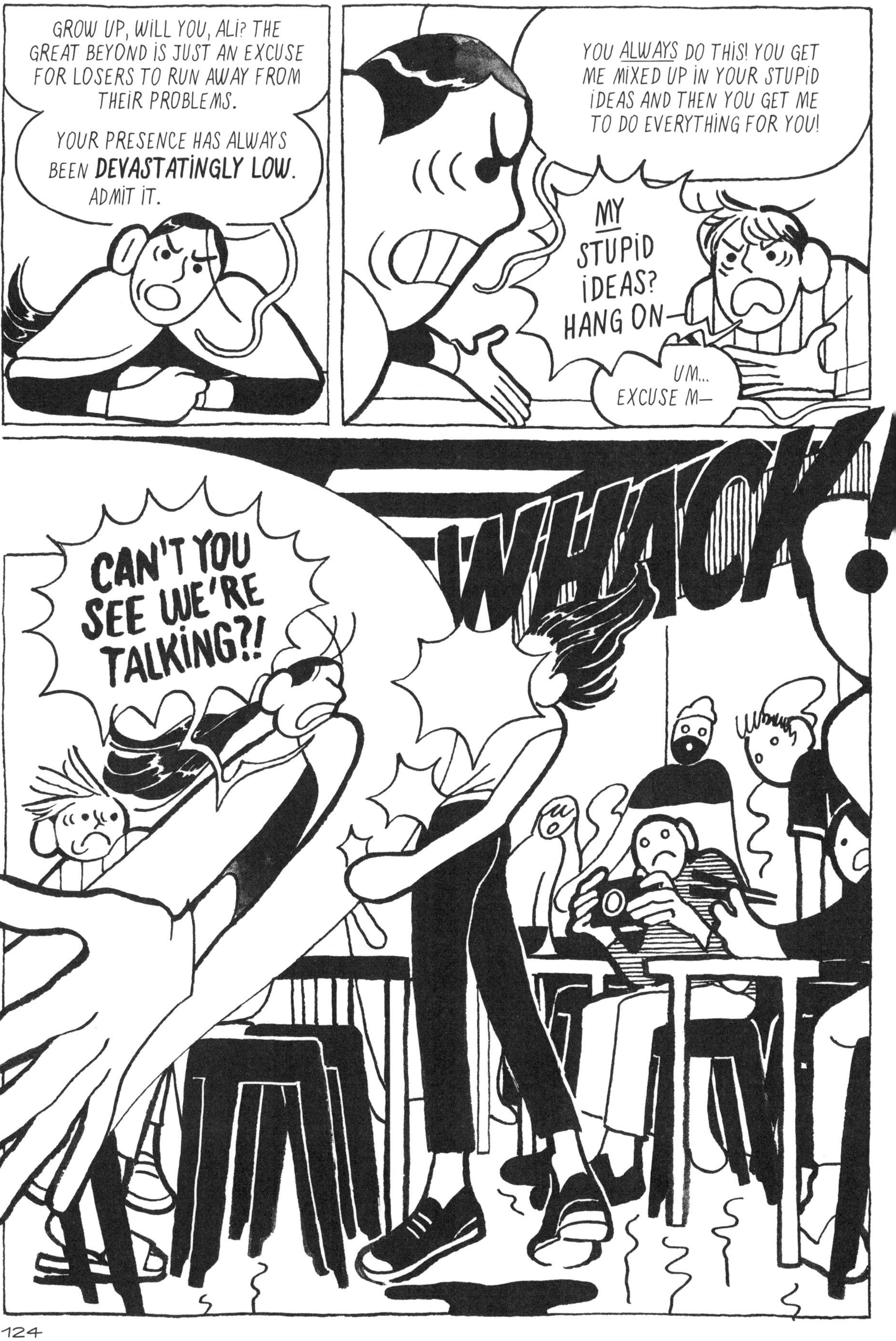
GROW UP, WILL YOU, ALI? THE GREAT BEYOND IS JUST AN EXCUSE FOR LOSERS TO RUN AWAY FROM THEIR PROBLEMS.
YOUR PRESENCE HAS ALWAYS BEEN DEVASTATINGLY LOW. ADMIT IT.
YOU ALWAYS DO THIS! YOU GET ME MIXED UP IN YOUR STUPID IDEAS AND THEN YOU GET ME TO DO EVERYTHING FOR YOU!
MY STUPID IDEAS? HANG ON—
UM... EXCUSE M—
WHACK!
CAN'T YOU SEE WE'RE TALKING?!

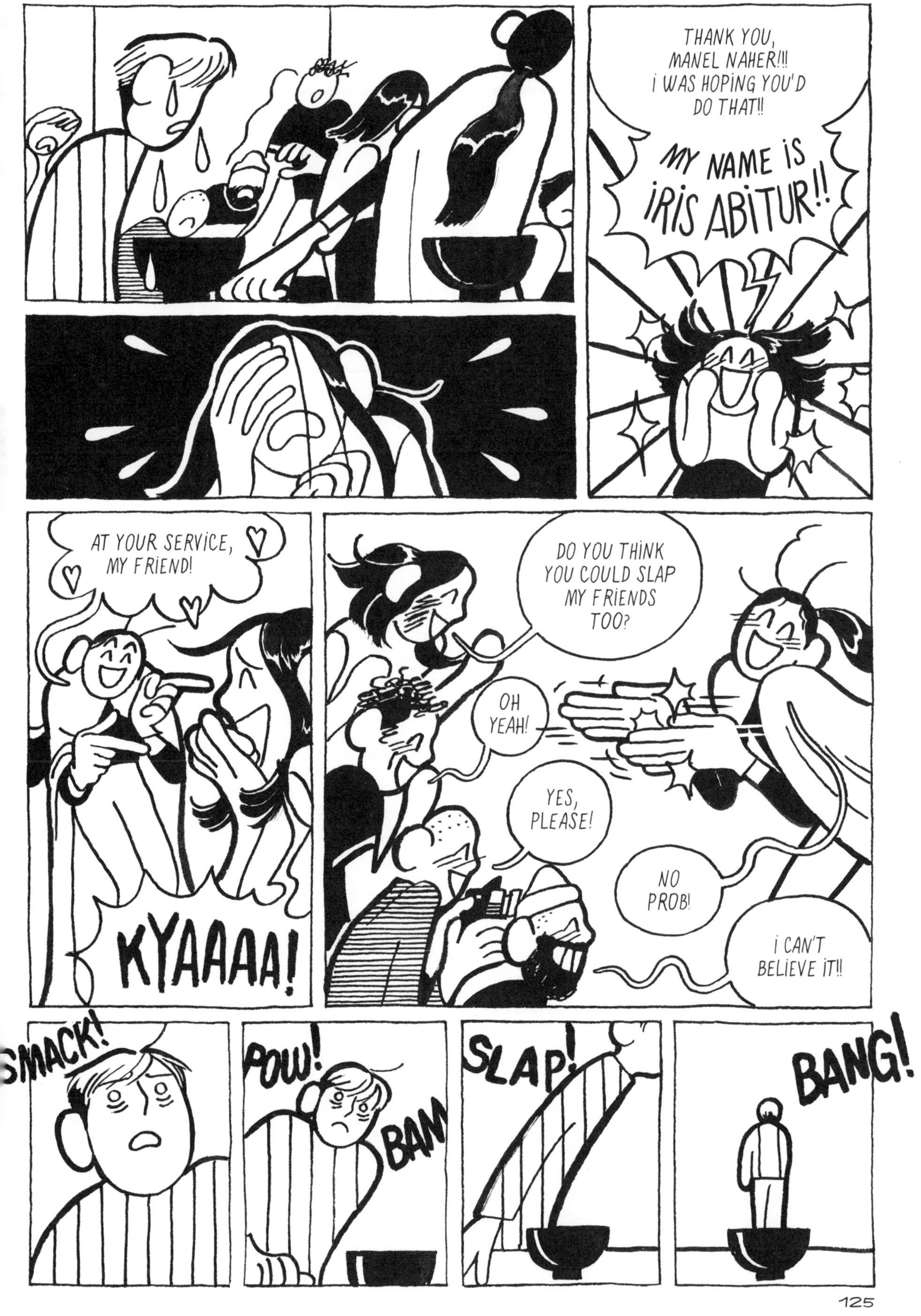
THANK YOU, MANEL NAHER!!! I WAS HOPING YOU'D DO THAT!!
MY NAME IS IRIS ABITUR!!
AT YOUR SERVICE, MY FRIEND!
KYAAAA!
DO YOU THINK YOU COULD SLAP MY FRIENDS TOO?
OH YEAH!
YES, PLEASE!
NO PROB!
I CAN'T BELIEVE IT!!
SMACK!
POW!
BAM
SLAP!
BANG!

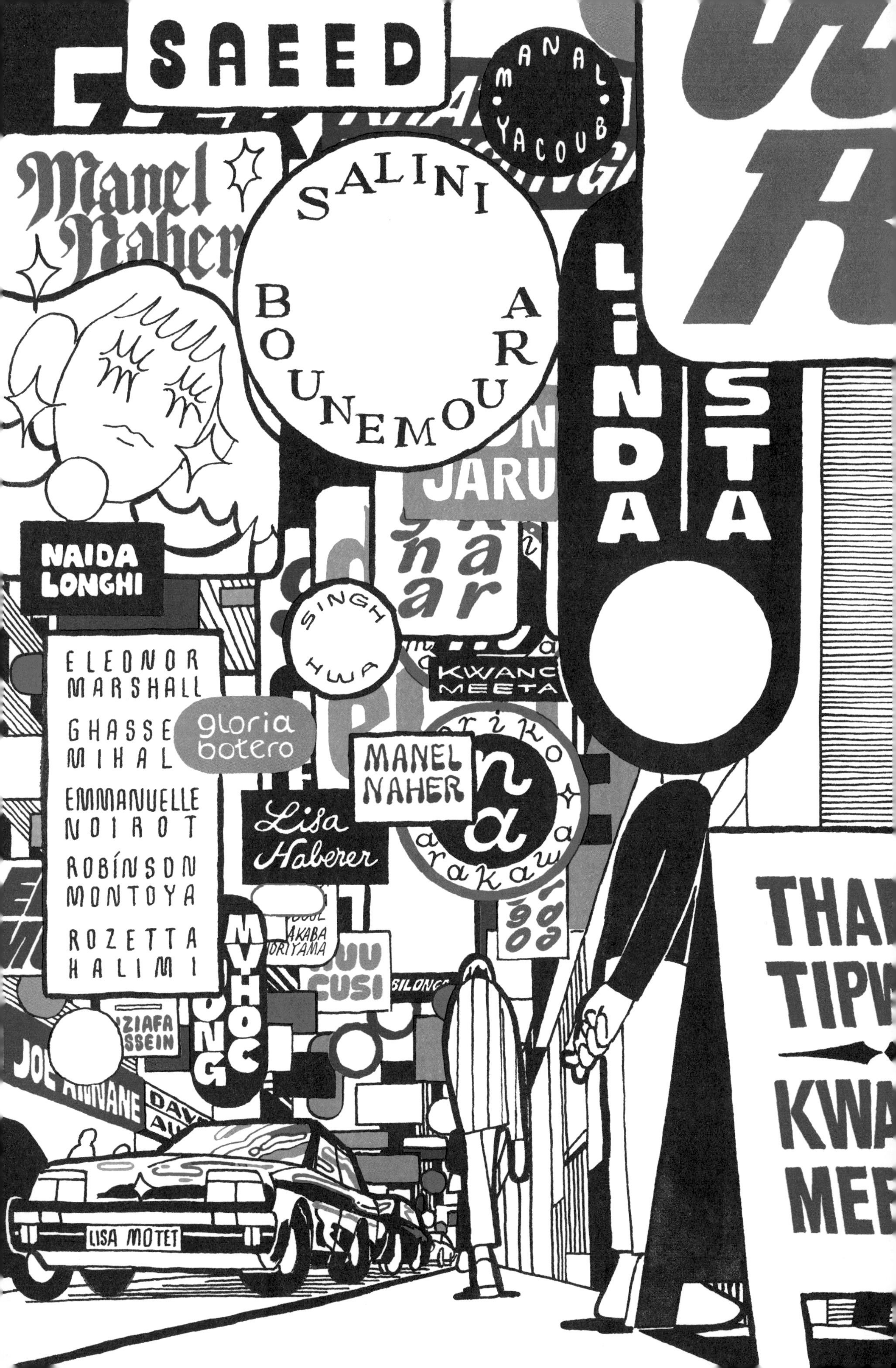
SAEED
MANAL YACOUB
Manel Naher
SALINI BOUNEMOUAR
LINDA
STA
JARU
NAIDA LONGHI
ELEONOR MARSHALL
GHASSE MIHAL
EMMANUELLE NOIROT
ROBÍNSON MONTOYA
ROZETTA HALIMI
gloria botero
SINGH HWA
KWANC MEETA
MANEL NAHER
Lisa Haberer
LISA MOTET

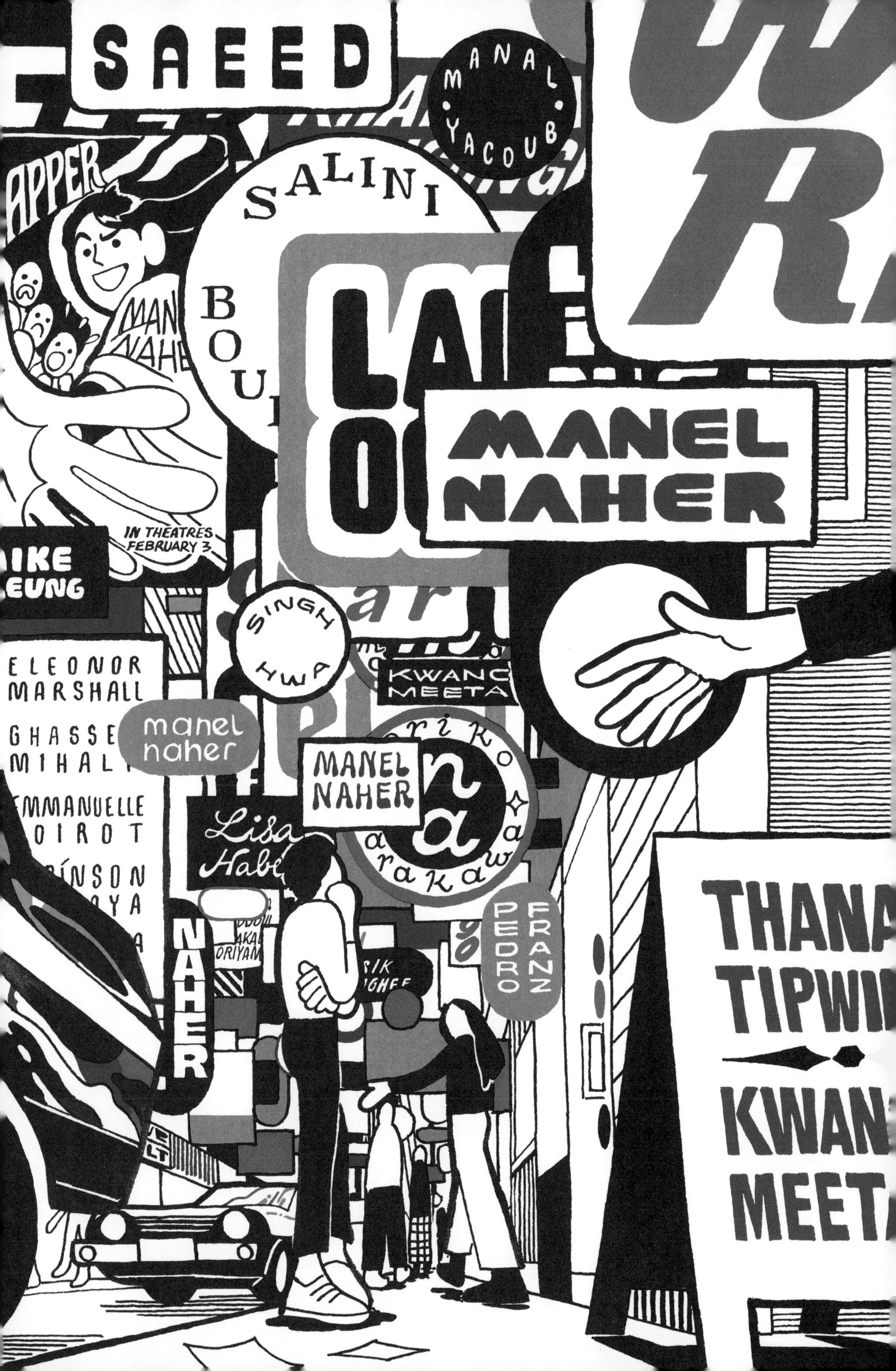
SAEED
MANAL YACOUB
SALINI
BOU
APPER
MANEL NAHER
IN THEATRES FEBRUARY 3
IKE
EUNG
MANEL NAHER
SINGH HWA
ELEONOR MARSHALL
GHASSE MIHAL
EMMANUELLE OIROT
manel naher
MANEL NAHER
Lisa Habe
riko arakawa
NAHER
PEDRO FRANZ
THANA TIPWI
KWAN MEETA

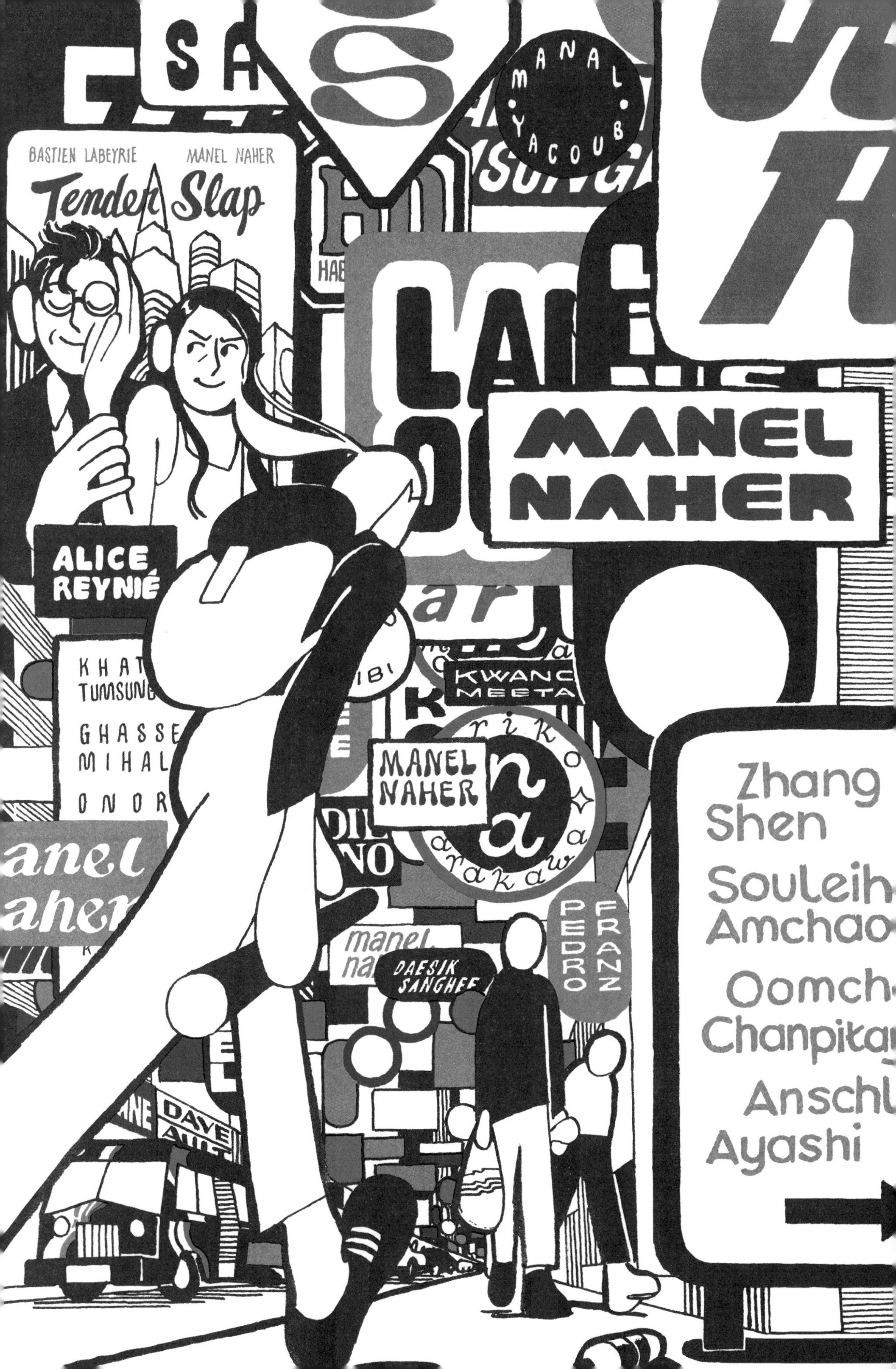

MANAL YACOUB
BASTIEN LABEYRIE
MANEL NAHER
Tender Slap
MANEL NAHER
ALICE REYNIÉ
MANEL NAHER
DAESIK SANGHEE
PEDRO FRANZ
Zhang Shen
Ayashi

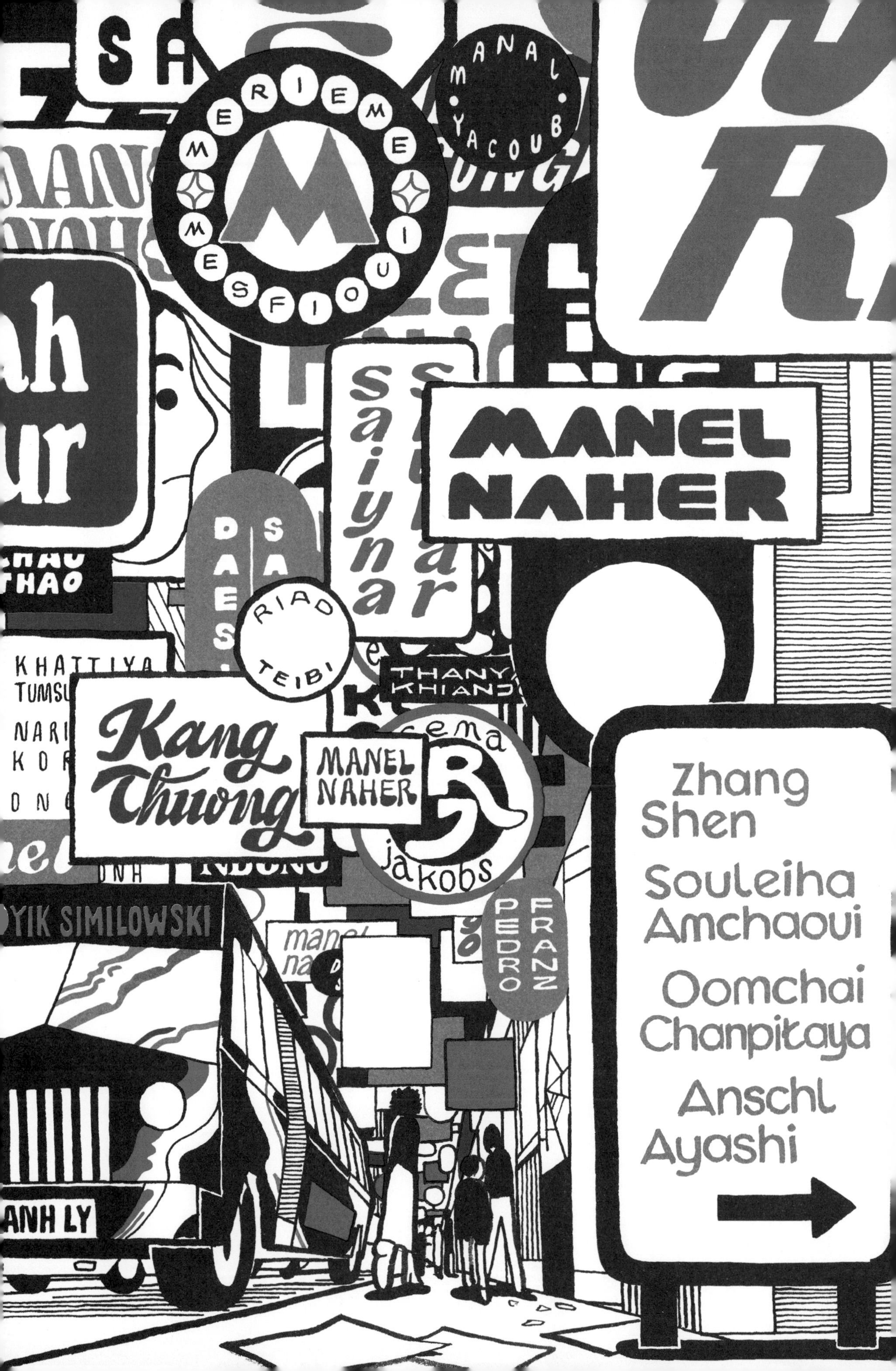
MERIEME MESFIOUI
MANAL YACOUB
Saiynar
MANEL NAHER
DAES
RIAD TEIBI
THAO
Kang Chuong
MANEL NAHER
cema
jakobs
PEDRO
FRANZ
YIK SIMILOWSKI
ANH LY
Zhang Shen
Souleiha Amchaoui
Oomchai Chanpitaya
Anschl Ayashi

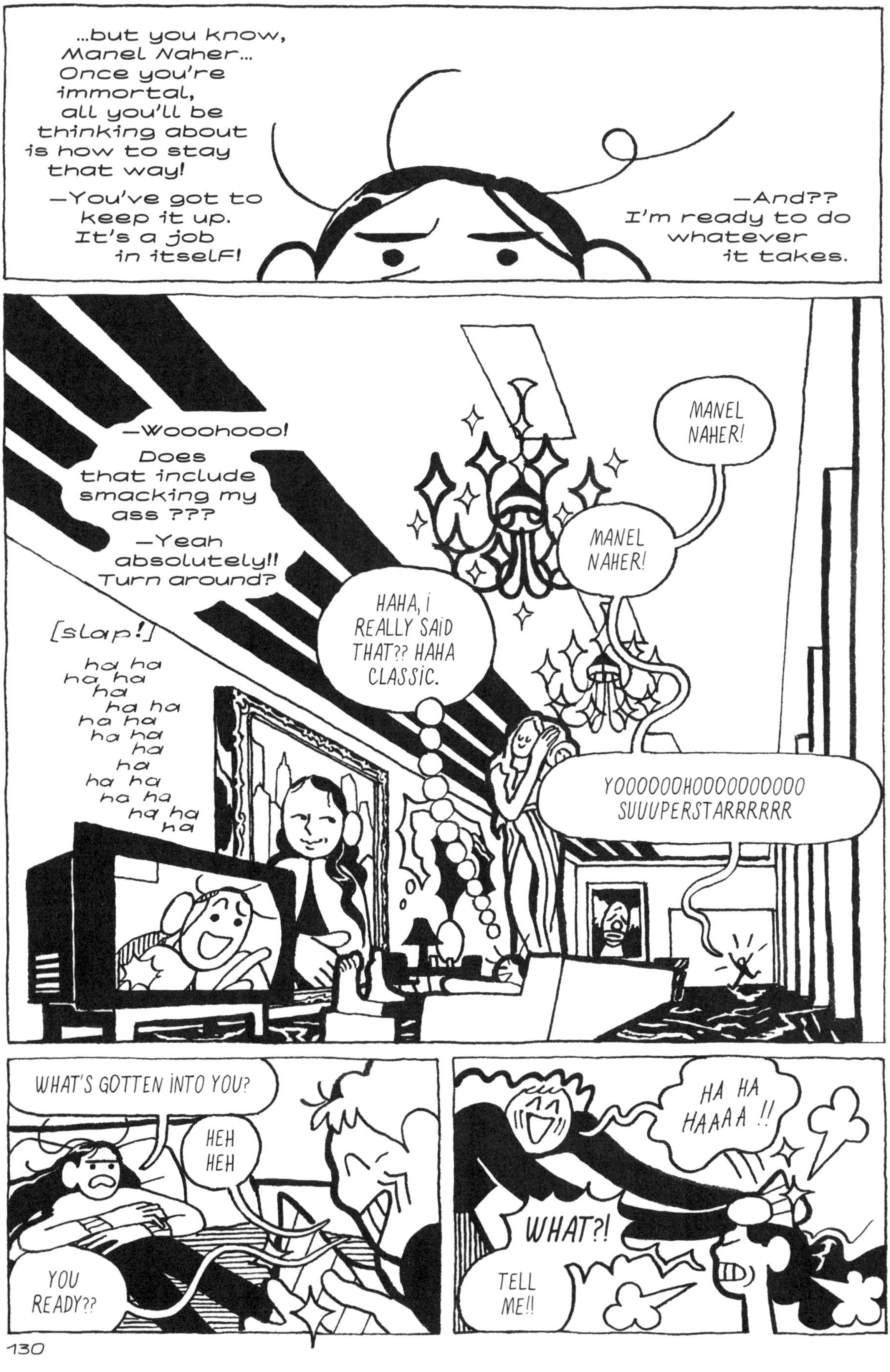
...but you know, Manel Naher... Once you're immortal, all you'll be thinking about is how to stay that way!
—You've got to keep it up. It's a job in itself!
—And?? I'm ready to do whatever it takes.
—Wooohooo! Does that include smacking my ass ???
—Yeah absolutely!! Turn around?
[slap!]
ha ha ha ha ha ha ha ha ha ha ha ha ha ha ha ha ha ha ha
HAHA, I REALLY SAID THAT?? HAHA CLASSIC.
MANEL NAHER!
MANEL NAHER!
YOOOOOOHOOOOOOOOOO SUUUPERSTARRRRRRR
WHAT'S GOTTEN INTO YOU?
HEH HEH
YOU READY??
HA HA HAAAA !!
WHAT?!
TELL ME!!

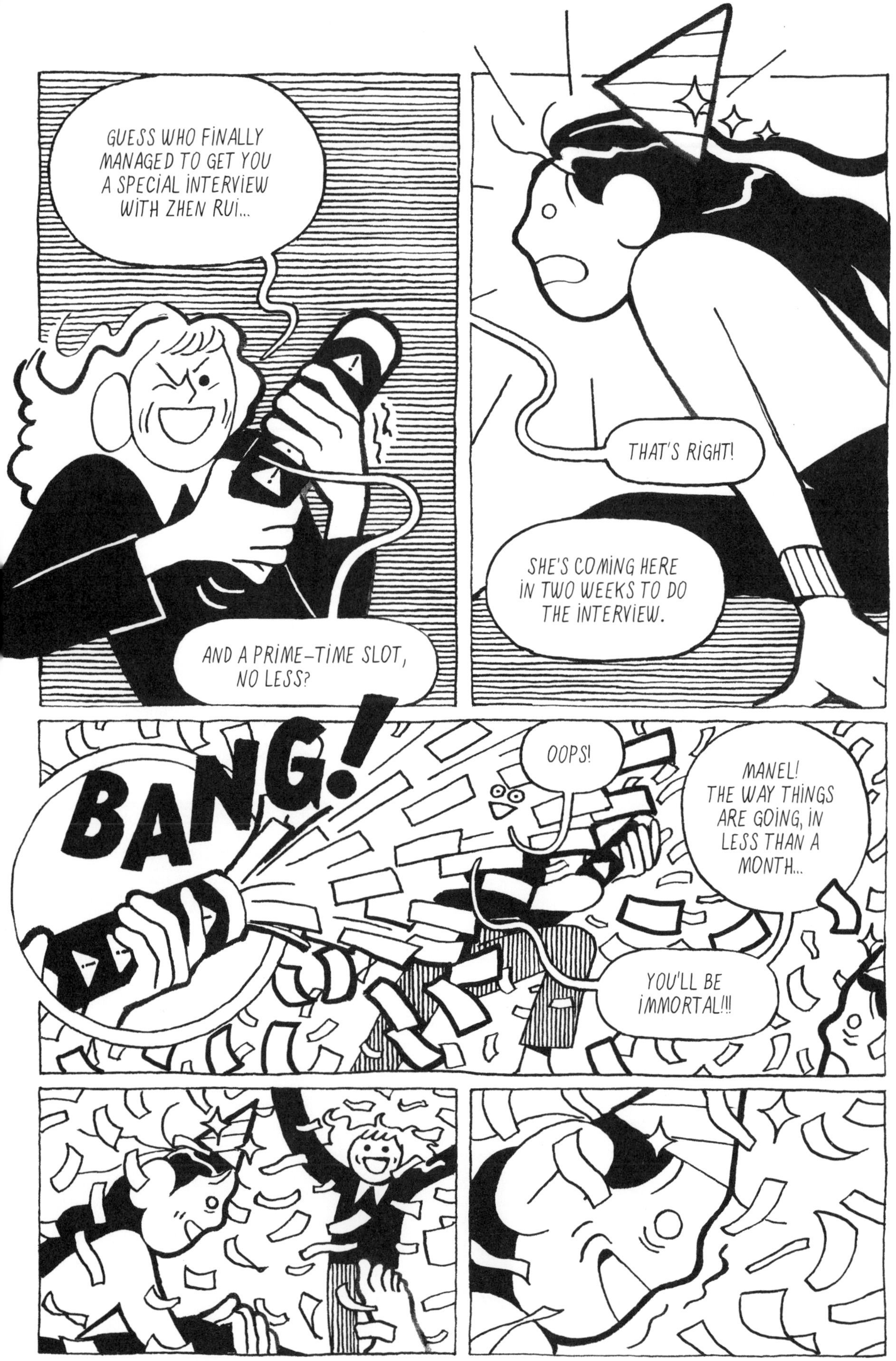
GUESS WHO FINALLY MANAGED TO GET YOU A SPECIAL INTERVIEW WITH ZHEN RUI...
AND A PRIME-TIME SLOT, NO LESS?
THAT'S RIGHT!
SHE'S COMING HERE IN TWO WEEKS TO DO THE INTERVIEW.
BANG!
OOPS!
MANEL! THE WAY THINGS ARE GOING, IN LESS THAN A MONTH...
YOU'LL BE IMMORTAL!!!

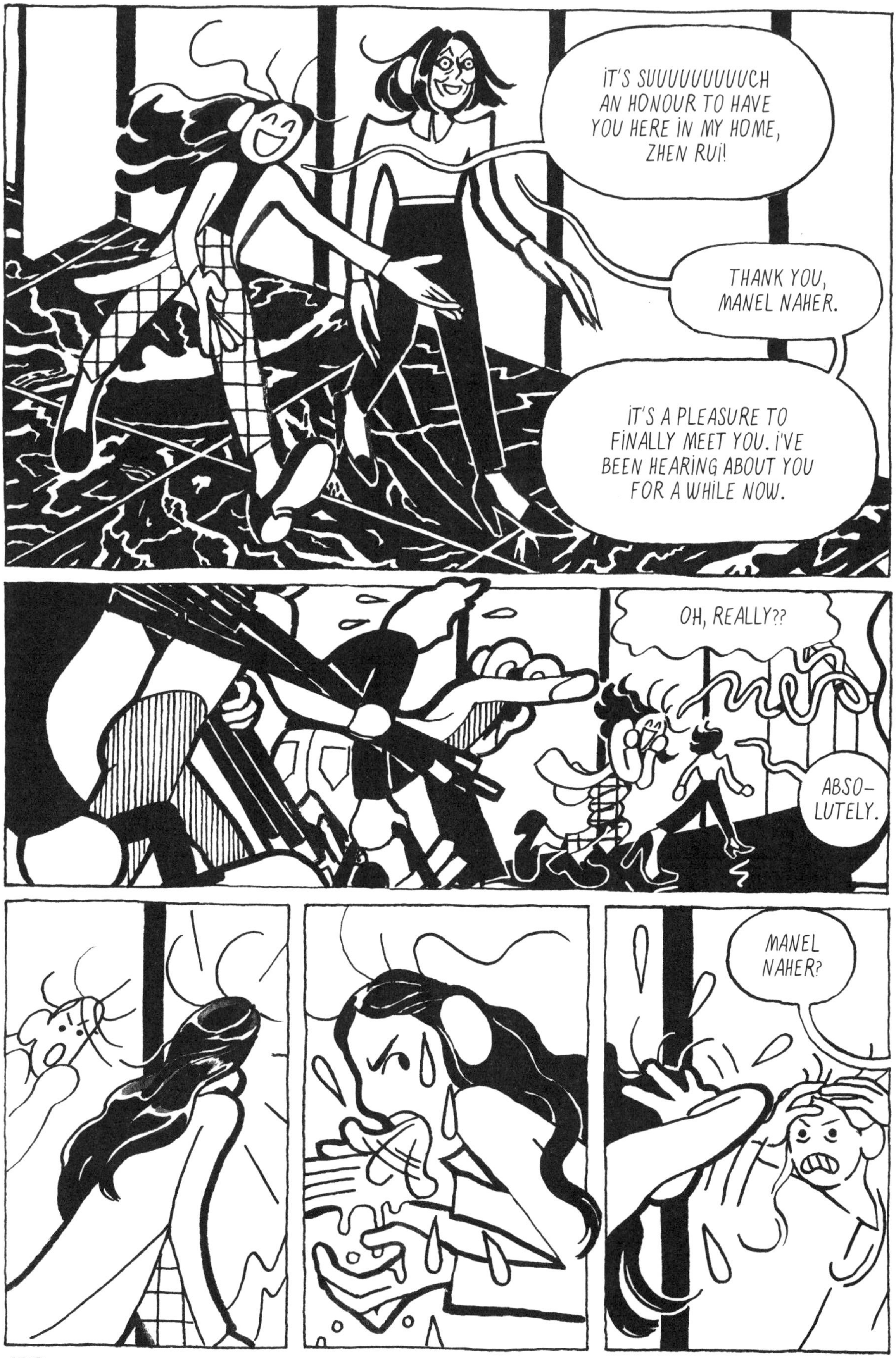
IT'S SUUUUUUUUUCH AN HONOUR TO HAVE YOU HERE IN MY HOME, ZHEN RUI!
THANK YOU, MANEL NAHER.
IT'S A PLEASURE TO FINALLY MEET YOU. I'VE BEEN HEARING ABOUT YOU FOR A WHILE NOW.
OH, REALLY??
ABSO-LUTELY.
MANEL NAHER?

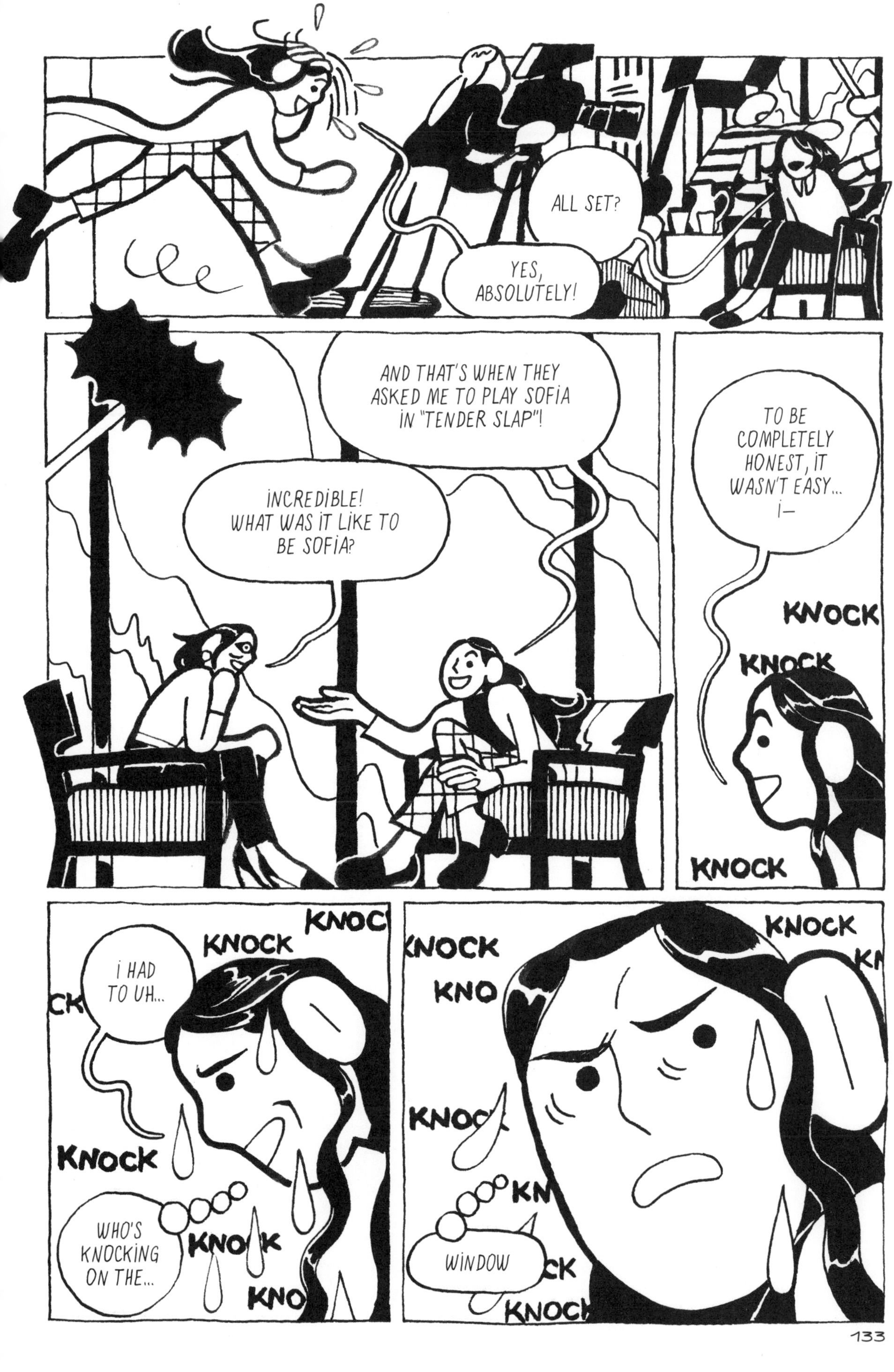
ALL SET?
YES, ABSOLUTELY!
AND THAT'S WHEN THEY ASKED ME TO PLAY SOFIA IN "TENDER SLAP"!
INCREDIBLE! WHAT WAS IT LIKE TO BE SOFIA?
TO BE COMPLETELY HONEST, IT WASN'T EASY... I—
KNOCK
KNOCK
KNOCK
KNOCK
KNOC
CK
I HAD TO UH...
KNOCK
WHO'S KNOCKING ON THE...
KNO
KNO
KNOCK
KNOCK
KNO
KNOC
KN
WINDOW
CK
KNOC

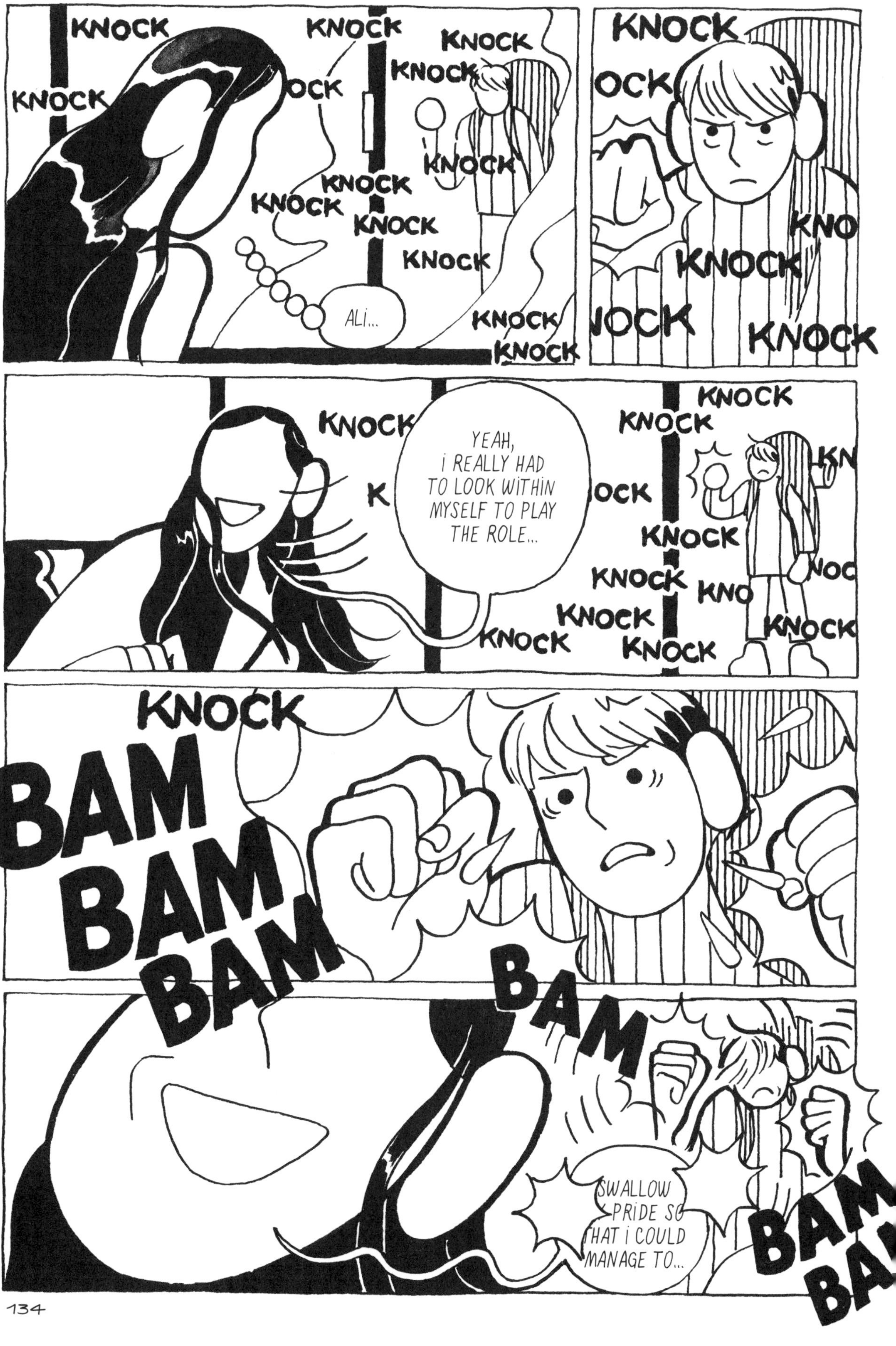
KNOCK
KNOCK
KNOCK
KNOCK
KNOCK
KNOCK
KNOCK
KNOCK
KNOCK
KNOCK
ALi...
KNOCK
KNOCK
KNOCK
KNOCK
KNOCK
KNOCK
KNOCK
YEAH, i REALLY HAD TO LOOK WiTHiN MYSELF TO PLAY THE ROLE...
KNOCK
KNOCK
KNOCK
KNOCK
KNOCK
KNOCK
KNOCK
KNOCK
BAM BAM BAM
BAM
SWALLOW PRiDE SO THAT i COULD MANAGE TO...

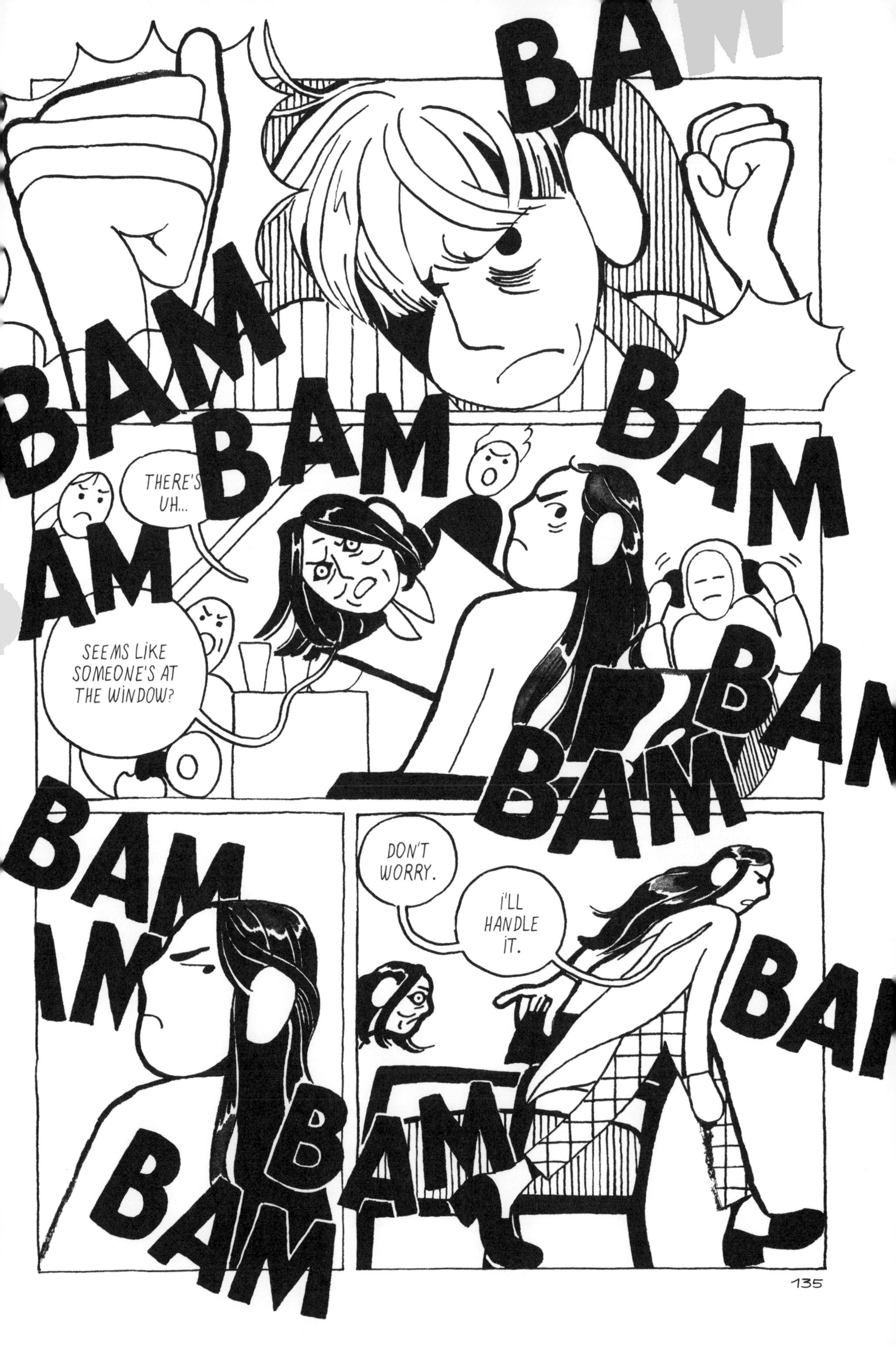
BAM
BAM
BAM
BAM
THERE'S UH...
SEEMS LIKE SOMEONE'S AT THE WINDOW?
BAM
BAM
BAM
DON'T WORRY.
I'LL HANDLE IT.
BAM
BAM
BAM

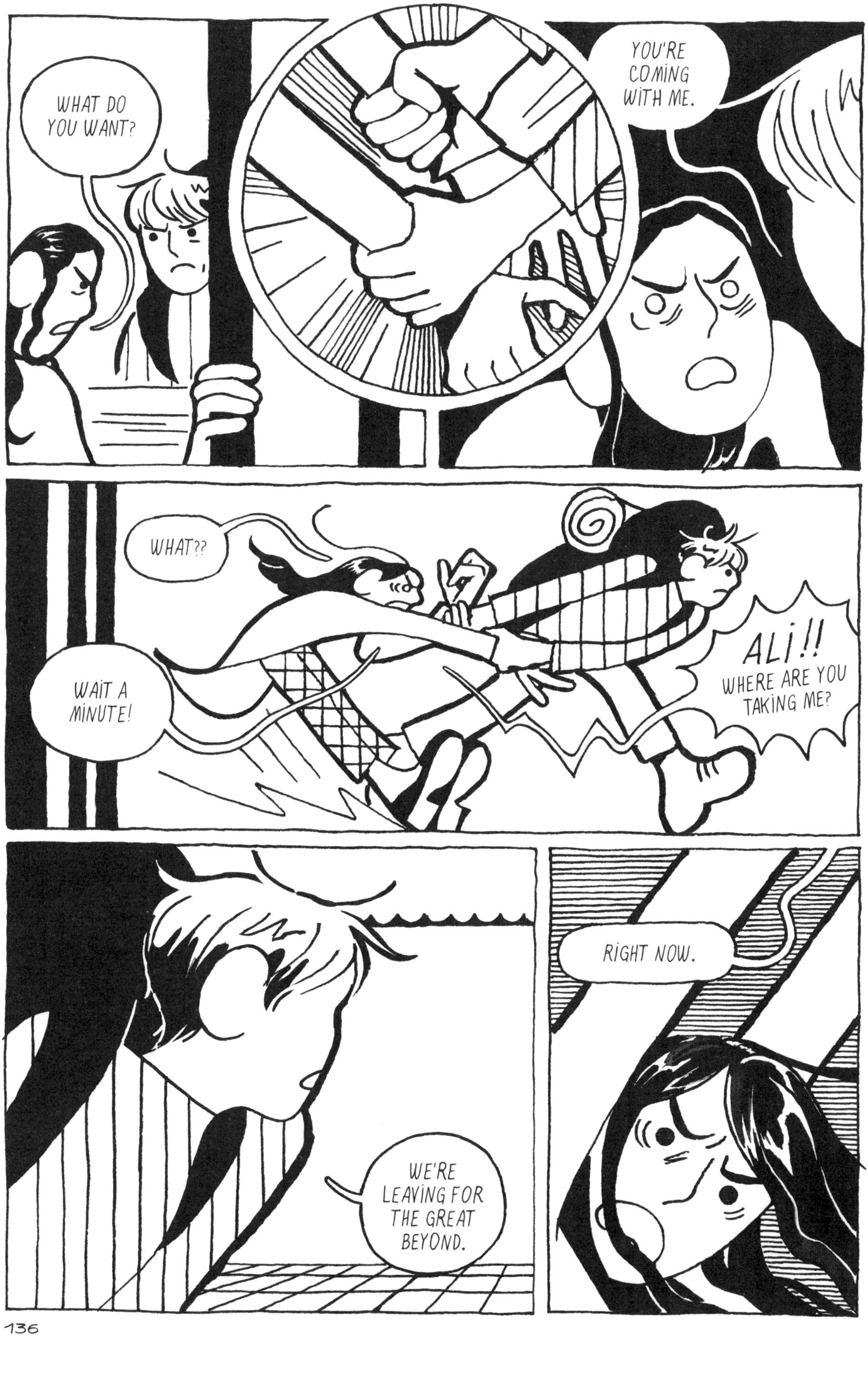
WHAT DO YOU WANT?
YOU'RE COMING WITH ME.
WHAT??
WAIT A MINUTE!
ALI!! WHERE ARE YOU TAKING ME?
WE'RE LEAVING FOR THE GREAT BEYOND.
RIGHT NOW.

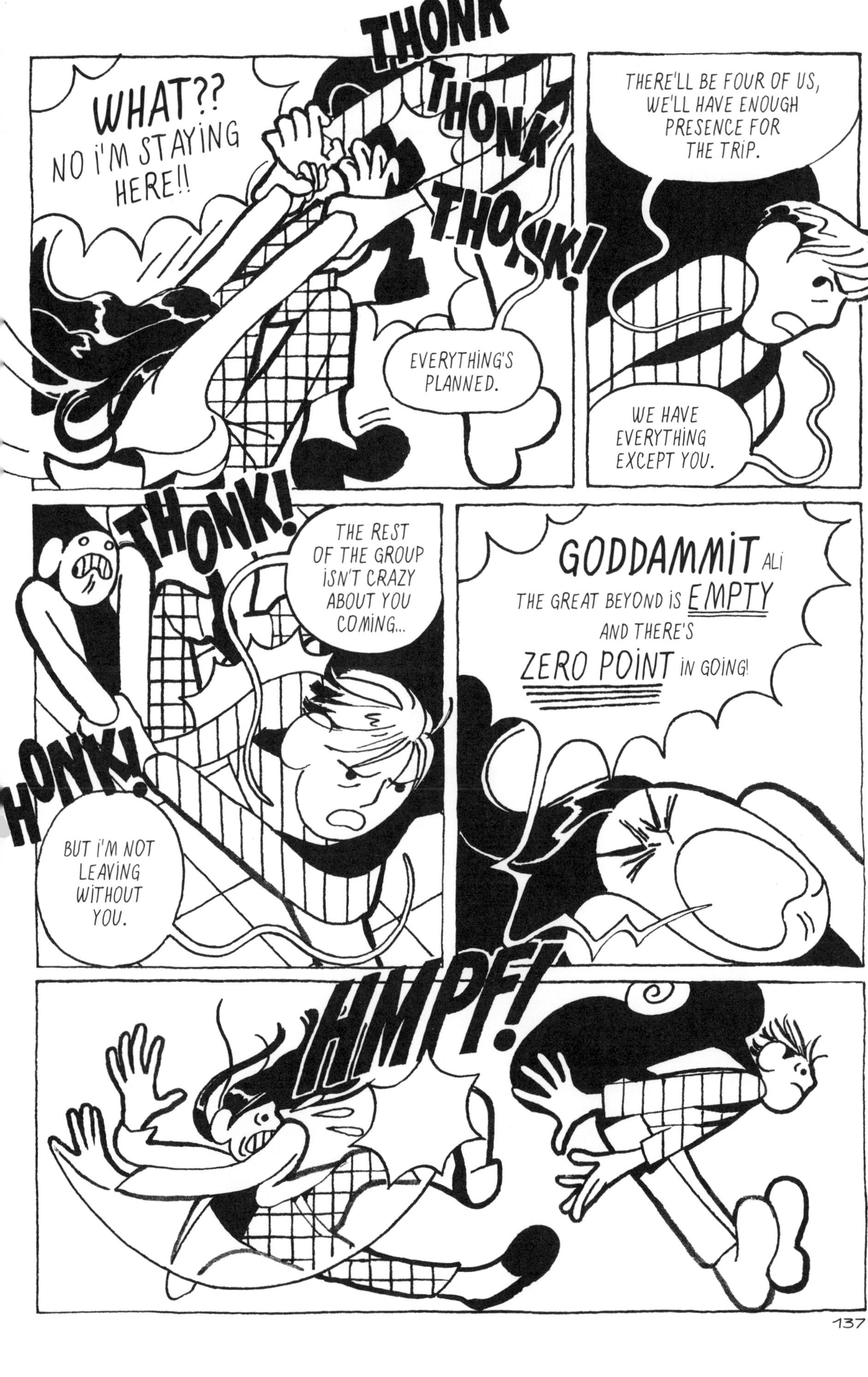
WHAT?? NO I'M STAYING HERE!!
THONK
THONK
THONK!
EVERYTHING'S PLANNED.
THERE'LL BE FOUR OF US, WE'LL HAVE ENOUGH PRESENCE FOR THE TRIP.
WE HAVE EVERYTHING EXCEPT YOU.
THONK!
THE REST OF THE GROUP ISN'T CRAZY ABOUT YOU COMING...
HONK!
BUT I'M NOT LEAVING WITHOUT YOU.
GODDAMMIT ALI THE GREAT BEYOND IS EMPTY AND THERE'S ZERO POINT IN GOING!
HMPF!

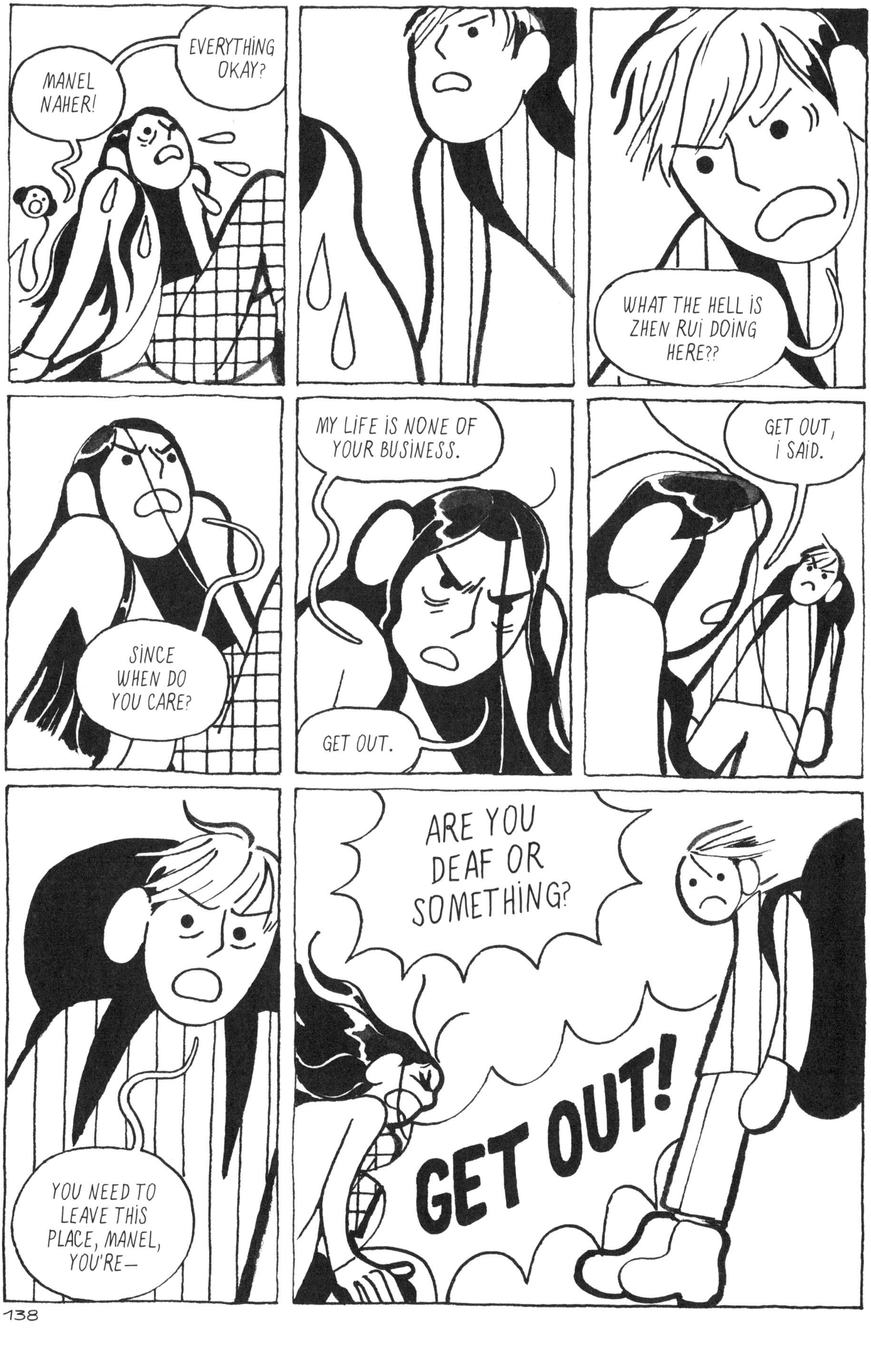
MANEL NAHER!
EVERYTHING OKAY?
WHAT THE HELL IS ZHEN RUI DOING HERE??
SINCE WHEN DO YOU CARE?
MY LIFE IS NONE OF YOUR BUSINESS.
GET OUT.
GET OUT, I SAID.
YOU NEED TO LEAVE THIS PLACE, MANEL, YOU'RE—
ARE YOU DEAF OR SOMETHING?
GET OUT!

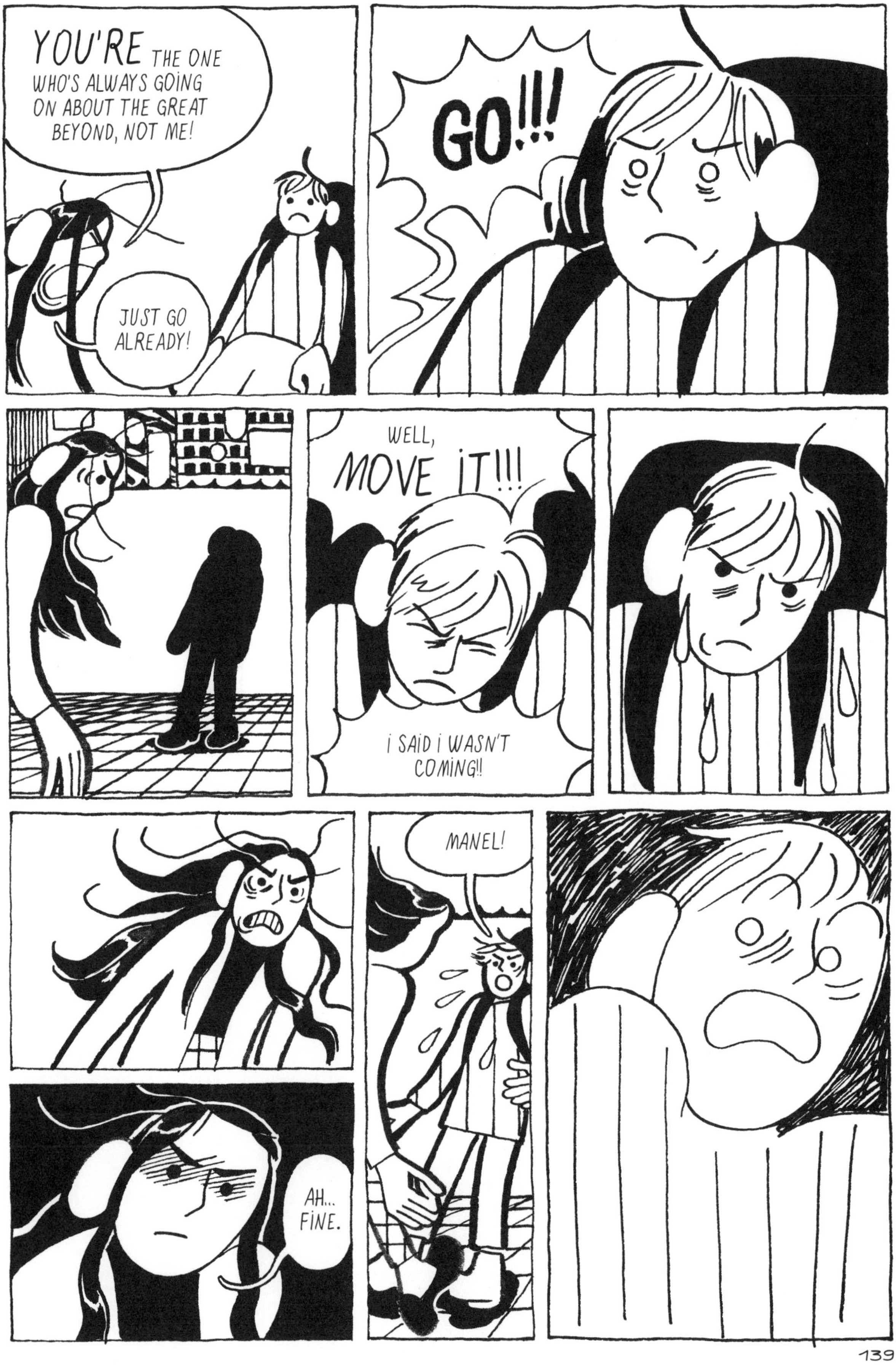
YOU'RE THE ONE WHO'S ALWAYS GOING ON ABOUT THE GREAT BEYOND, NOT ME!
JUST GO ALREADY!
GO!!!
WELL, MOVE IT!!!
I SAID I WASN'T COMING!!
MANEL!
AH... FINE.

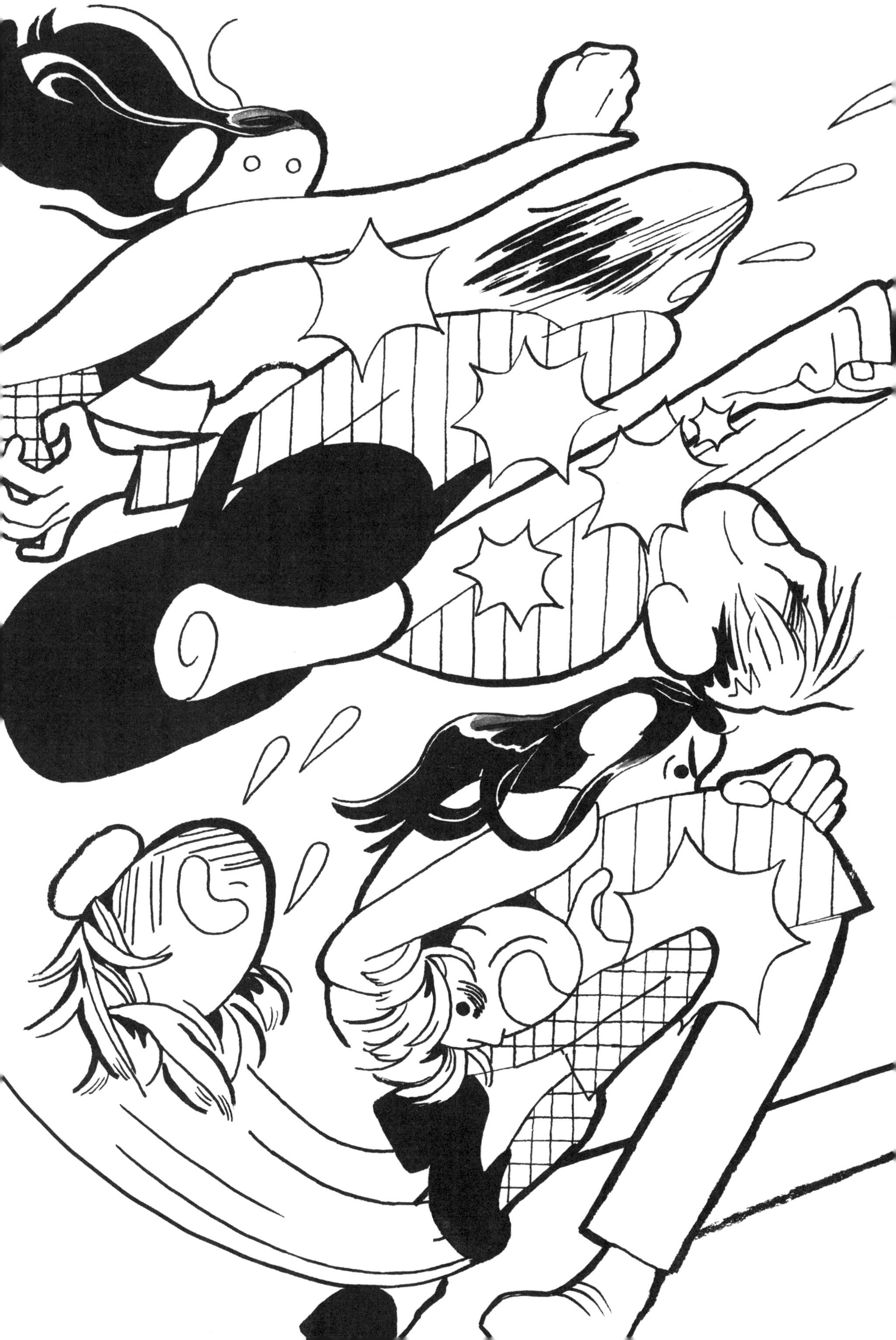

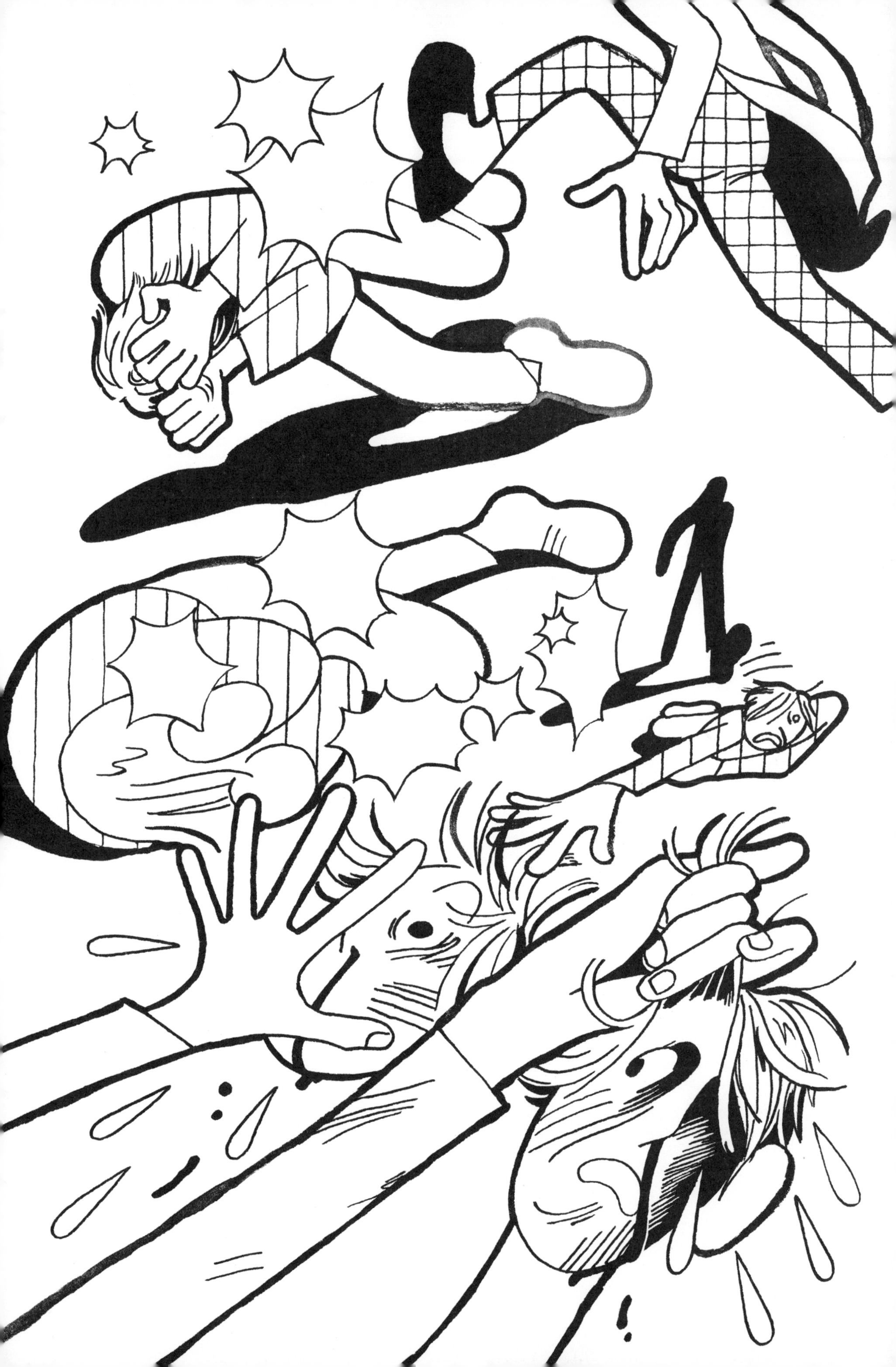

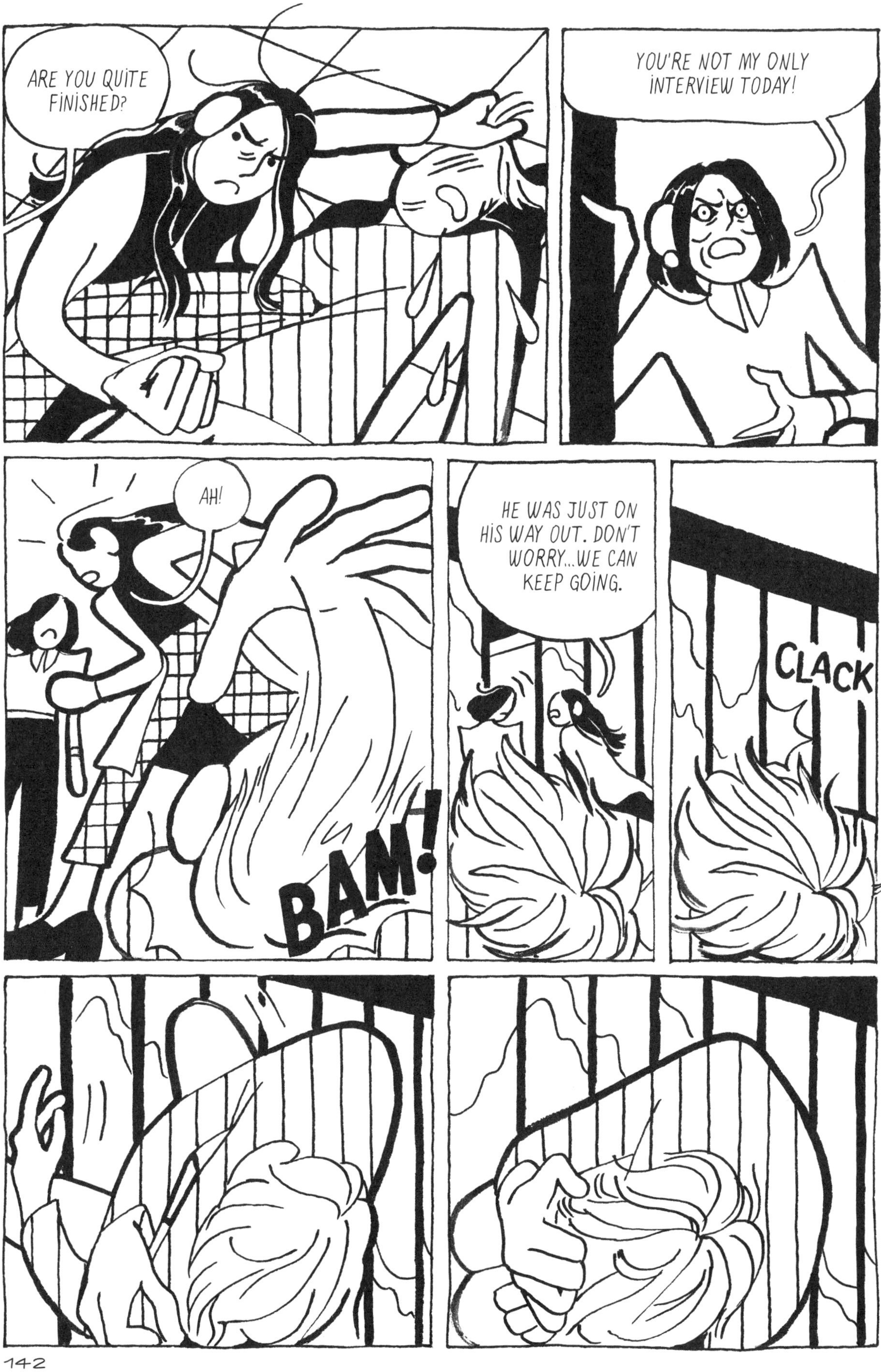
ARE YOU QUITE FINISHED?
YOU'RE NOT MY ONLY INTERVIEW TODAY!
AH!
BAM!
HE WAS JUST ON HIS WAY OUT. DON'T WORRY...WE CAN KEEP GOING.
CLACK

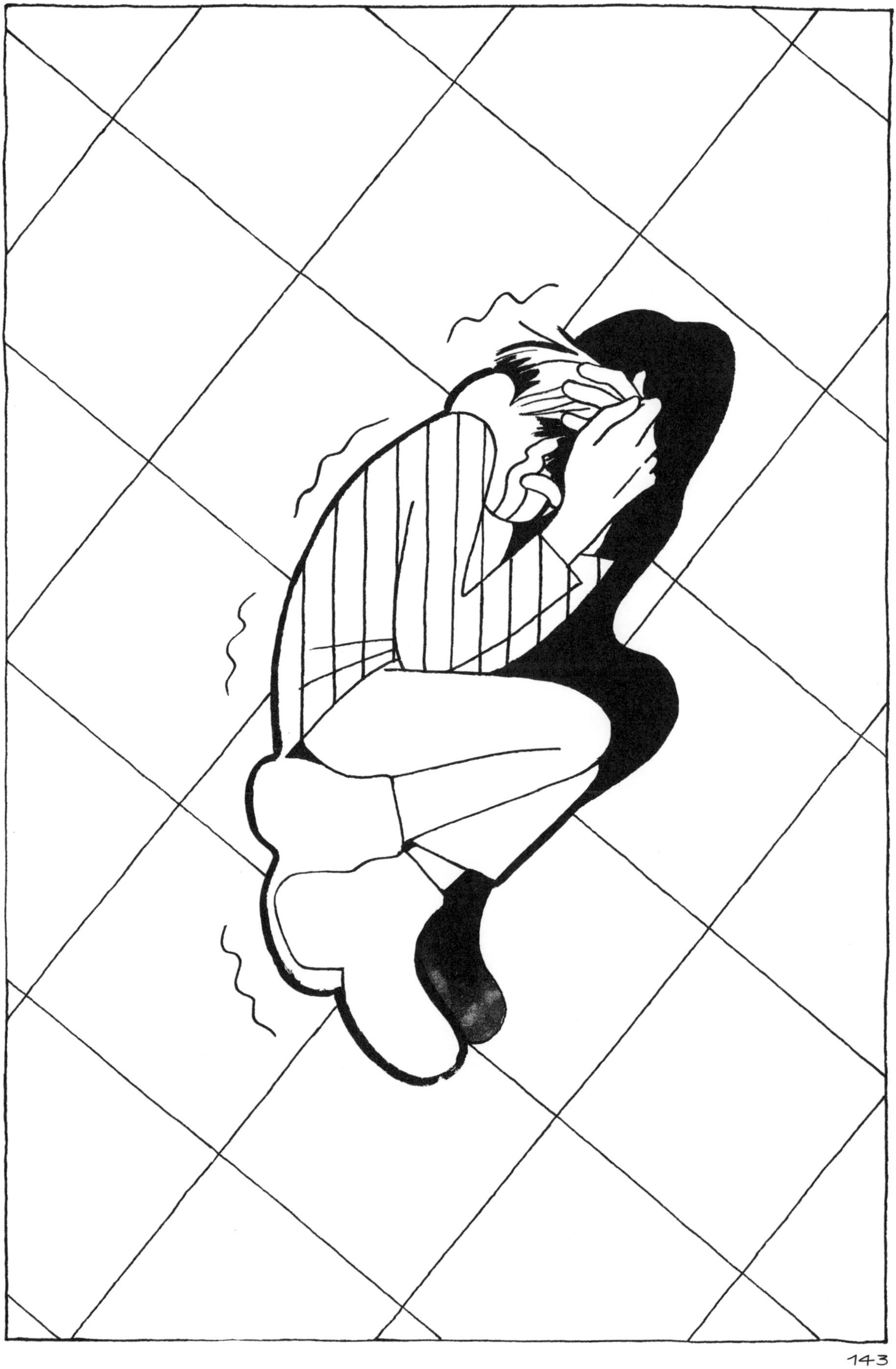

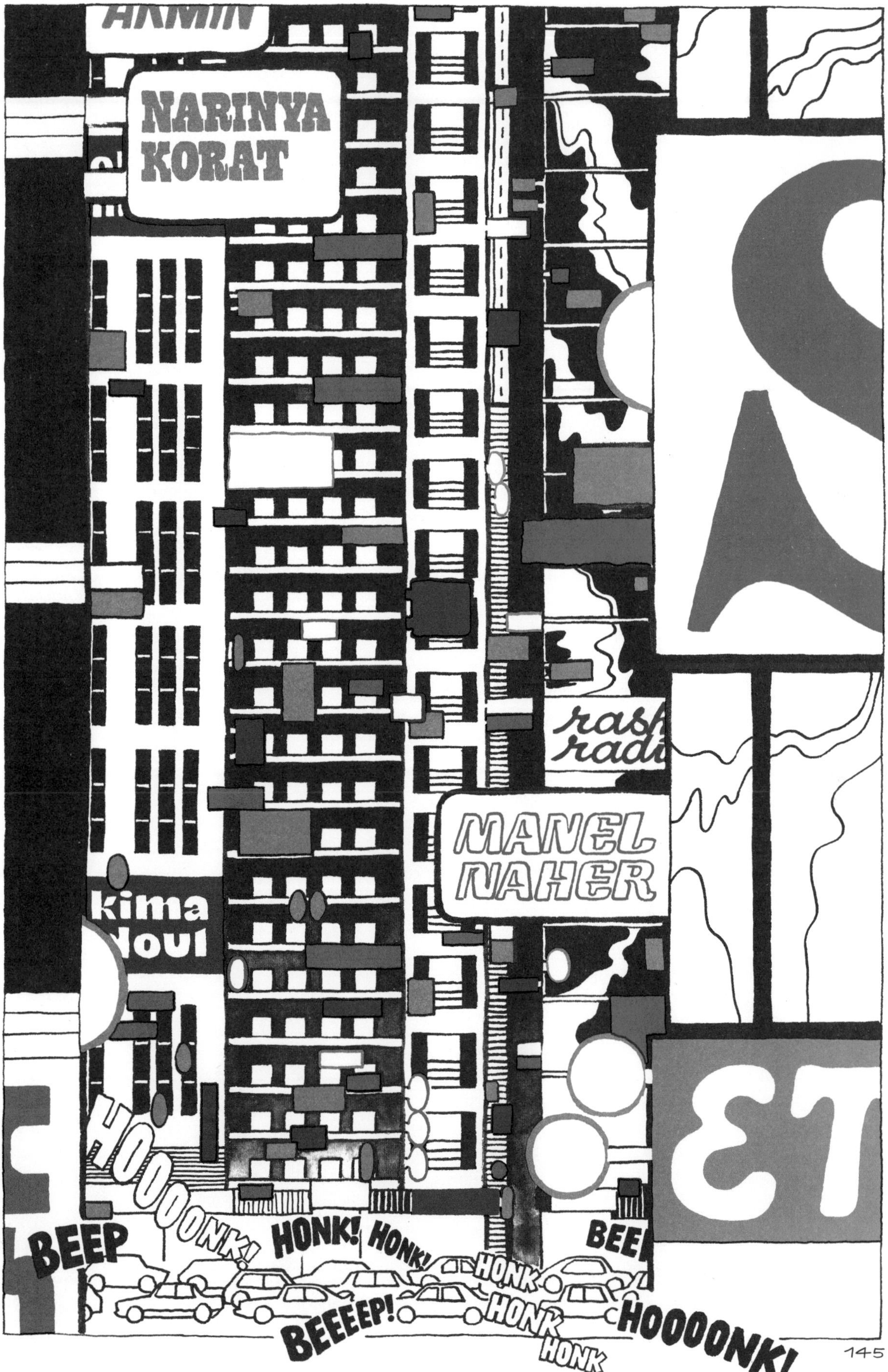
NARINYA
KORAT
kima
doul
rash
radi
MANEL
NAHER
ET
HOOOONK!
BEEP
HONK!
HONK!
HONK
BEEEEP!
HONK
HONK
HOOOONK!
BEE

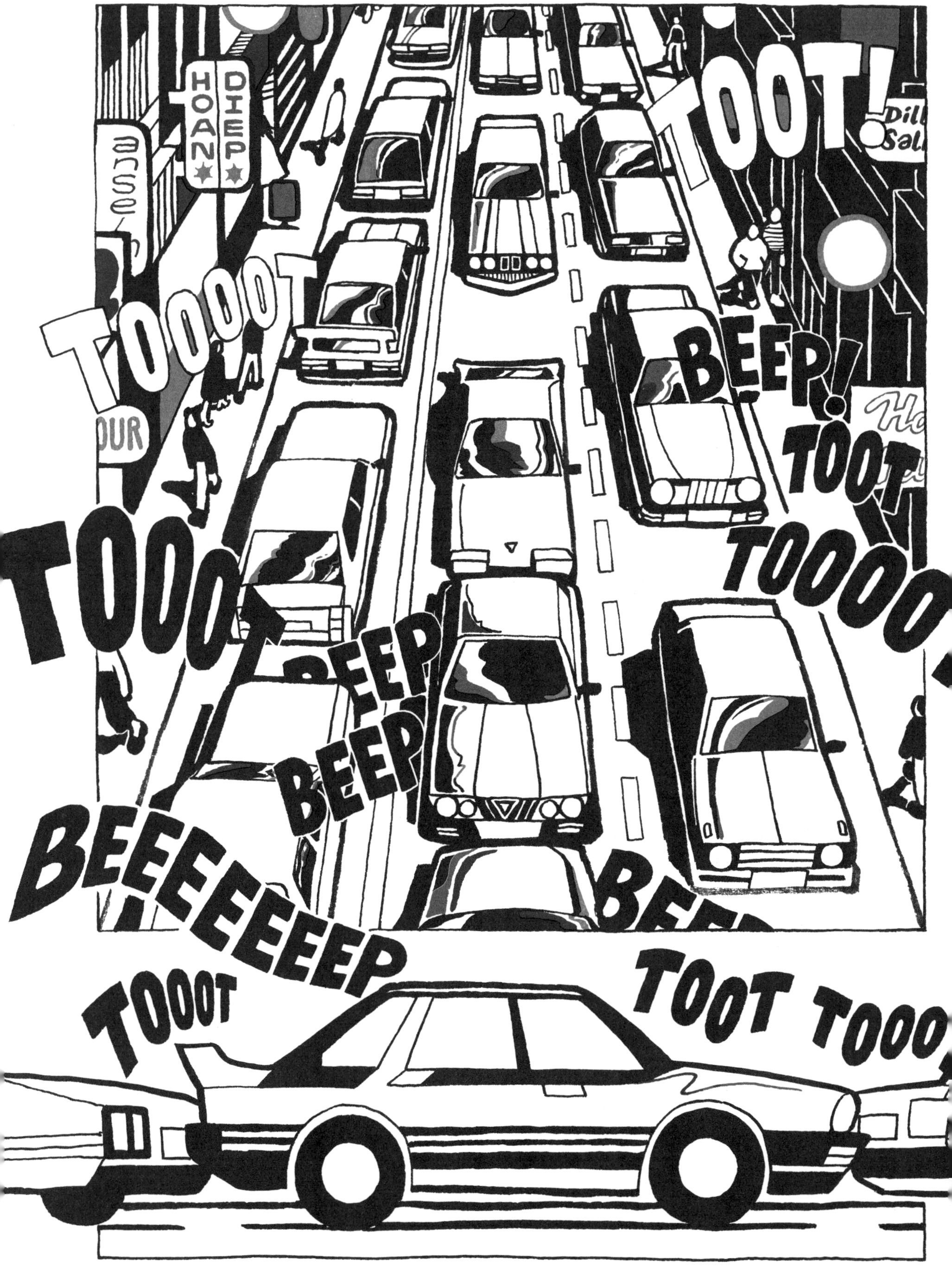

HOAN
DIEP
TOOT!
TOOOOT
BEEP!
TOOT
TOOOT
BEEP
BEEP
BEEEEEEEEEP
TOOOT
TOOT

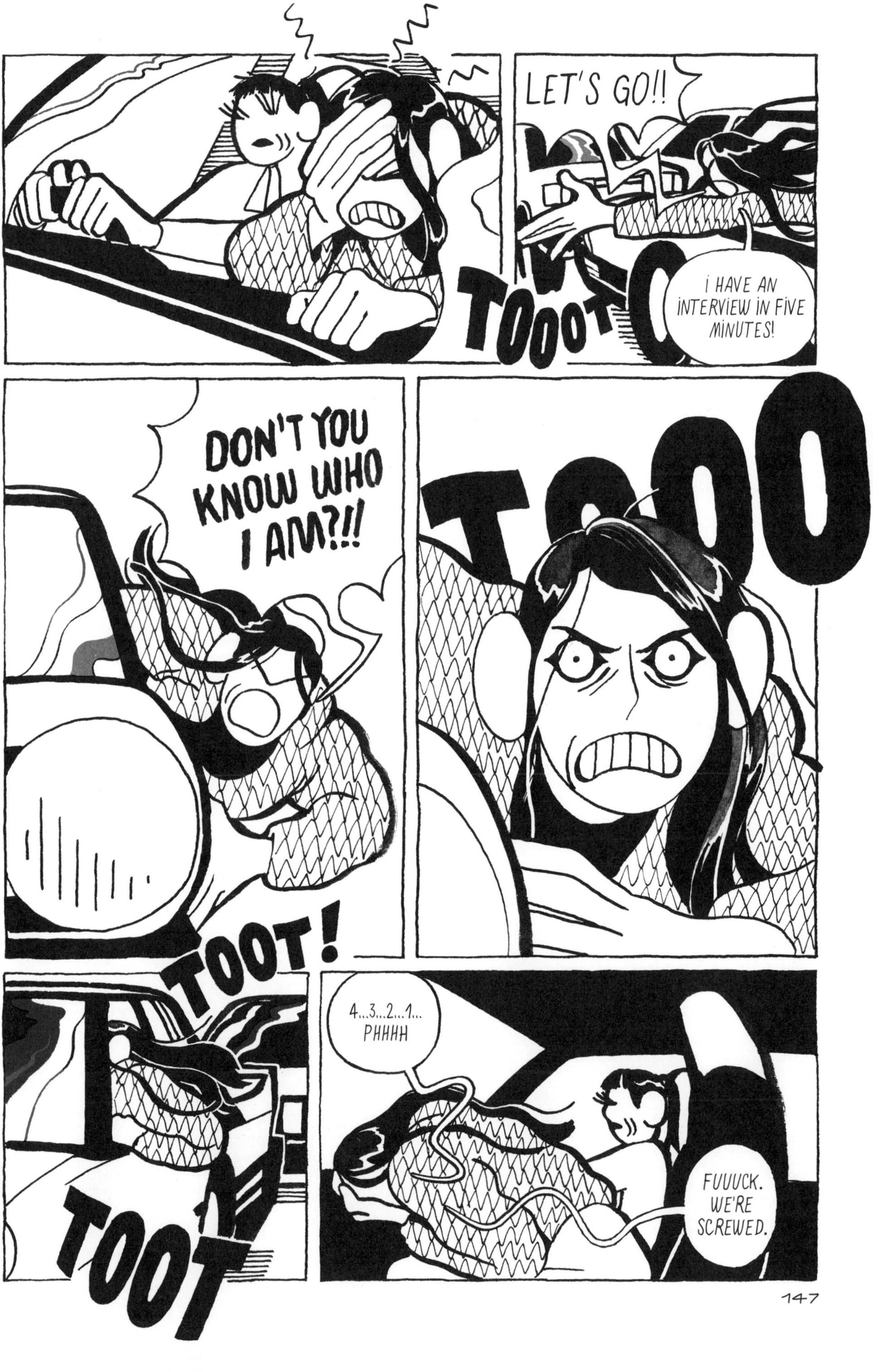
LET'S GO!!
TOOOT
I HAVE AN INTERVIEW IN FIVE MINUTES!
DON'T YOU KNOW WHO I AM?!!
TOOT!
TOOO
TOOT
TOOT
4...3...2...1... PHHHH
FUUUCK. WE'RE SCREWED.

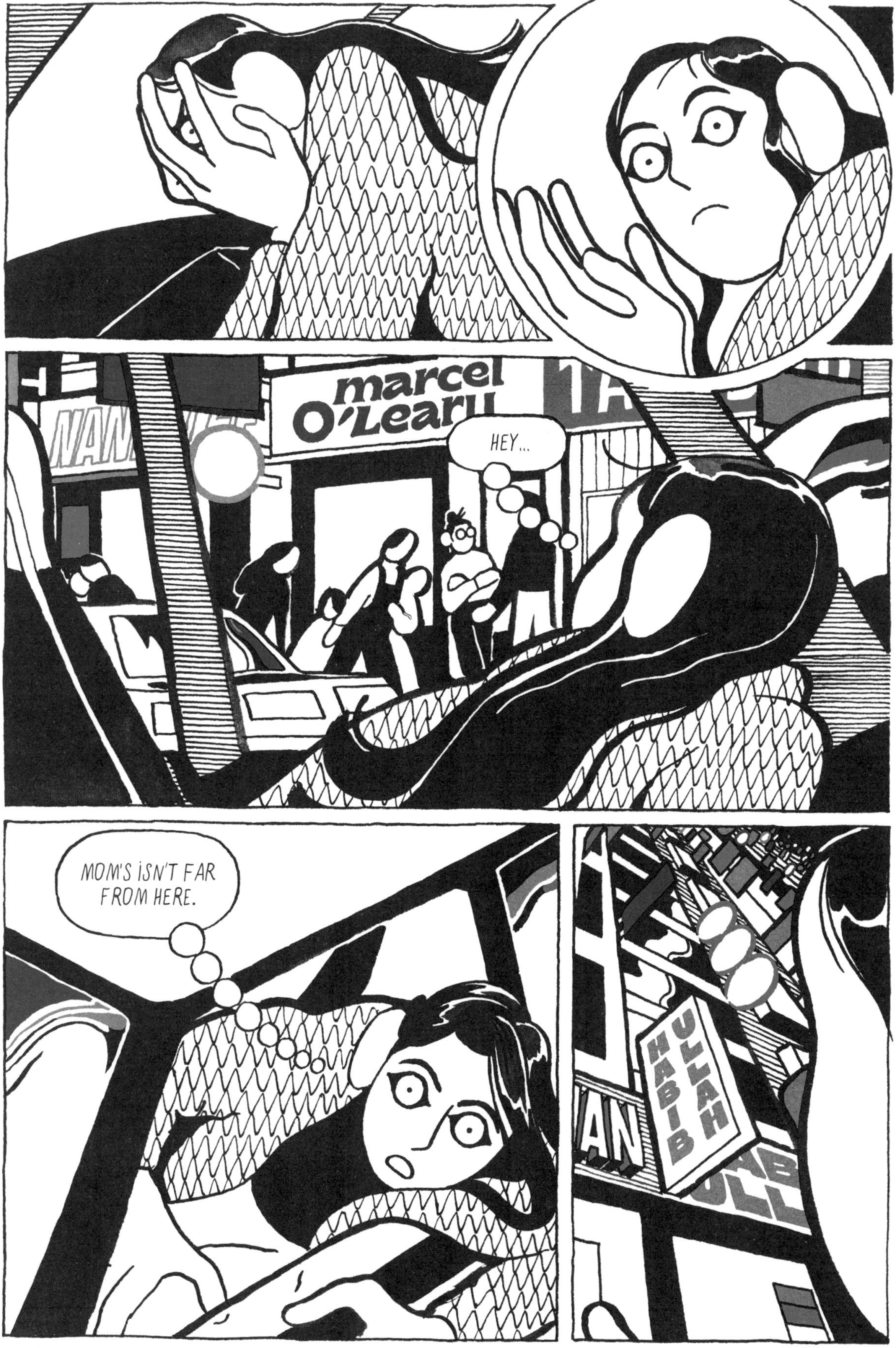
marcel
O'Leary
HEY...
MOM'S ISN'T FAR FROM HERE.
HABIB ULLAH

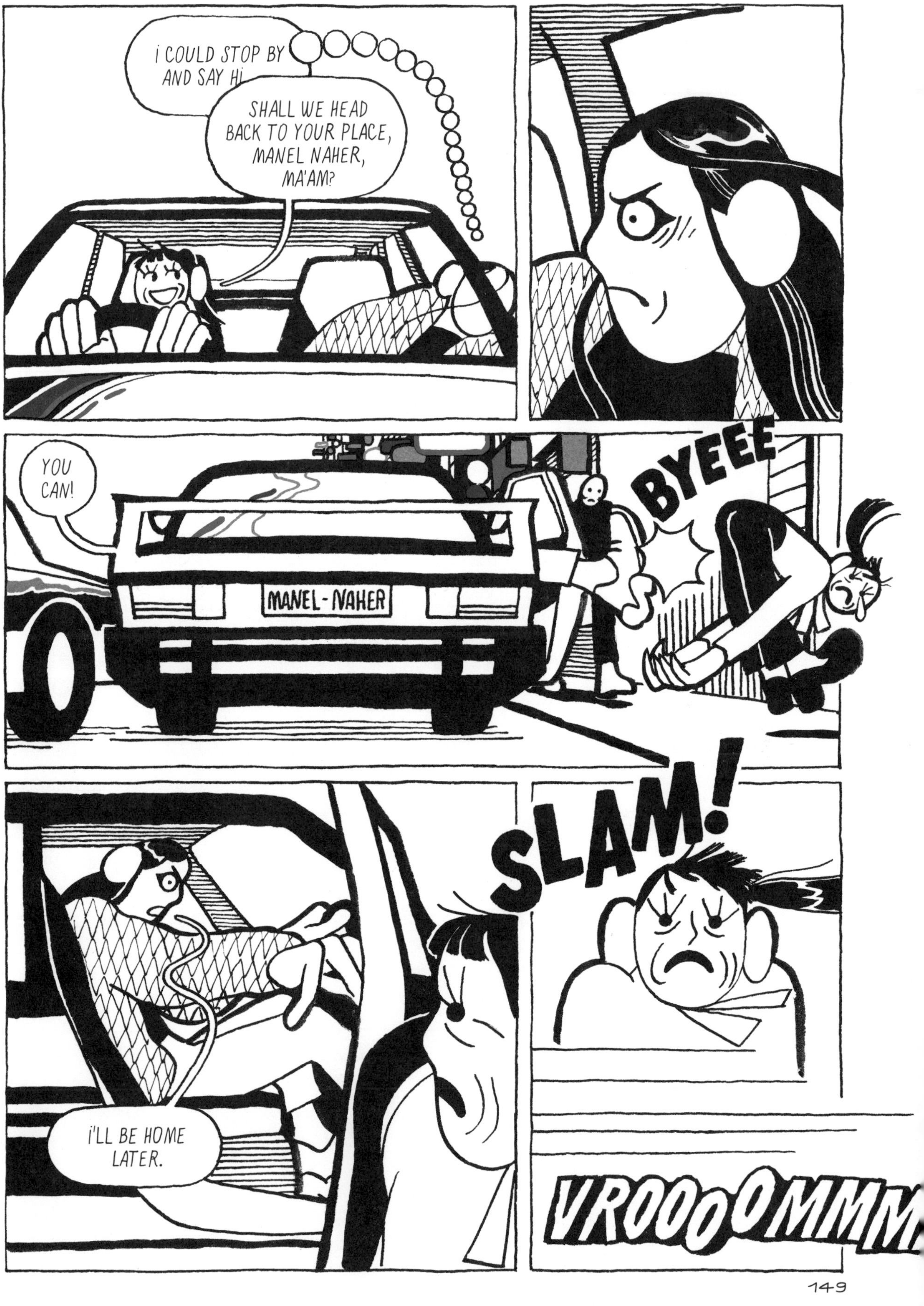
i COULD STOP BY AND SAY Hi
SHALL WE HEAD BACK TO YOUR PLACE, MANEL NAHER, MA'AM?
YOU CAN!
MANEL-NAHER
BYEEE
SLAM!
i'LL BE HOME LATER.
VROOOOOMMMM

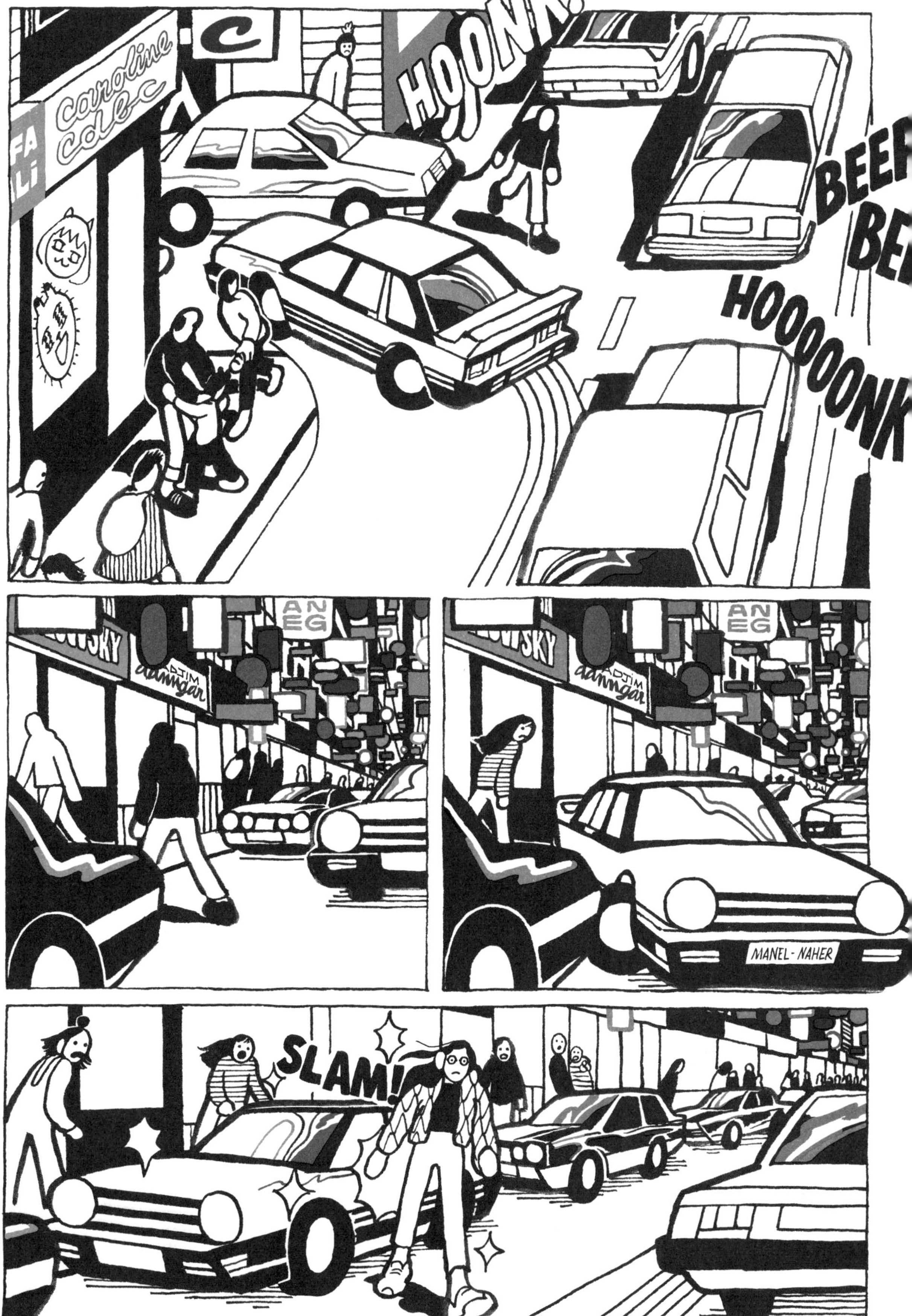
HOONK!
HOOOOOONK
AN EG
MANEL-NAHER
SLAM!

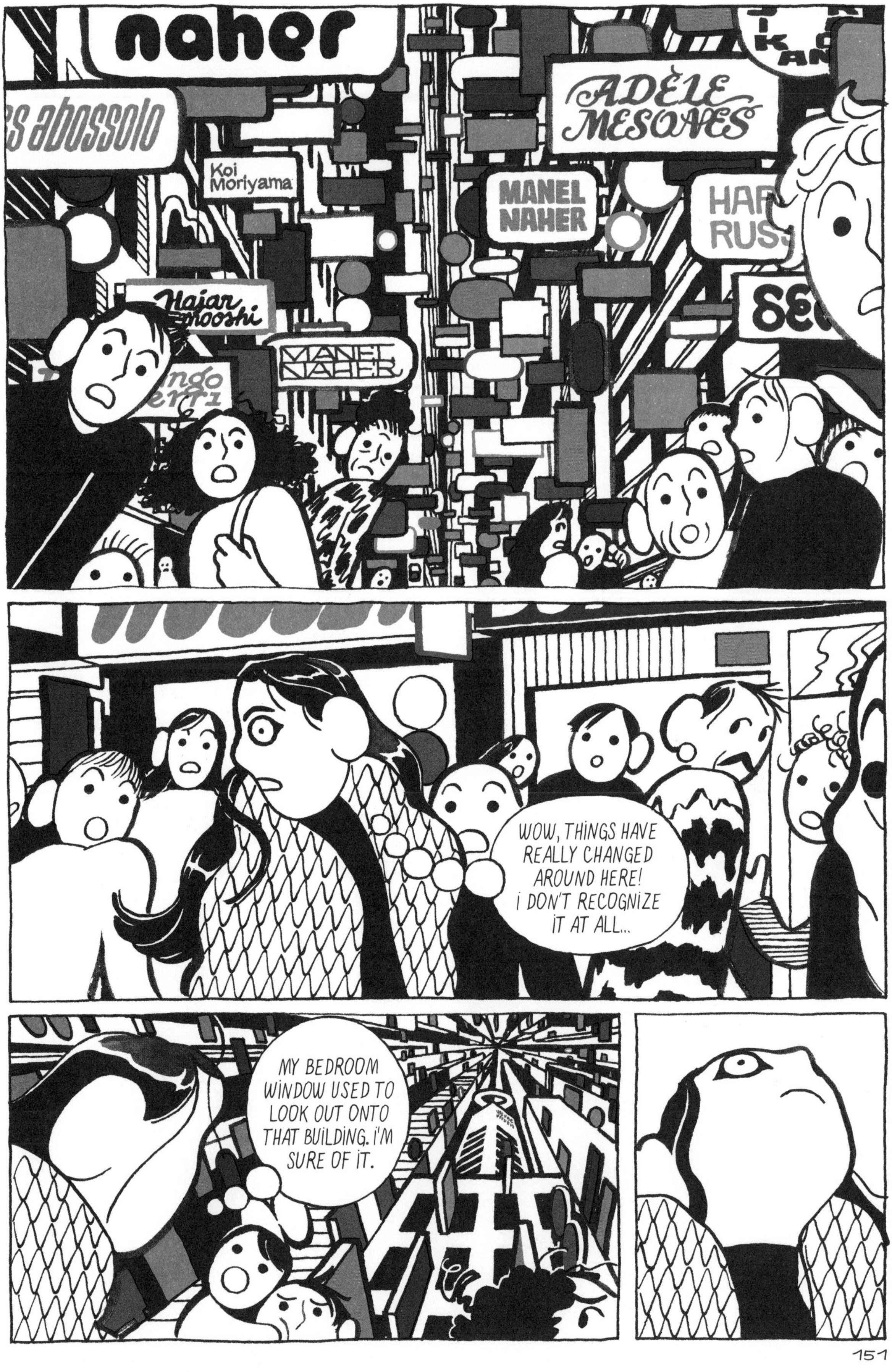
naher
ADÈLE MESONES
Koi Moriyama
MANEL NAHER
WOW, THINGS HAVE REALLY CHANGED AROUND HERE! I DON'T RECOGNIZE IT AT ALL...
MY BEDROOM WINDOW USED TO LOOK OUT ONTO THAT BUILDING. I'M SURE OF IT.

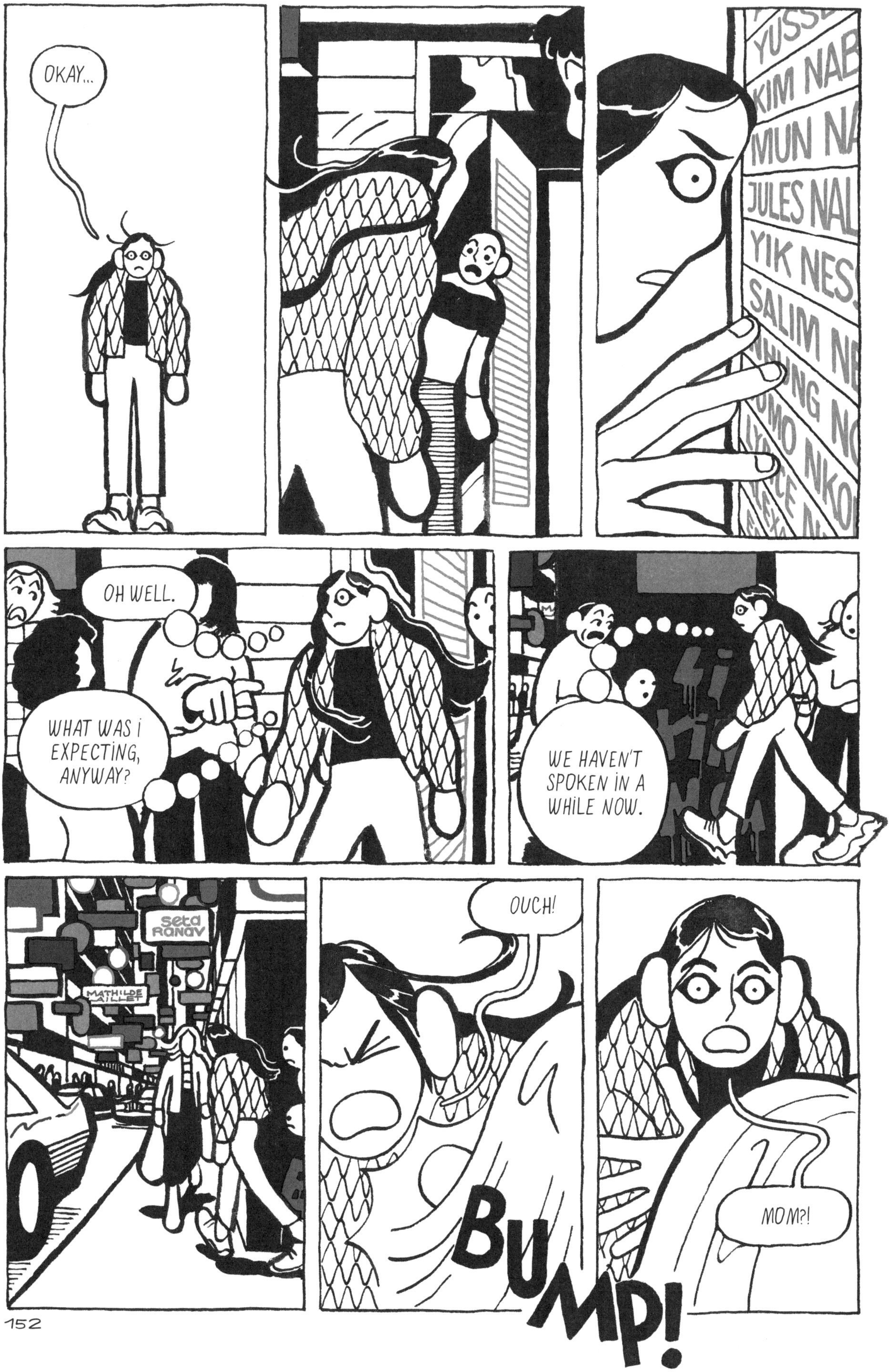
OKAY...
KIM NAB
MUN NA
JULES NAL
YIK NES
SALIM NE
OH WELL.
WHAT WAS I EXPECTING, ANYWAY?
WE HAVEN'T SPOKEN IN A WHILE NOW.
Seta Ranav
OUCH!
BUMP!
MOM?!

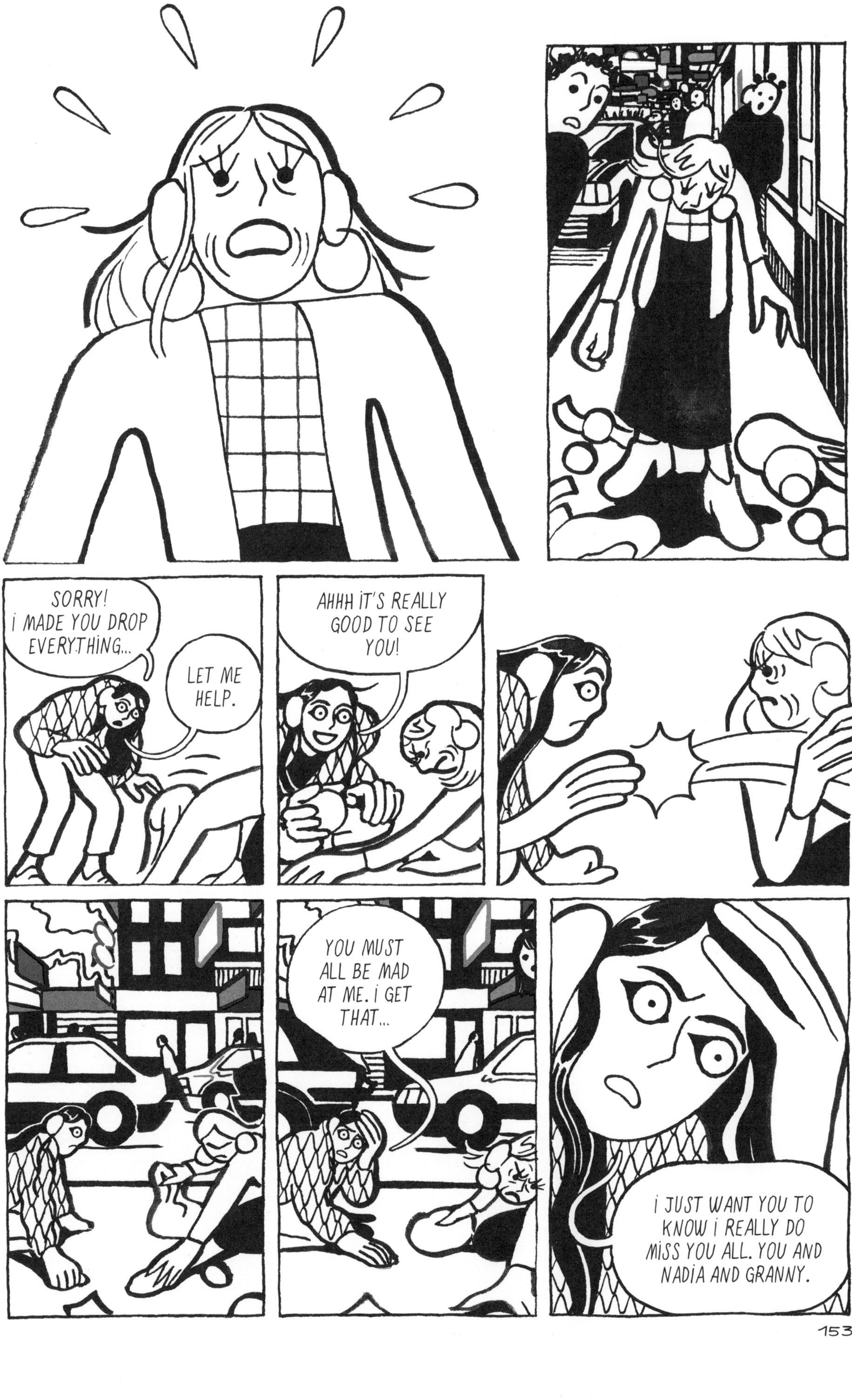
SORRY! I MADE YOU DROP EVERYTHING...
LET ME HELP.
AHHH IT'S REALLY GOOD TO SEE YOU!
YOU MUST ALL BE MAD AT ME. I GET THAT...
I JUST WANT YOU TO KNOW I REALLY DO MISS YOU ALL. YOU AND NADIA AND GRANNY.

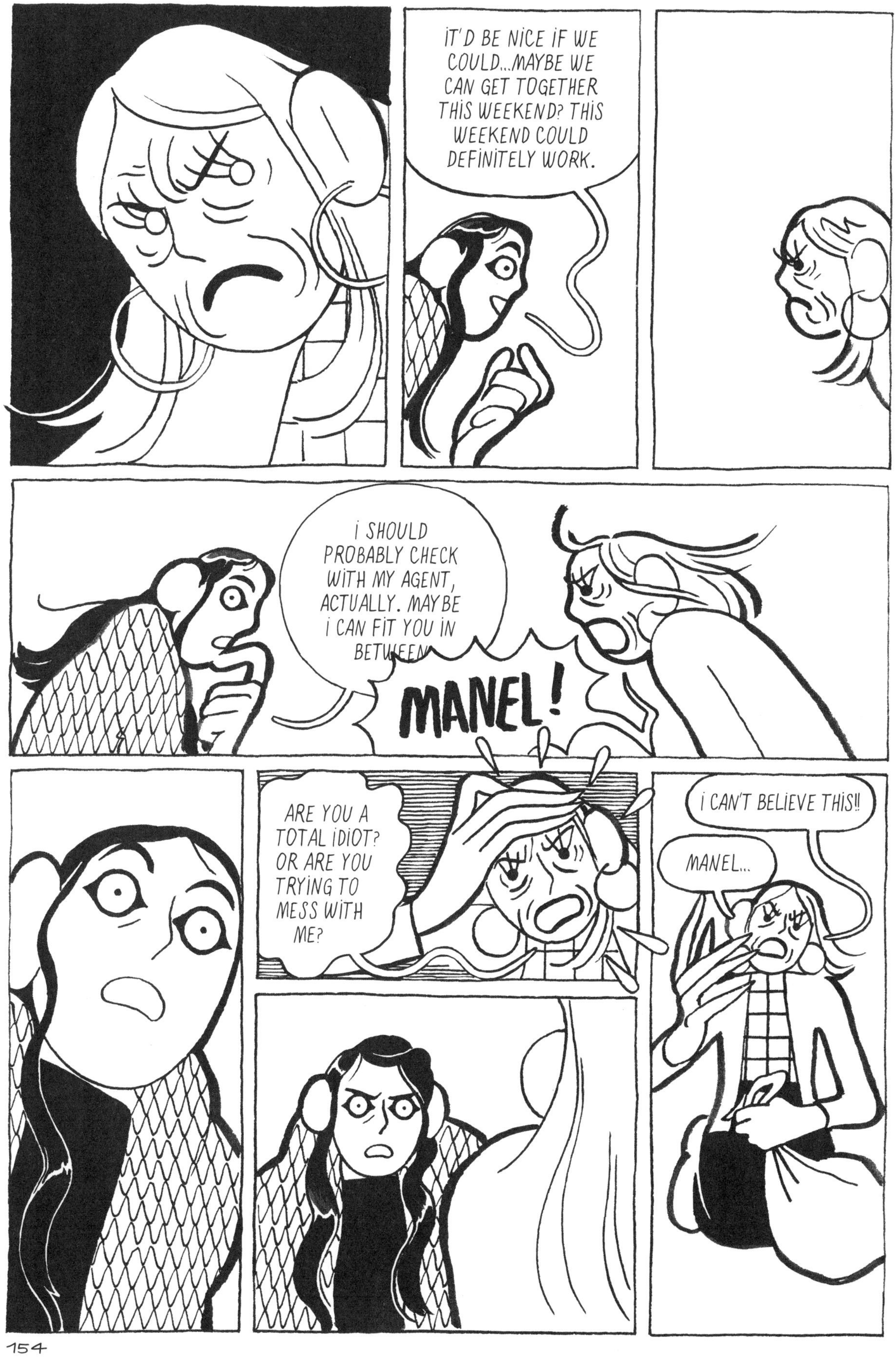
IT'D BE NICE IF WE COULD...MAYBE WE CAN GET TOGETHER THIS WEEKEND? THIS WEEKEND COULD DEFINITELY WORK.
I SHOULD PROBABLY CHECK WITH MY AGENT, ACTUALLY. MAYBE I CAN FIT YOU IN BETWEEN
MANEL!
ARE YOU A TOTAL IDIOT? OR ARE YOU TRYING TO MESS WITH ME?
I CAN'T BELIEVE THIS!!
MANEL...

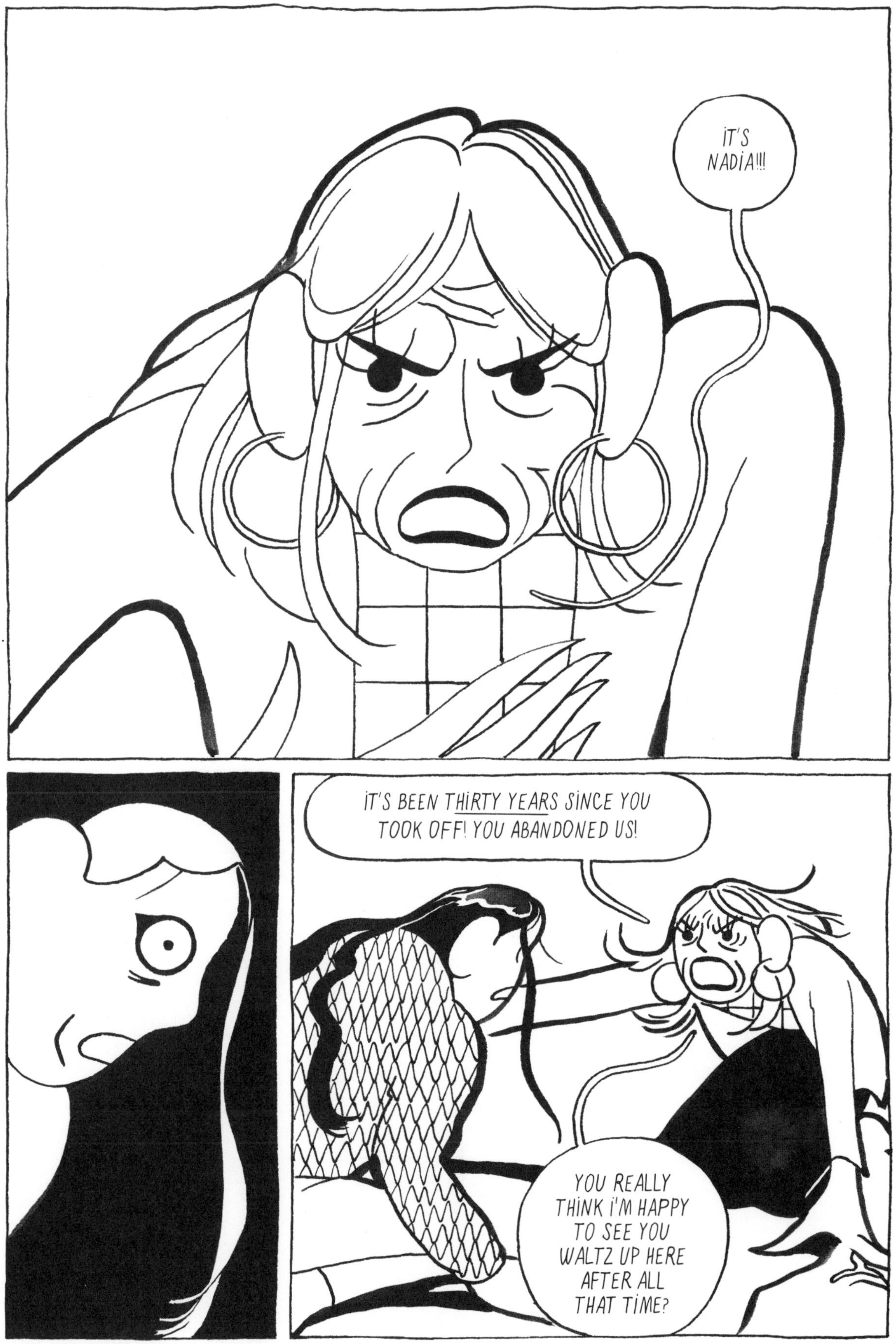
IT'S NADIA!!!
IT'S BEEN THIRTY YEARS SINCE YOU TOOK OFF! YOU ABANDONED US!
YOU REALLY THINK I'M HAPPY TO SEE YOU WALTZ UP HERE AFTER ALL THAT TIME?

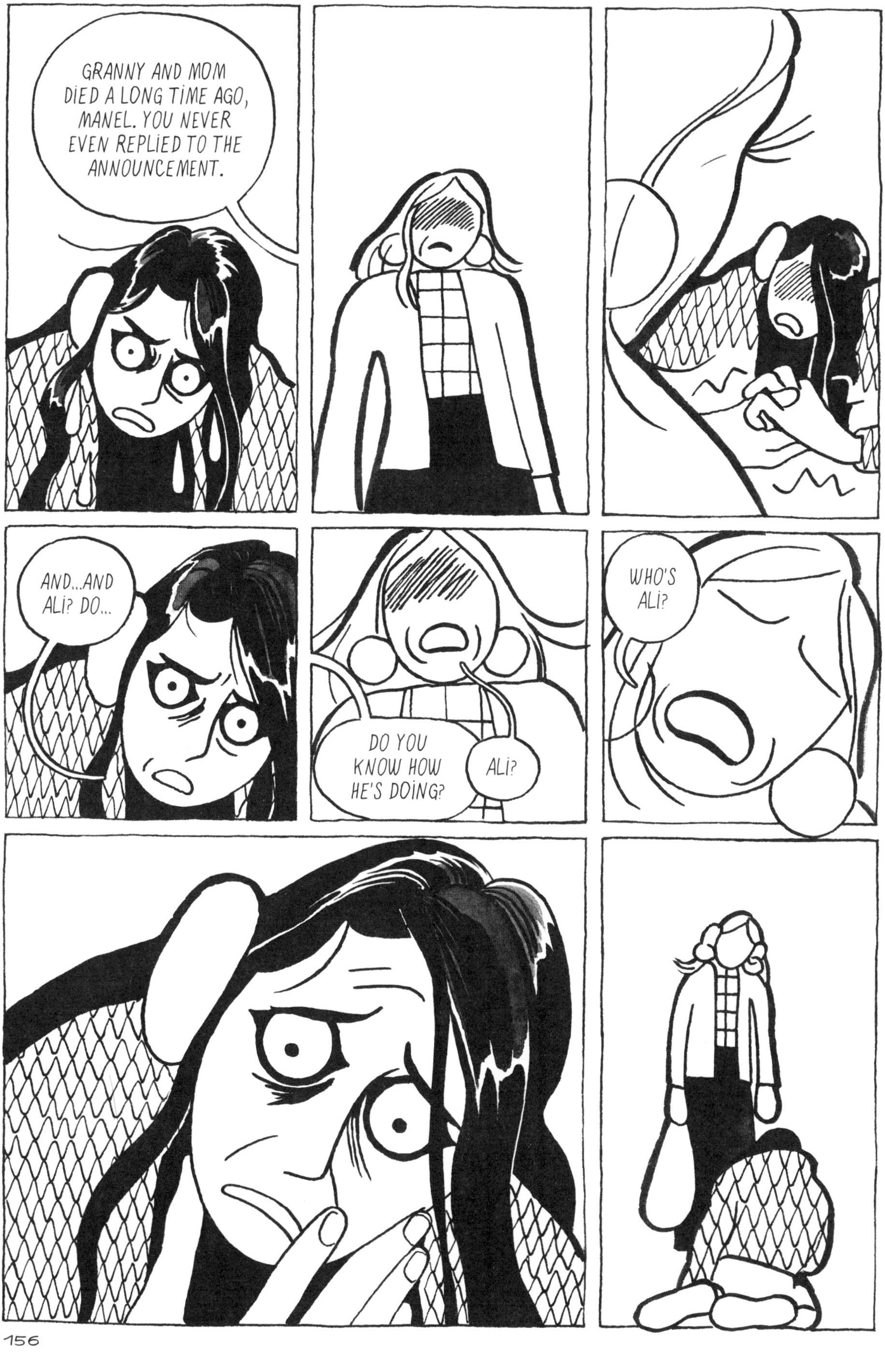
GRANNY AND MOM DIED A LONG TIME AGO, MANEL. YOU NEVER EVEN REPLIED TO THE ANNOUNCEMENT.
AND...AND ALI? DO...
DO YOU KNOW HOW HE'S DOING?
ALI?
WHO'S ALI?

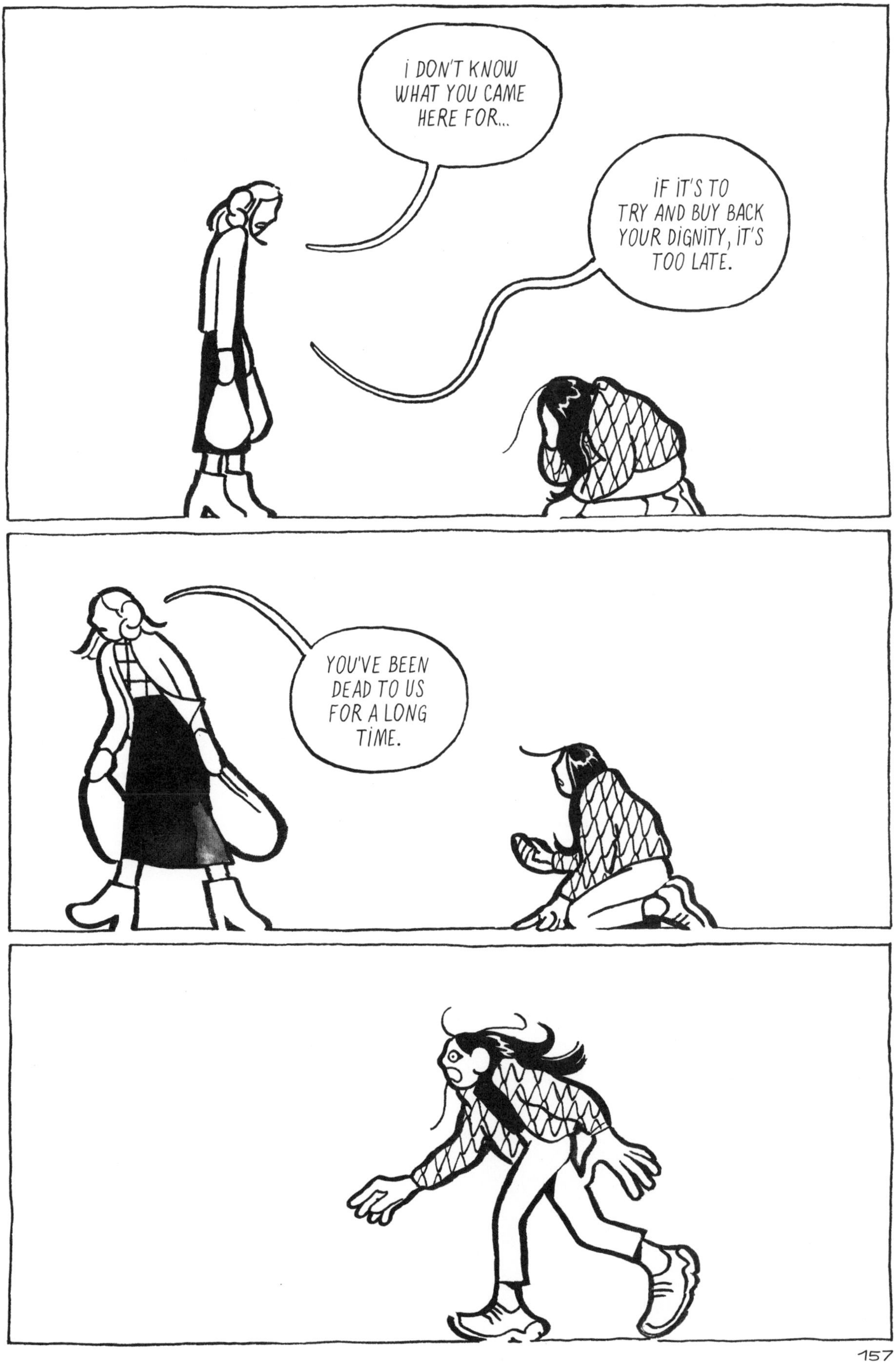
I DON'T KNOW WHAT YOU CAME HERE FOR...
IF IT'S TO TRY AND BUY BACK YOUR DIGNITY, IT'S TOO LATE.
YOU'VE BEEN DEAD TO US FOR A LONG TIME.

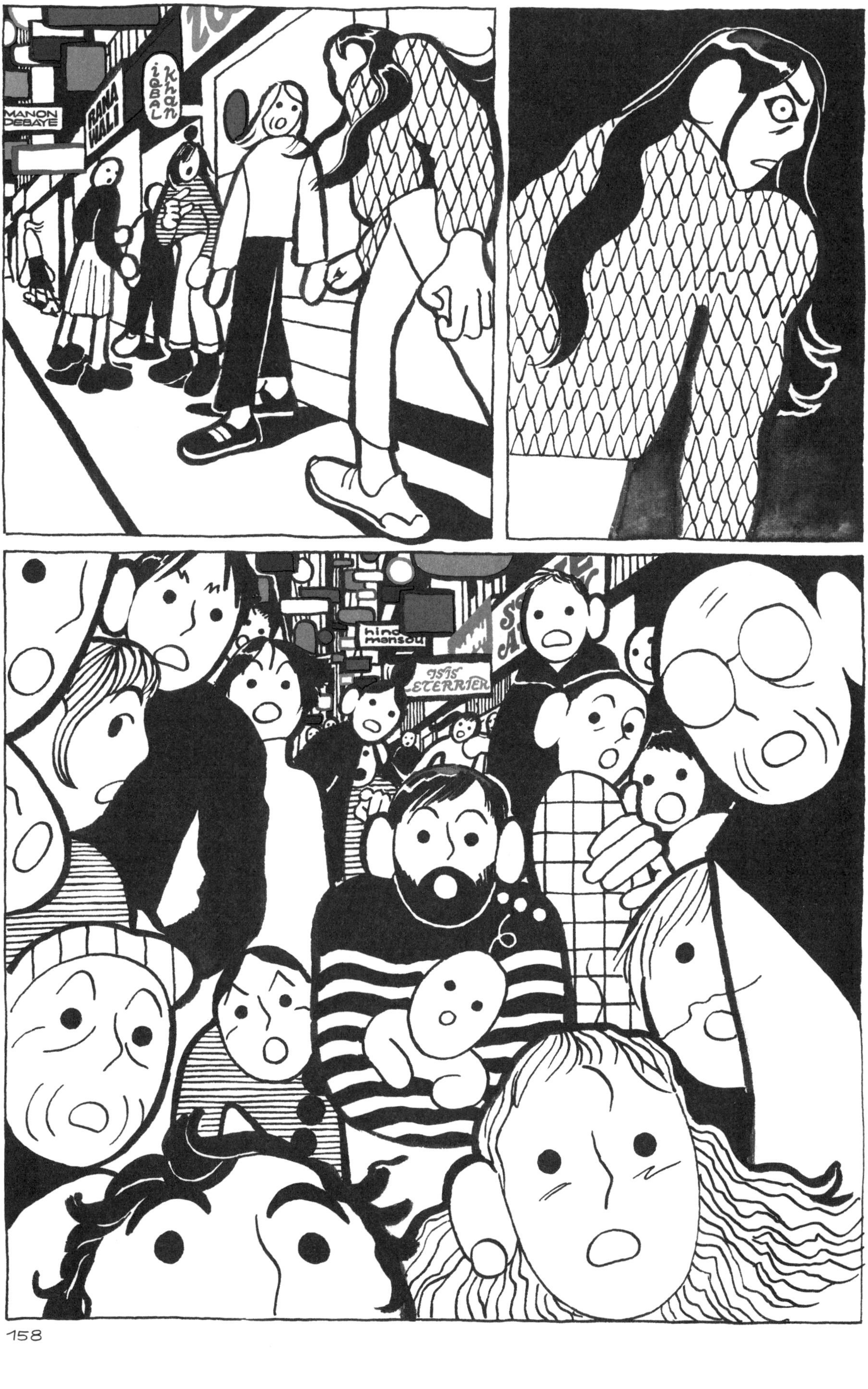
MANON DEBAYE
RANA WALI
iqbal khan
ISIS LETERRIER

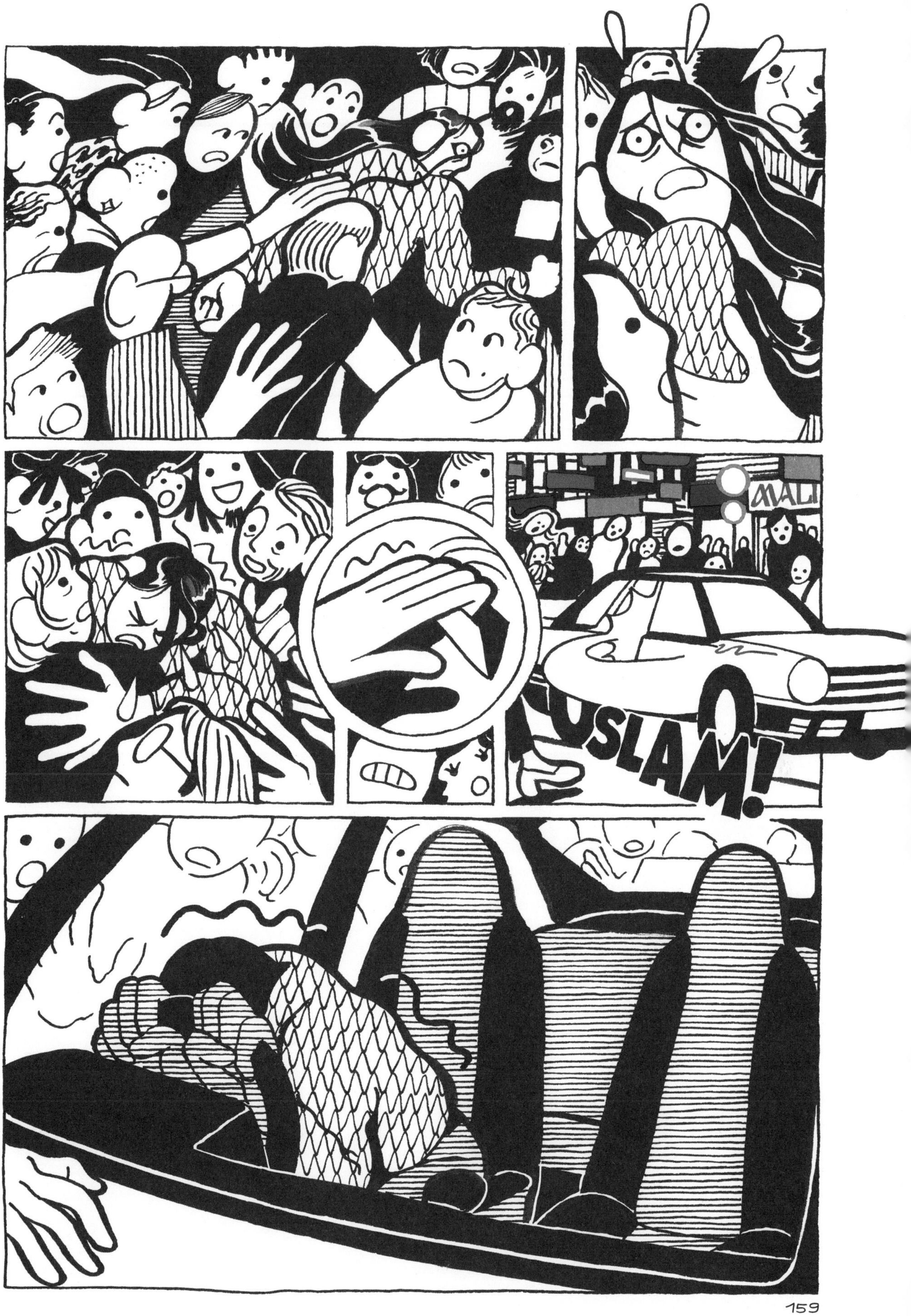
MALI
SLAM!

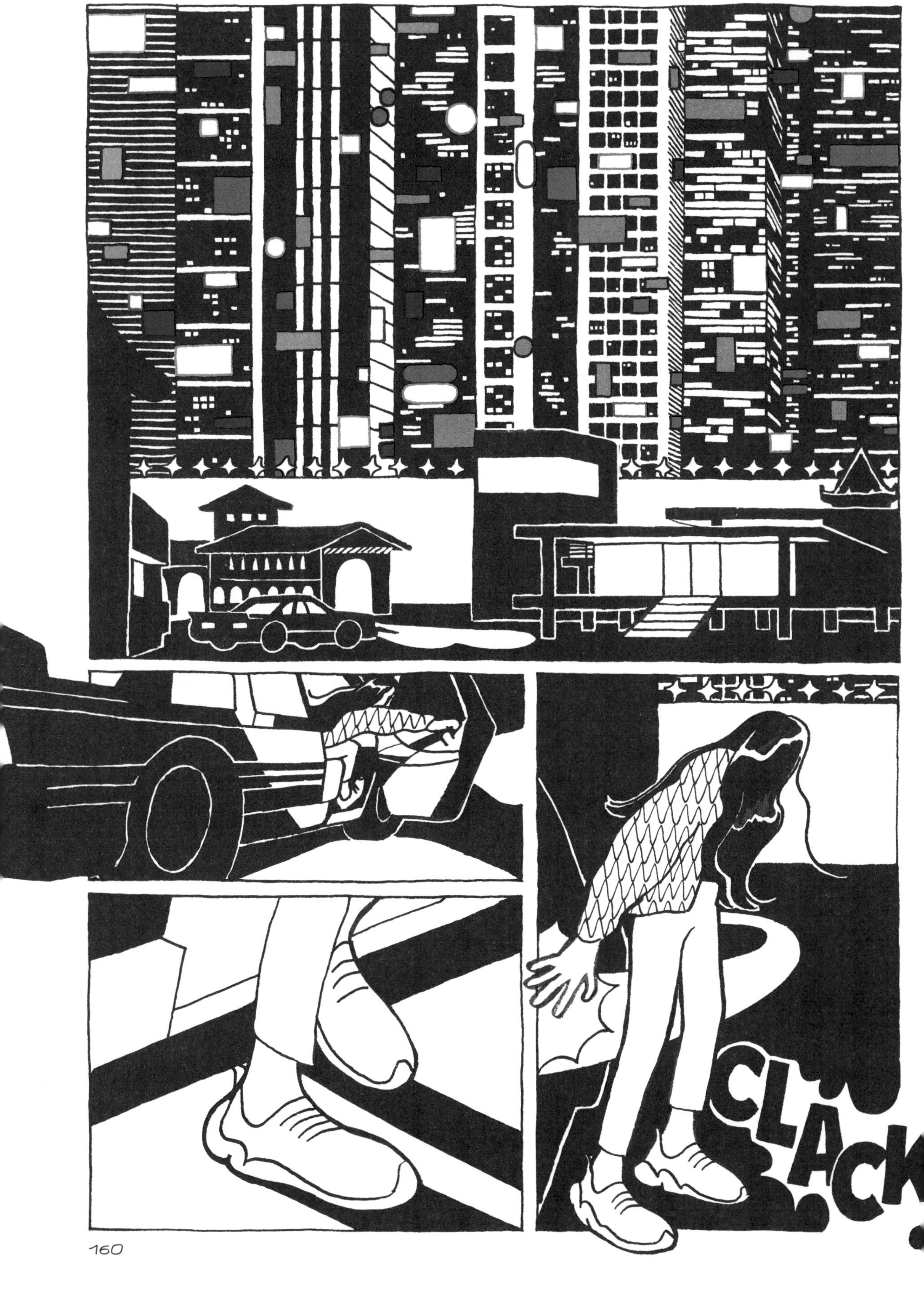
CLACK

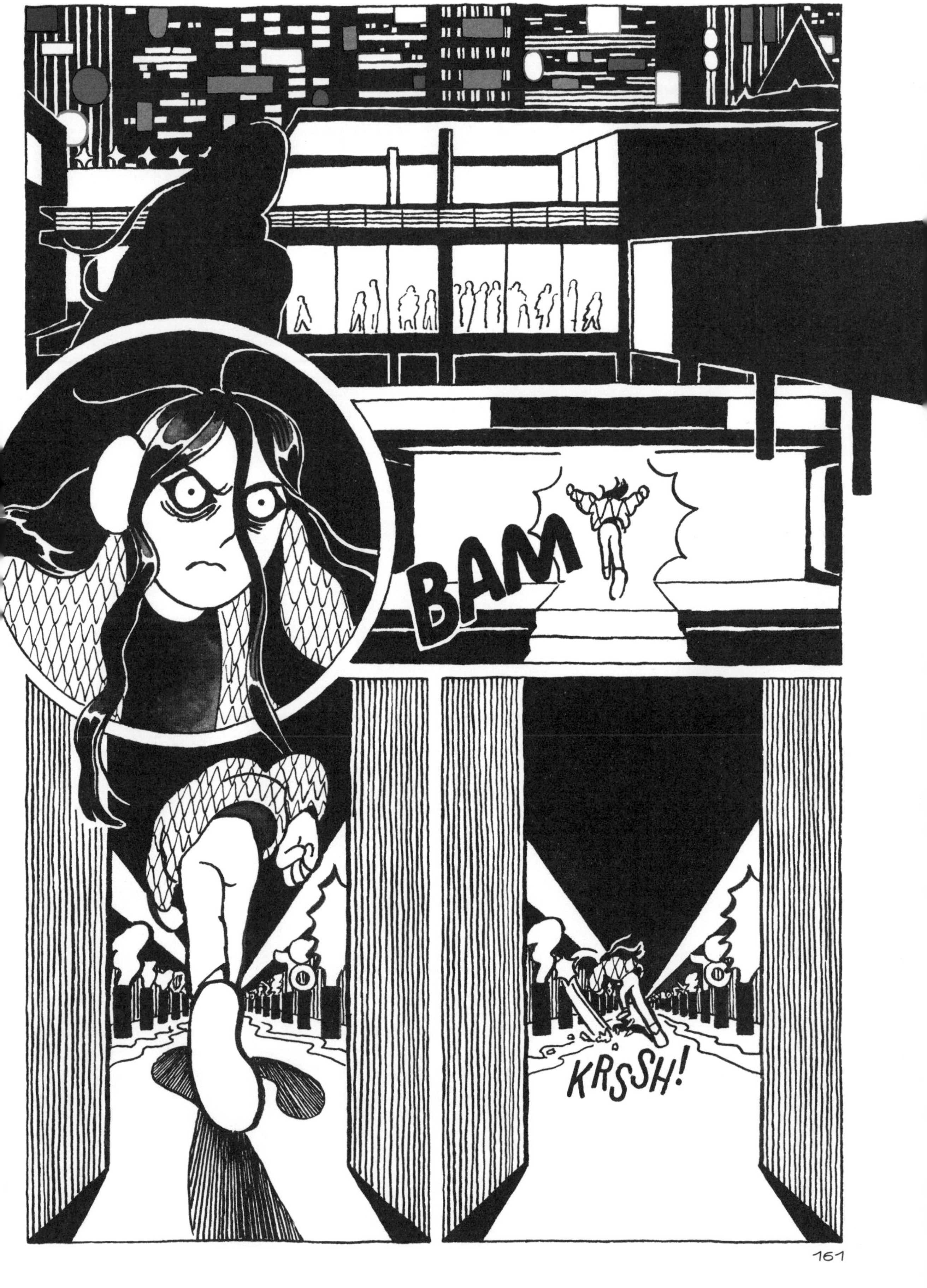
BAM
KRSSH!

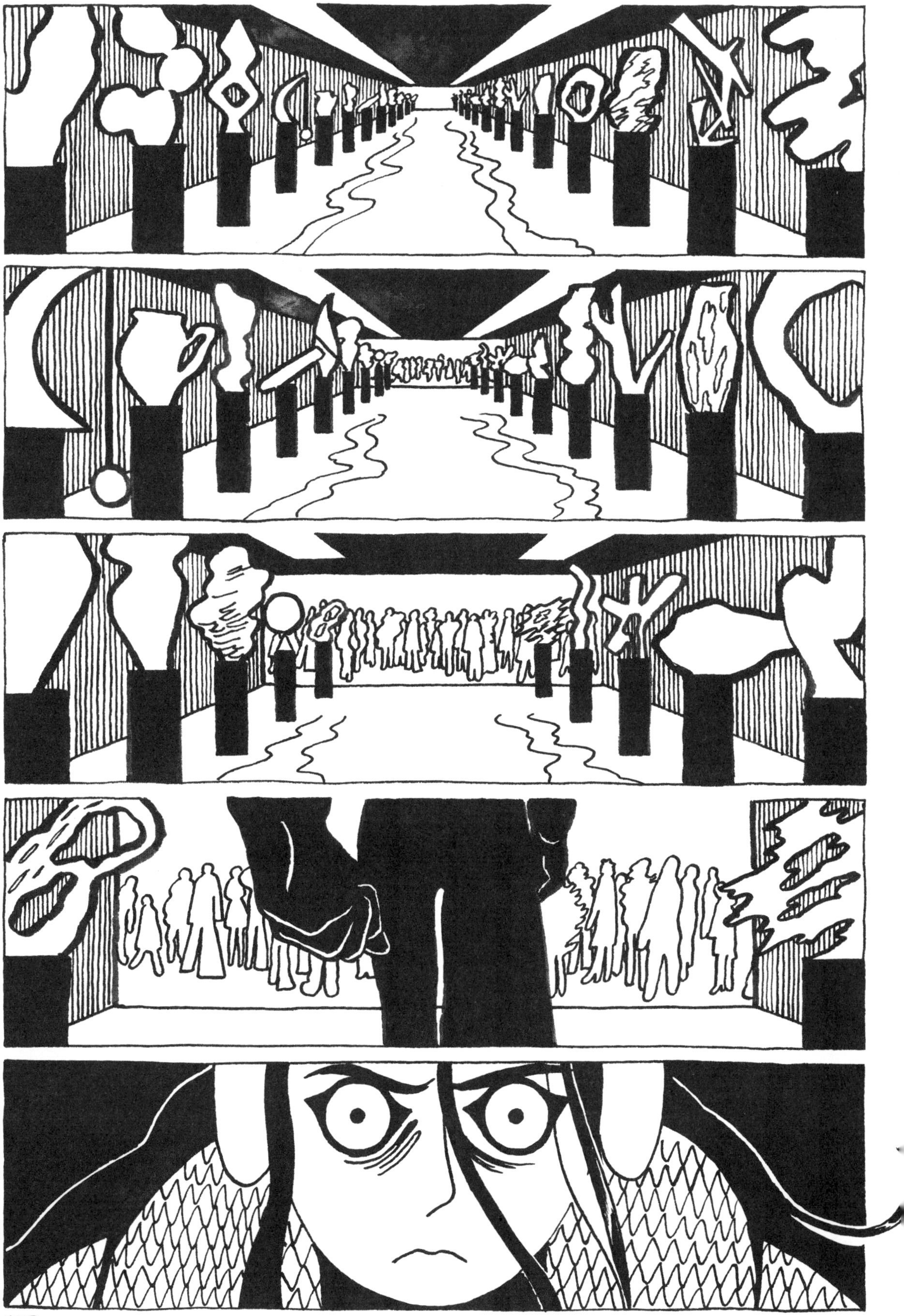

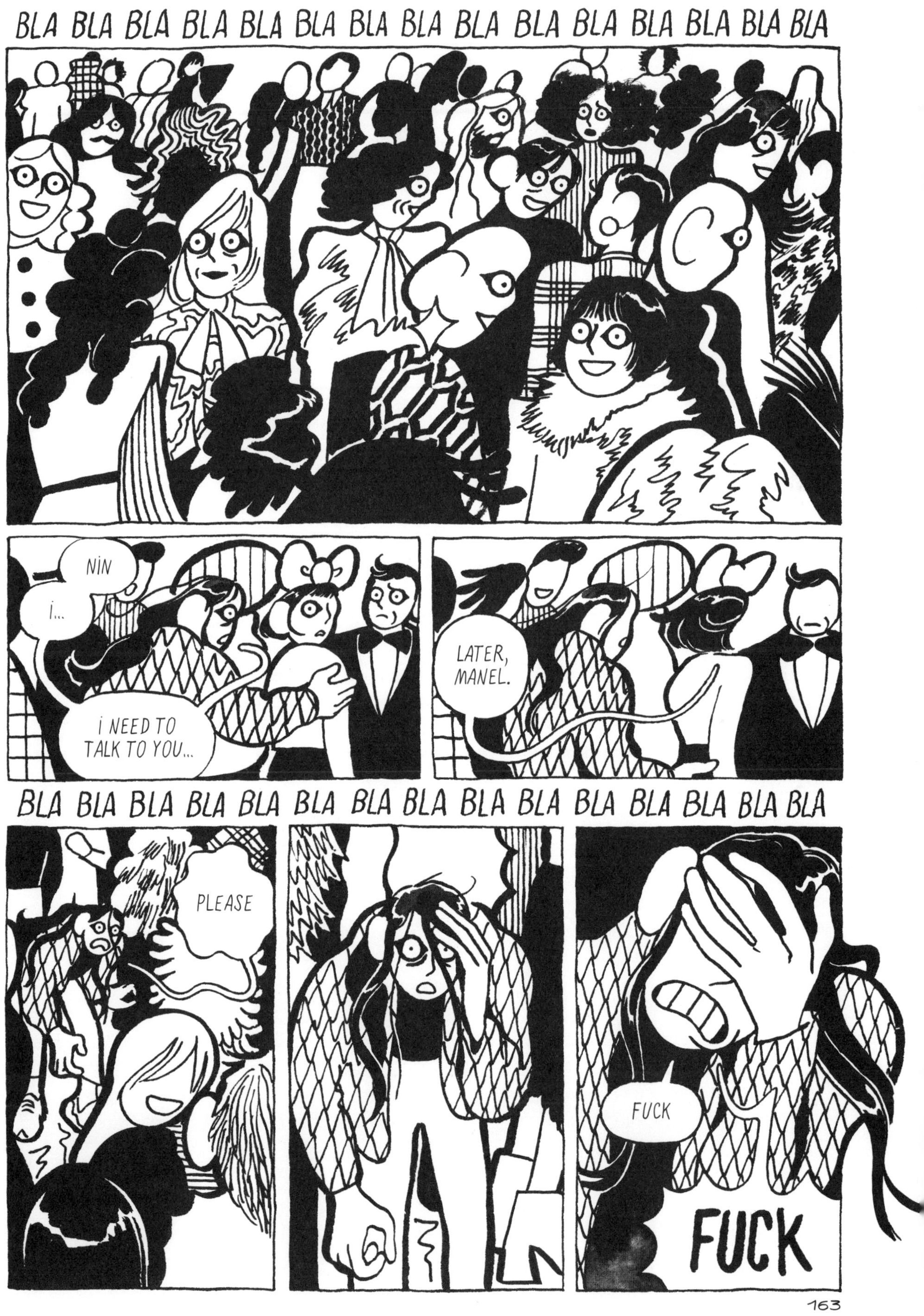
BLA BLA BLA BLA BLA BLA BLA BLA BLA BLA BLA BLA BLA BLA BLA
NIN
I...
I NEED TO TALK TO YOU...
LATER, MANEL.
BLA BLA BLA BLA BLA BLA BLA BLA BLA BLA BLA BLA BLA BLA BLA
PLEASE
FUCK
FUCK

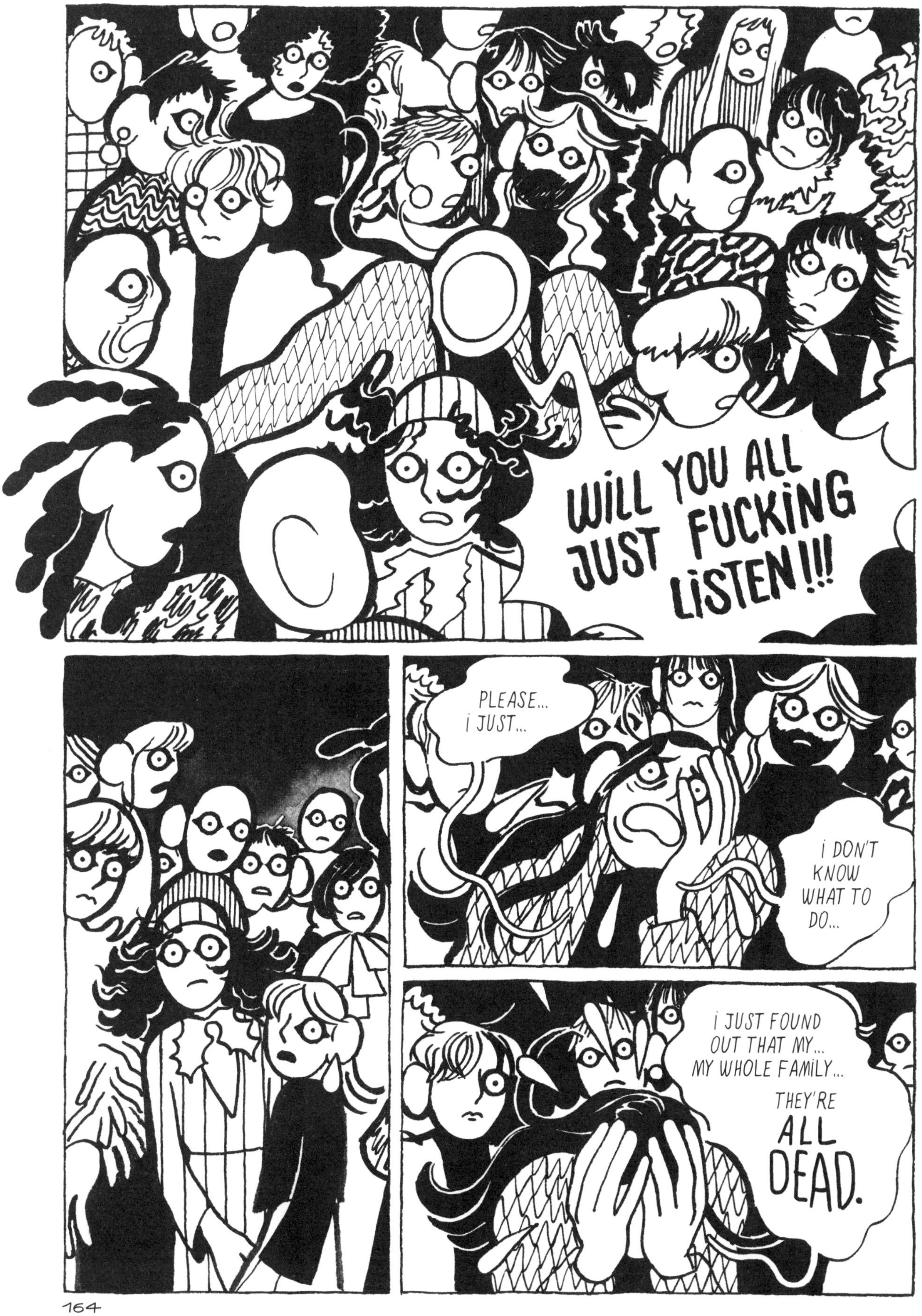
WILL YOU ALL JUST FUCKING LISTEN!!!
PLEASE... I JUST...
I DON'T KNOW WHAT TO DO...
I JUST FOUND OUT THAT MY... MY WHOLE FAMILY...
THEY'RE ALL DEAD.

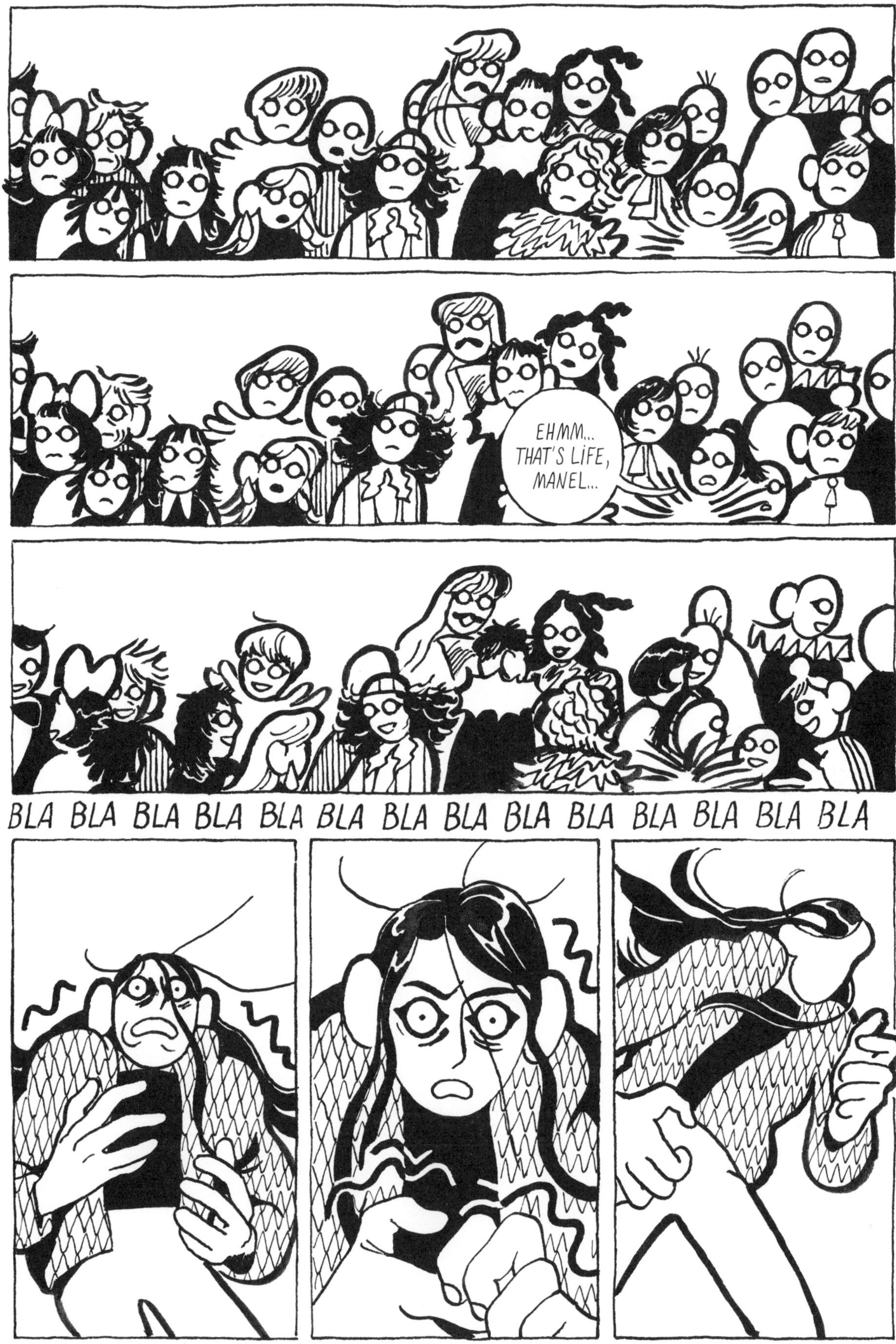
EHMM...
THAT'S LIFE,
MANEL...
BLA BLA BLA BLA BLA BLA BLA BLA BLA BLA BLA BLA BLA BLA

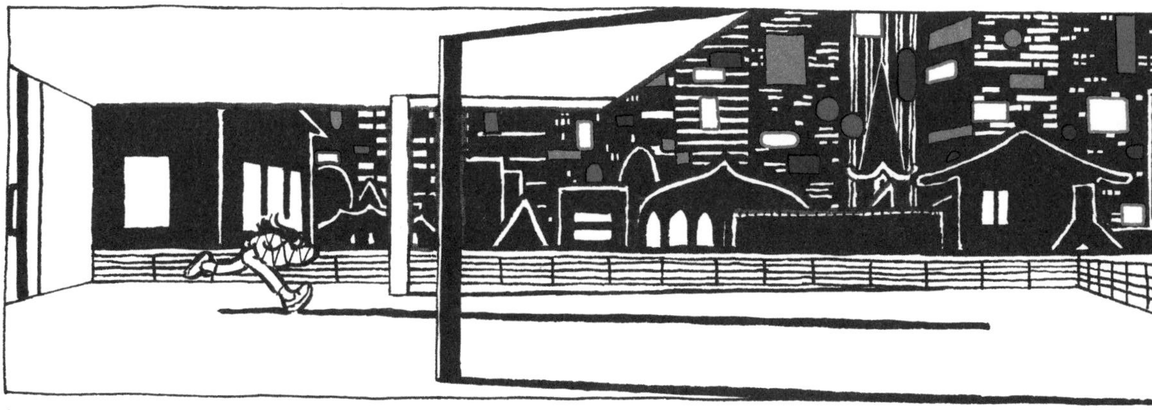

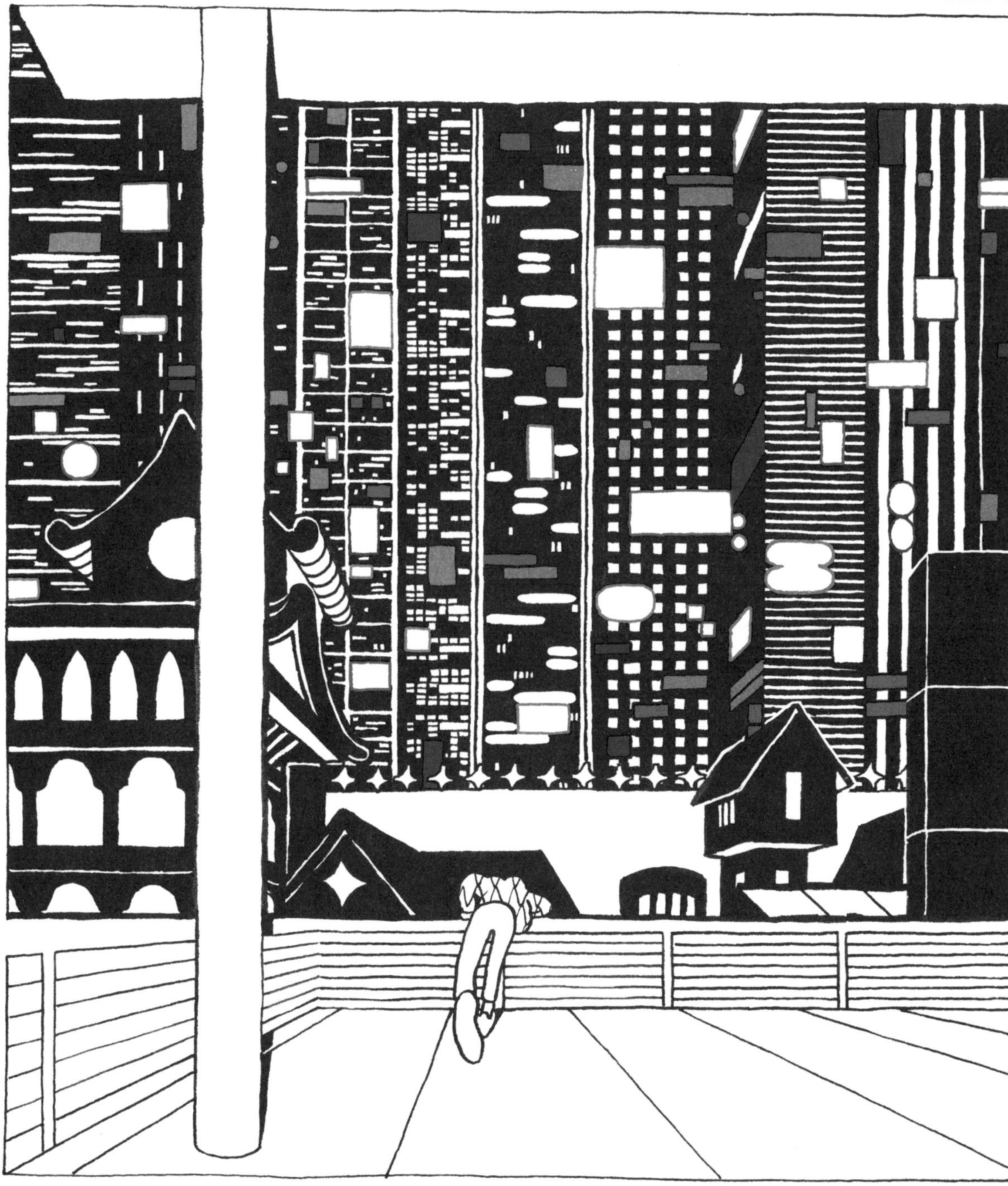

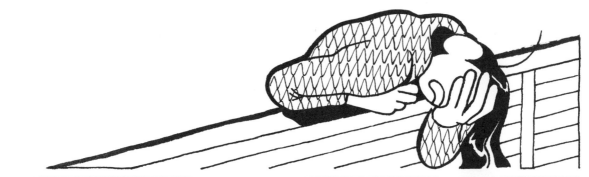

AN IMMORTAL LOSING HER SHIT? HAHA

BEEN A WHILE SINCE I SAW THAT KINDA DISPLAY...

I'M GLAD I STUCK AROUND!

SHK!

SSSSSST

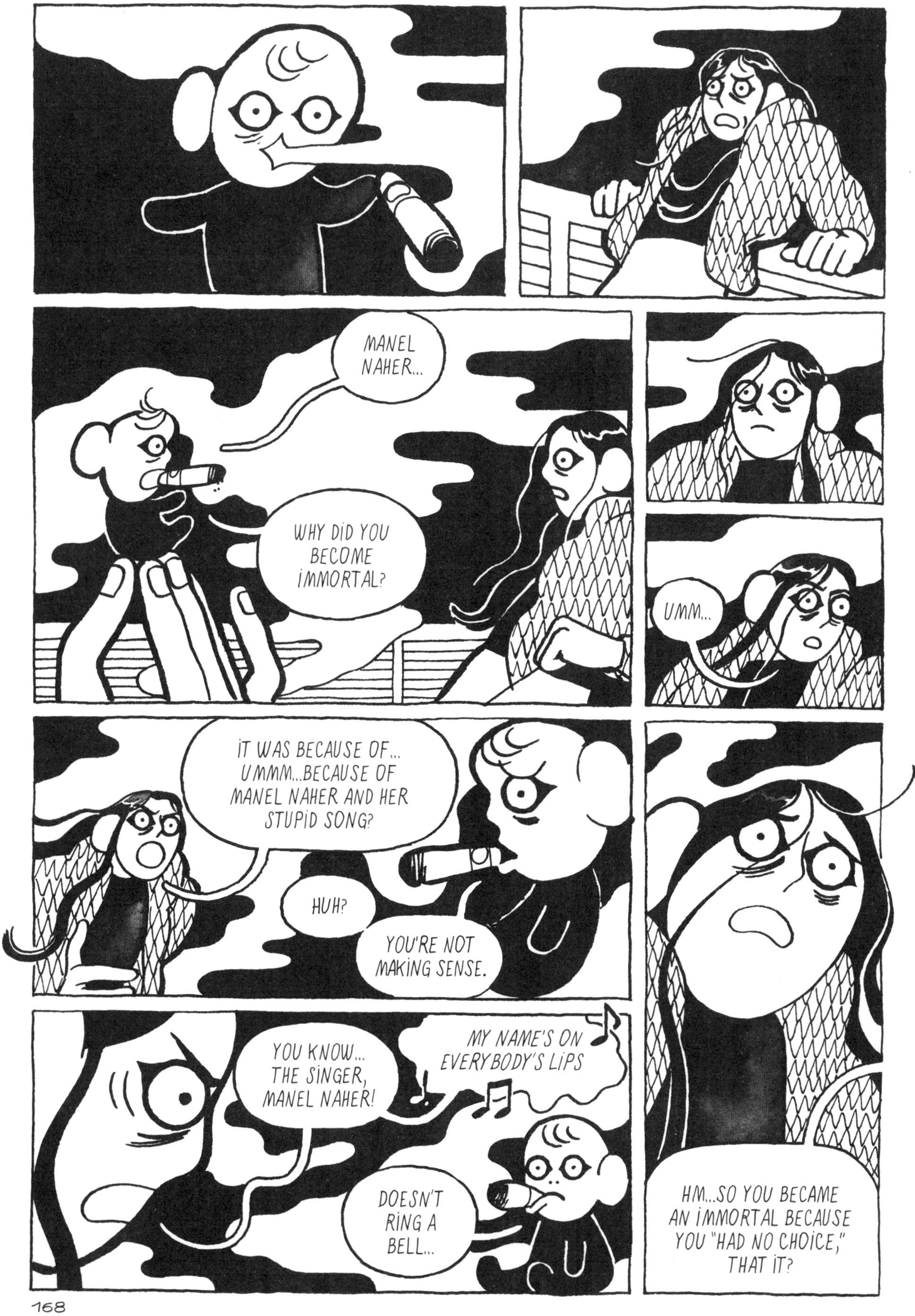
MANEL NAHER...
WHY DID YOU BECOME IMMORTAL?
UMM...
IT WAS BECAUSE OF... UMMM...BECAUSE OF MANEL NAHER AND HER STUPID SONG?
HUH?
YOU'RE NOT MAKING SENSE.
HM...SO YOU BECAME AN IMMORTAL BECAUSE YOU "HAD NO CHOICE," THAT IT?
YOU KNOW... THE SINGER, MANEL NAHER!
MY NAME'S ON EVERYBODY'S LIPS
DOESN'T RING A BELL...

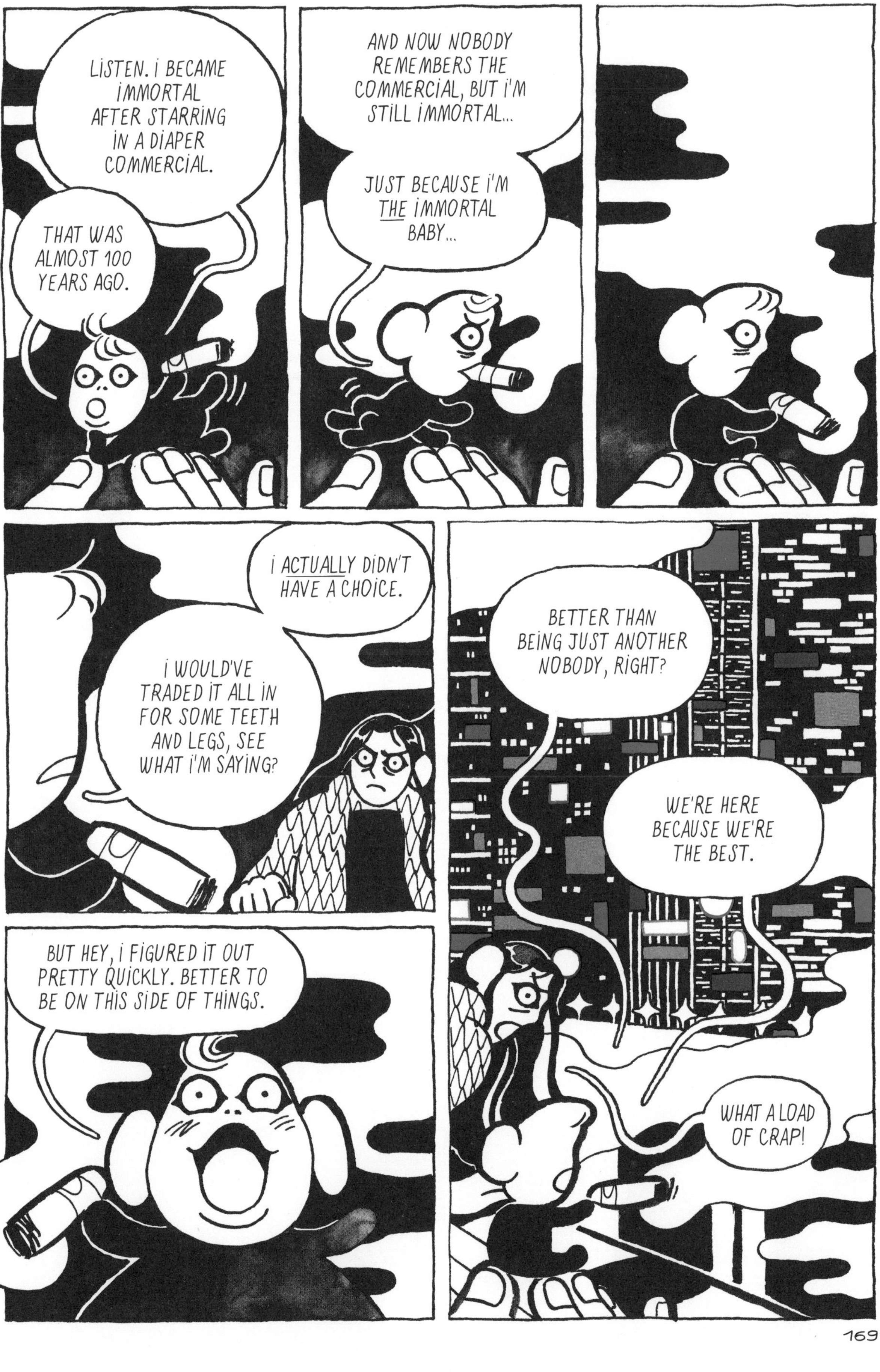
LISTEN. I BECAME IMMORTAL AFTER STARRING IN A DIAPER COMMERCIAL.
THAT WAS ALMOST 100 YEARS AGO.
AND NOW NOBODY REMEMBERS THE COMMERCIAL, BUT I'M STILL IMMORTAL...
JUST BECAUSE I'M THE IMMORTAL BABY...
I ACTUALLY DIDN'T HAVE A CHOICE.
I WOULD'VE TRADED IT ALL IN FOR SOME TEETH AND LEGS, SEE WHAT I'M SAYING?
BUT HEY, I FIGURED IT OUT PRETTY QUICKLY. BETTER TO BE ON THIS SIDE OF THINGS.
BETTER THAN BEING JUST ANOTHER NOBODY, RIGHT?
WE'RE HERE BECAUSE WE'RE THE BEST.
WHAT A LOAD OF CRAP!

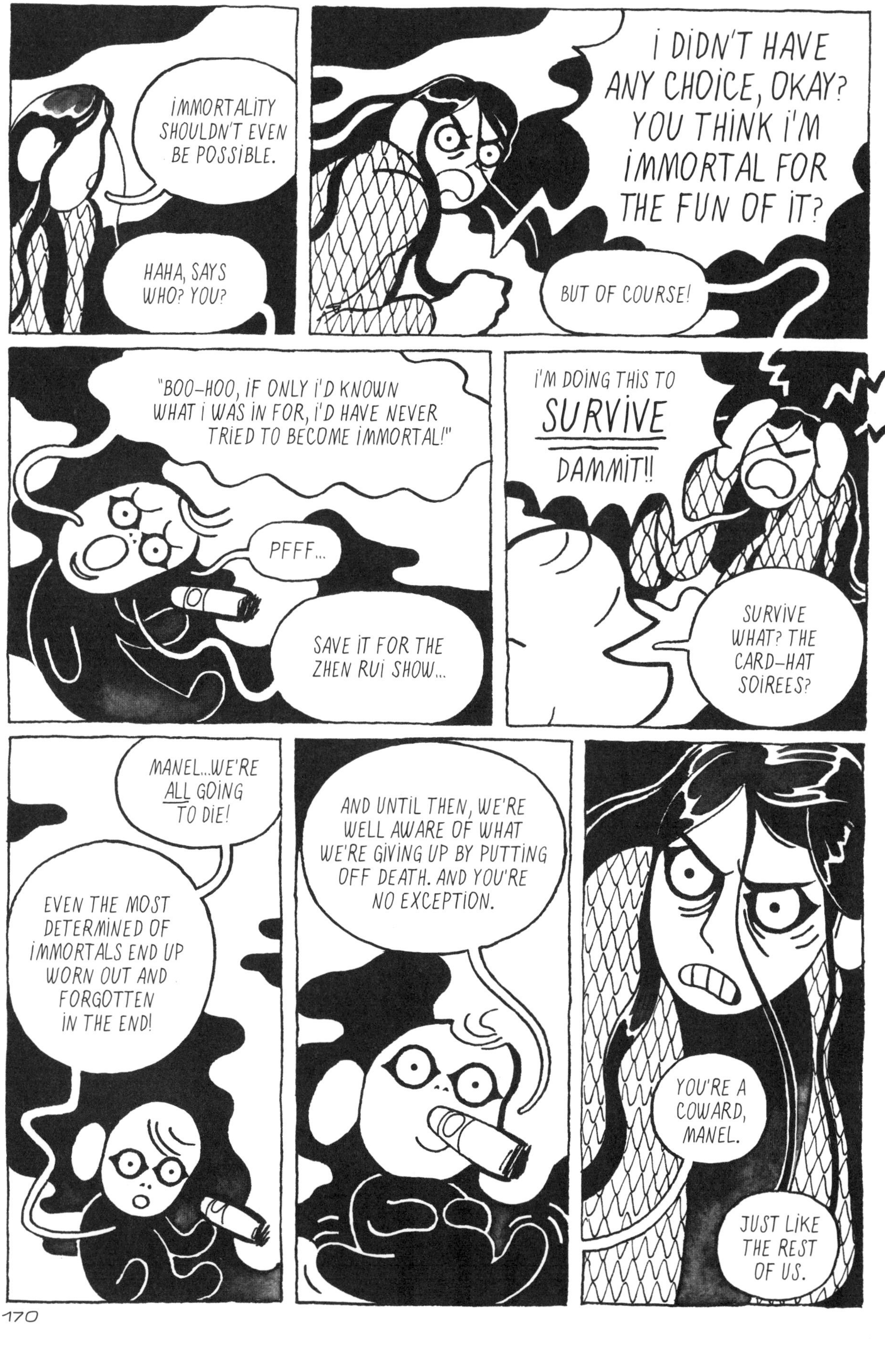

IMMORTALITY SHOULDN'T EVEN BE POSSIBLE.
HAHA, SAYS WHO? YOU?
I DIDN'T HAVE ANY CHOICE, OKAY? YOU THINK I'M IMMORTAL FOR THE FUN OF IT?
BUT OF COURSE!
"BOO-HOO, IF ONLY I'D KNOWN WHAT I WAS IN FOR, I'D HAVE NEVER TRIED TO BECOME IMMORTAL!"
PFFF...
SAVE IT FOR THE ZHEN RUI SHOW...
I'M DOING THIS TO SURVIVE DAMMIT!!
SURVIVE WHAT? THE CARD-HAT SOIREES?
MANEL...WE'RE ALL GOING TO DIE!
EVEN THE MOST DETERMINED OF IMMORTALS END UP WORN OUT AND FORGOTTEN IN THE END!
AND UNTIL THEN, WE'RE WELL AWARE OF WHAT WE'RE GIVING UP BY PUTTING OFF DEATH. AND YOU'RE NO EXCEPTION.
YOU'RE A COWARD, MANEL.
JUST LIKE THE REST OF US.

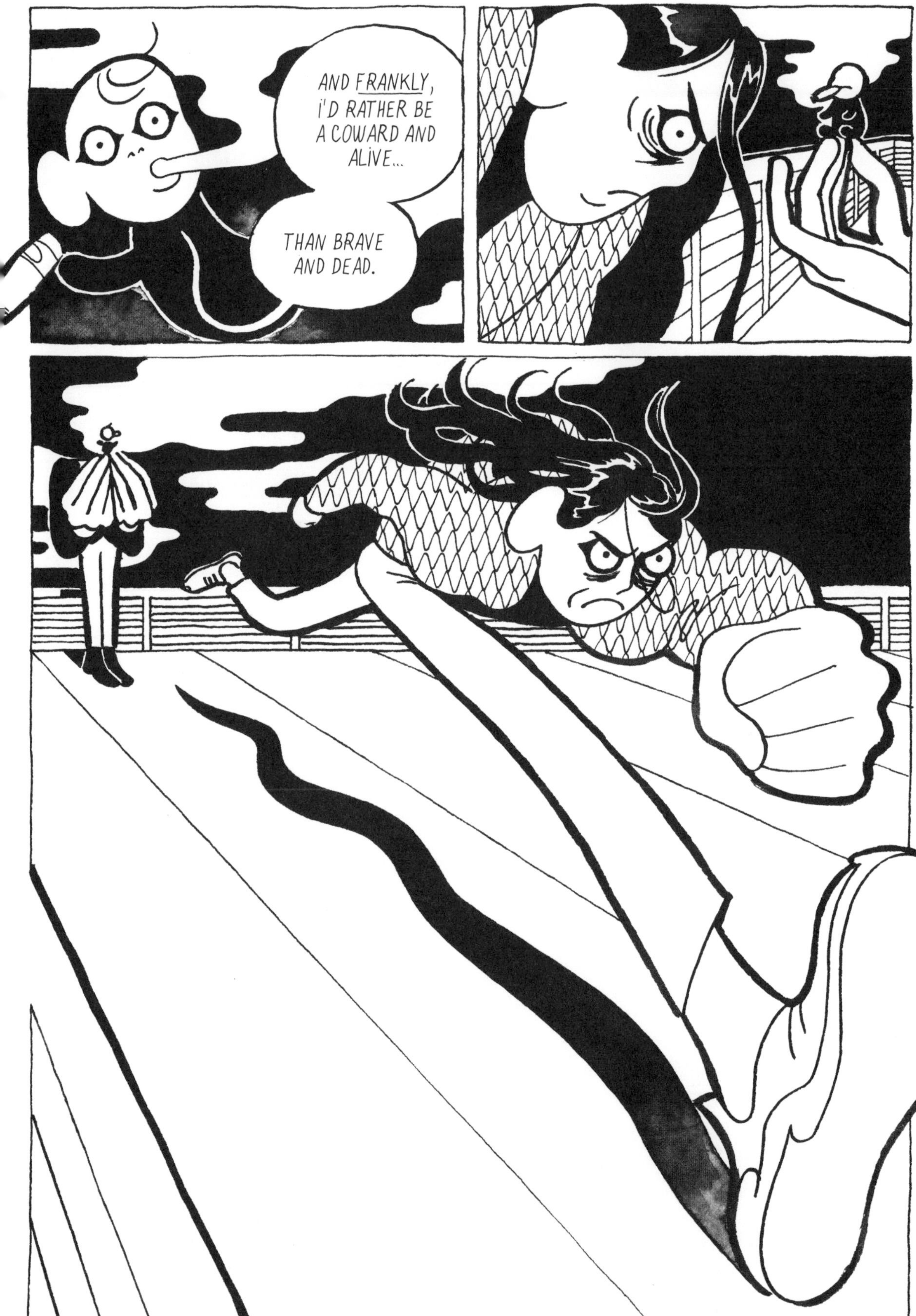
AND FRANKLY, I'D RATHER BE A COWARD AND ALIVE...
THAN BRAVE AND DEAD.

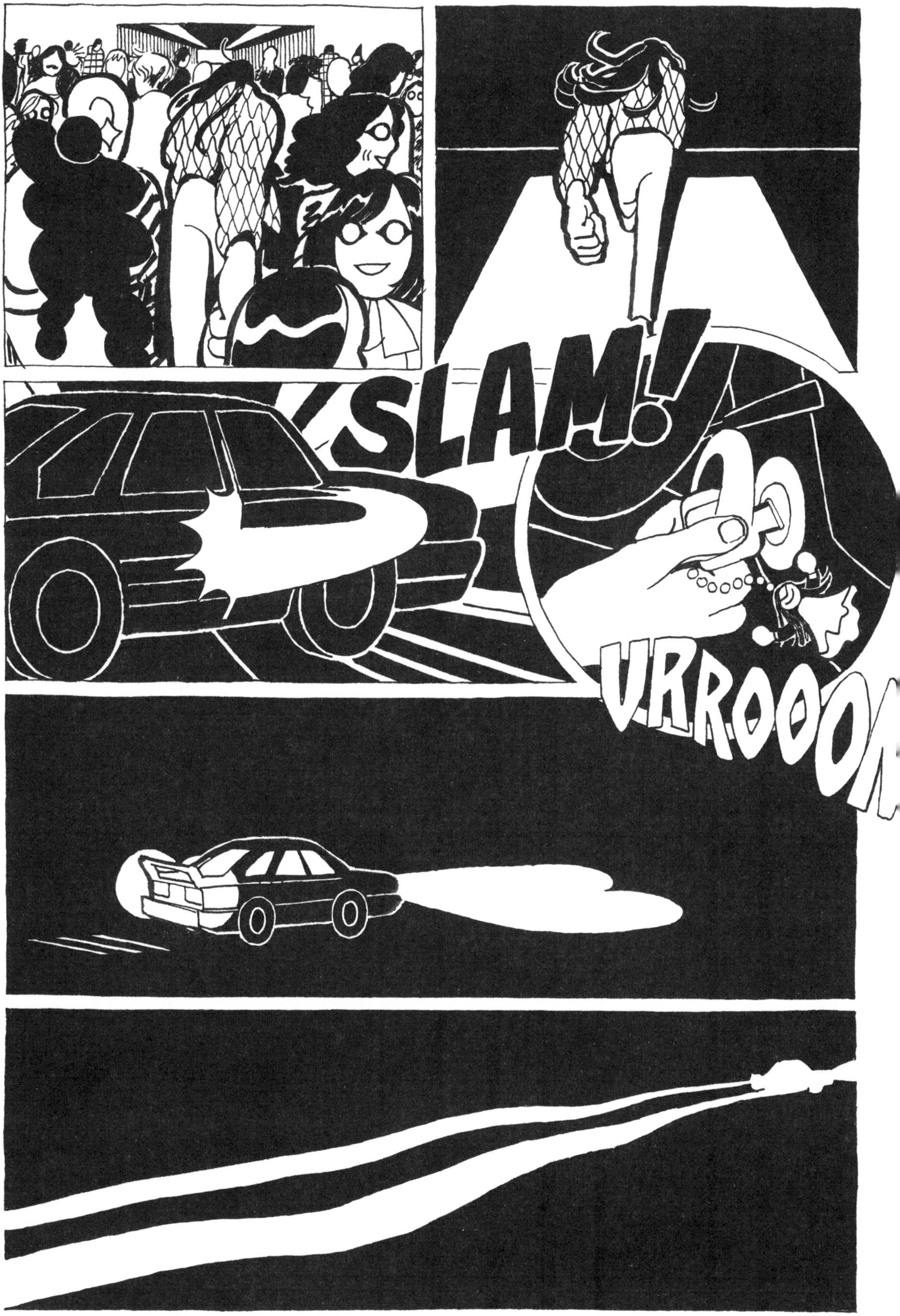
SLAM!
VRROOOM

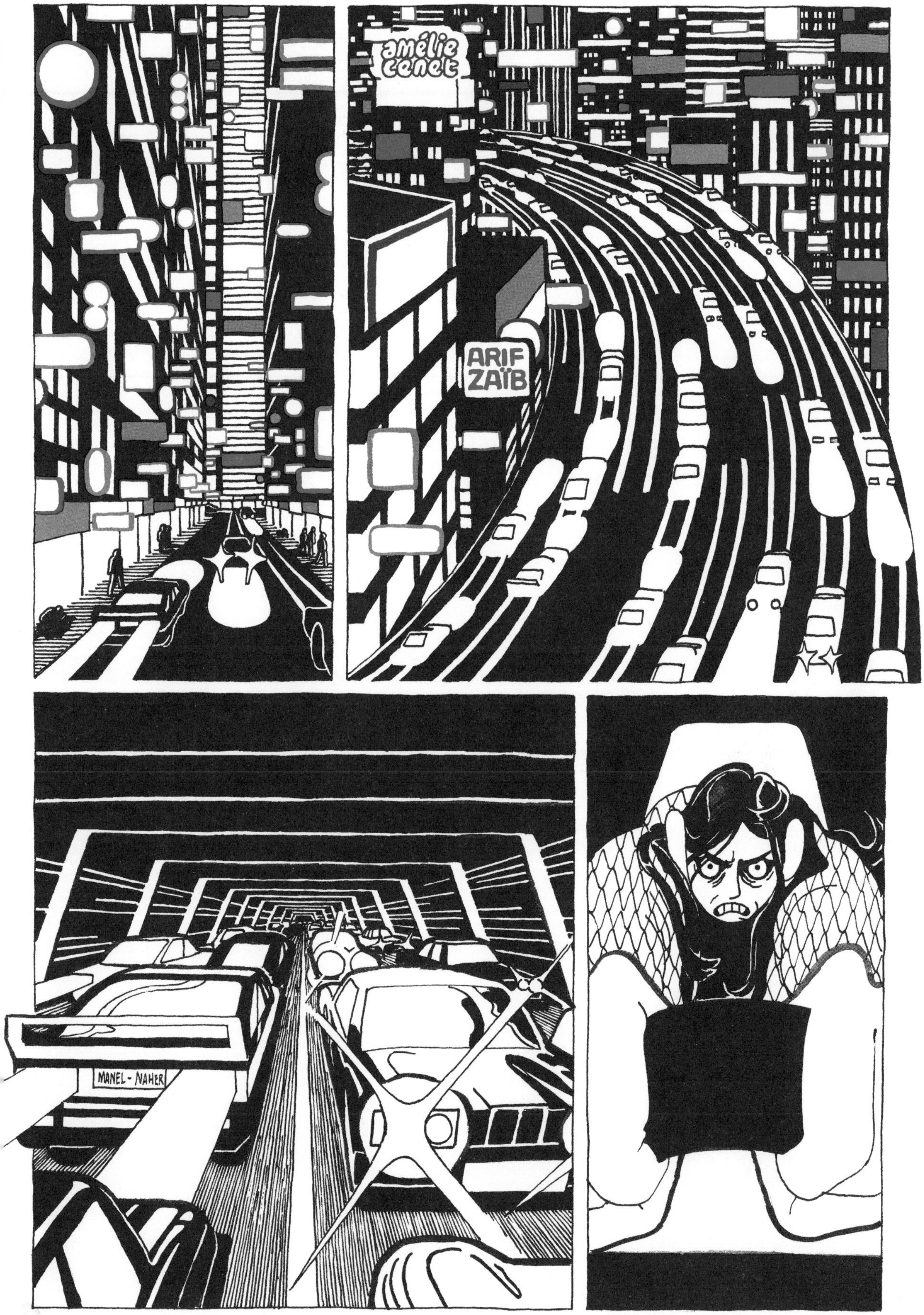
amélie cenet
ARIF ZAÏB
MANEL-NAHER

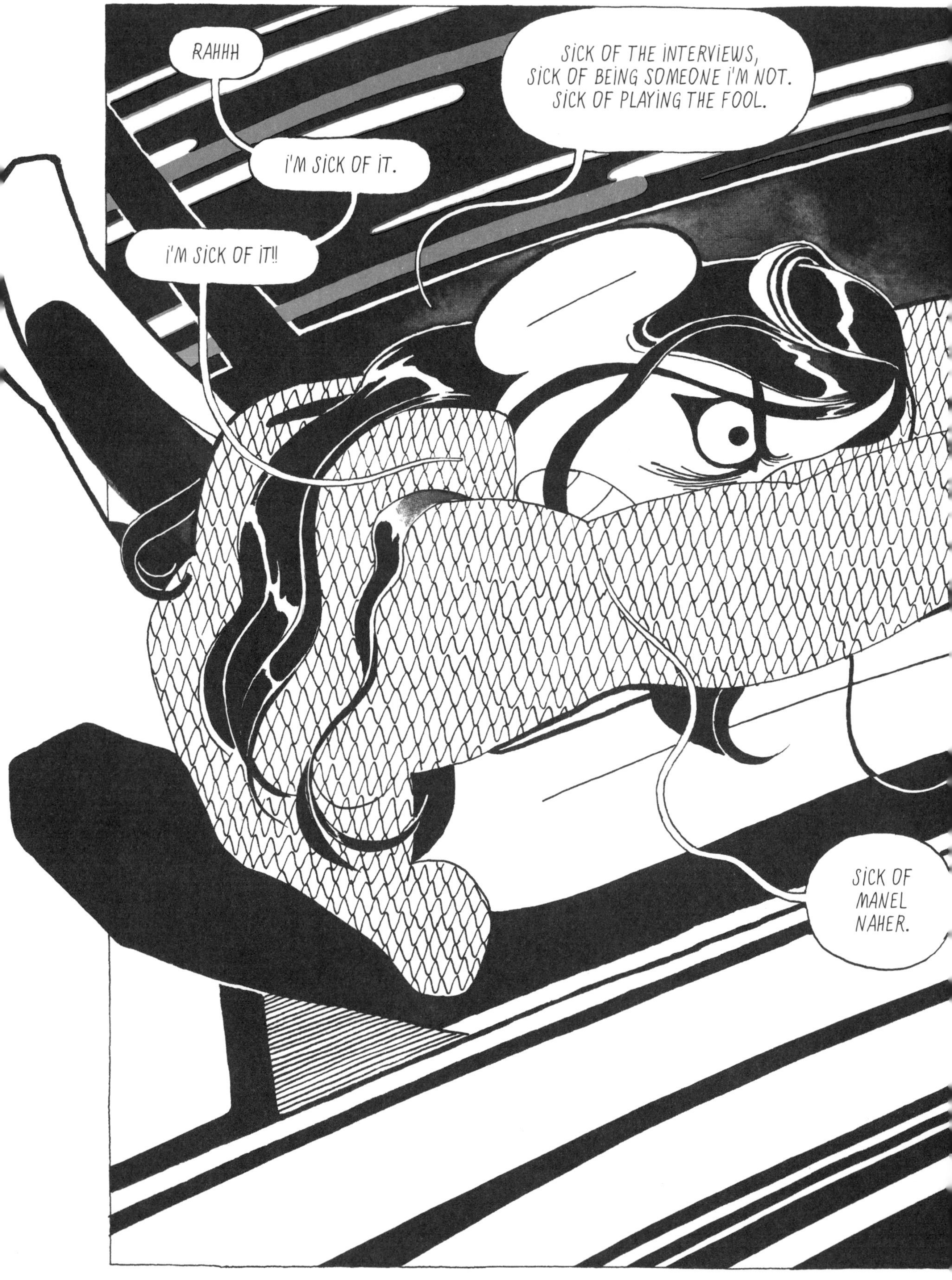
RAHHH
I'M SICK OF IT.
I'M SICK OF IT!!
SICK OF THE INTERVIEWS, SICK OF BEING SOMEONE I'M NOT. SICK OF PLAYING THE FOOL.
SICK OF MANEL NAHER.

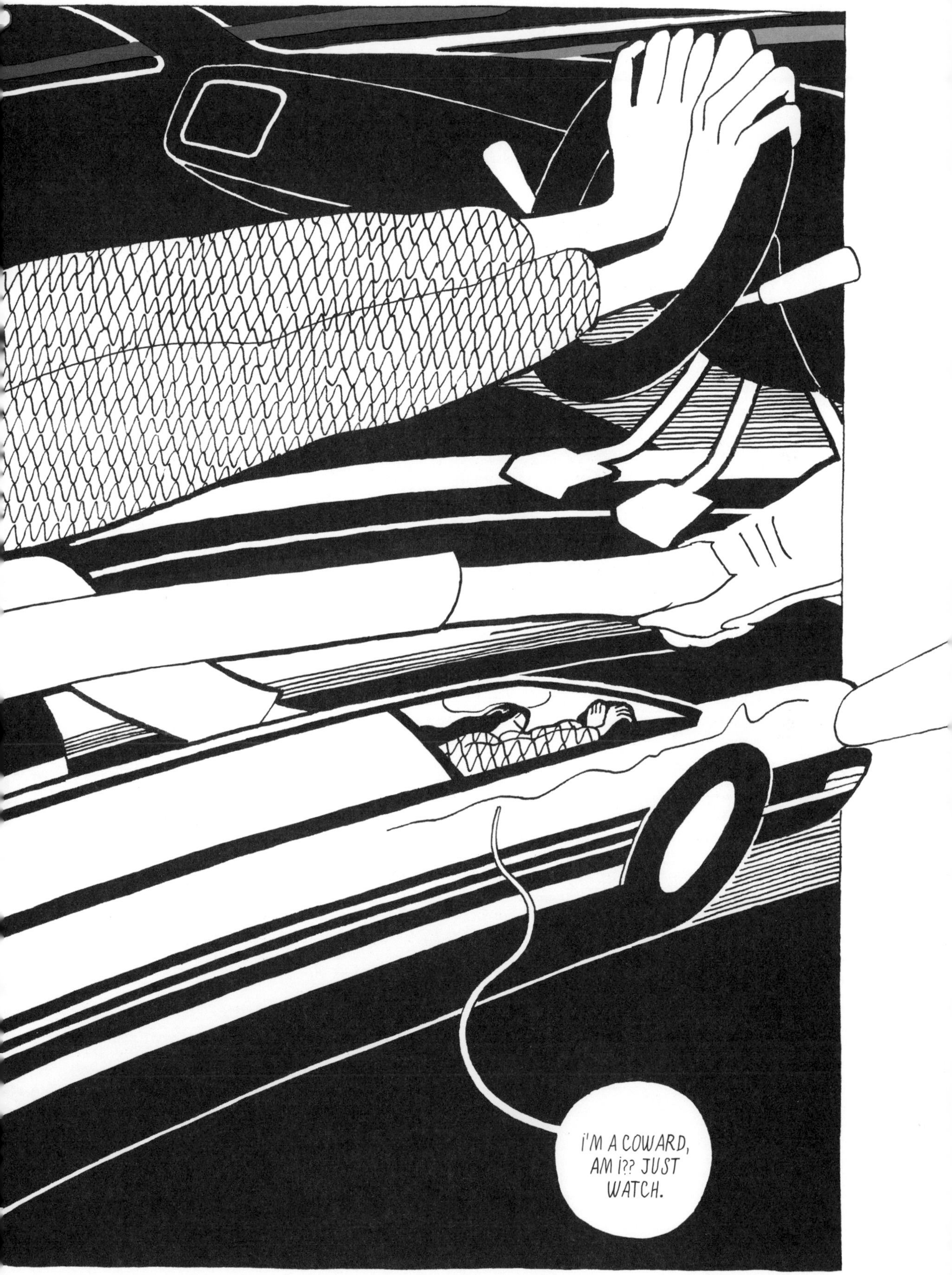
I'M A COWARD, AM I?? JUST WATCH.

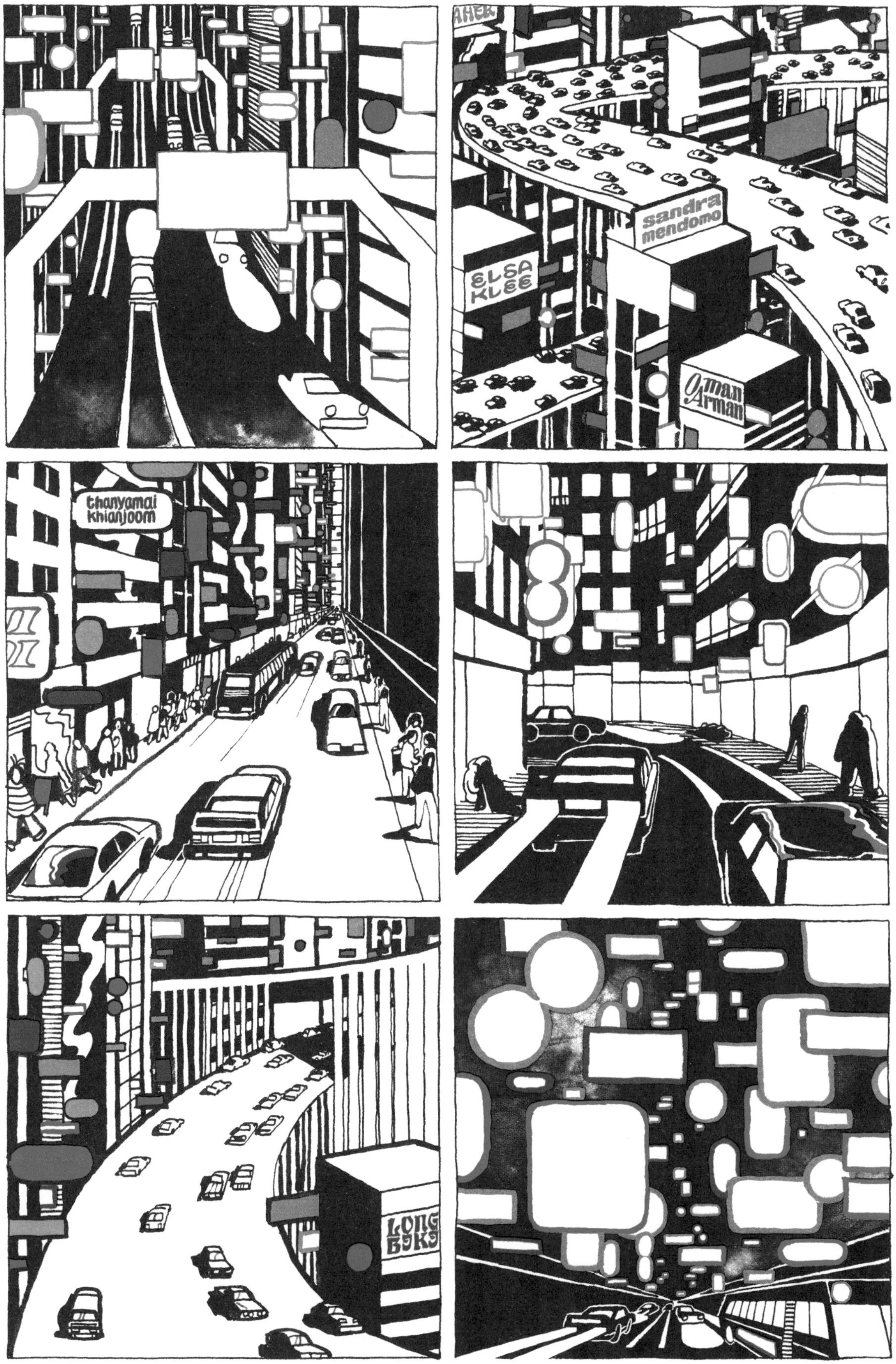
sandra mendomo
ELSA KLEE
man Arman
thanyamai khianjoom
LONG

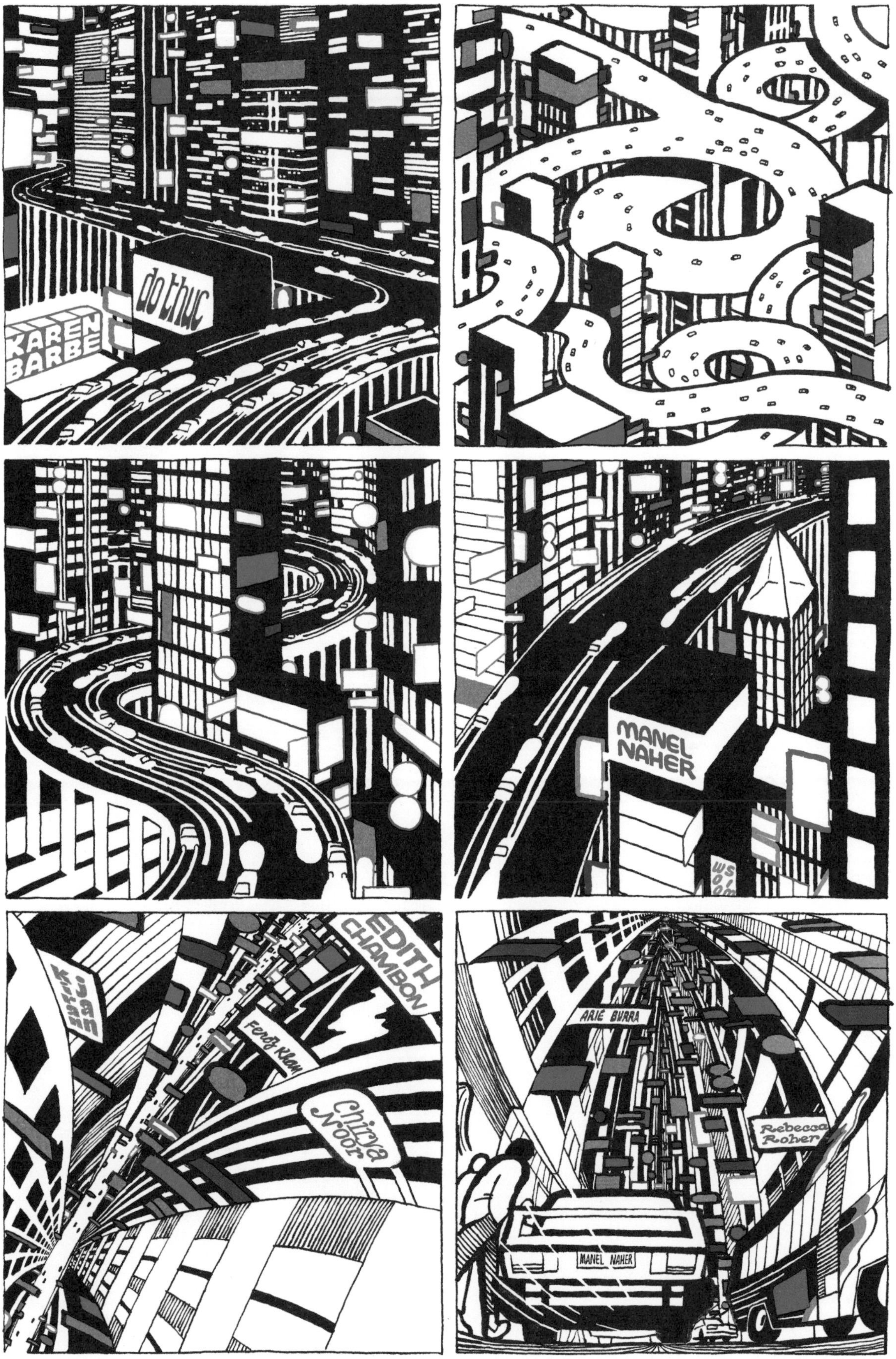
KAREN BARBE
do thuc
MANEL NAHER
EDITH CHAMBON
Feng Klem
Chirya Noor
ARIÉ BURRA
Rebecca Rolver
MANEL NAHER

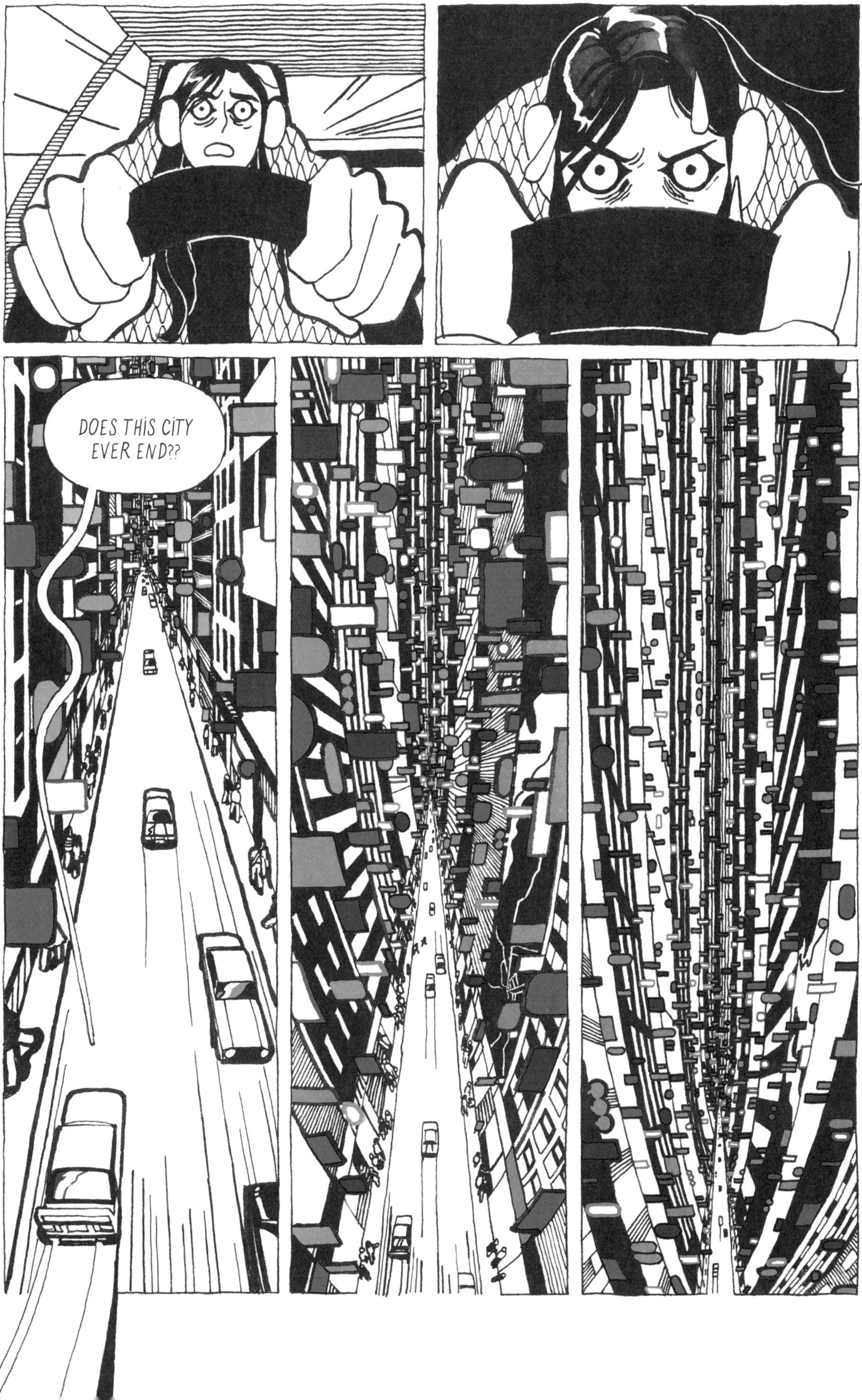
DOES THIS CITY EVER END??

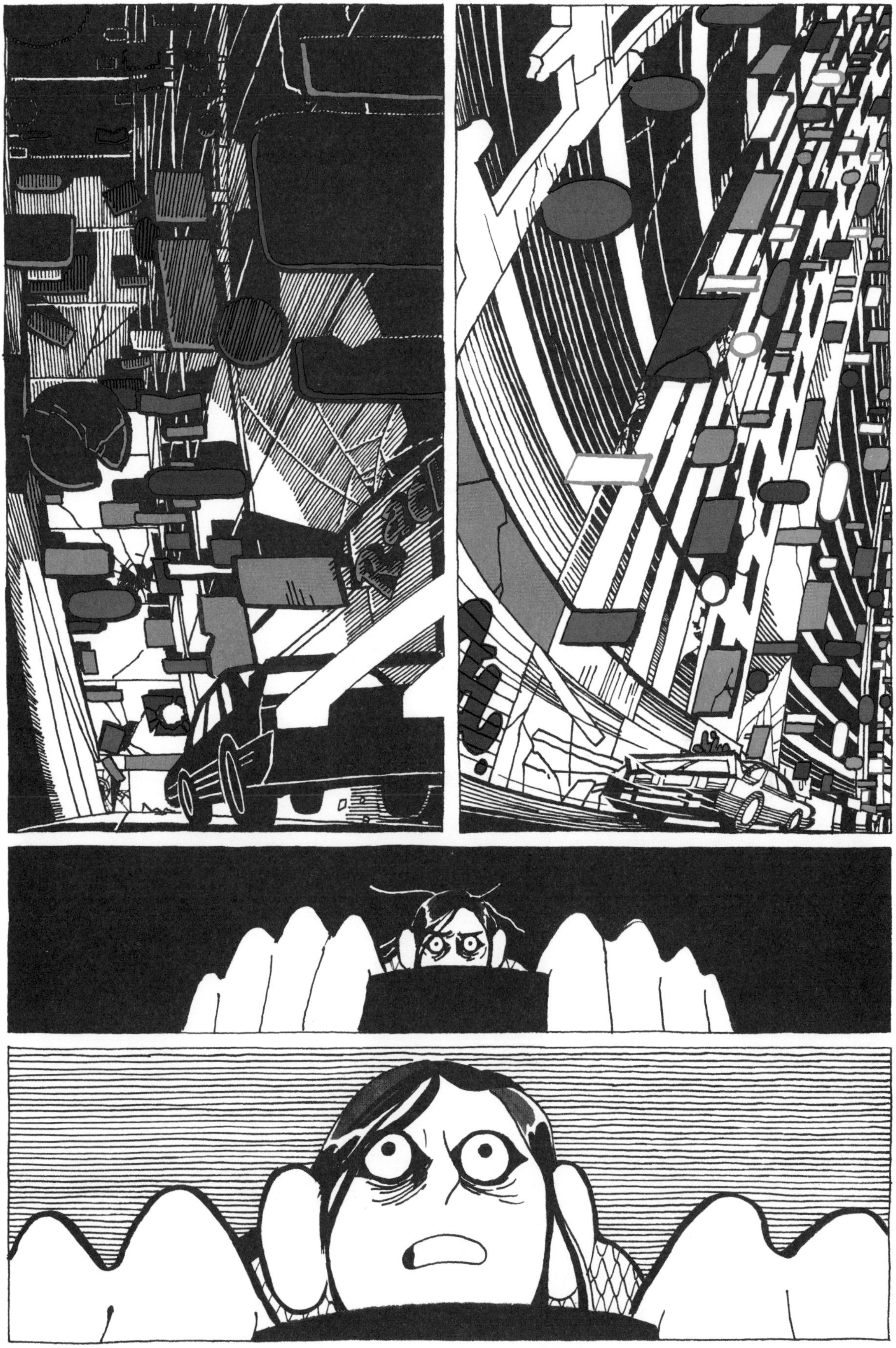

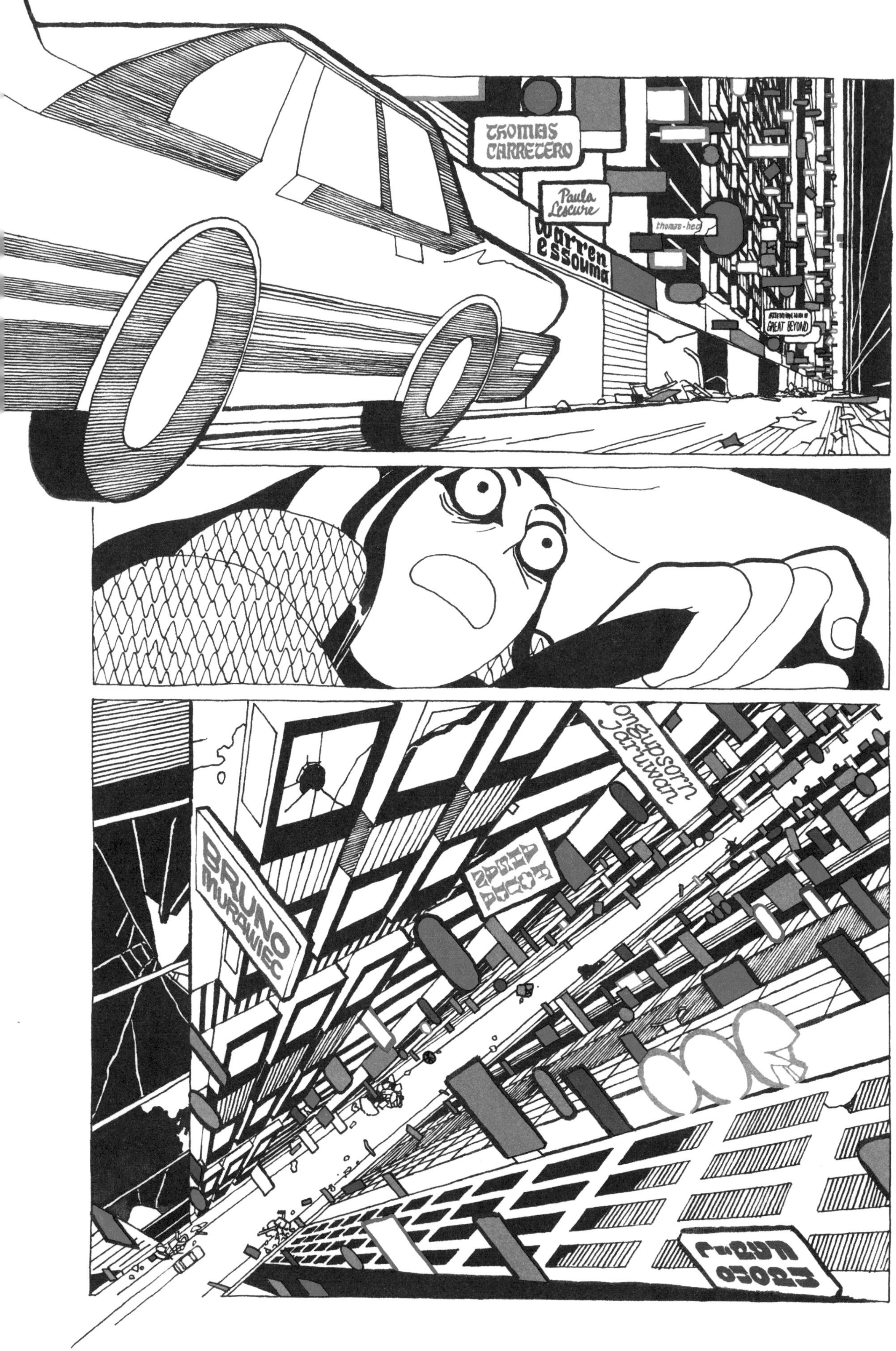
THOMAS CARRETERO
Paula Lescure
Warren Essouma
thomas-hec
GREAT BEYOND
BRUNO MURAWIEC
ongupsorn Jaruwan

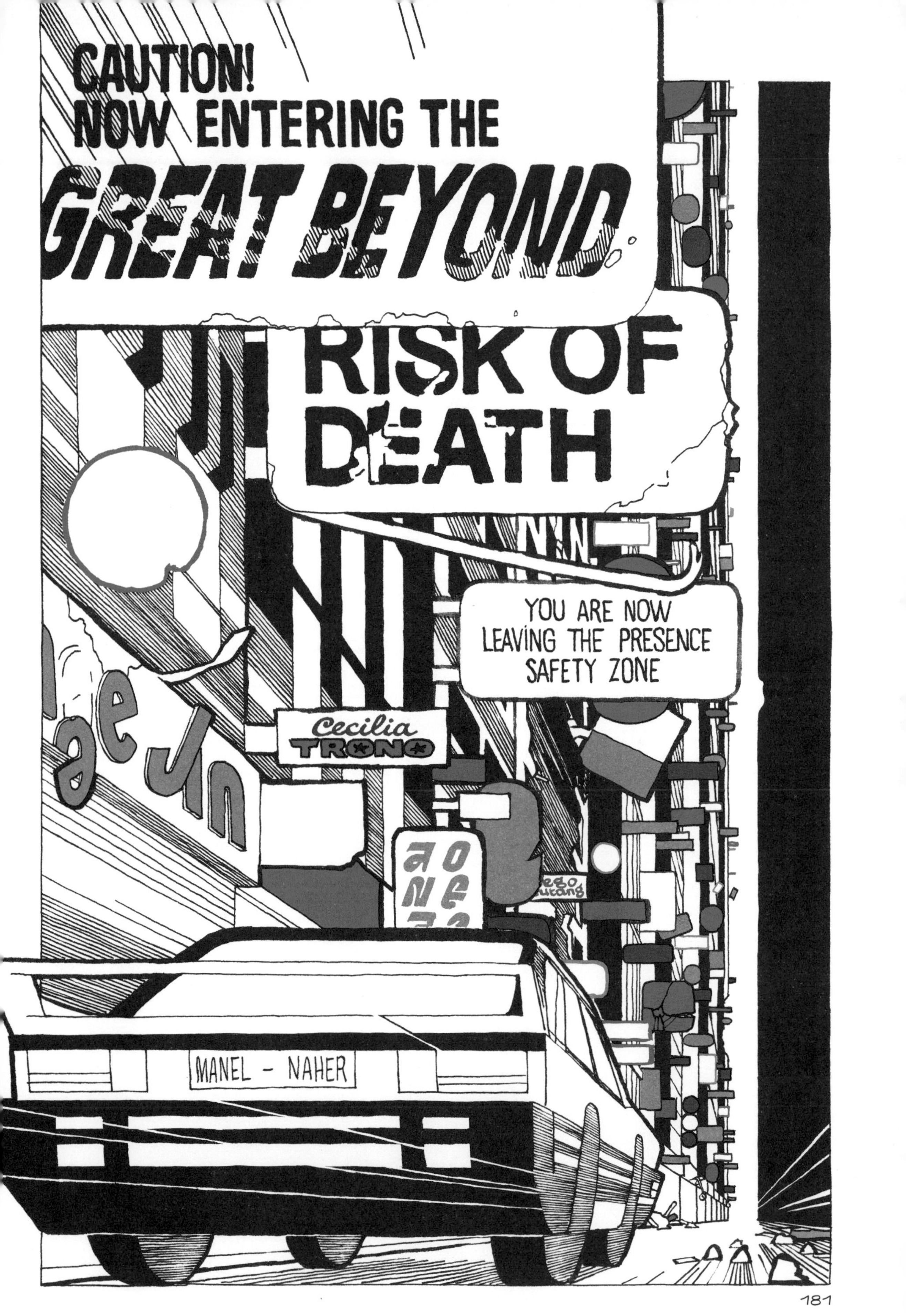
CAUTION!
NOW ENTERING THE
GREAT BEYOND
RISK OF DEATH
YOU ARE NOW LEAVING THE PRESENCE SAFETY ZONE
Cecilia TRONO
MANEL - NAHER

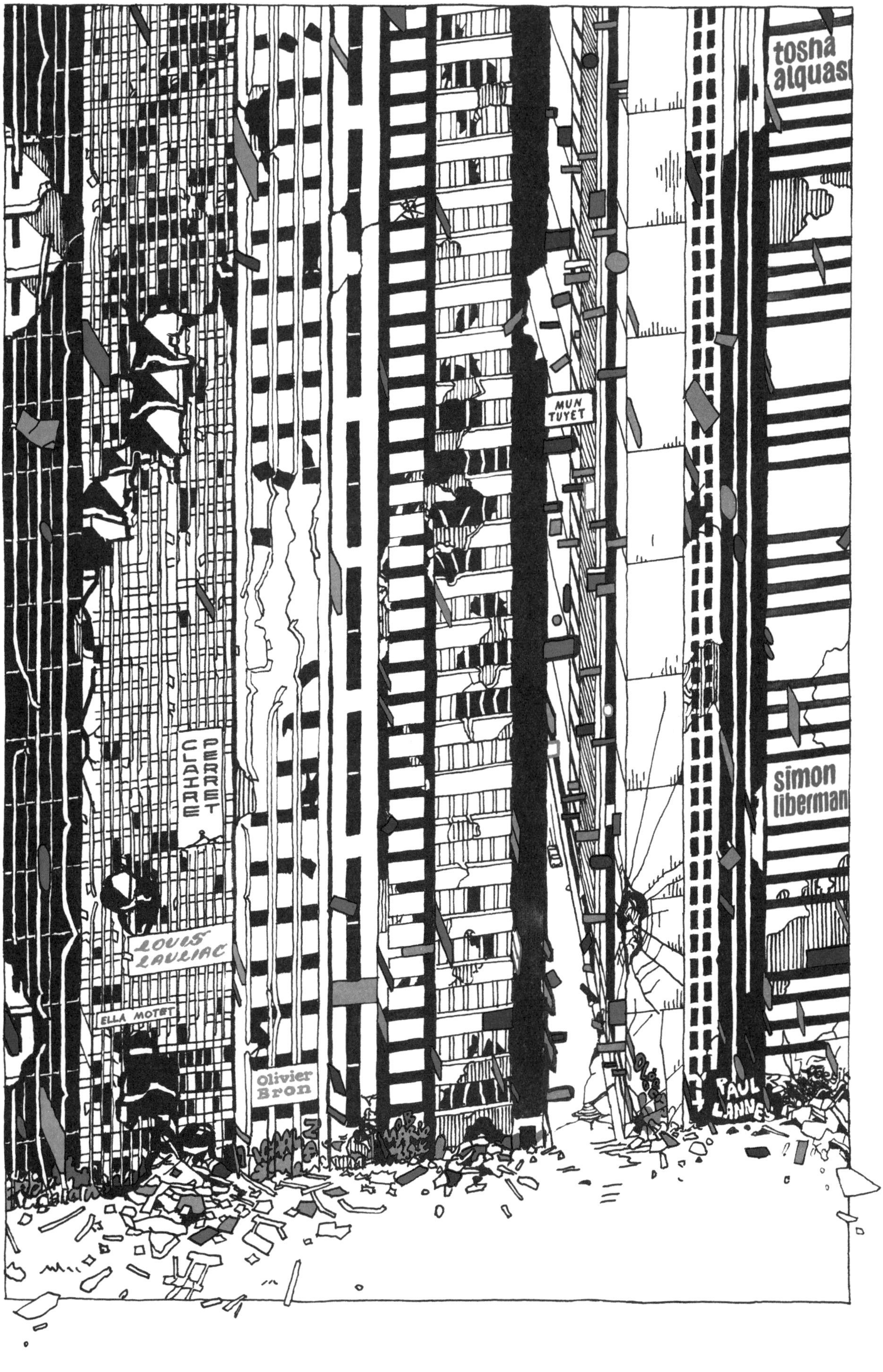
tosha
alquas
MUN
TUYET
CLAIRE
PERRET
simon
liberman
LOUIS
LAULIAC
ELLA MOTET
Olivier
Bron
PAUL
LANNES

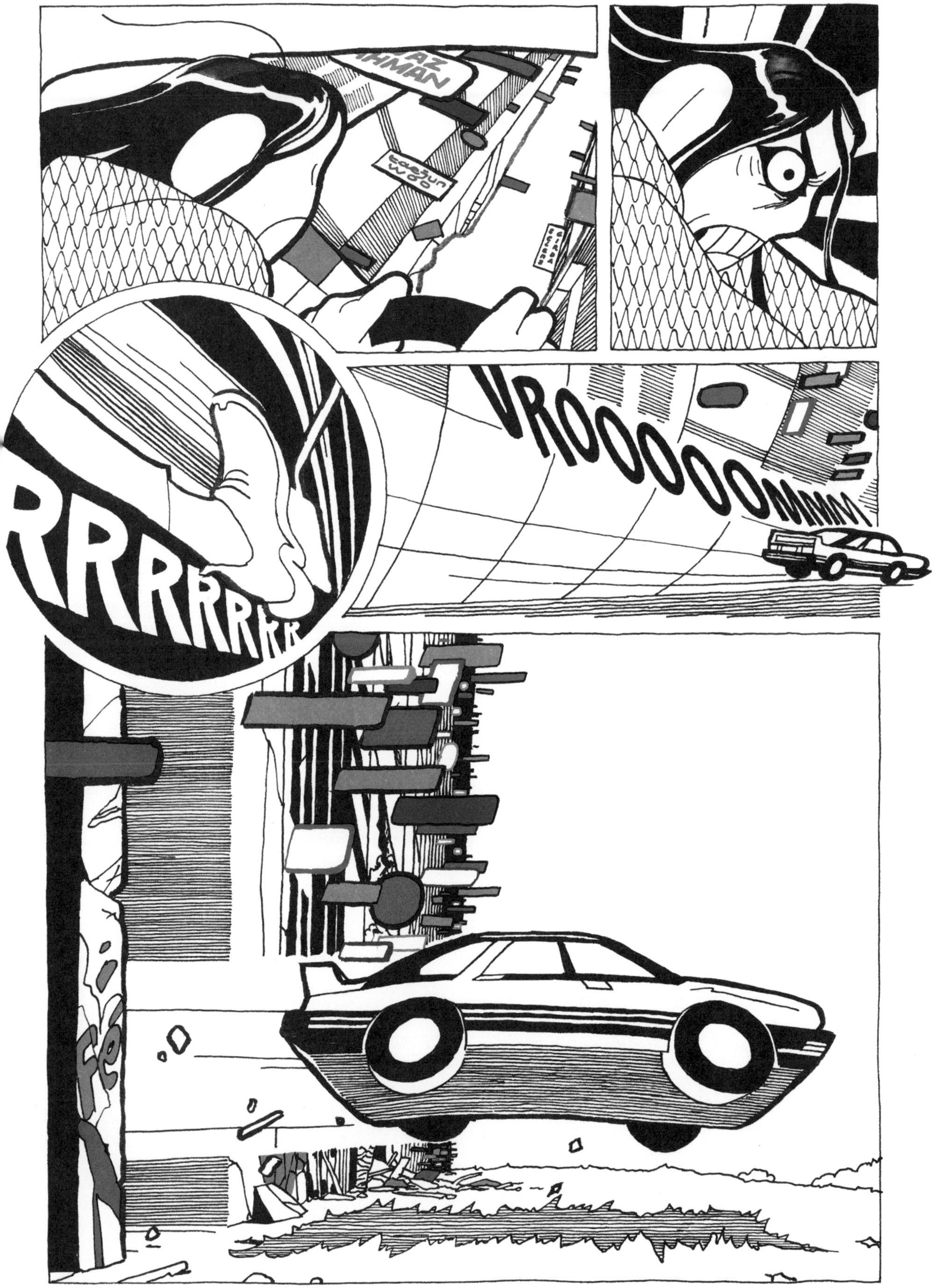
taejun woo
VROOOOOMMMM
RRRRRRRRR

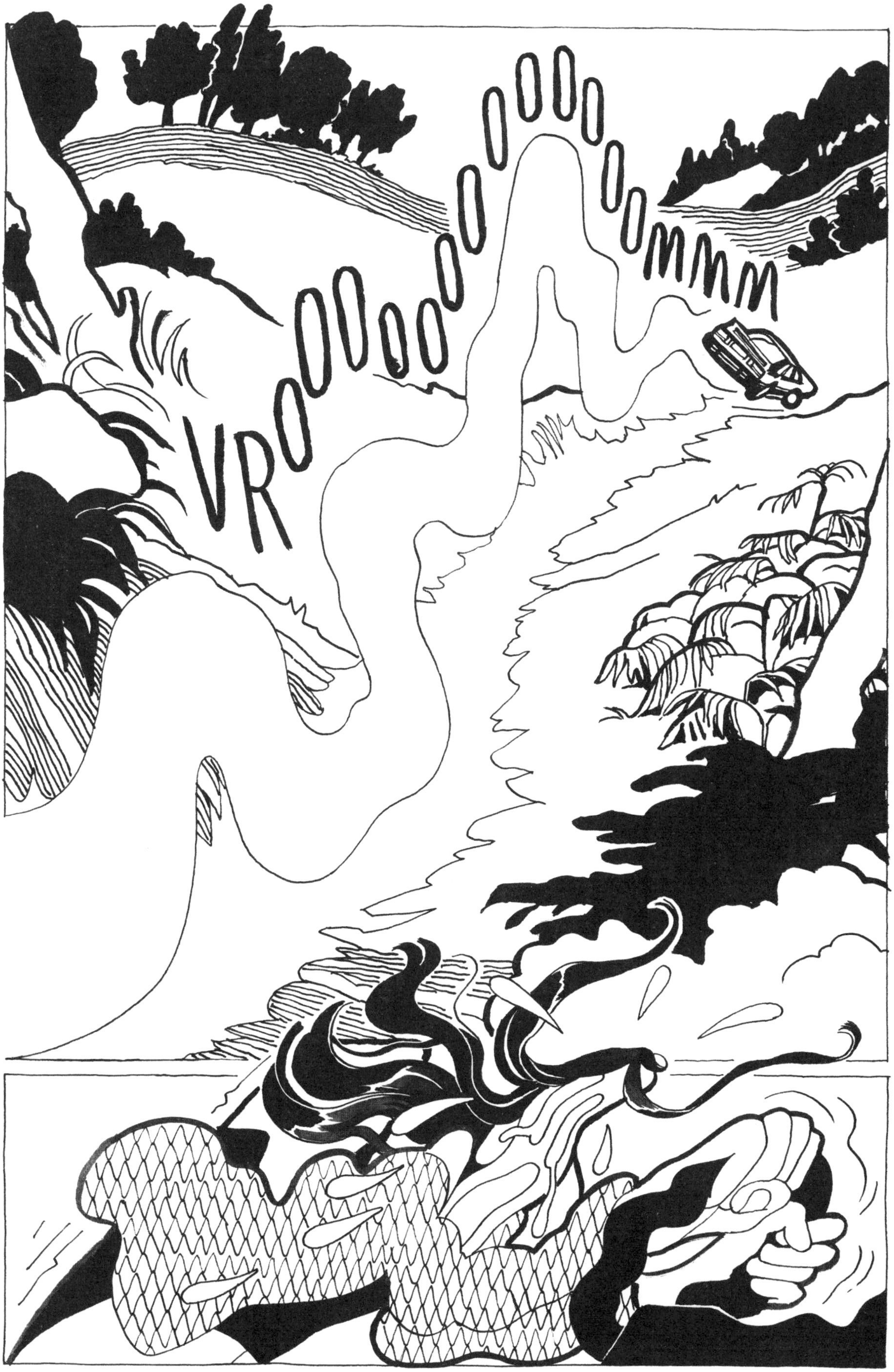
VROOOOOOOOOOOOOOMMMM

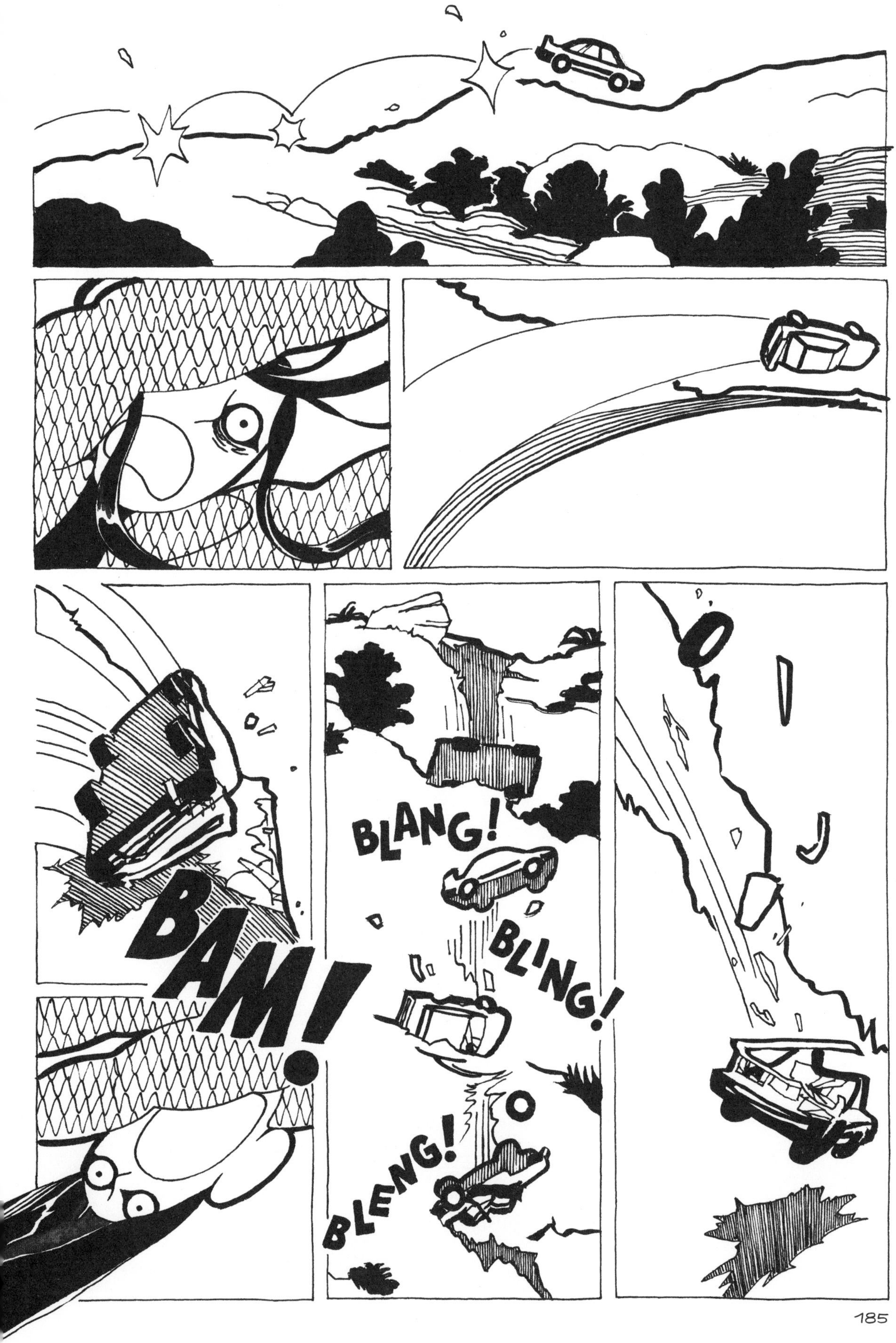
BAM!
BLANG!
BLING!
BLENG!

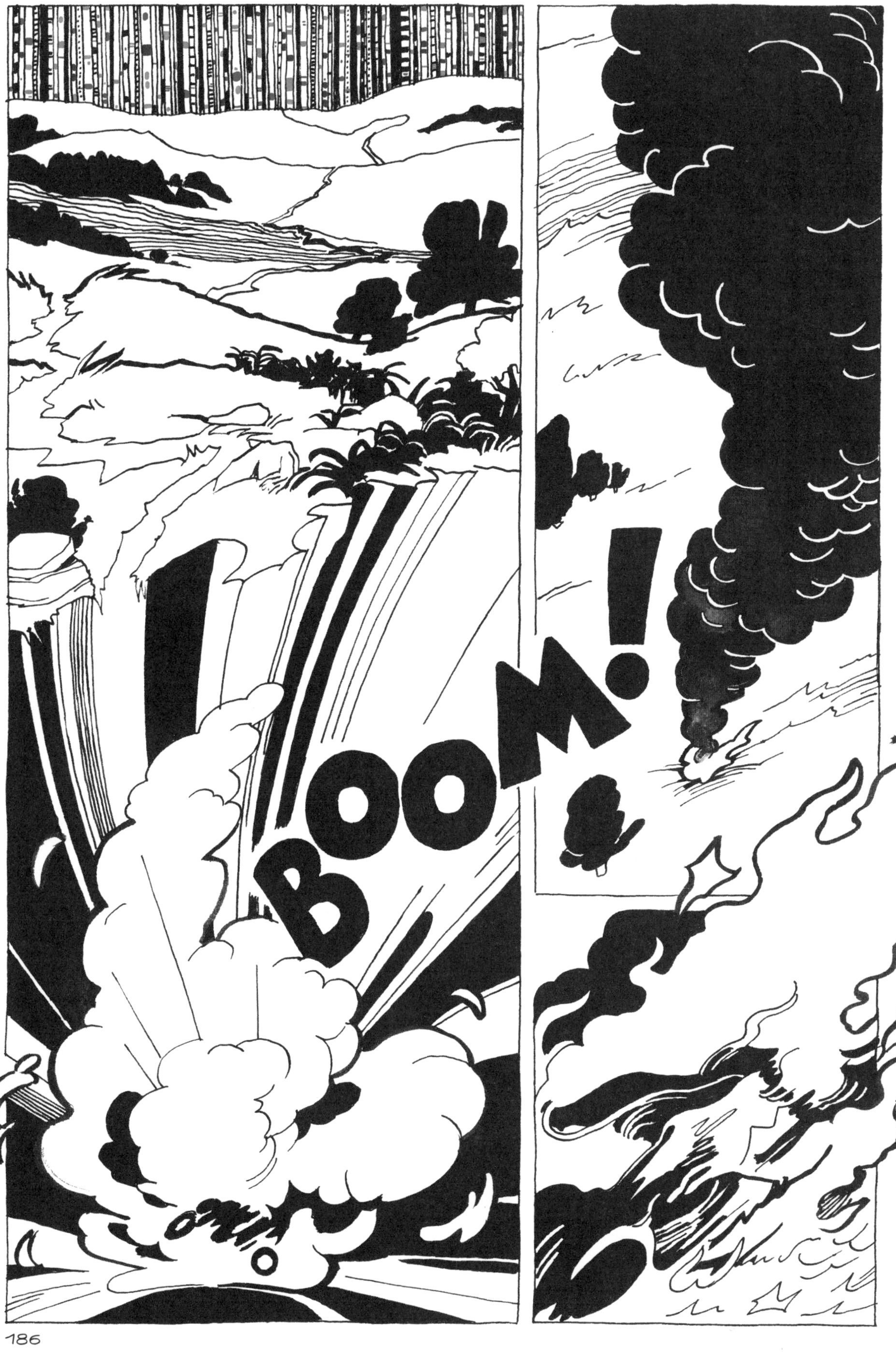
BOOM!

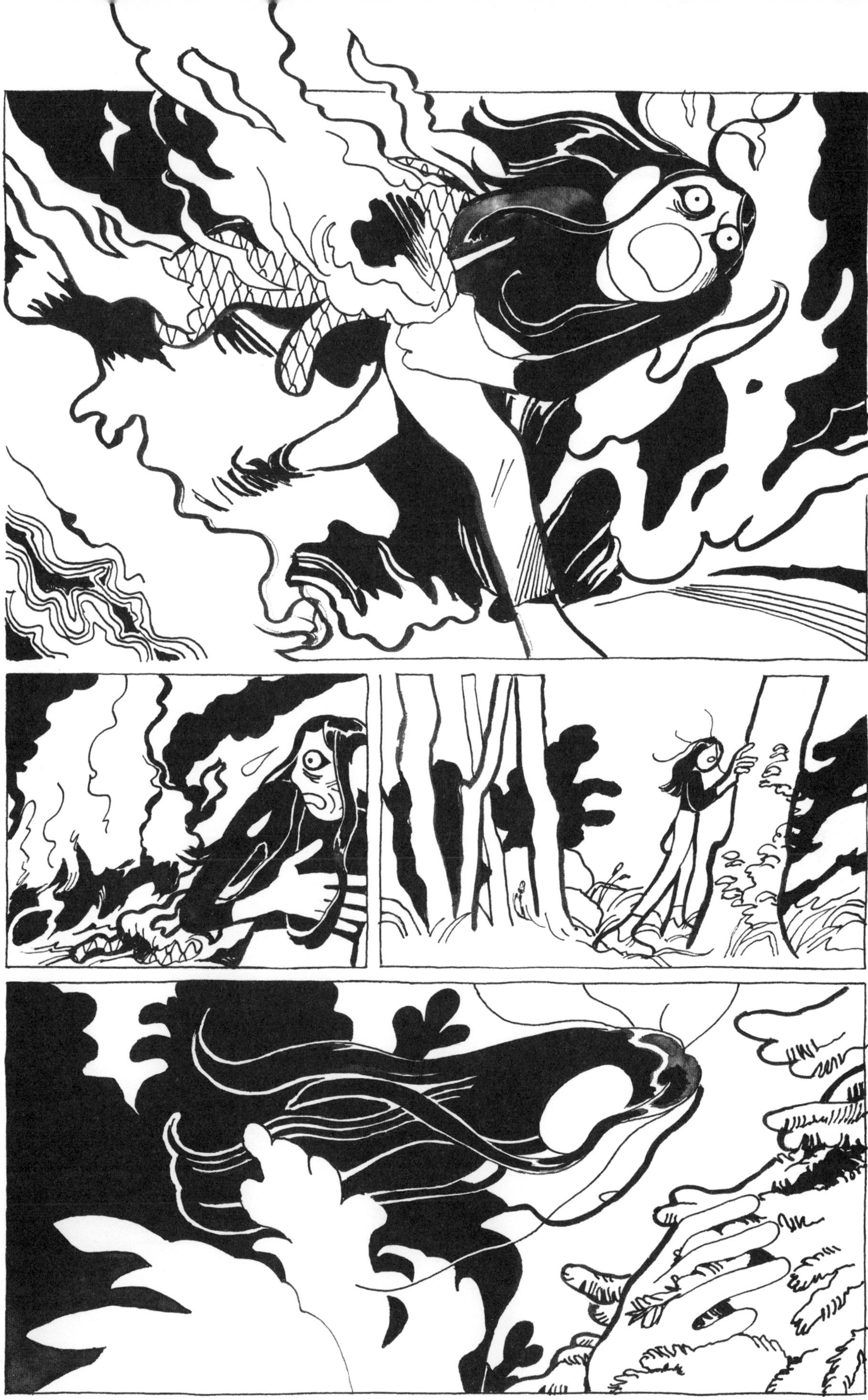

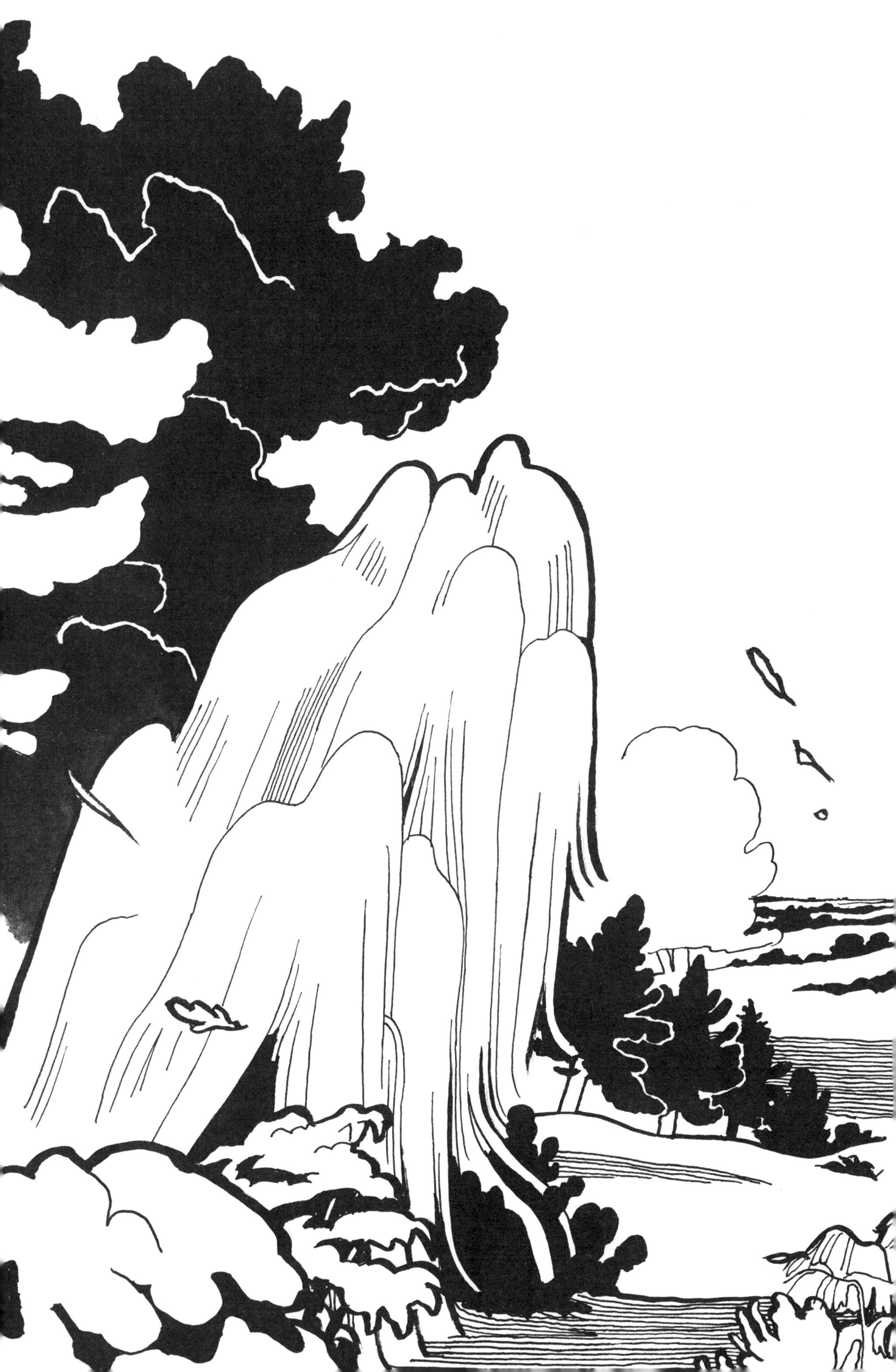

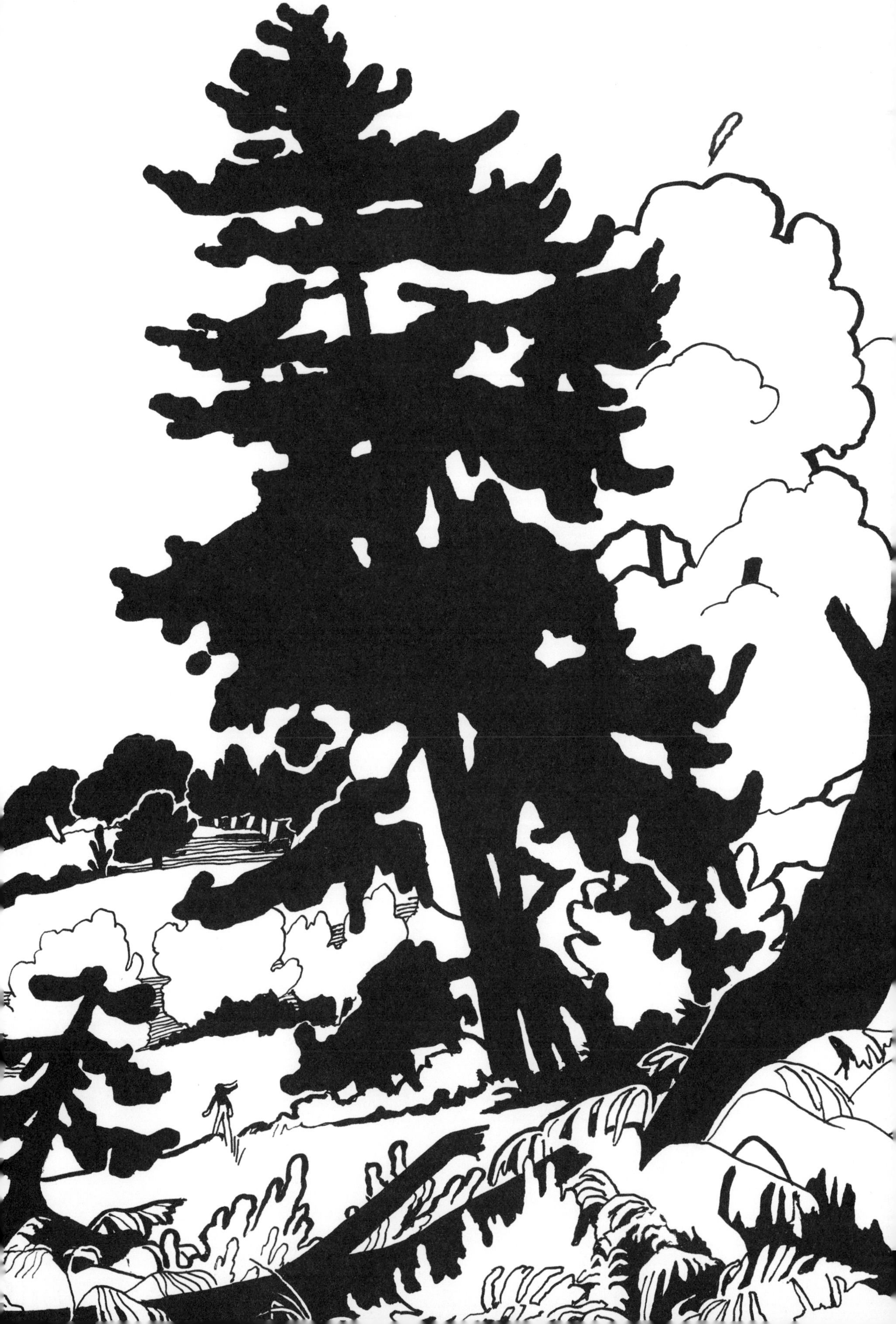

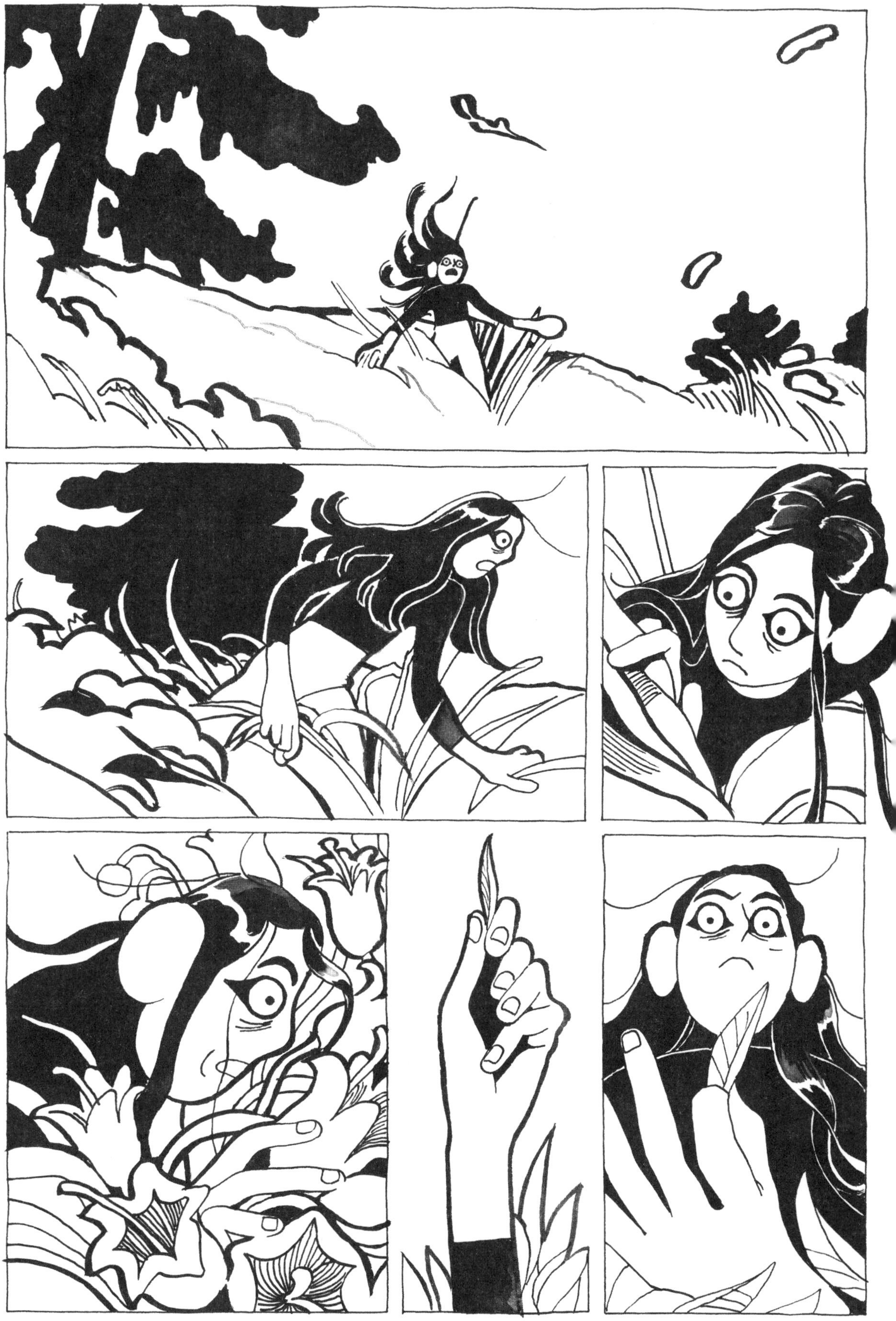

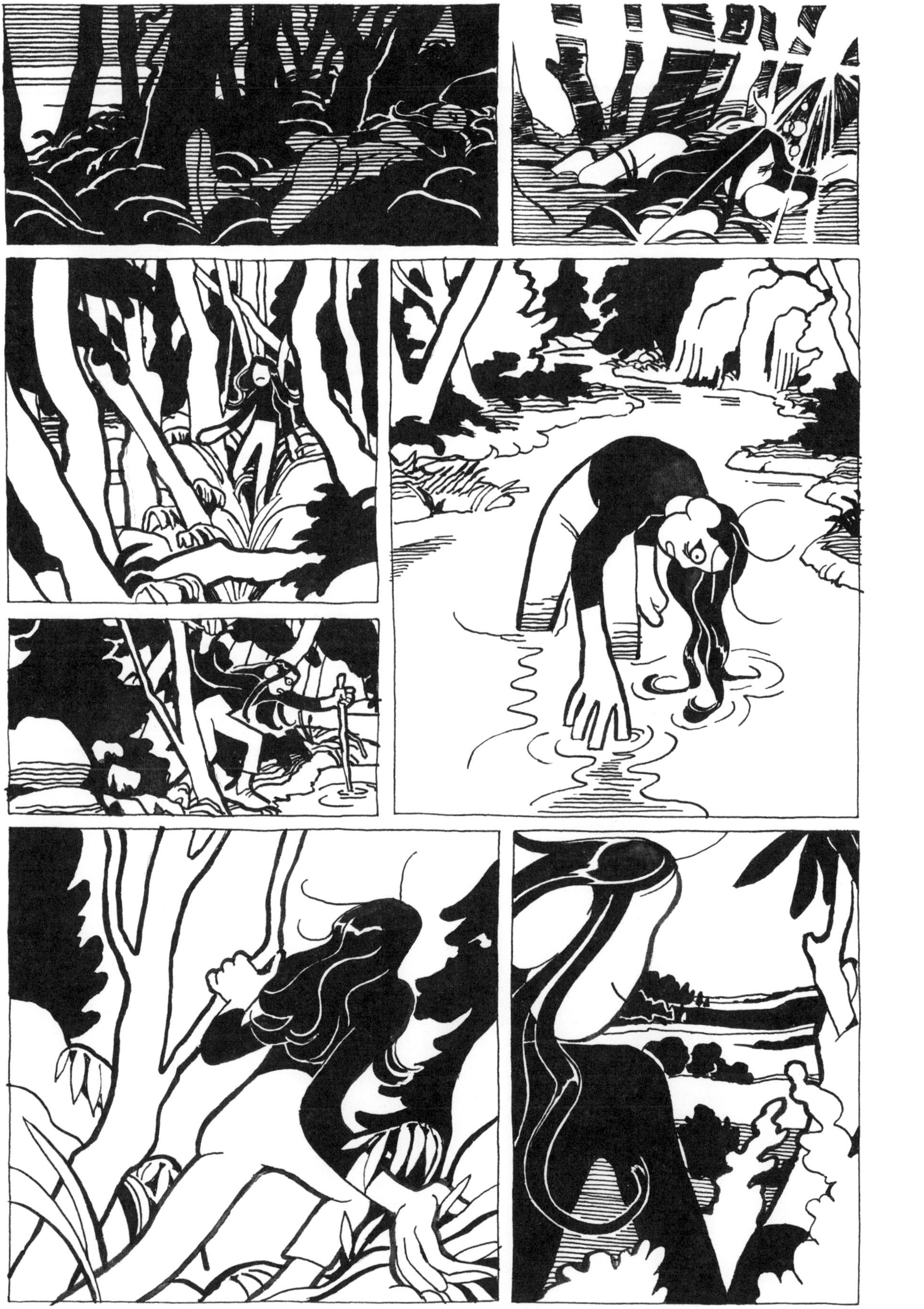

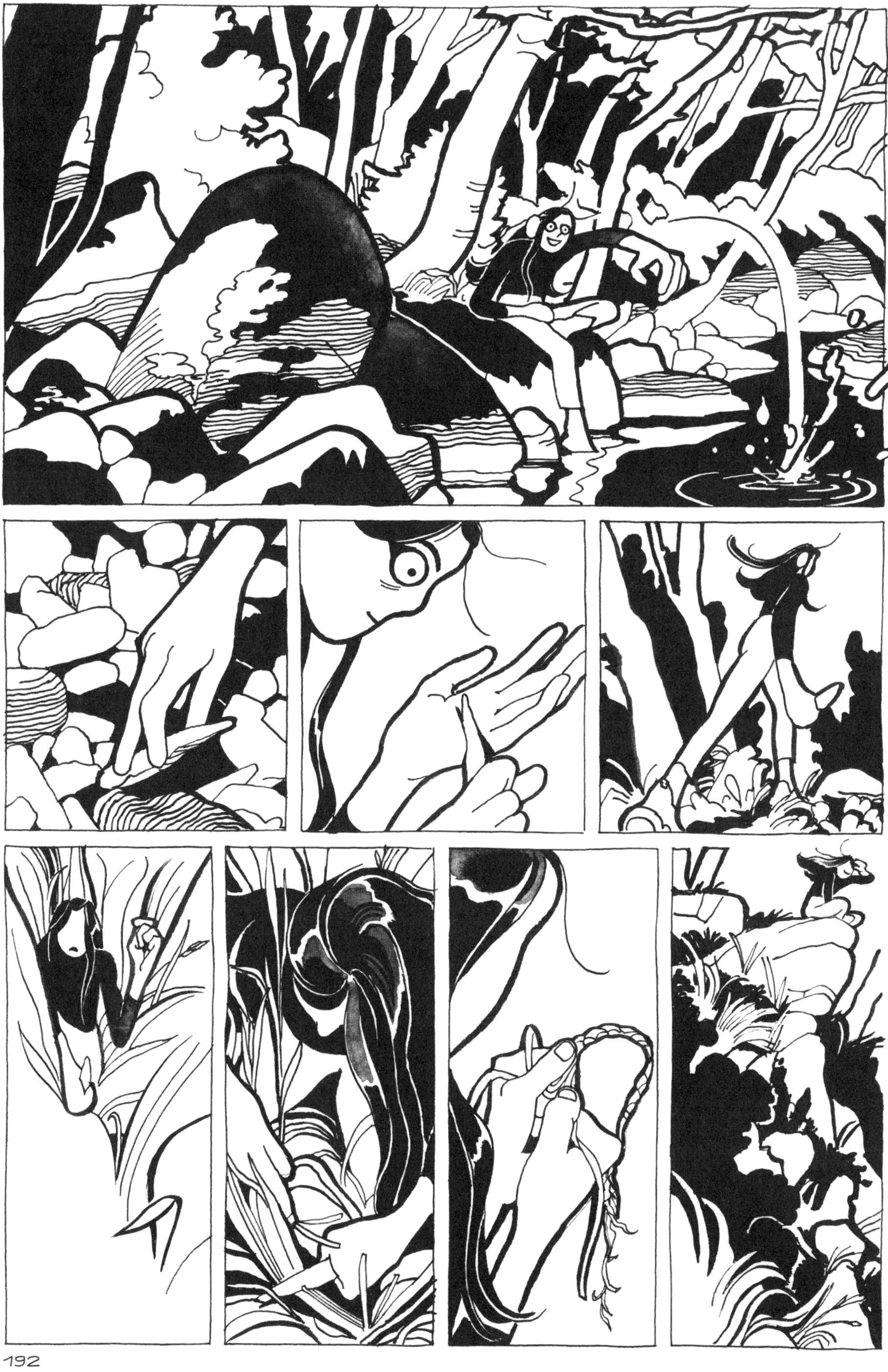

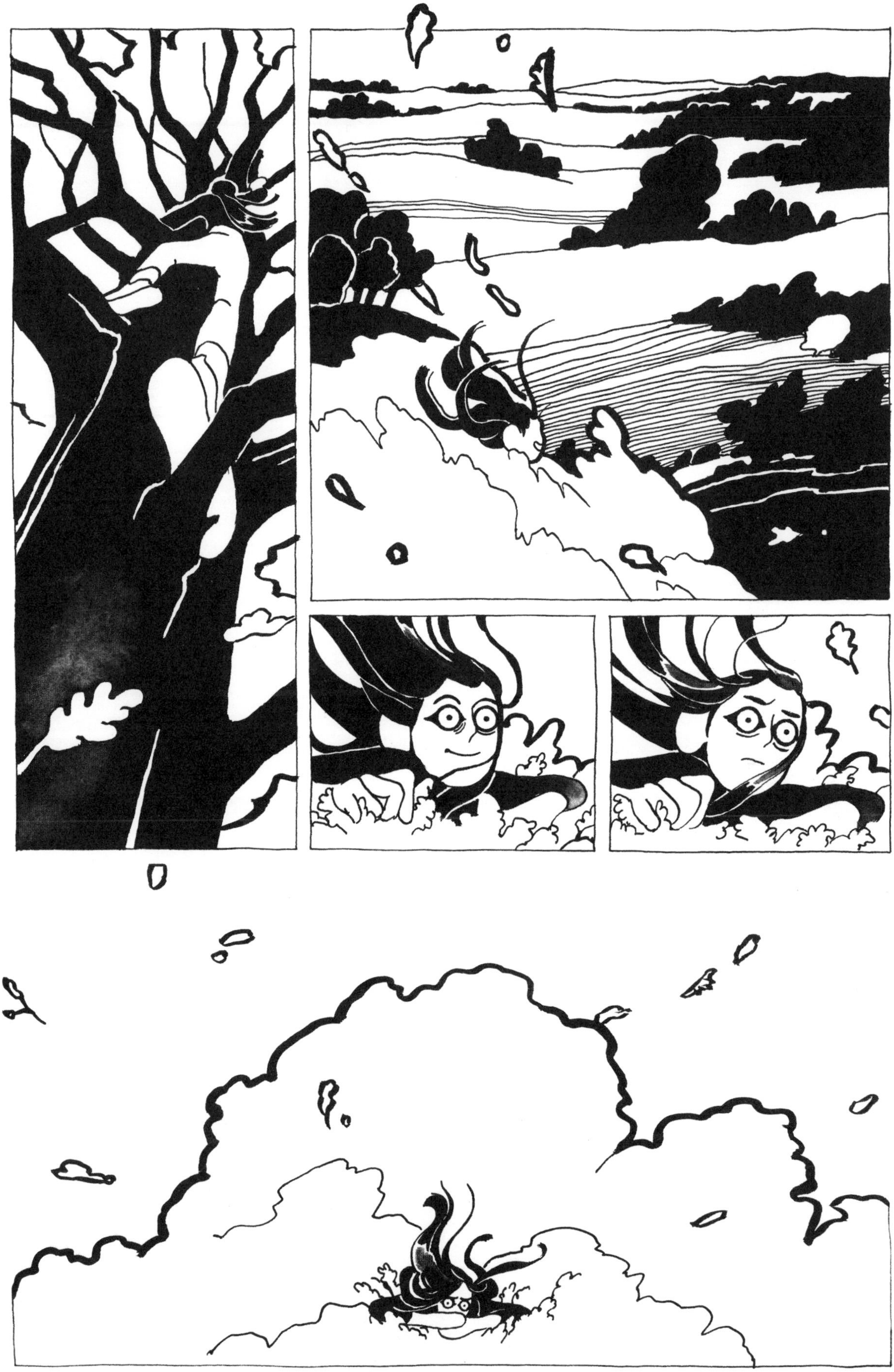

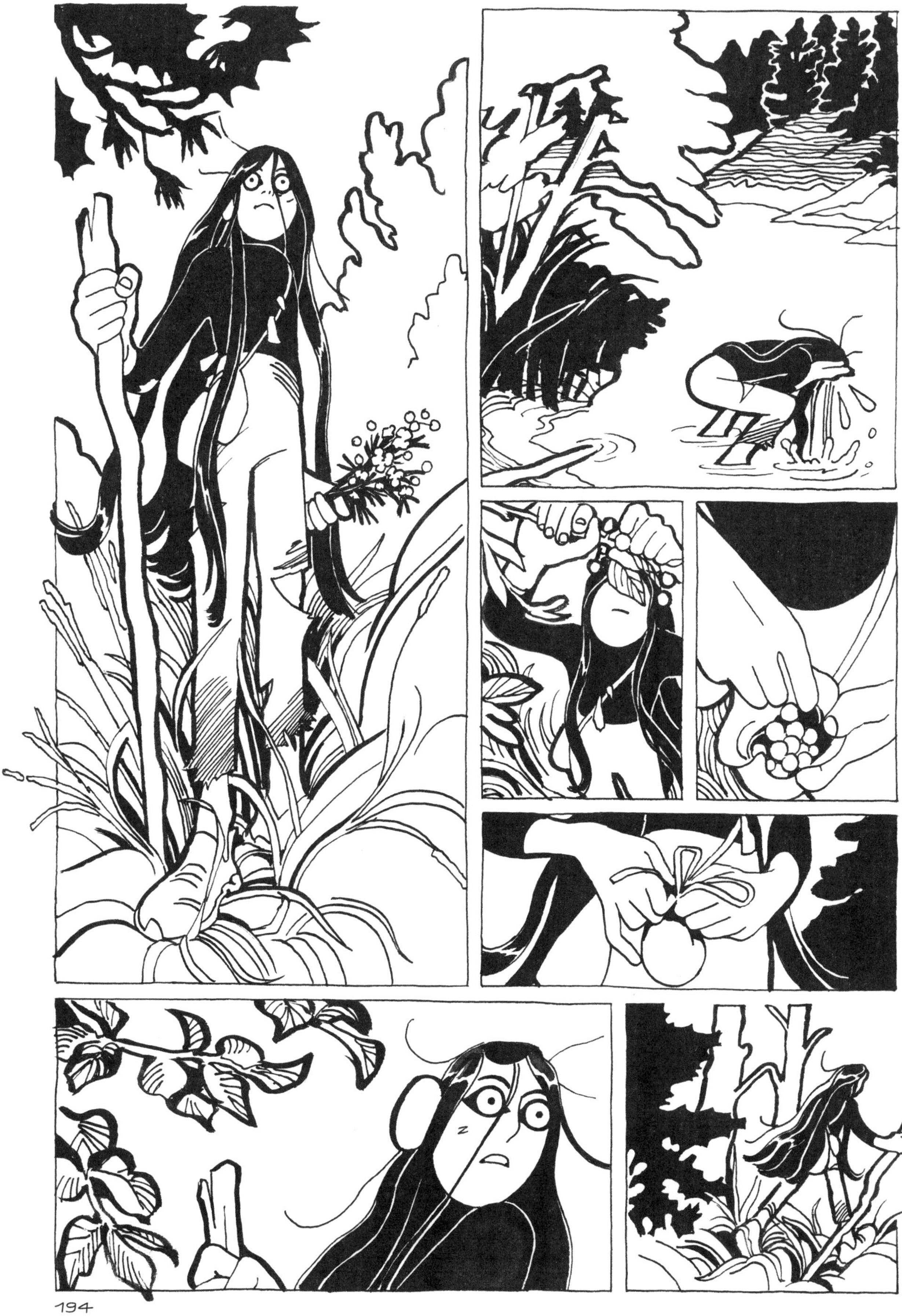

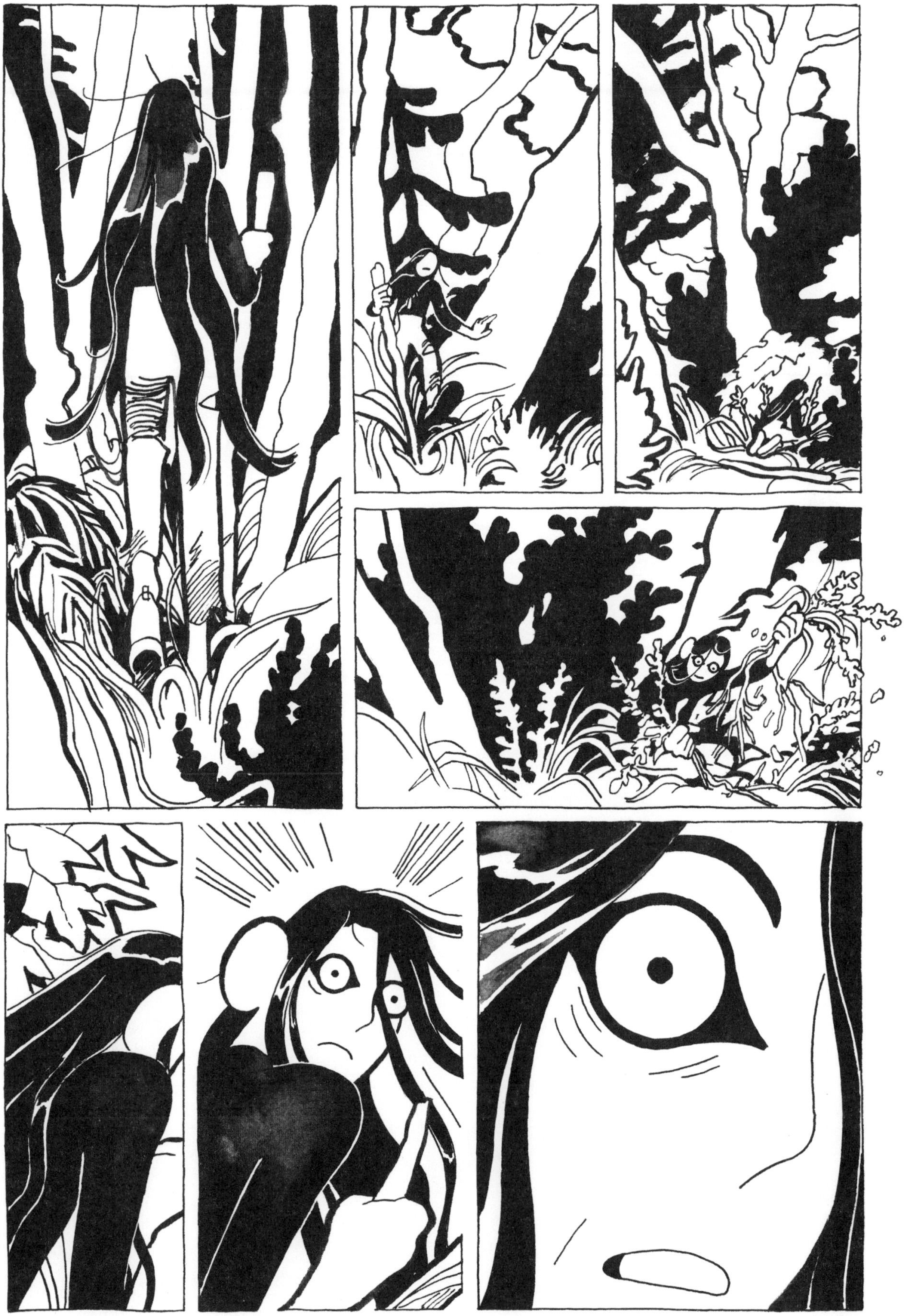

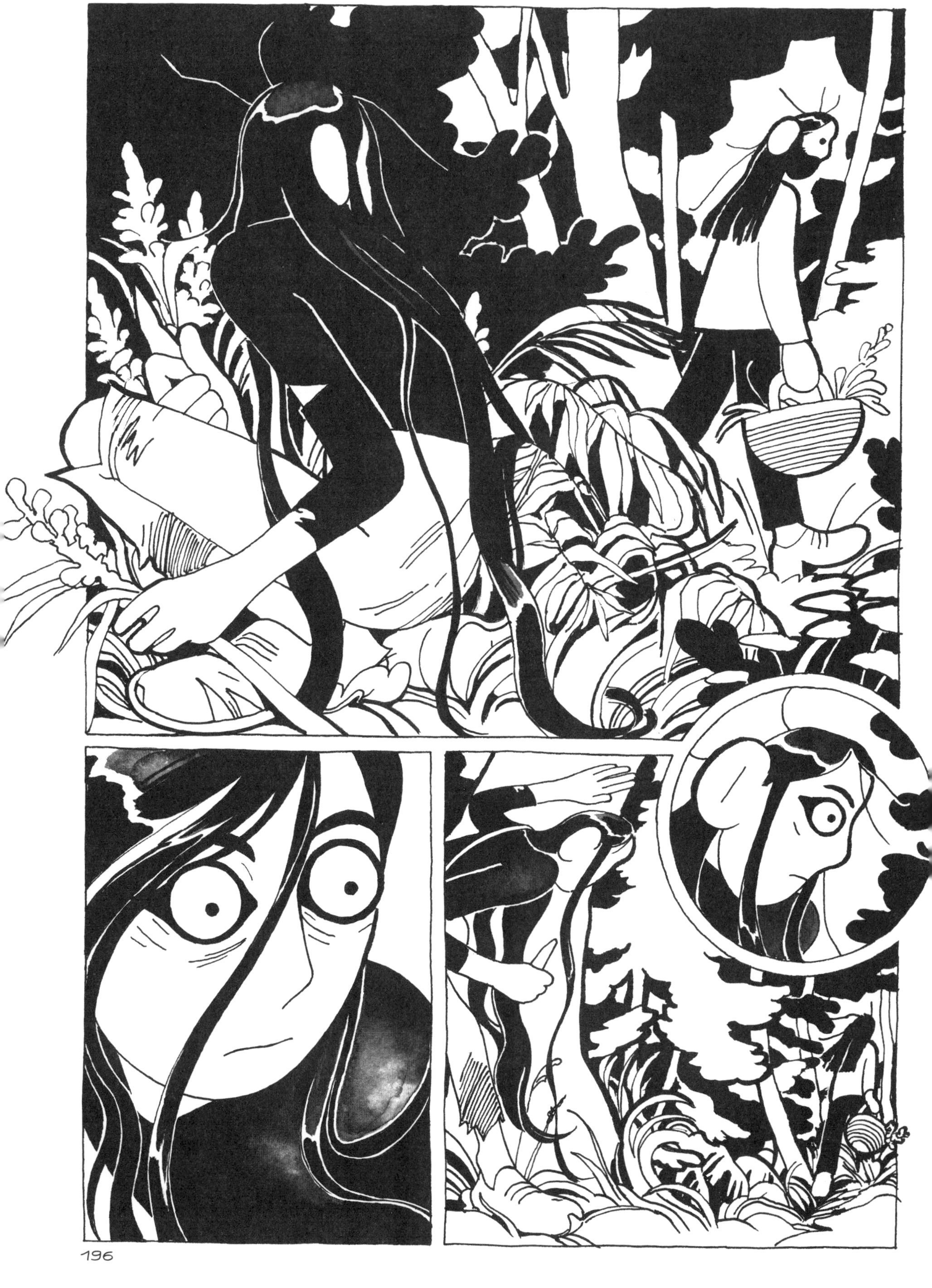

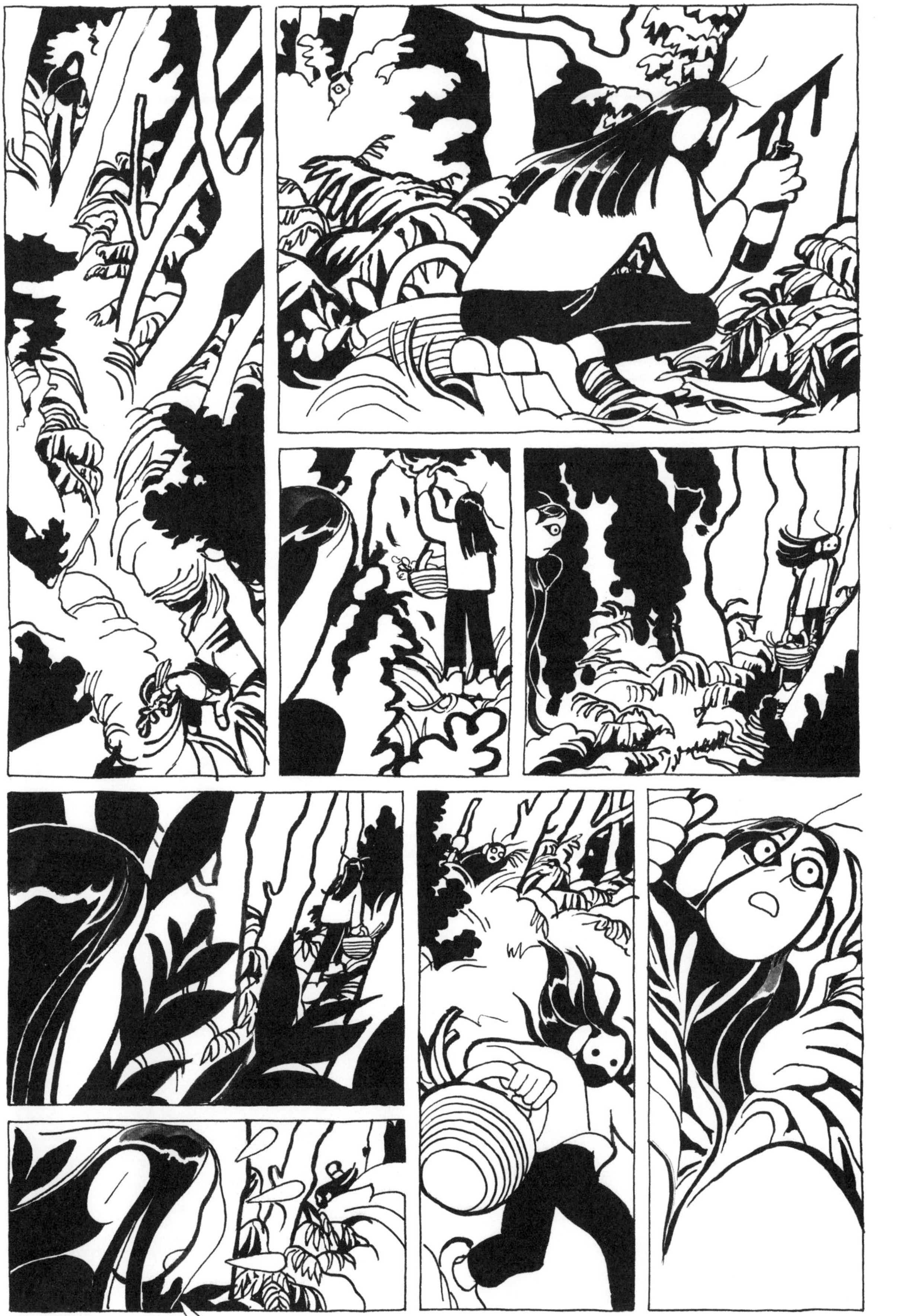

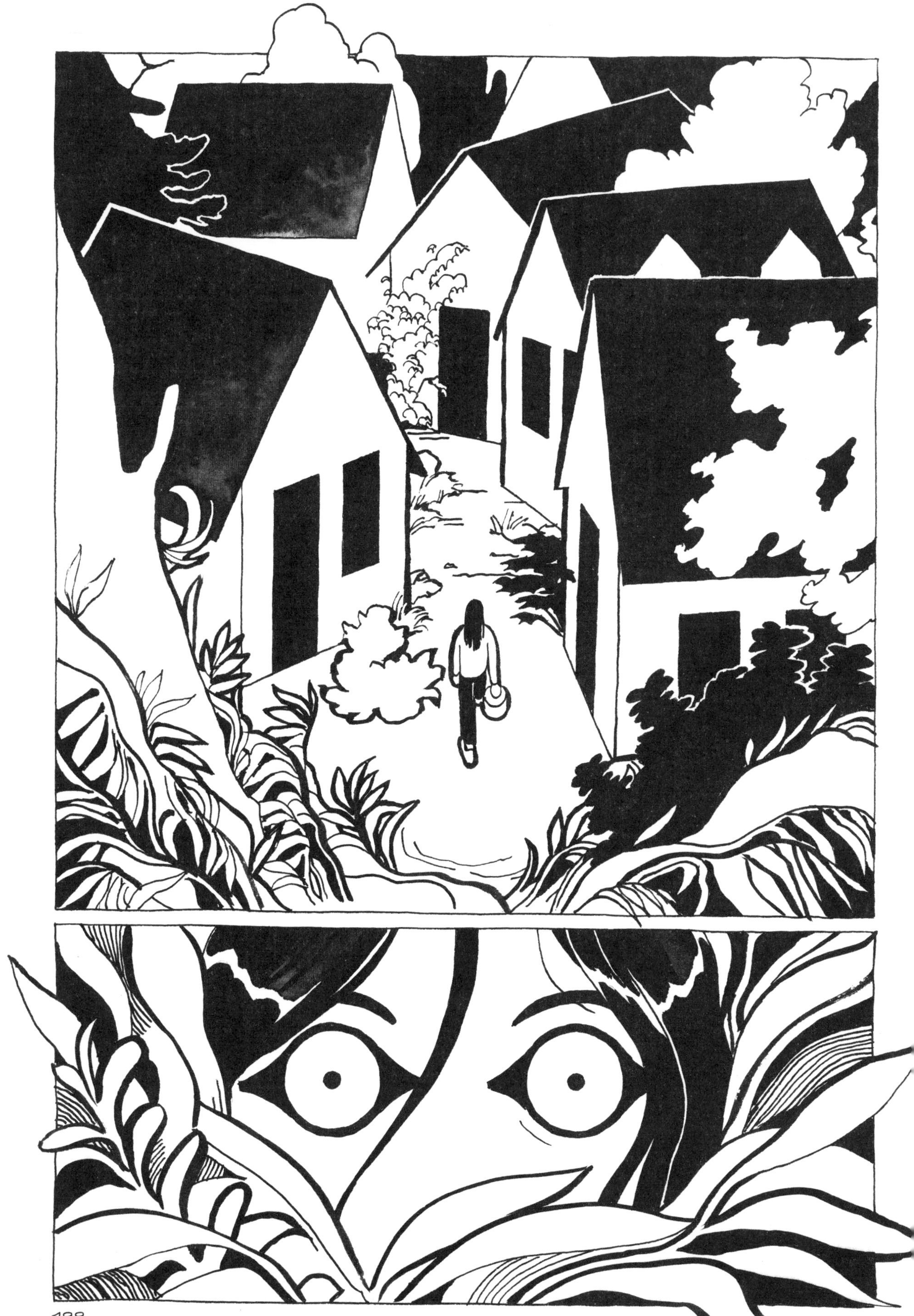

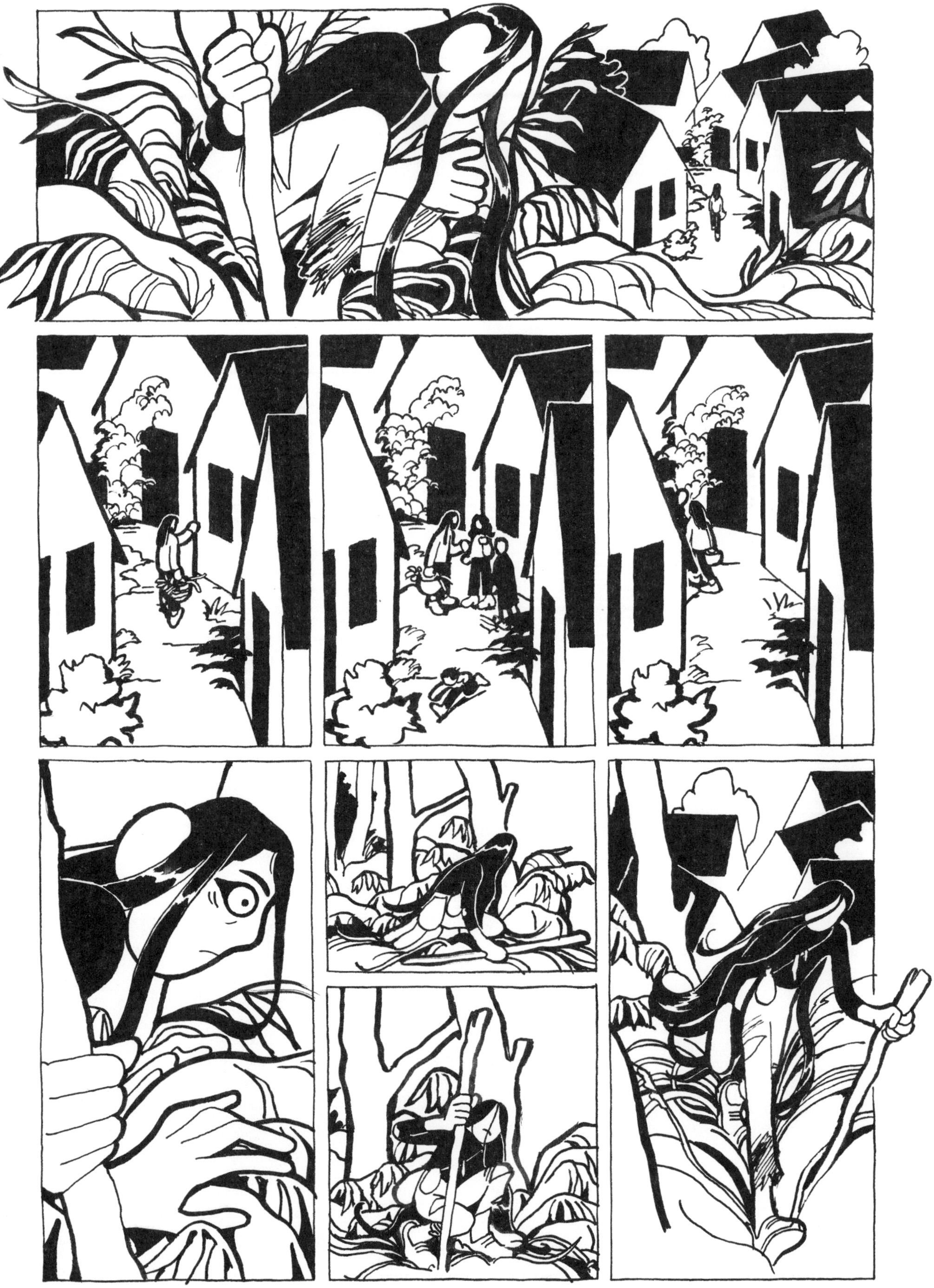

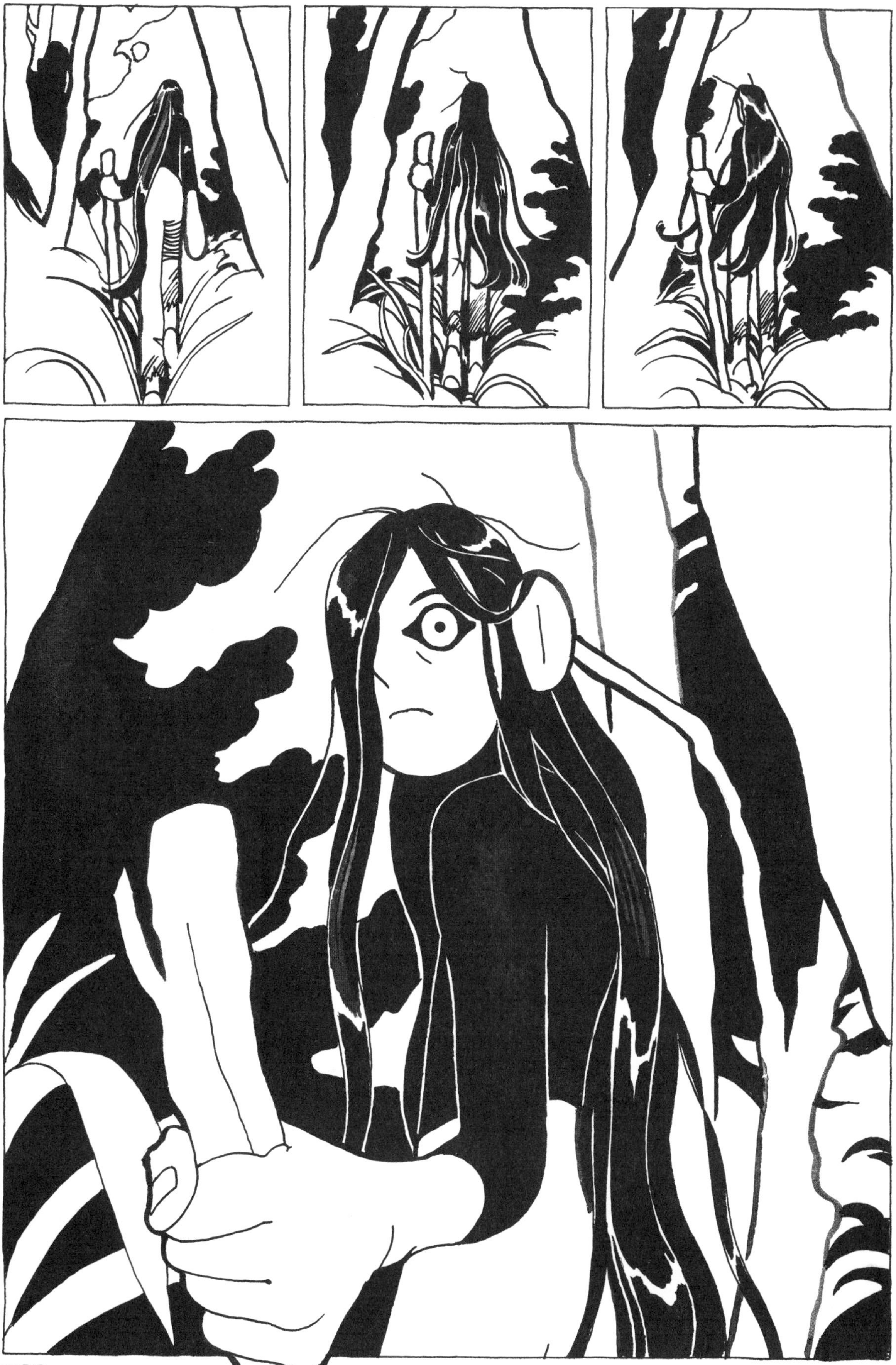

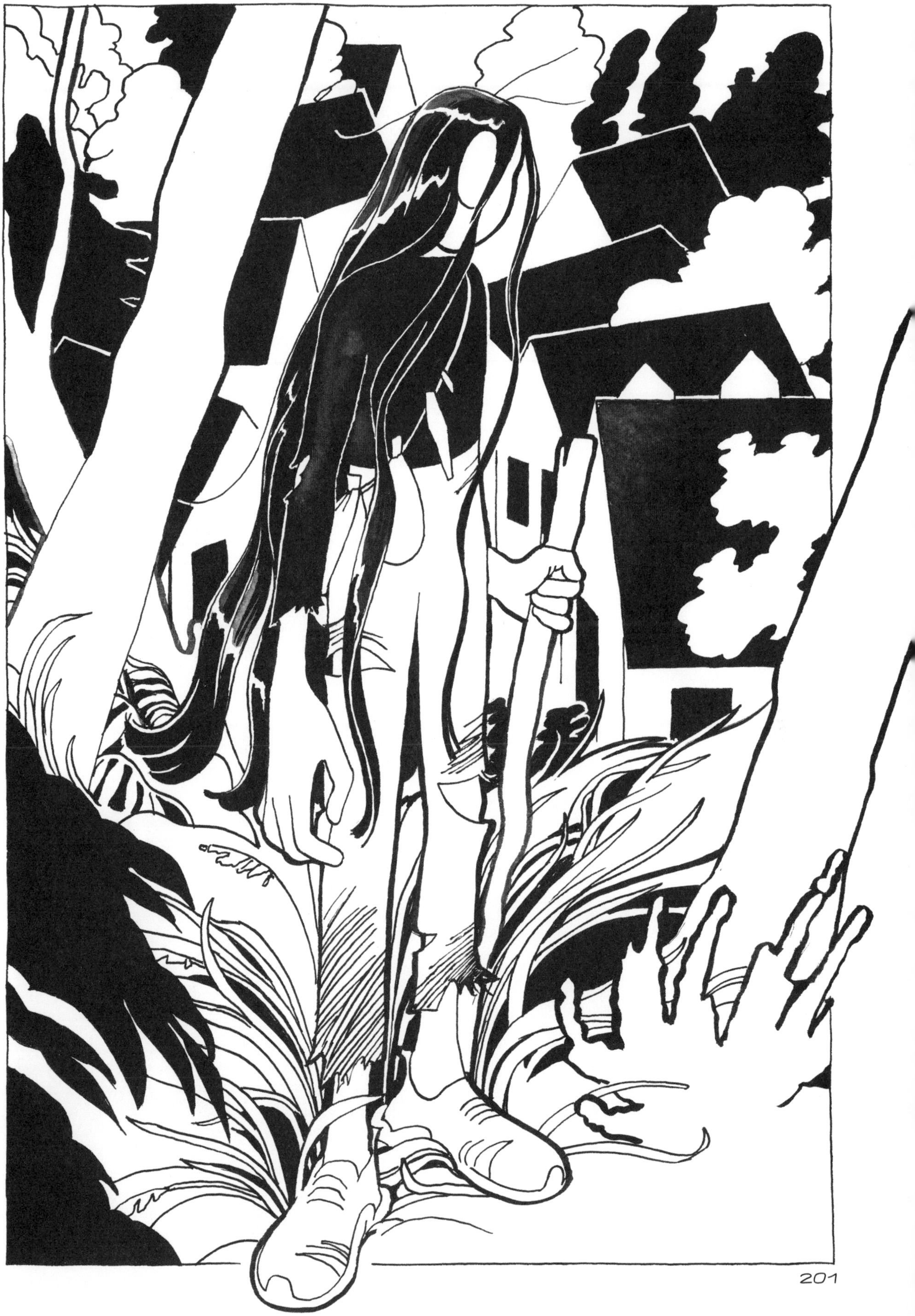

LÉA MURAWIEC is an avid manga fan who began making her own comics at a very young age. She studied graphic design at the École Estienne and later shifted her focus to comics at the École européenne supérieure de l'image in Angoulême. She is the co-founder of Éditions Flutiste, an independent small press spotlighting emerging cartoonists.

ALESHIA JENSEN is a former bookseller who translates novels, non-fiction, and comics from French to English. Her translations and co-translations include graphic novels by Julie Delporte, Camille Jourdy, Axelle Lenoir, Mirion Malle, and Pascal Girard.

FSC
www.fsc.org
MIX
Paper | Supporting
responsible forestry
FSC® C005748

drawnandquarterly.com • ISBN 978-1-77046-677-7 • First English edition: October 2023 Printed in China • 10 9 8 7 6 5 4 3 2 1 • Cataloguing data available from Library and Archives Canada

Published in the USA by Drawn & Quarterly, a client publisher of Farrar, Straus and Giroux. Published in Canada by Drawn & Quarterly, a client publisher of Raincoast Books. Published in the United Kingdom by Drawn & Quarterly, a client publisher of Publishers Group UK.

Drawn & Quarterly reconnaît l'aide financière du gouvernement du Québec par l'entremise de la Société de développement des entreprises culturelles (SODEC) pour nos activités d'édition.

Drawn & Quarterly acknowledges the support of the Government of Canada for our publishing program.

SODEC
Québec 🔲🔲   Canadä

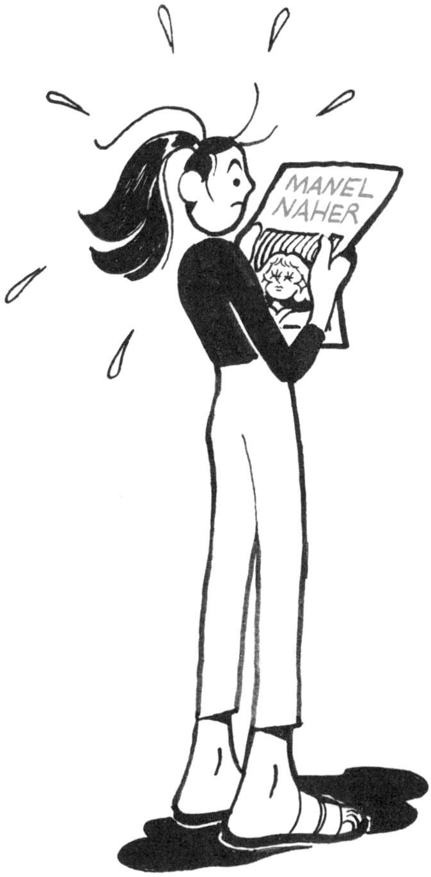
MANEL
NAHER

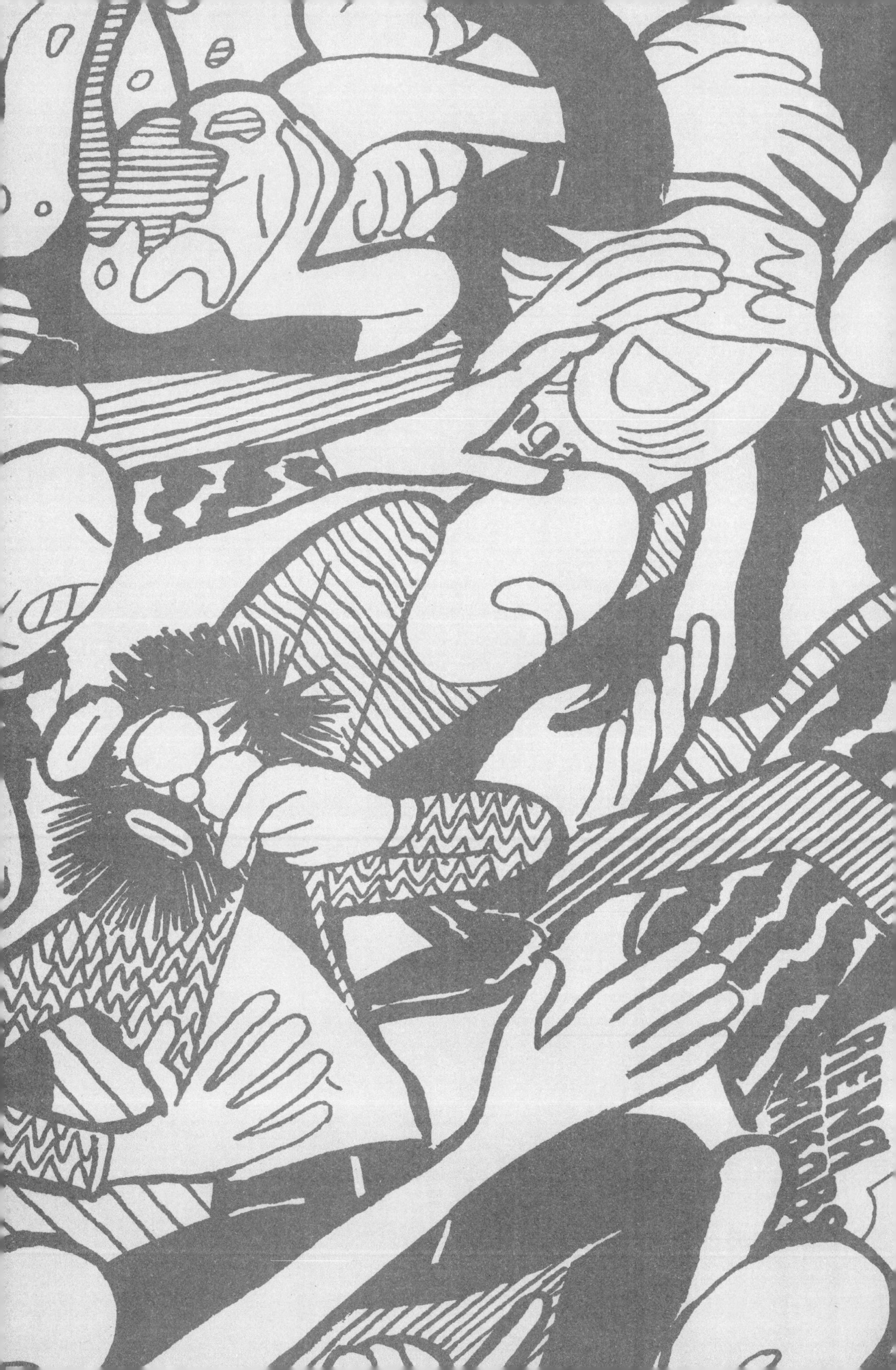